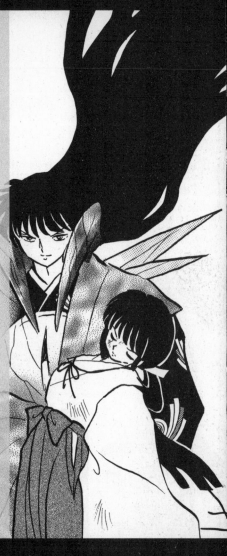

THE STORY THUS FAR

Long ago, in the "Warring States" era of Japan's Muromachi period, dog-like half demon Inuyasha attempted to steal the Shikon Jewel—or "Jewel of Four Souls"—from a village. The village priestess, Kikyo, put a stop to his thievery with an enchanted arrow. Pinned to a tree, Inuyasha fell into a deep sleep, while mortally wounded Kikyo took the jewel with her into her funeral pyre. Years passed...

In the present day, Kagome, a Japanese high school girl, is pulled down into a well and transported into the past. There she discovers trapped Inuyasha—and frees him.

When the Shikon Jewel mysteriously reappears, demons attack. In the ensuing battle, the jewel *shatters*!

Now Inuyasha is bound to Kagome with a powerful spell, and the grudging companions must battle to reclaim the shattered shards of the Shikon Jewel to keep them out of evil hands...

LAST VOLUME Inuyasha has a vision of the day half a century ago when Kikyo, Kagome's ancestor, perished. Then their archenemy Naraku entraps the reanimated Kikyo and Inuyasha. Kagome rescues them but is unable to heal Kikyo's miasma wounds with her bow, which has been tainted by Naraku. Meanwhile, Byakuya tracks down Kohaku and tries to return him to Naraku but is intercepted by Sesshomaru. Kagome and company travel to Mount Azusa to obtain an untainted bowstring. Kagome passes the resident spirit guardian's test and is awarded a new Sacred Bow that can purify...

CHARACTERS

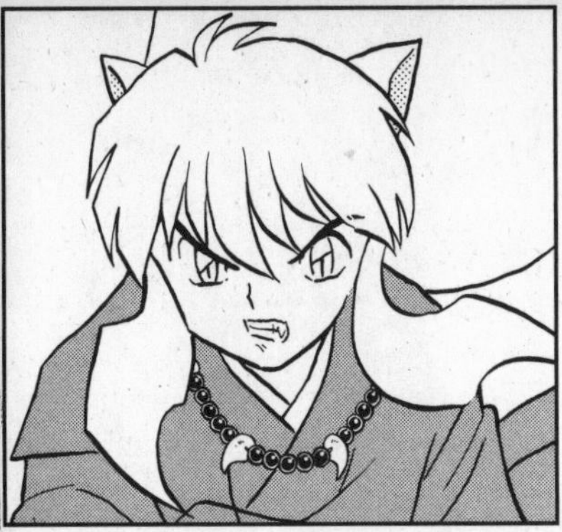

INUYASHA
Half-demon hybrid, son of a human mother and demon father. His necklace is enchanted, allowing Kagome to control him with a word.

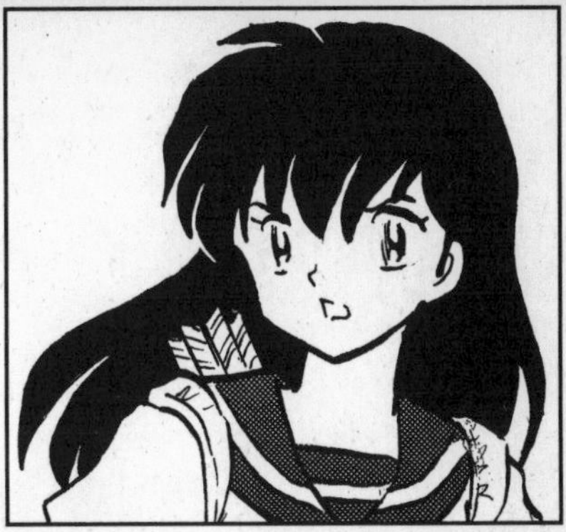

KAGOME
Modern-day Japanese schoolgirl who can travel back and forth between the past and present through an enchanted well.

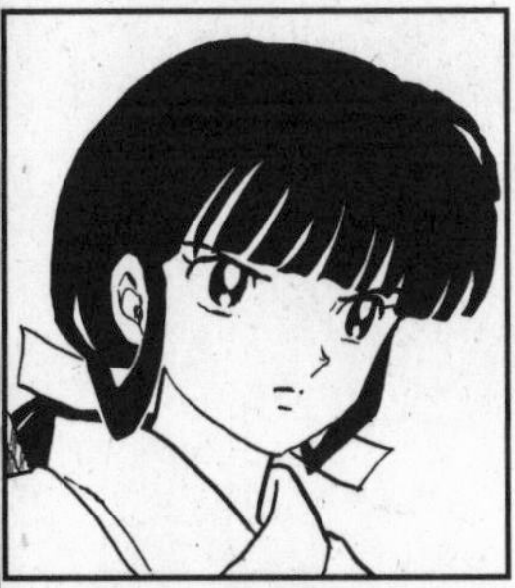

KIKYO
A powerful priestess once in charge of protecting the Shikon Jewel who has been brought back to life. Kagome is her reincarnation.

SESSHOMARU
Inuyasha's completely demon half brother. The brothers have the same demon father. Sesshomaru covets the sword left to Inuyasha by their father.

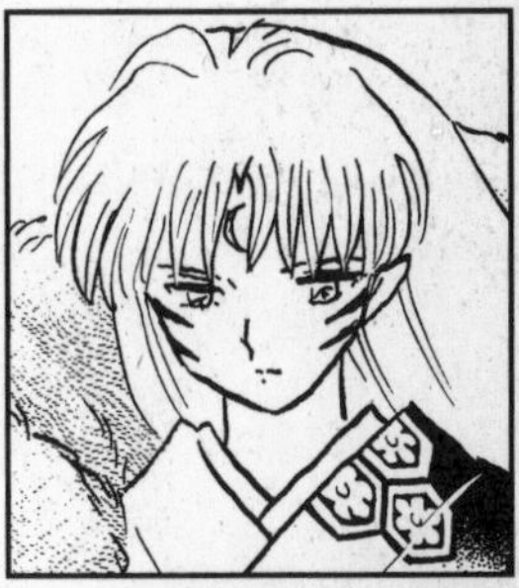

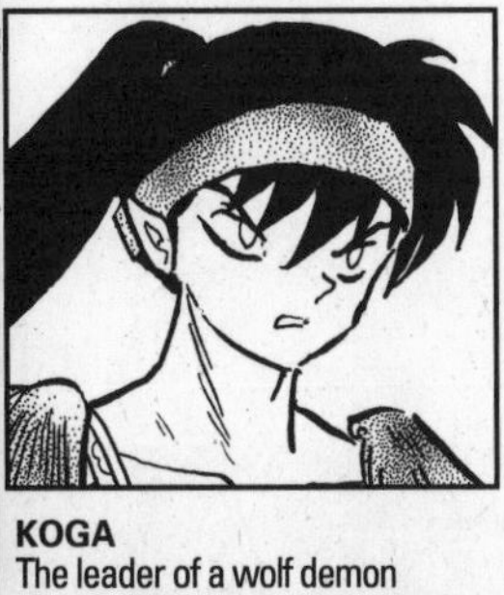

KOGA
The leader of a wolf demon clan. A Shikon shard in each of his legs imbues him with super speed. Enamored of Kagome, Koga quarrels with Inuyasha frequently.

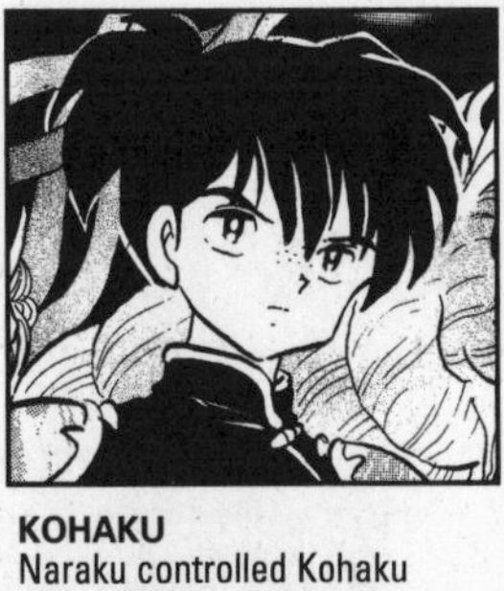

KOHAKU
Naraku controlled Kohaku with a Shikon shard and resurrected him after death to do his bidding. Kohaku regained his memories and is trying to redeem himself by helping Kikyo and Sesshomaru.

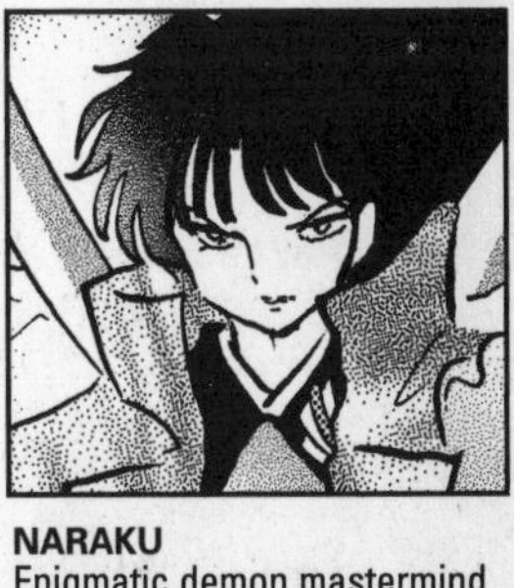

NARAKU
Enigmatic demon mastermind behind the miseries of nearly everyone in the story. He has the power to create multiple incarnations of himself from his body. He will stop at nothing to obtain all the shards of the Shikon Jewel.

SCROLL 1

TRAPPED COMPANIONS

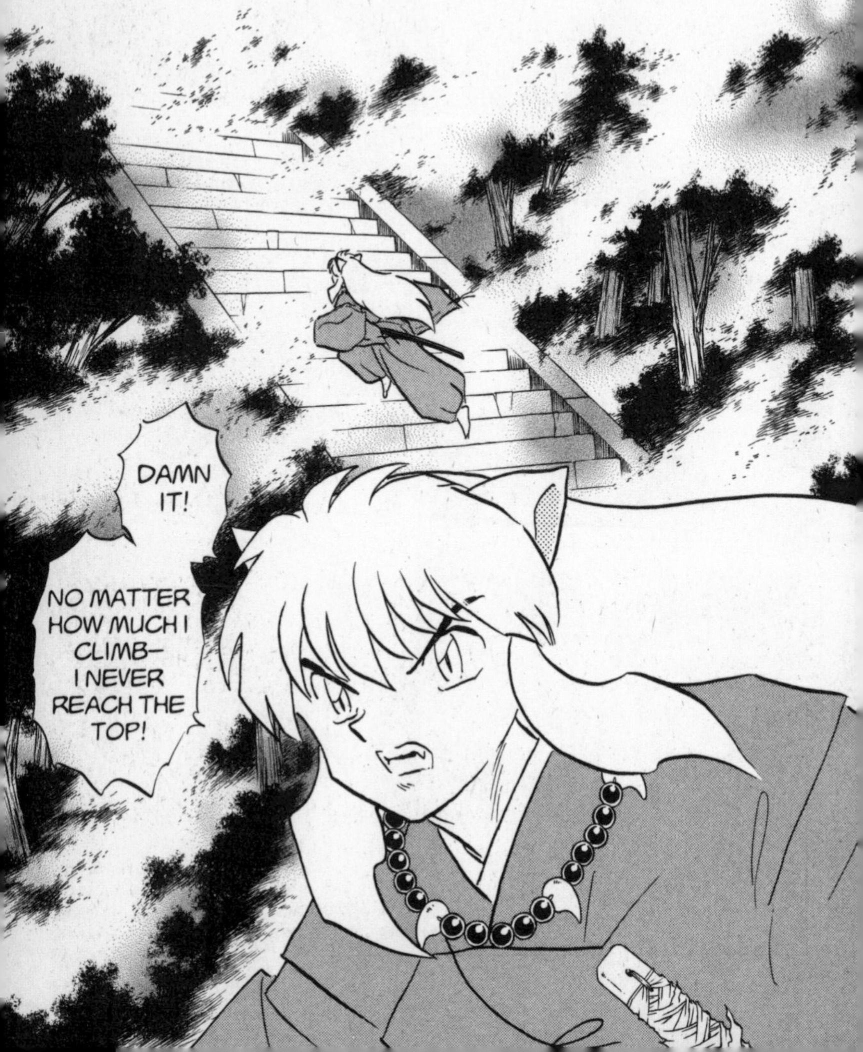
DAMN IT!
NO MATTER HOW MUCH I CLIMB— I NEVER REACH THE TOP!

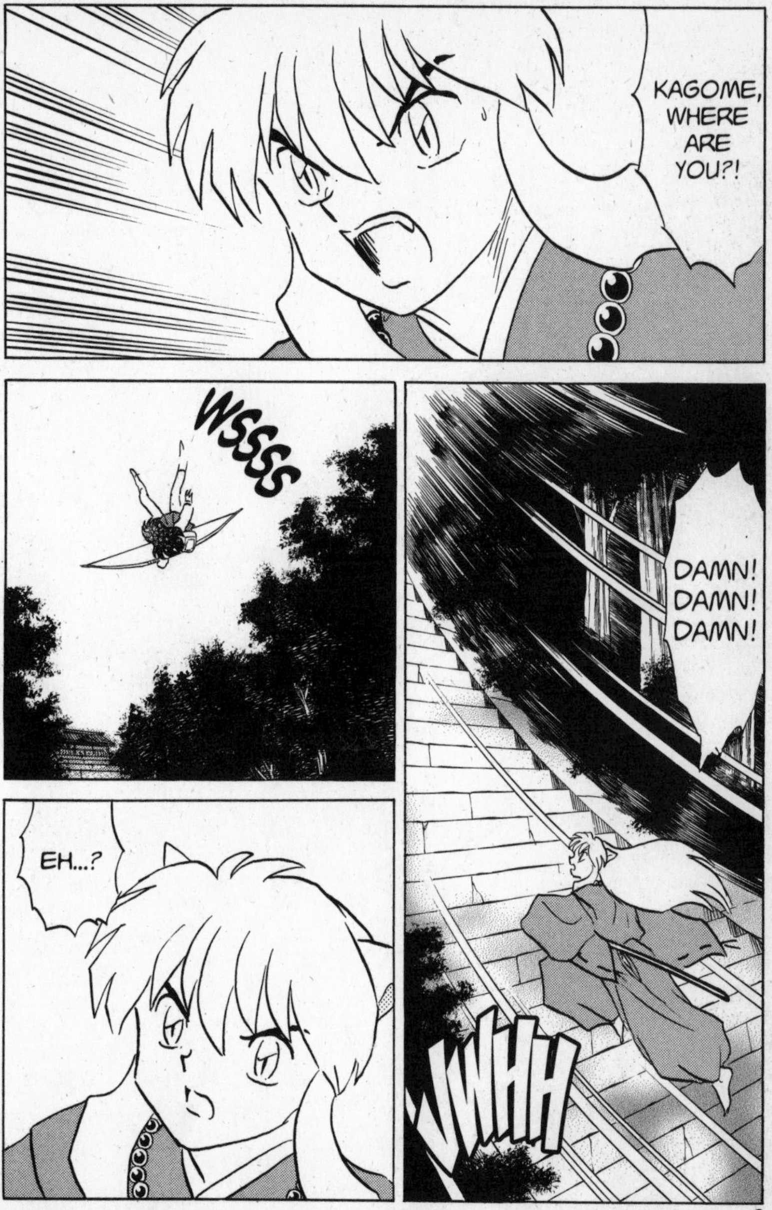
KAGOME, WHERE ARE YOU?!
DAMN! DAMN! DAMN!
JWHH
WSSSS
EH...?

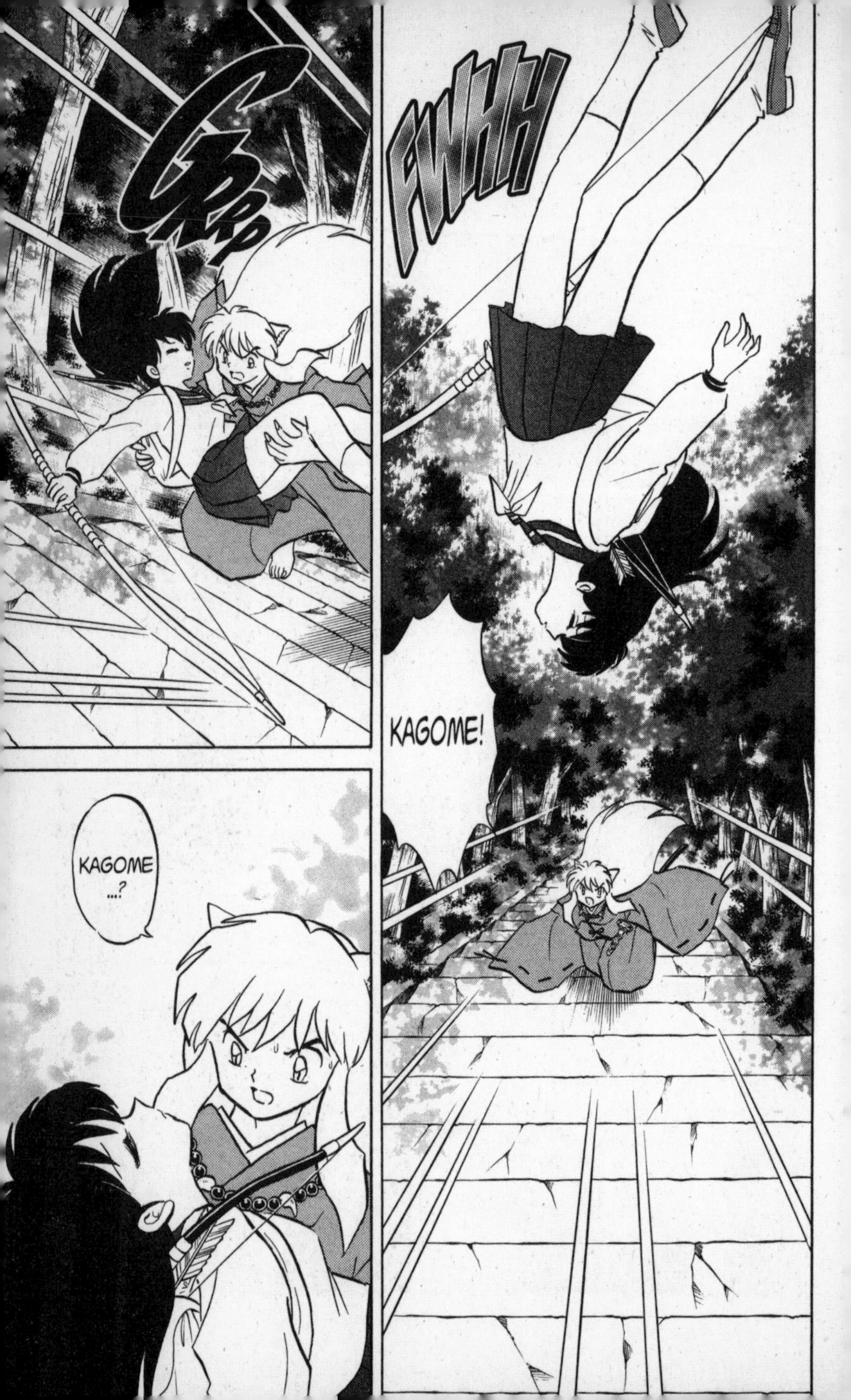
FWHH
KAGOME!
GRRP
KAGOME ...?

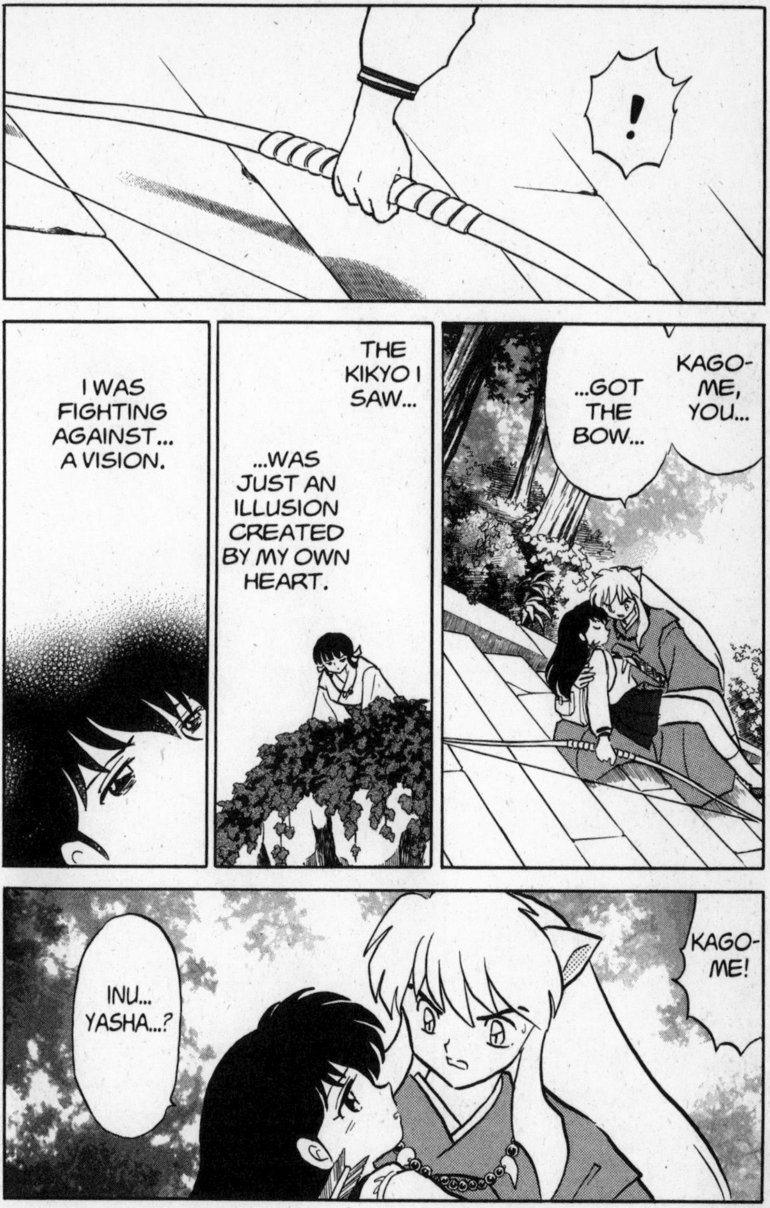
!
KAGO-ME, YOU...
...GOT THE BOW...
THE KIKYO I SAW...
...WAS JUST AN ILLUSION CREATED BY MY OWN HEART.
I WAS FIGHTING AGAINST... A VISION.
KAGO-ME!
INU... YASHA...?

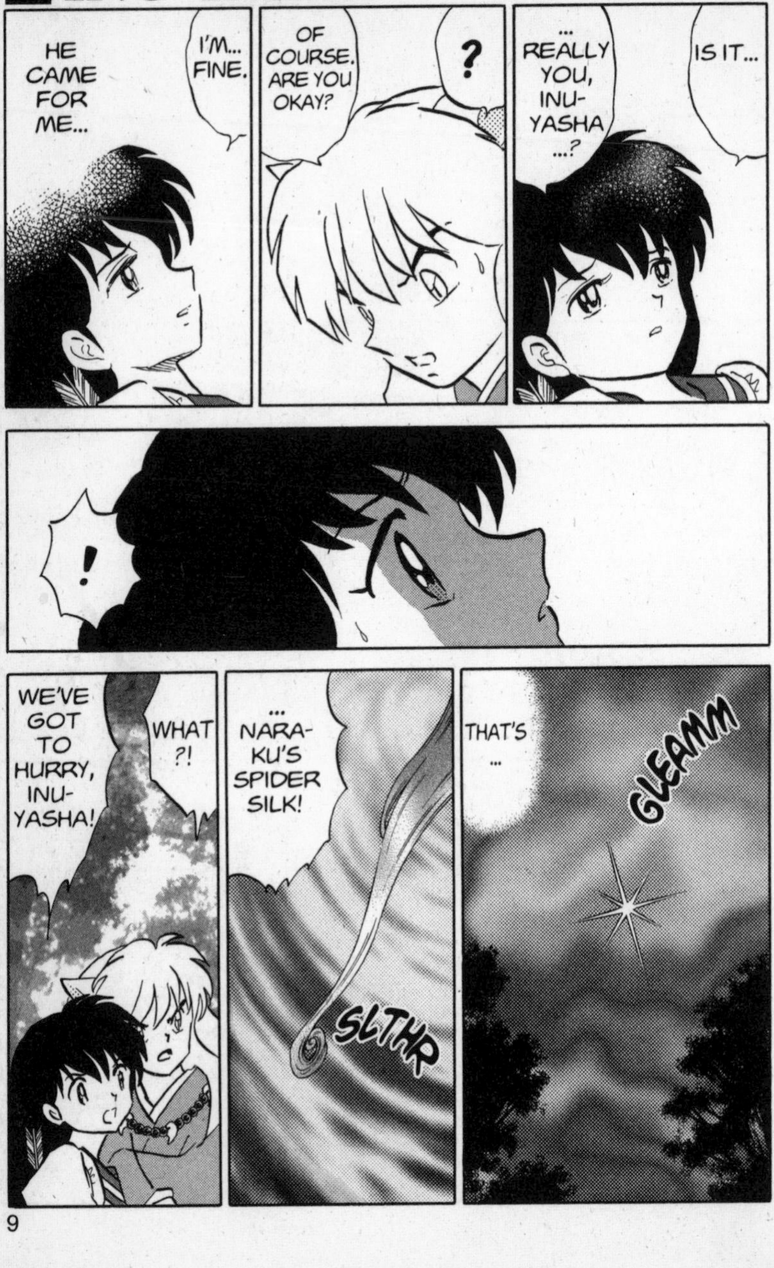
IS IT...
...REALLY YOU, INU-YASHA...?
?
OF COURSE. ARE YOU OKAY?
I'M... FINE.
HE CAME FOR ME...
!
GLEAMM
THAT'S...
...NARAKU'S SPIDER SILK!
SLTHR
WHAT?!
WE'VE GOT TO HURRY, INU-YASHA!

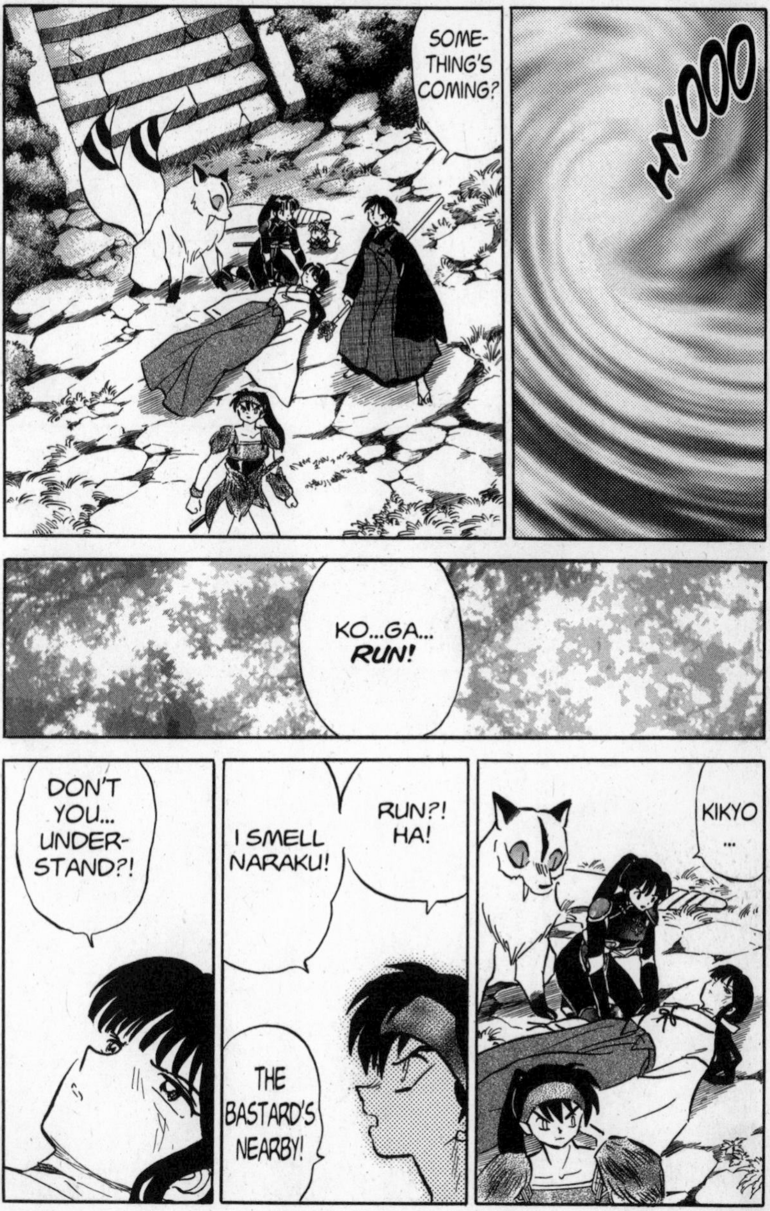
HYOOO
SOME-THING'S COMING?
KO...GA... RUN!
KIKYO ...
RUN?! HA!
I SMELL NARAKU!
THE BASTARD'S NEARBY!
DON'T YOU... UNDER-STAND?!

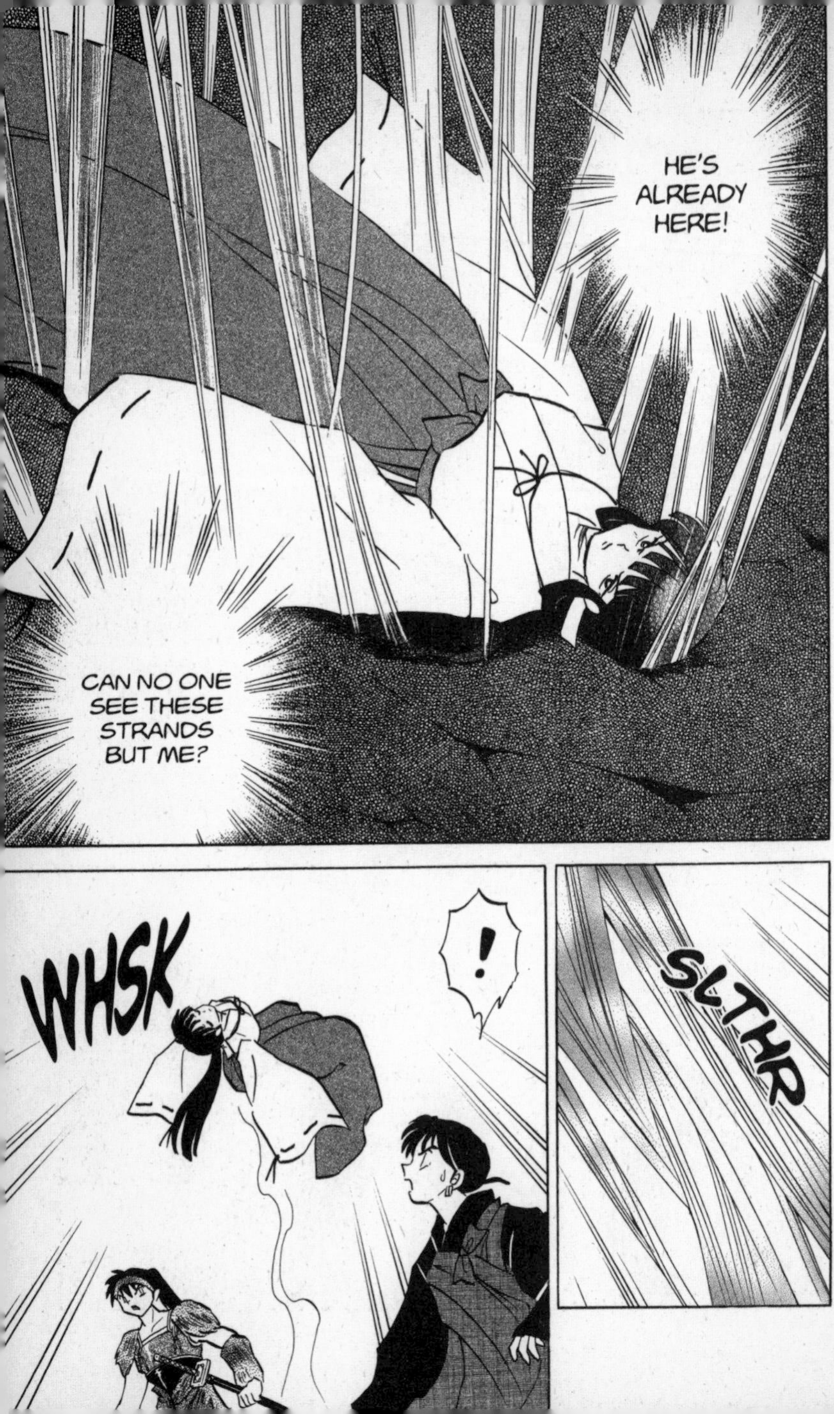
HE'S ALREADY HERE!
CAN NO ONE SEE THESE STRANDS BUT ME?
SLTHR
!
WHSK

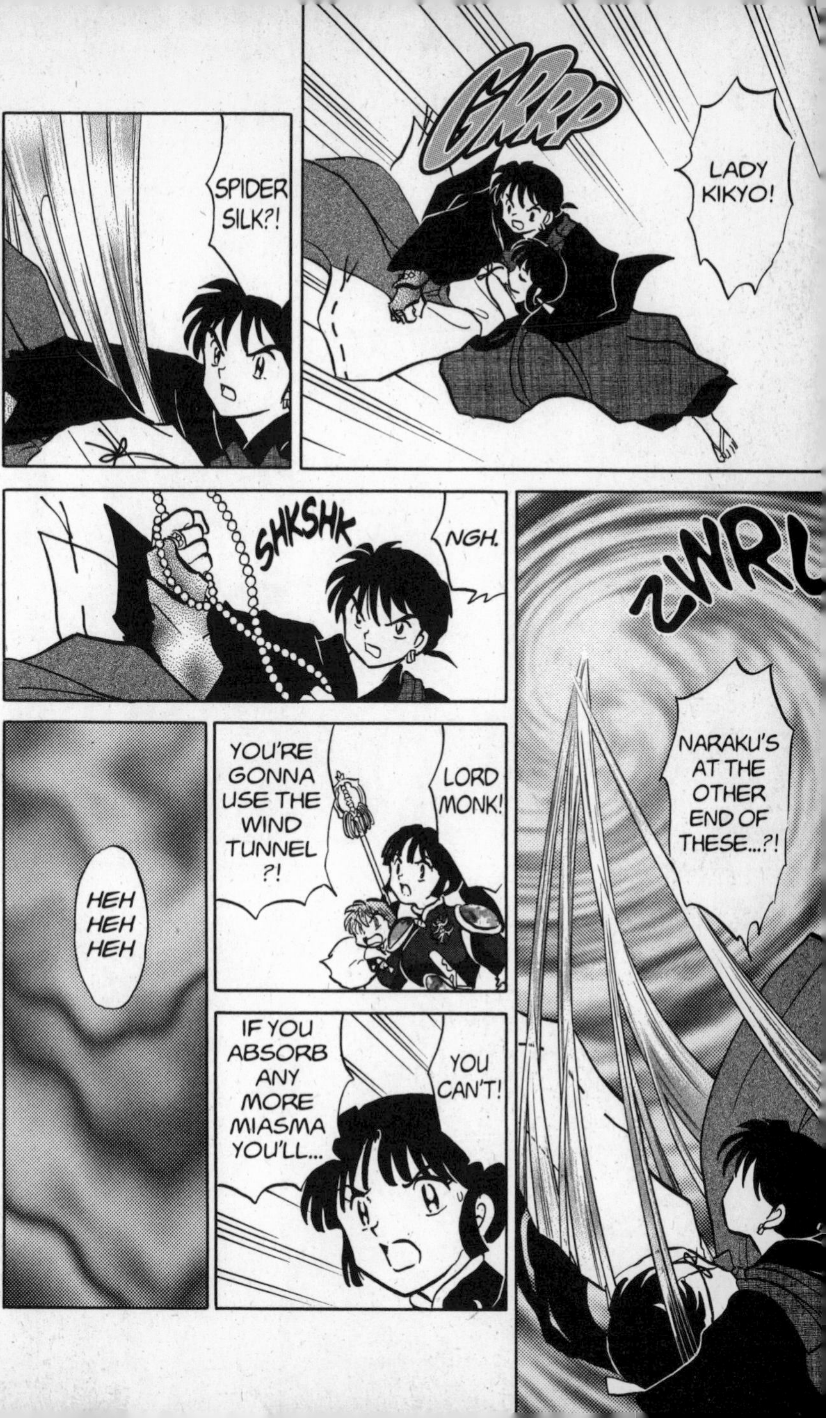
GRRR
LADY KIKYO!
SPIDER SILK?!
ZWRL
NARAKU'S AT THE OTHER END OF THESE...?!
SHKSHK
NGH.
LORD MONK!
YOU'RE GONNA USE THE WIND TUNNEL ?!
YOU CAN'T!
IF YOU ABSORB ANY MORE MIASMA YOU'LL...
HEH HEH HEH

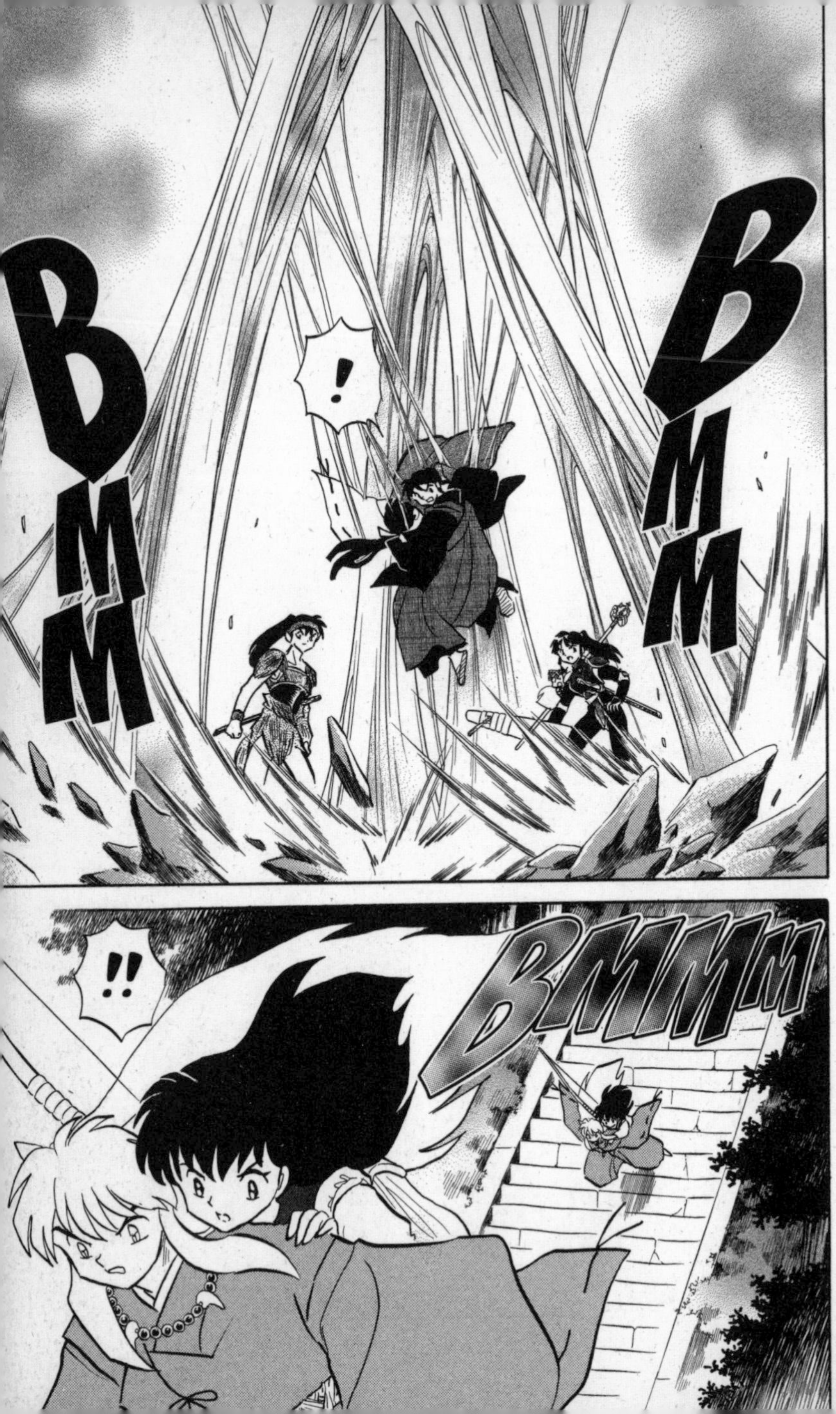
BMMM
!
BMMM
BMMM
!!

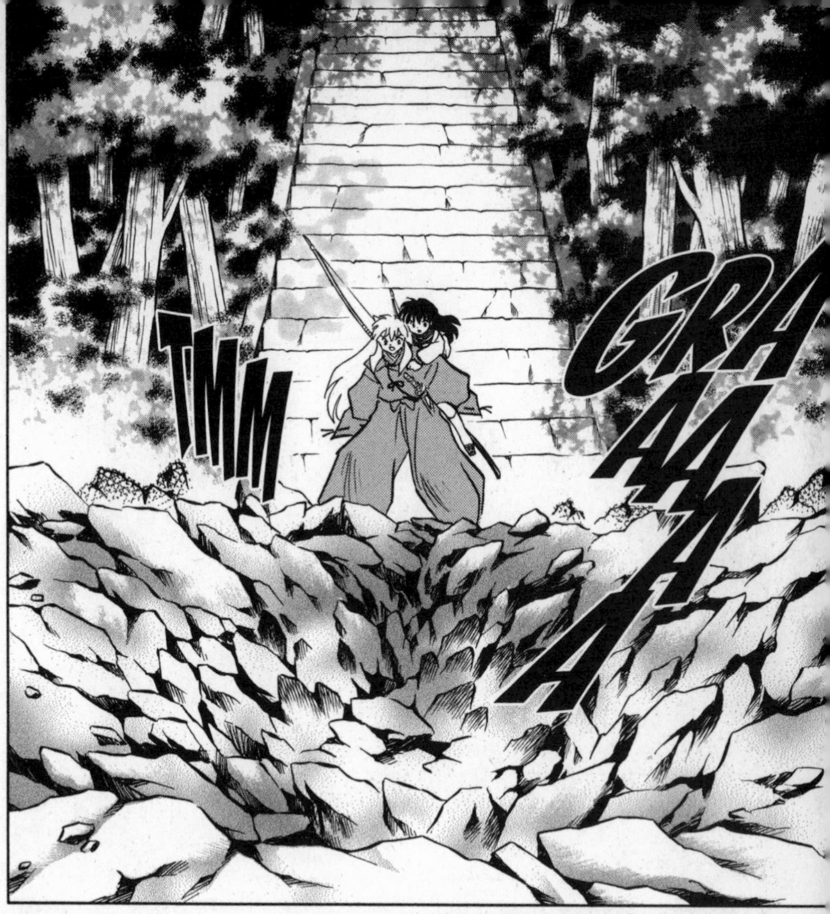
GRAAAAA
TMM
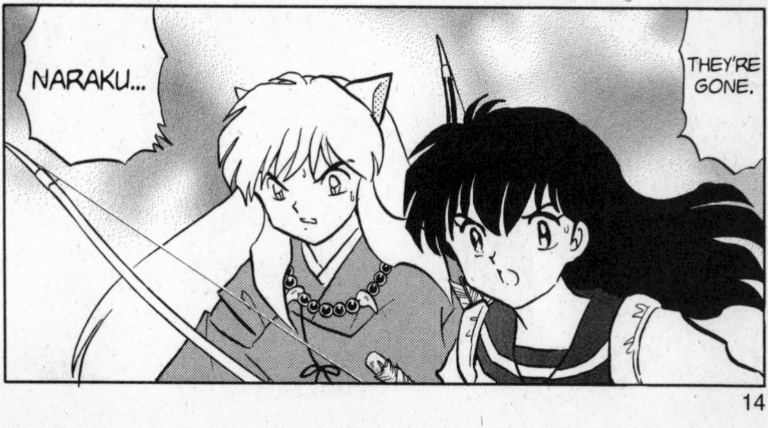
THEY'RE GONE.
NARAKU...

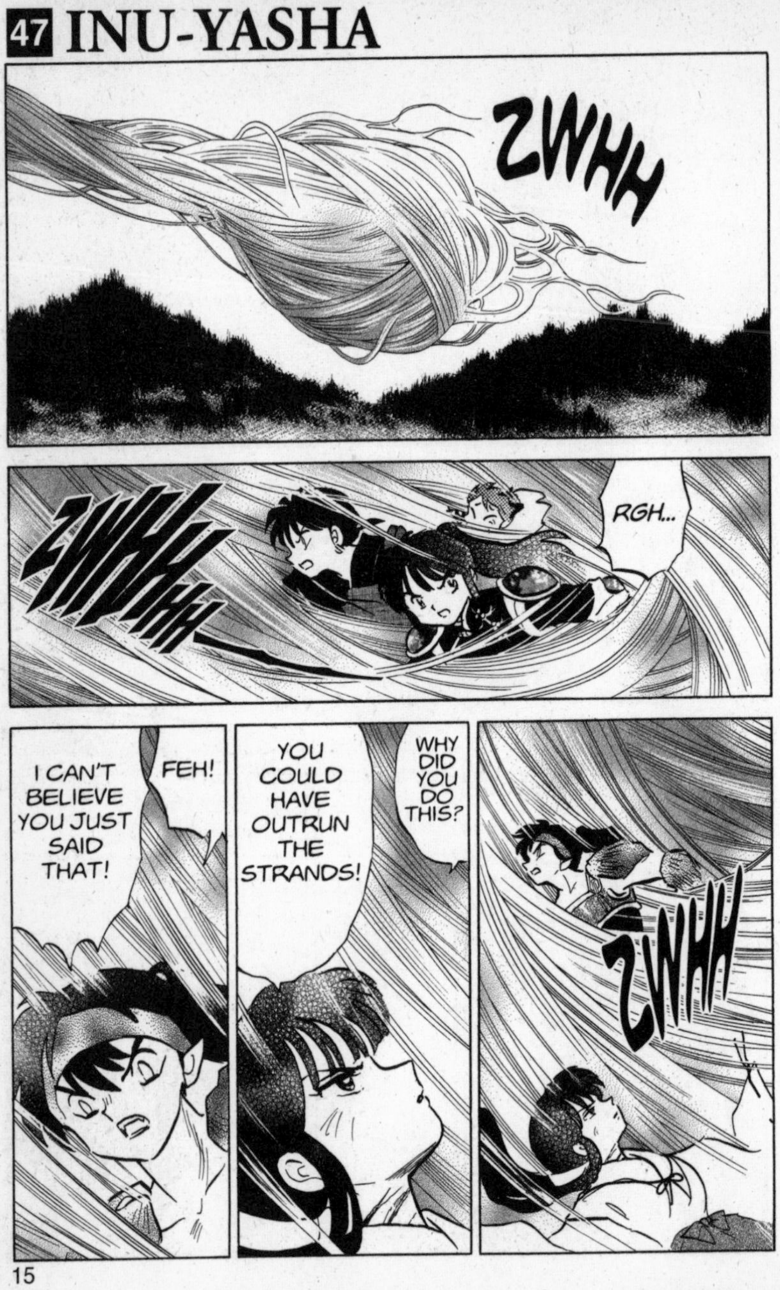
ZWHH
RGH...
ZWHHH
ZWHH
WHY DID YOU DO THIS?
YOU COULD HAVE OUTRUN THE STRANDS!
FEH!
I CAN'T BELIEVE YOU JUST SAID THAT!

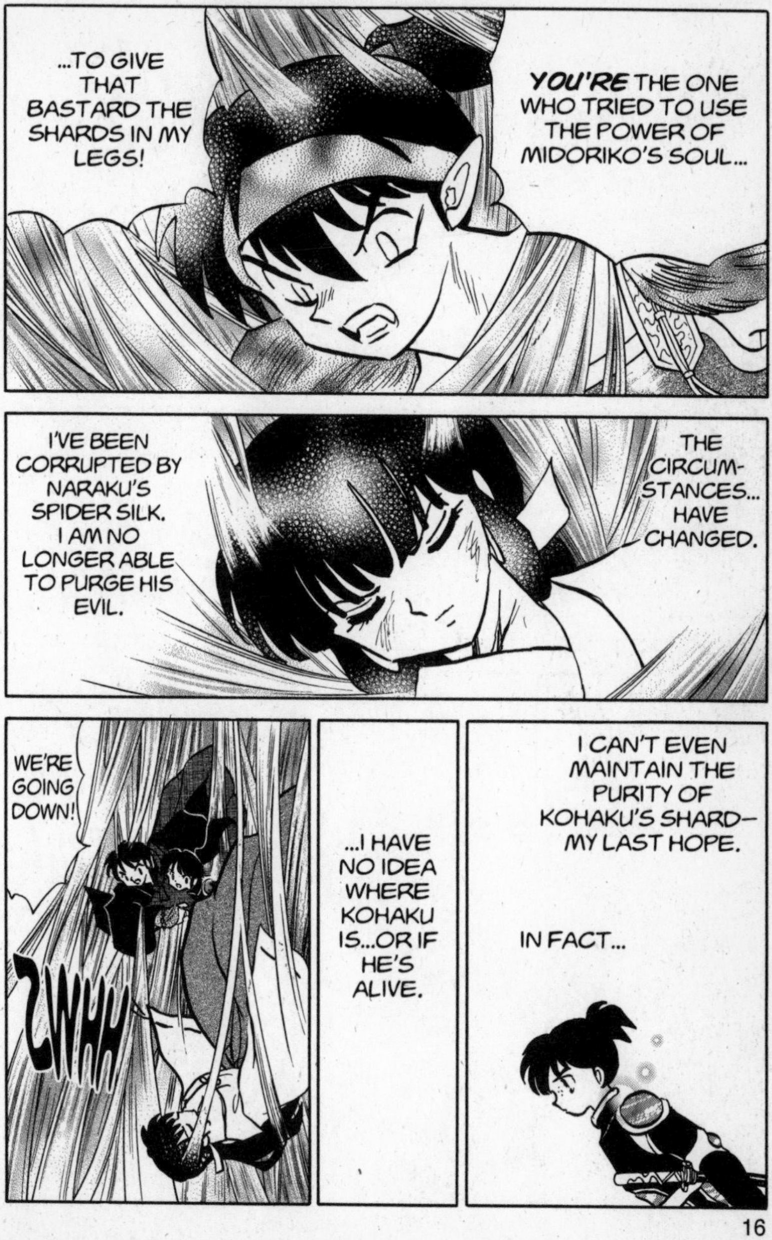
YOU'RE THE ONE WHO TRIED TO USE THE POWER OF MIDORIKO'S SOUL...
...TO GIVE THAT BASTARD THE SHARDS IN MY LEGS!
THE CIRCUM-STANCES... HAVE CHANGED.
I'VE BEEN CORRUPTED BY NARAKU'S SPIDER SILK. I AM NO LONGER ABLE TO PURGE HIS EVIL.
I CAN'T EVEN MAINTAIN THE PURITY OF KOHAKU'S SHARD—MY LAST HOPE.
IN FACT...
...I HAVE NO IDEA WHERE KOHAKU IS...OR IF HE'S ALIVE.
WE'RE GOING DOWN!
ZWHH

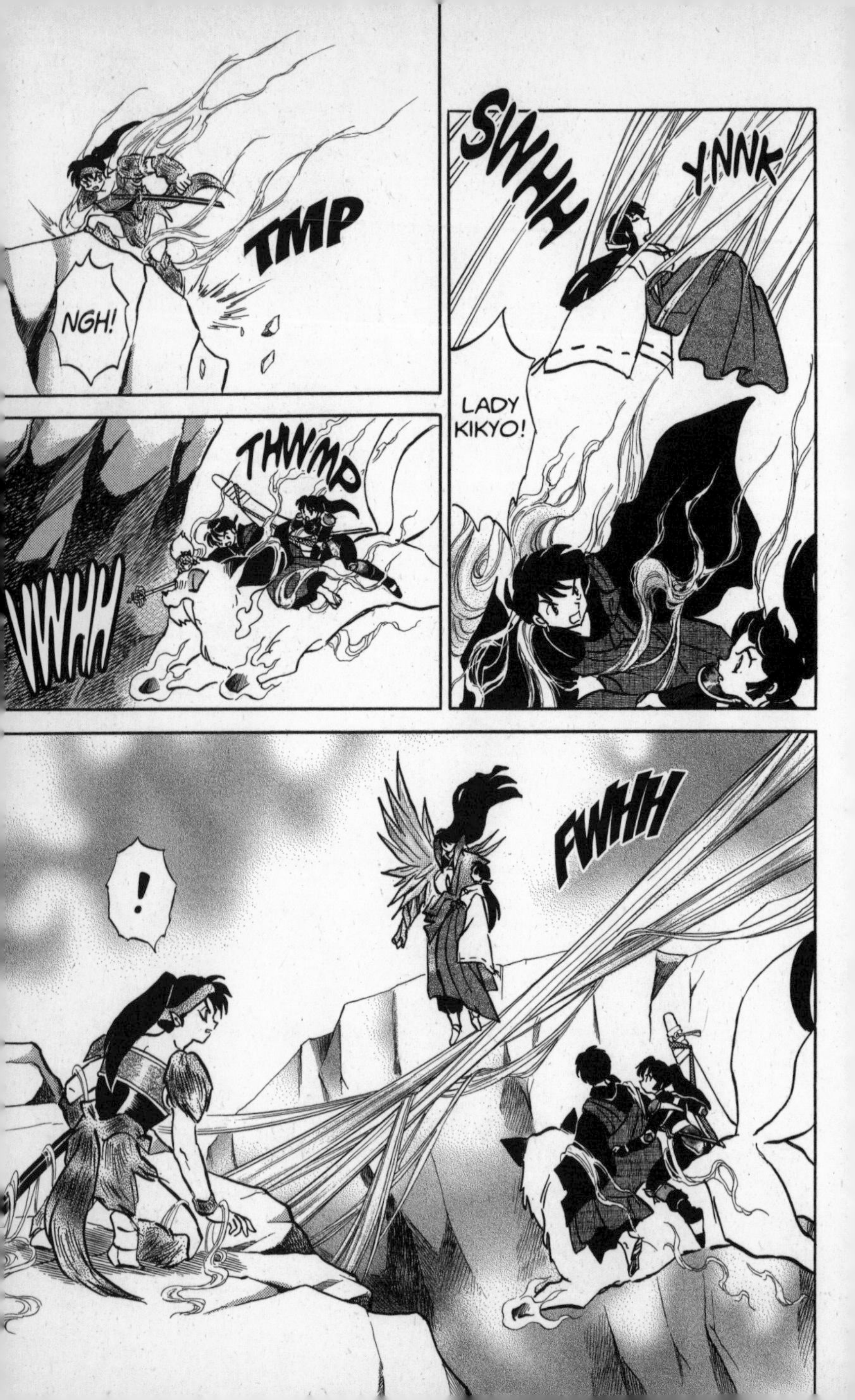
SWHH
YNNK
LADY KIKYO!
TMP
NGH!
THWMP
VWHH
FWHH
!

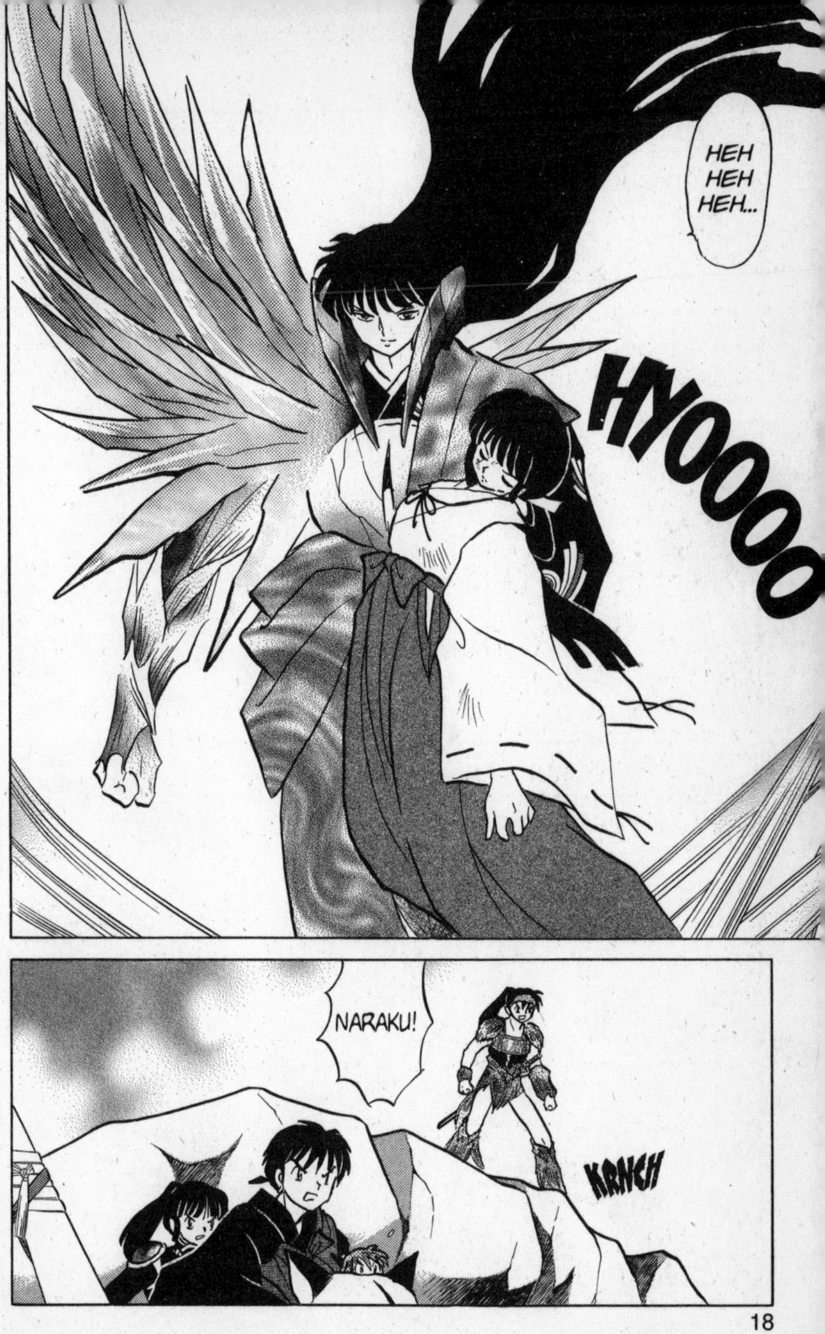
HEH
HEH
HEH...
HYOOOOO
NARAKU!
KRNCH

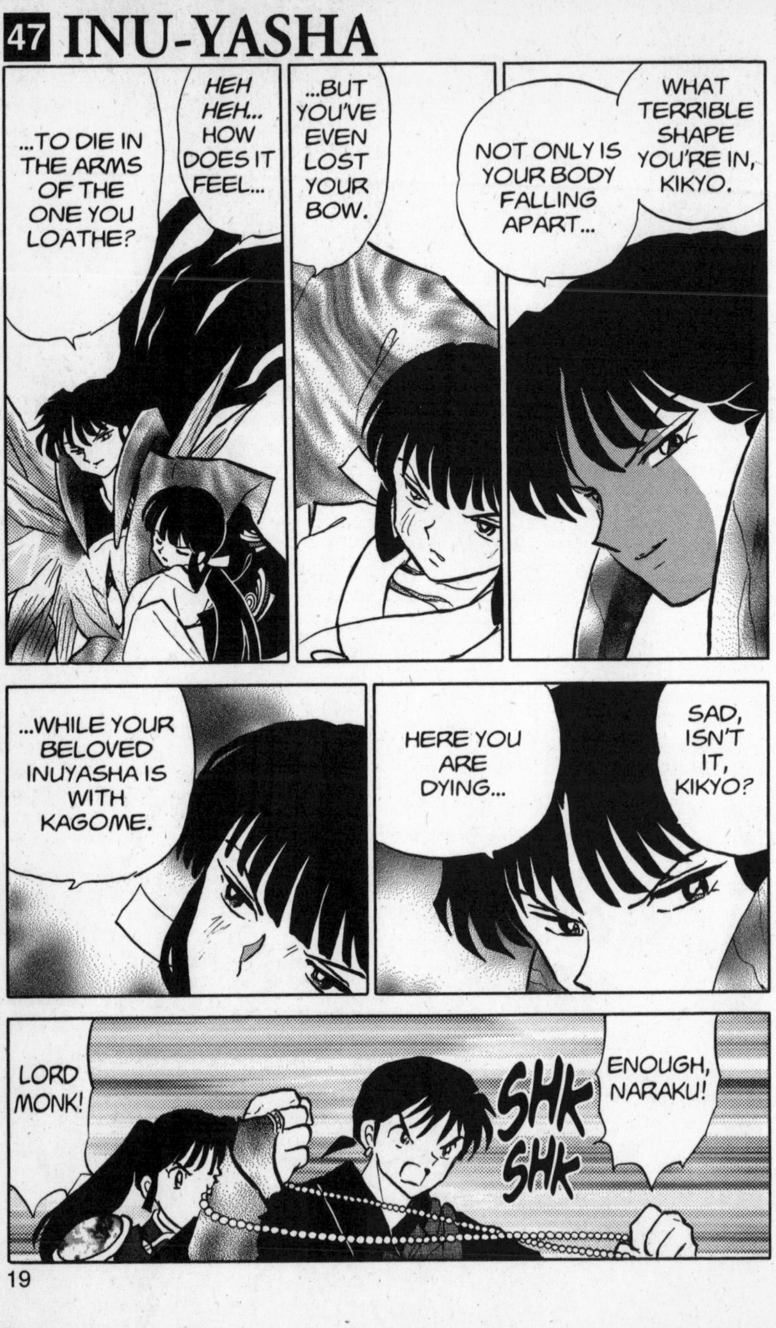
WHAT TERRIBLE SHAPE YOU'RE IN, KIKYO.
NOT ONLY IS YOUR BODY FALLING APART...
...BUT YOU'VE EVEN LOST YOUR BOW.
HEH HEH... HOW DOES IT FEEL...
...TO DIE IN THE ARMS OF THE ONE YOU LOATHE?
SAD, ISN'T IT, KIKYO?
HERE YOU ARE DYING...
...WHILE YOUR BELOVED INUYASHA IS WITH KAGOME.
ENOUGH, NARAKU!
SHK SHK
LORD MONK!

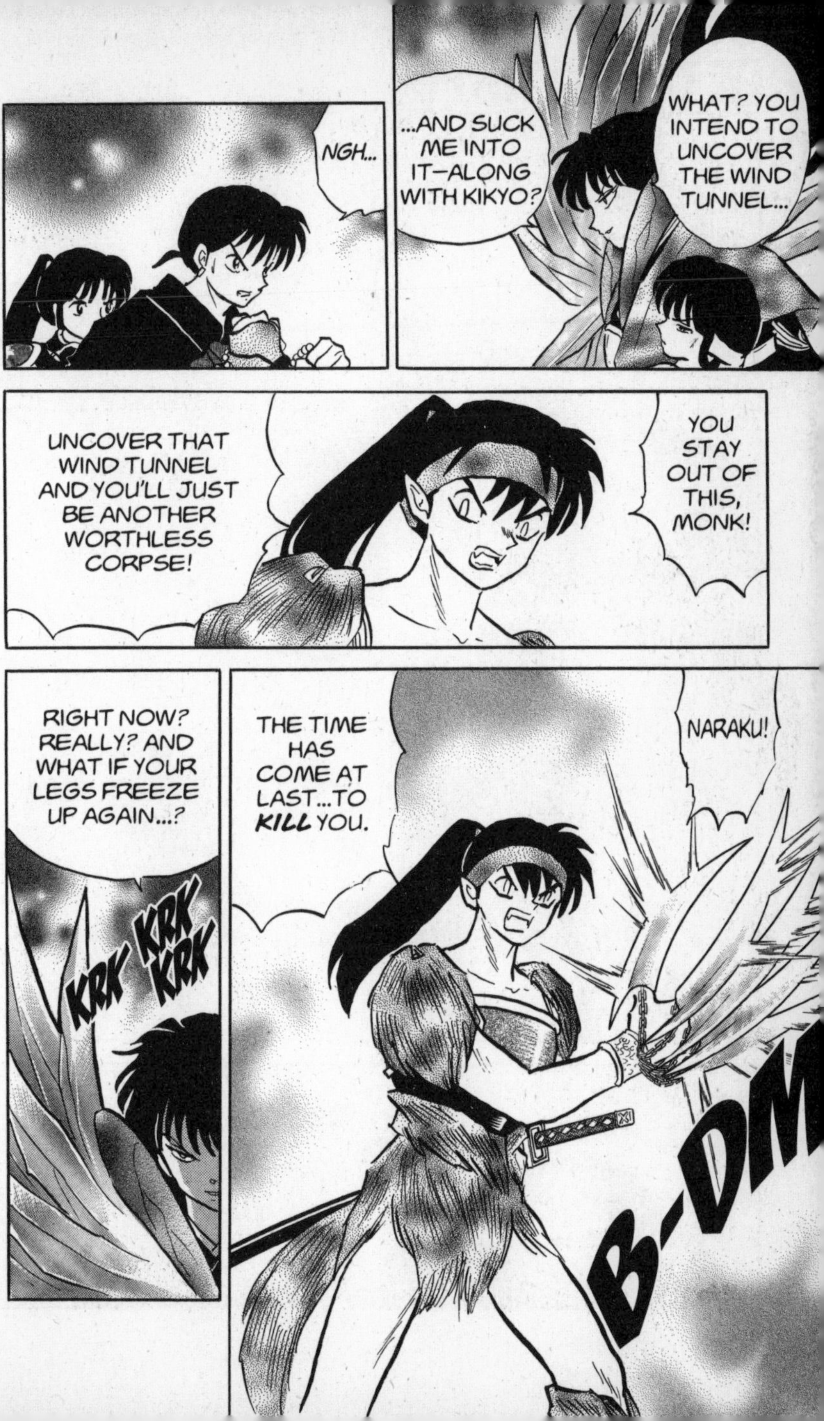
WHAT? YOU INTEND TO UNCOVER THE WIND TUNNEL...
...AND SUCK ME INTO IT—ALONG WITH KIKYO?
NGH...
YOU STAY OUT OF THIS, MONK!
UNCOVER THAT WIND TUNNEL AND YOU'LL JUST BE ANOTHER WORTHLESS CORPSE!
NARAKU!
THE TIME HAS COME AT LAST...TO **KILL** YOU.
B-DM
RIGHT NOW? REALLY? AND WHAT IF YOUR LEGS FREEZE UP AGAIN...?
KRK KRK KRK KRK

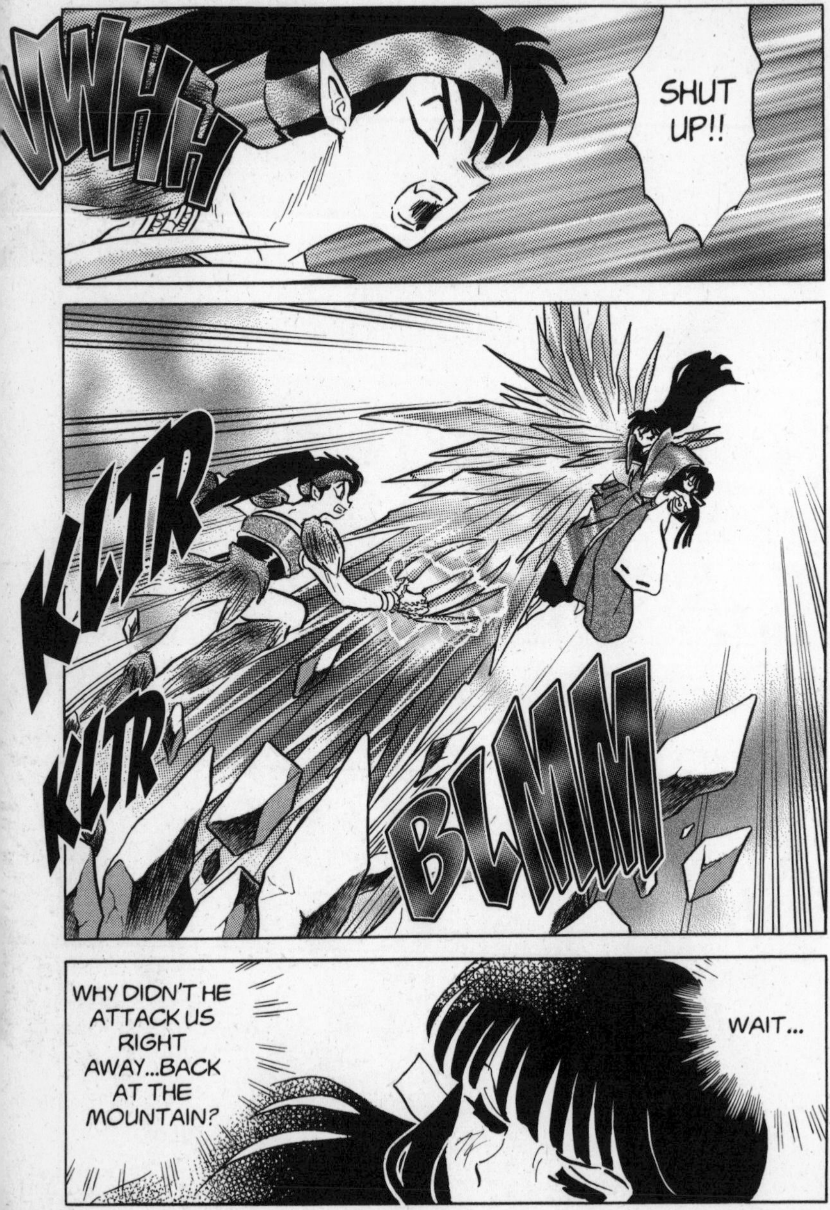
SHUT UP!!
VWHH
BLMM
KLTR
KLTR
WAIT...
WHY DIDN'T HE ATTACK US RIGHT AWAY...BACK AT THE MOUNTAIN?

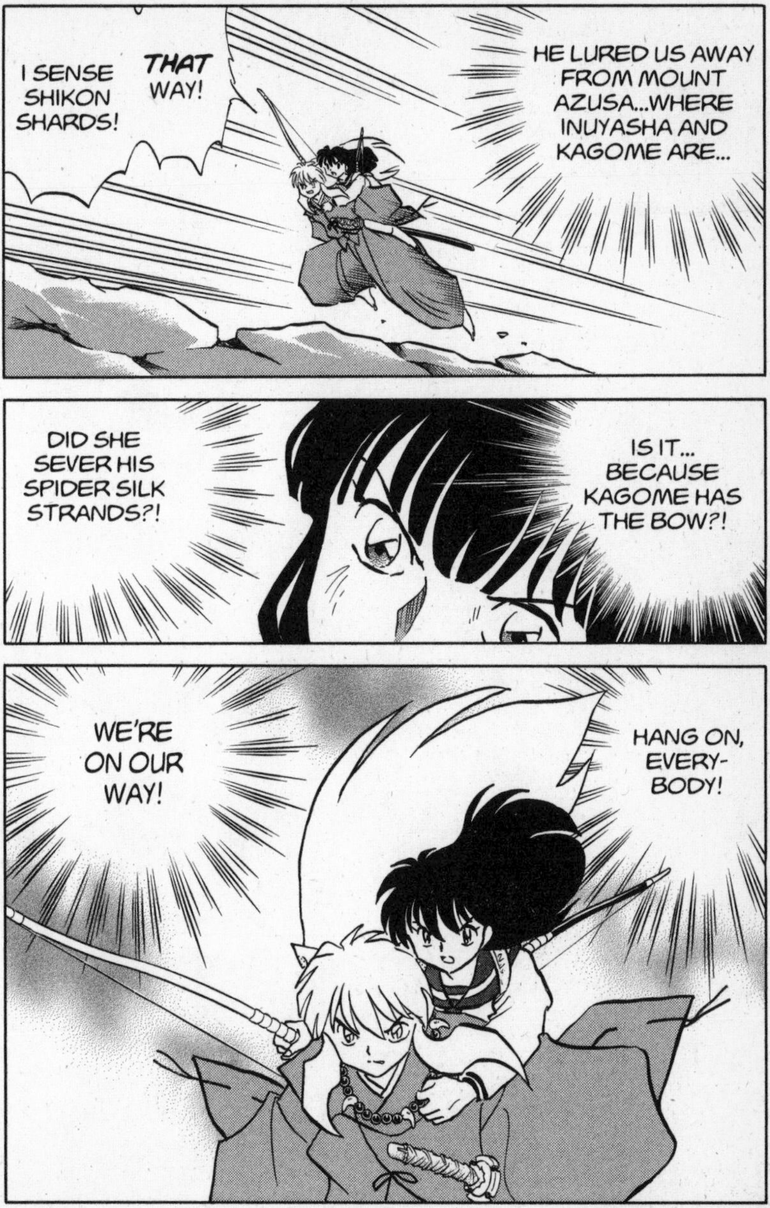
HE LURED US AWAY FROM MOUNT AZUSA...WHERE INUYASHA AND KAGOME ARE...
THAT WAY!
I SENSE SHIKON SHARDS!
IS IT... BECAUSE KAGOME HAS THE BOW?!
DID SHE SEVER HIS SPIDER SILK STRANDS?!
HANG ON, EVERY-BODY!
WE'RE ON OUR WAY!

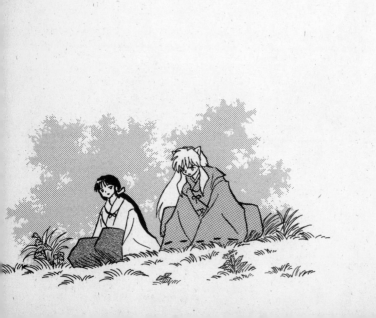

SCROLL 2

HEARTS LINKED

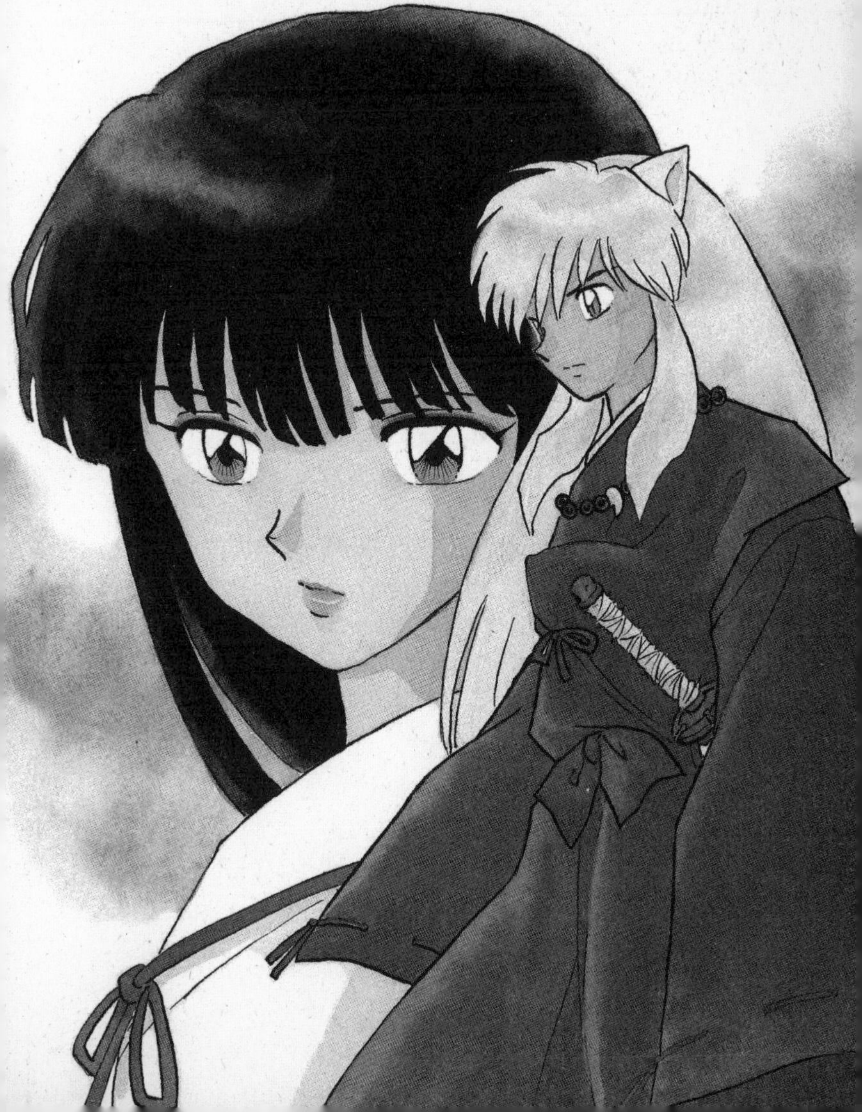

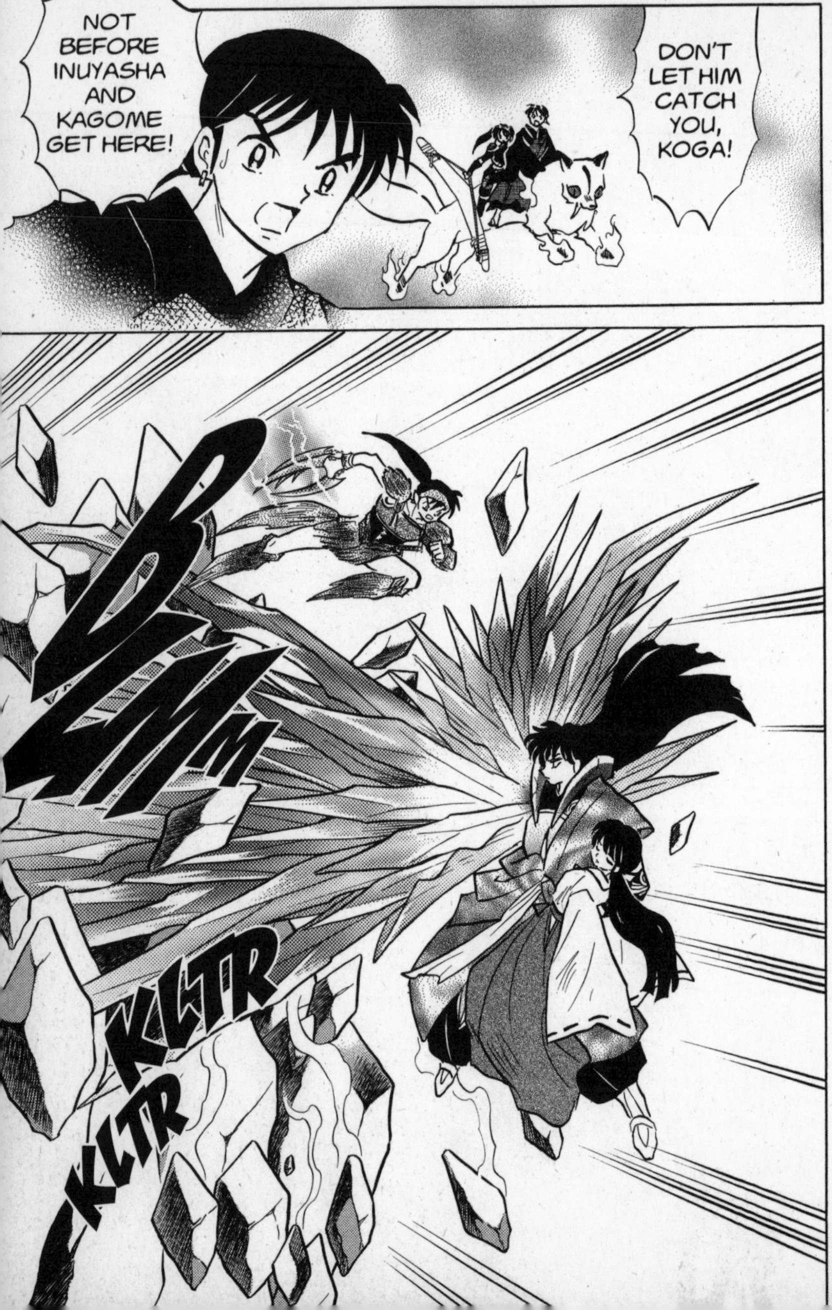
DON'T LET HIM CATCH YOU, KOGA!
NOT BEFORE INUYASHA AND KAGOME GET HERE!
BZMM
KLTR
KLTR

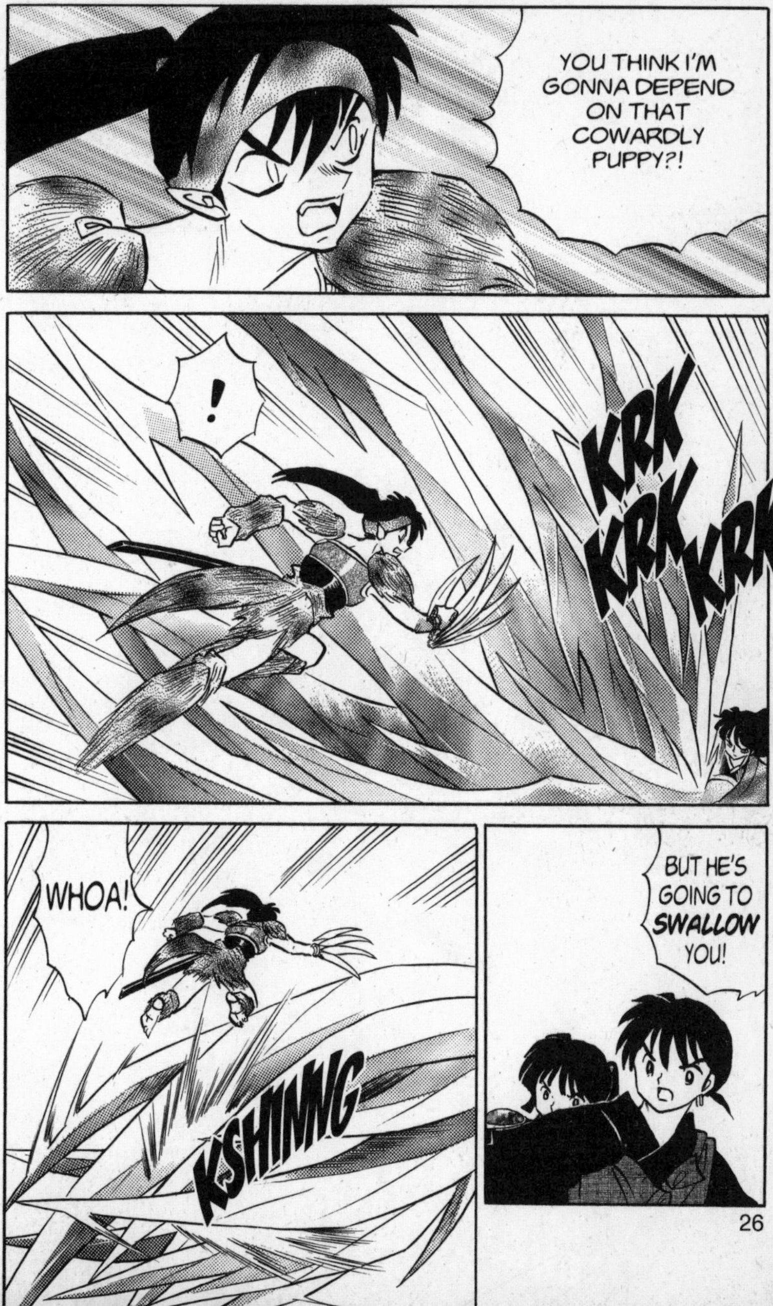
YOU THINK I'M GONNA DEPEND ON THAT COWARDLY PUPPY?!
!
KRK KRK KRK KRK
BUT HE'S GOING TO SWALLOW YOU!
WHOA!
KSHIINNG

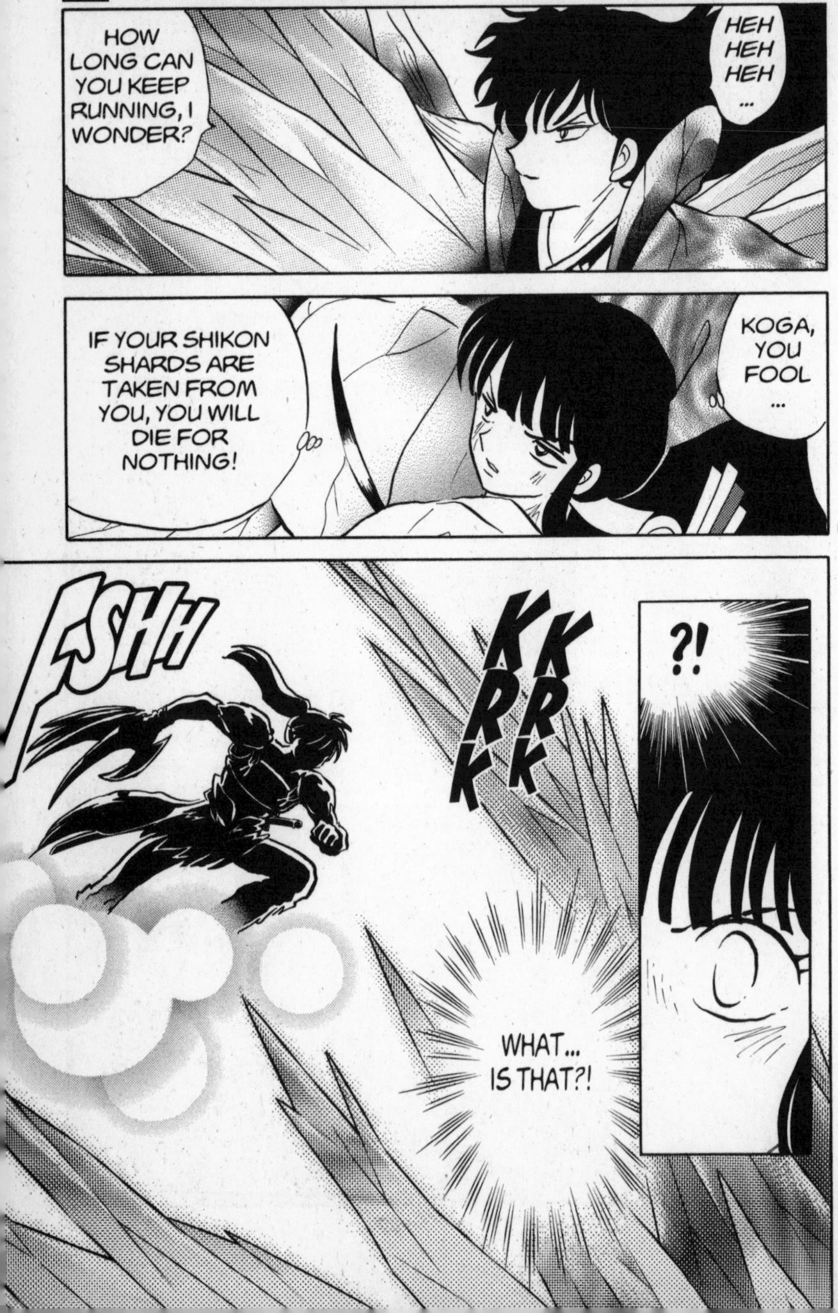
HEH HEH HEH ...
HOW LONG CAN YOU KEEP RUNNING, I WONDER?
KOGA, YOU FOOL ...
IF YOUR SHIKON SHARDS ARE TAKEN FROM YOU, YOU WILL DIE FOR NOTHING!
?!
WHAT... IS THAT?!
KKRRKK
FSHH

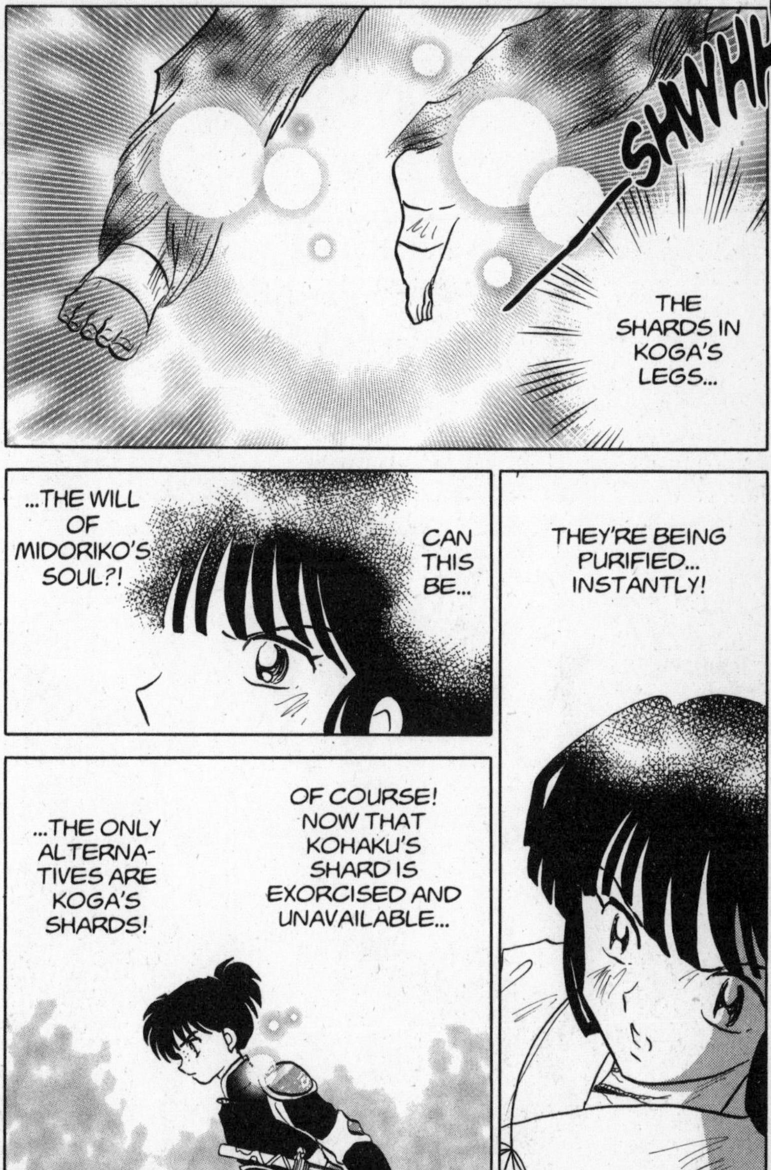
SHWHH
THE SHARDS IN KOGA'S LEGS...
THEY'RE BEING PURIFIED... INSTANTLY!
CAN THIS BE...
...THE WILL OF MIDORIKO'S SOUL?!
OF COURSE! NOW THAT KOHAKU'S SHARD IS EXORCISED AND UNAVAILABLE...
...THE ONLY ALTERNATIVES ARE KOGA'S SHARDS!

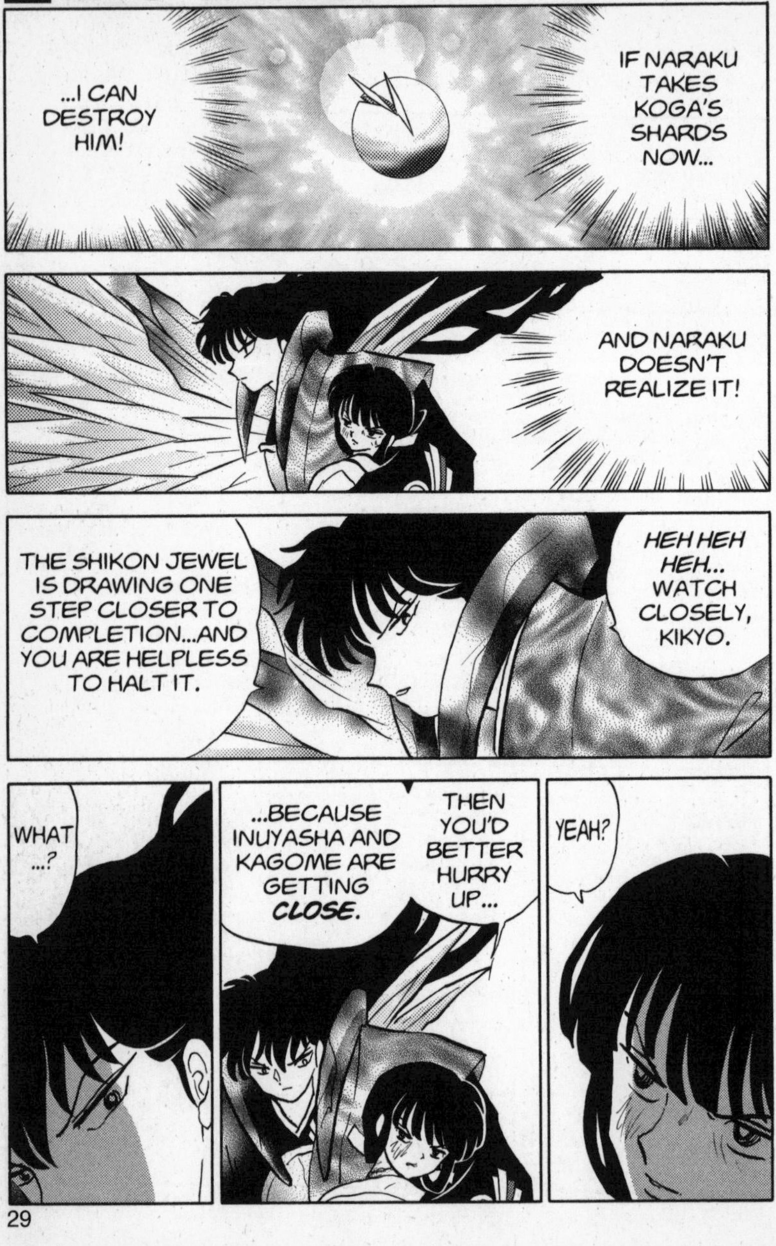
IF NARAKU TAKES KOGA'S SHARDS NOW...
...I CAN DESTROY HIM!
AND NARAKU DOESN'T REALIZE IT!
HEH HEH HEH... WATCH CLOSELY, KIKYO.
THE SHIKON JEWEL IS DRAWING ONE STEP CLOSER TO COMPLETION...AND YOU ARE HELPLESS TO HALT IT.
YEAH?
THEN YOU'D BETTER HURRY UP...
...BECAUSE INUYASHA AND KAGOME ARE GETTING *CLOSE*.
WHAT ...?

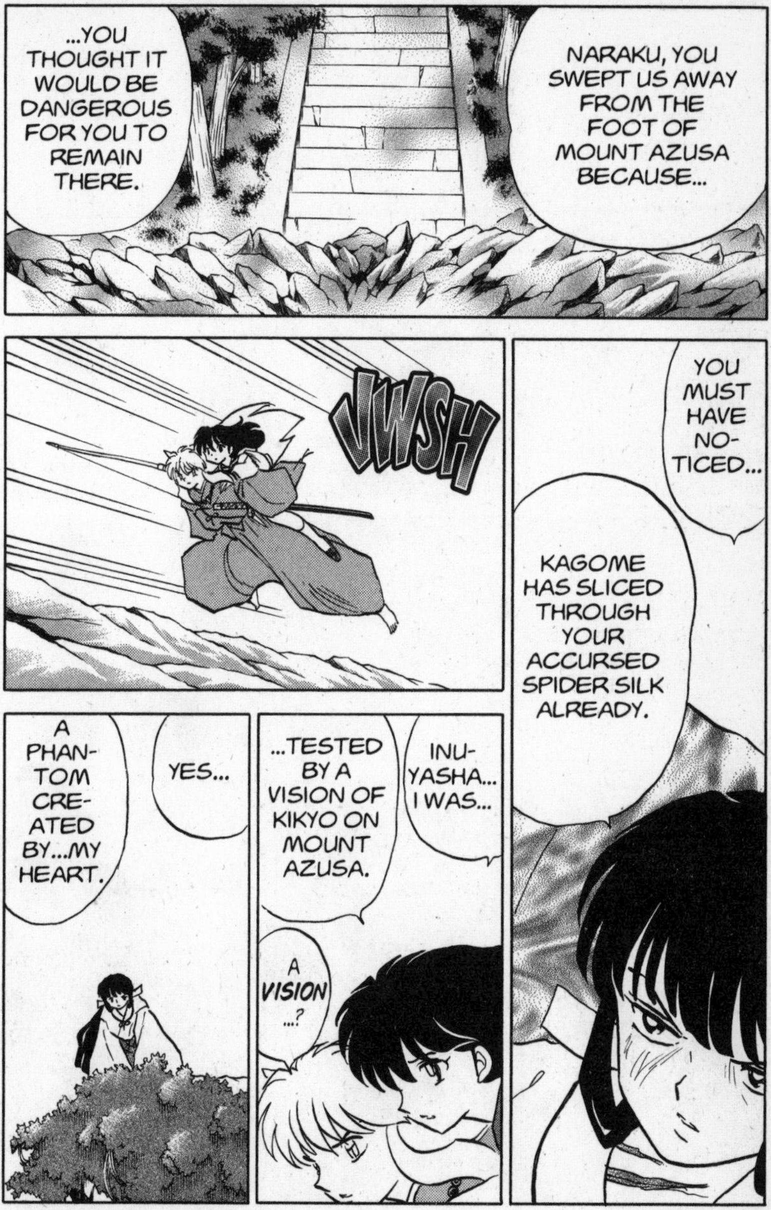
NARAKU, YOU SWEPT US AWAY FROM THE FOOT OF MOUNT AZUSA BECAUSE...
...YOU THOUGHT IT WOULD BE DANGEROUS FOR YOU TO REMAIN THERE.
YOU MUST HAVE NO-TICED...
KAGOME HAS SLICED THROUGH YOUR ACCURSED SPIDER SILK ALREADY.
JWSH
INU-YASHA... I WAS...
...TESTED BY A VISION OF KIKYO ON MOUNT AZUSA.
A VISION...?
YES...
A PHAN-TOM CRE-ATED BY...MY HEART.

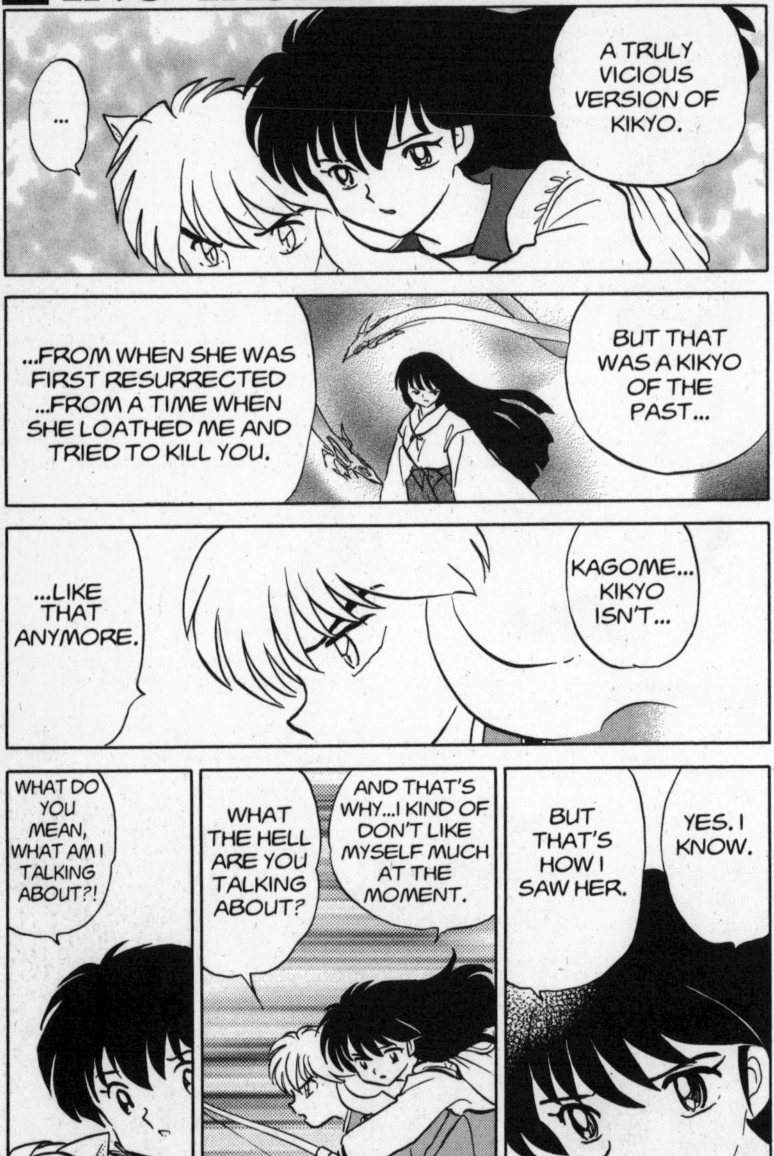
A TRULY VICIOUS VERSION OF KIKYO.
...
BUT THAT WAS A KIKYO OF THE PAST...
...FROM WHEN SHE WAS FIRST RESURRECTED ...FROM A TIME WHEN SHE LOATHED ME AND TRIED TO KILL YOU.
KAGOME... KIKYO ISN'T...
...LIKE THAT ANYMORE.
YES. I KNOW.
BUT THAT'S HOW I SAW HER.
AND THAT'S WHY...I KIND OF DON'T LIKE MYSELF MUCH AT THE MOMENT.
WHAT THE HELL ARE YOU TALKING ABOUT?
WHAT DO YOU MEAN, WHAT AM I TALKING ABOUT?!

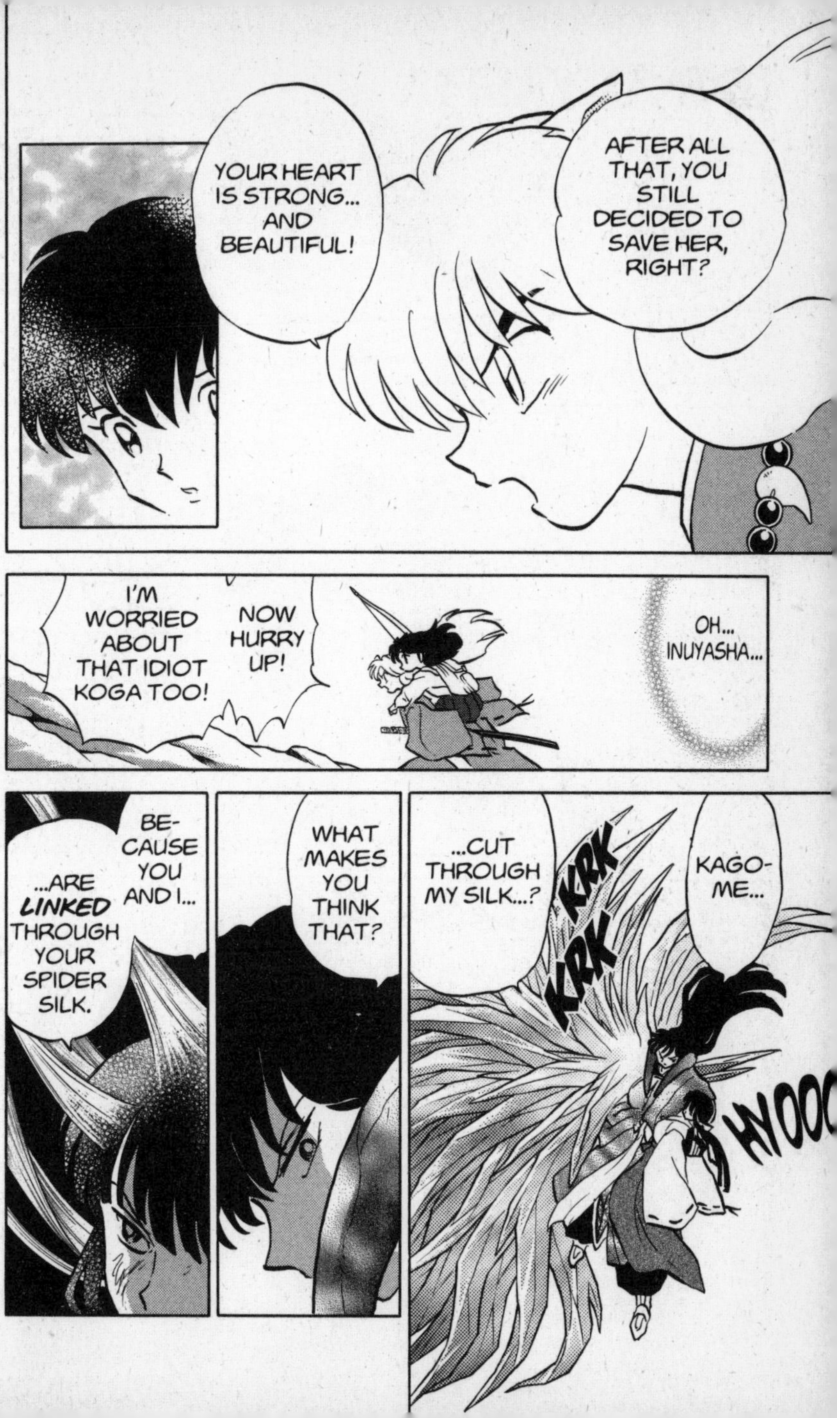
AFTER ALL THAT, YOU STILL DECIDED TO SAVE HER, RIGHT?
YOUR HEART IS STRONG... AND BEAUTIFUL!
OH... INUYASHA...
NOW HURRY UP!
I'M WORRIED ABOUT THAT IDIOT KOGA TOO!
KAGO-ME...
...CUT THROUGH MY SILK...?
KRK KRK
HYOO
WHAT MAKES YOU THINK THAT?
BE-CAUSE YOU AND I...
...ARE ***LINKED*** THROUGH YOUR SPIDER SILK.

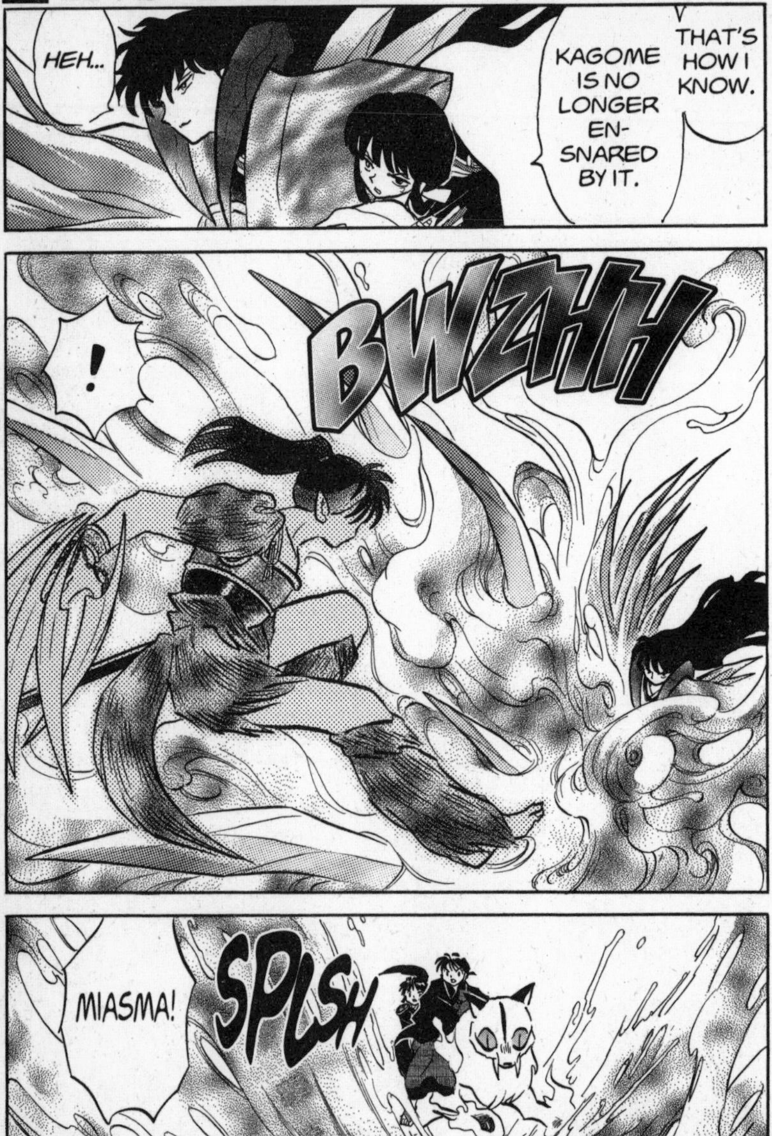
THAT'S HOW I KNOW.
KAGOME IS NO LONGER EN-SNARED BY IT.
HEH...
BWZHH
!
SPLSH
MIASMA!

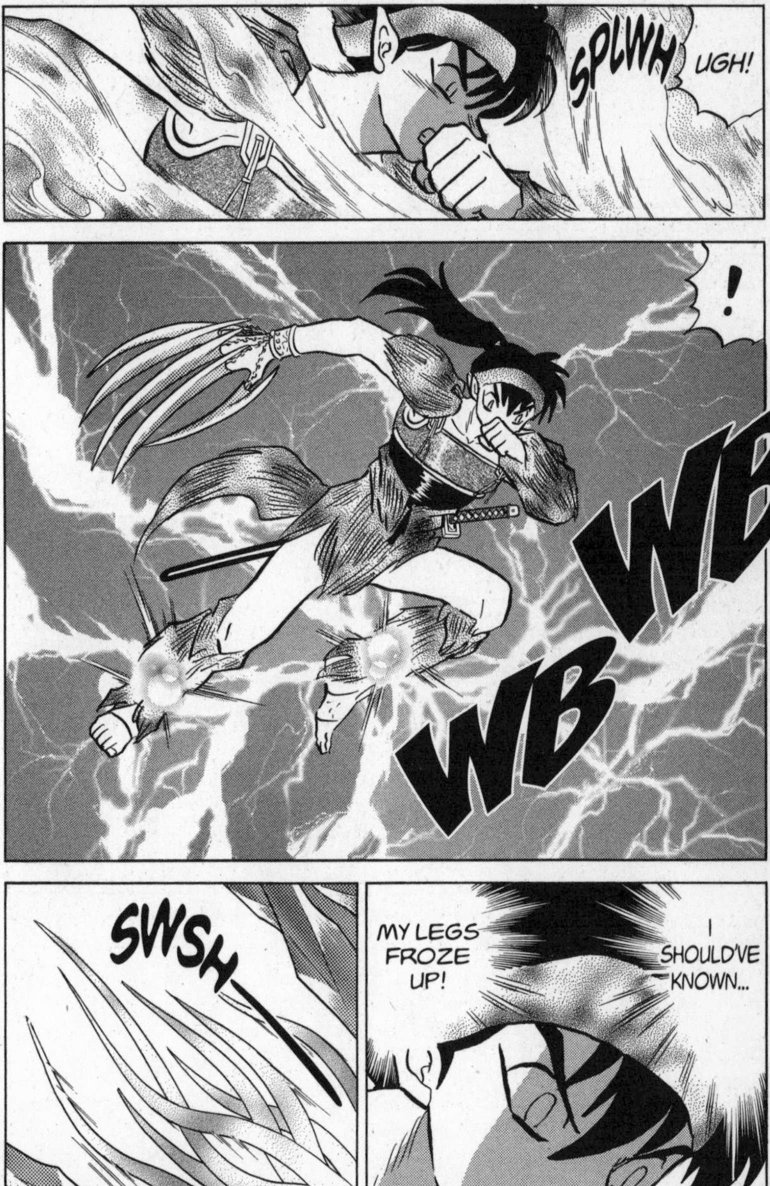
UGH!
SPLWH
!
WB WB
WB
I SHOULD'VE KNOWN...
MY LEGS FROZE UP!
SWSH

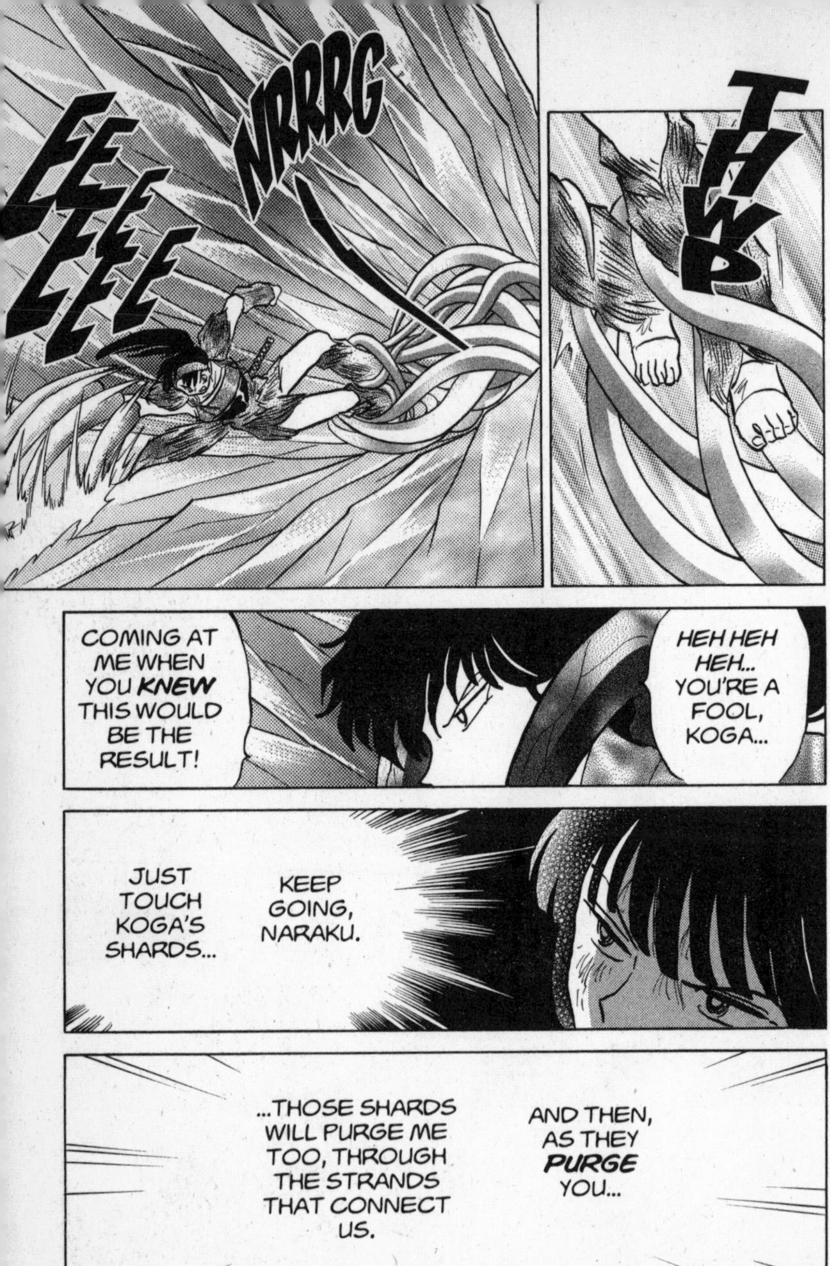
THWP
NRRRG
EEEEEE
HEH HEH HEH... YOU'RE A FOOL, KOGA...
COMING AT ME WHEN YOU *KNEW* THIS WOULD BE THE RESULT!
KEEP GOING, NARAKU.
JUST TOUCH KOGA'S SHARDS...
AND THEN, AS THEY *PURGE* YOU...
...THOSE SHARDS WILL PURGE ME TOO, THROUGH THE STRANDS THAT CONNECT US.

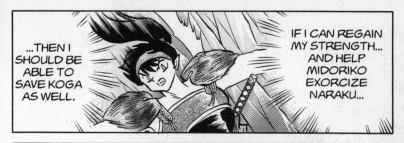

IF I CAN REGAIN MY STRENGTH... AND HELP MIDORIKO EXORCIZE NARAKU...
...THEN I SHOULD BE ABLE TO SAVE KOGA AS WELL.
I WILL **NOT** DIE, NARAKU...
NOT WHILE I'M ENTRAPPED IN YOUR FOUL ARMS, AT LEAST!
JUST HURRY... INUYASHA.
JWH
JWBJWH
TP

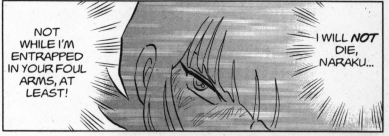

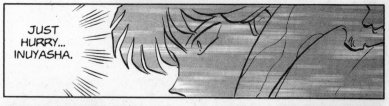

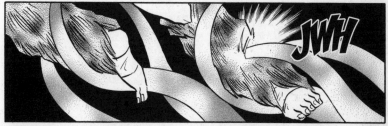

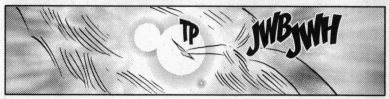

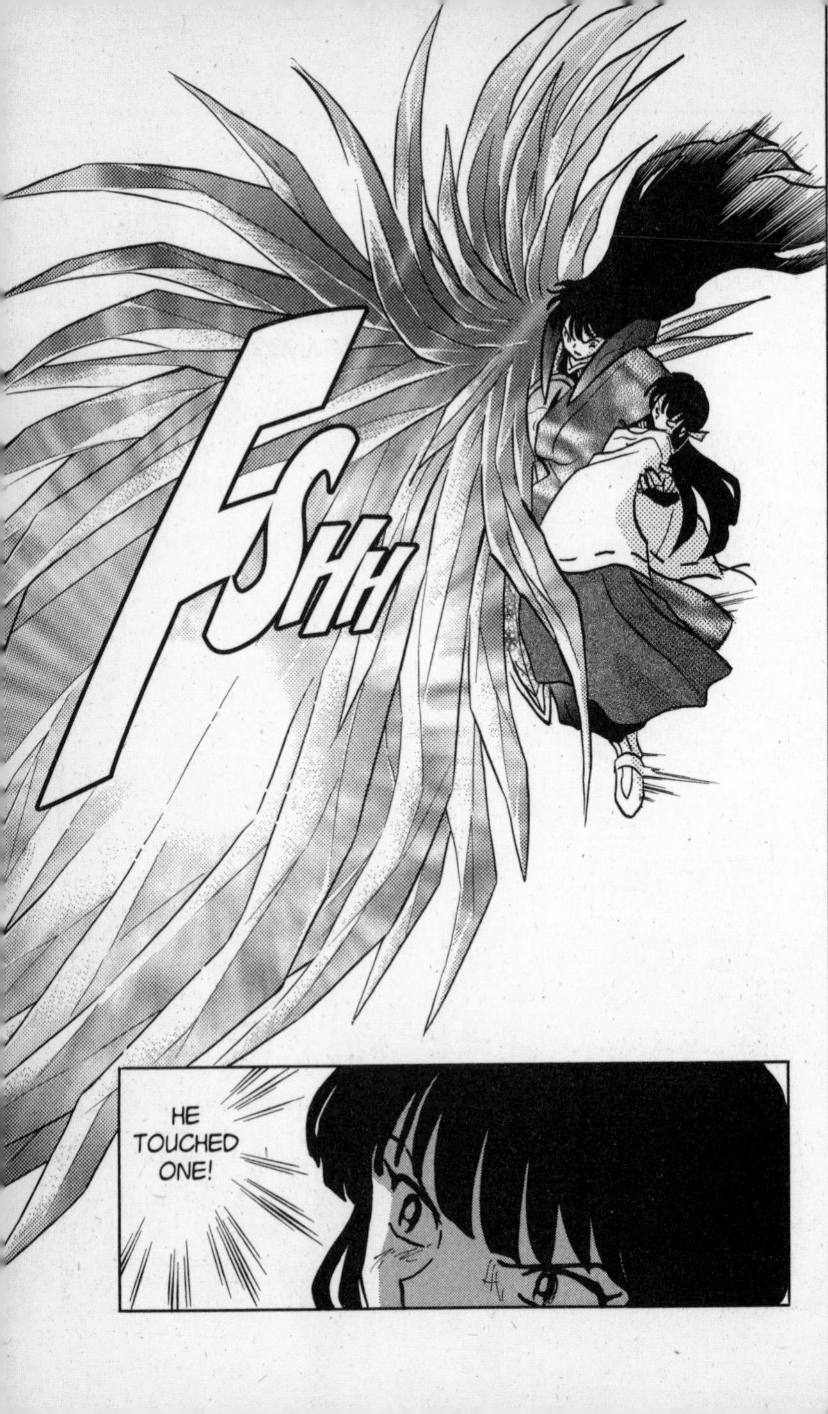
FSHH
HE TOUCHED ONE!

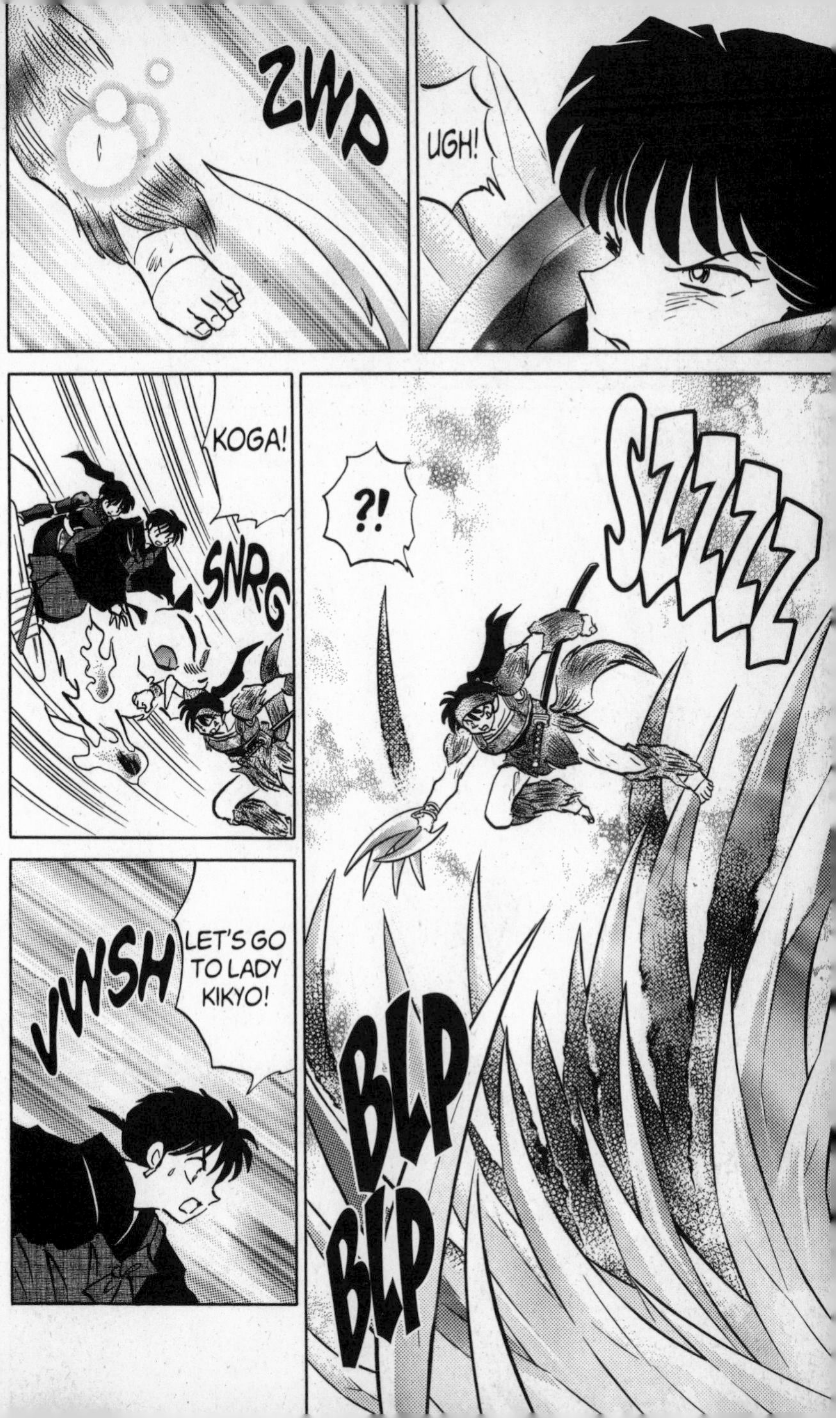
UGH!
ZWP
?!
SZZZZ
BLP
BLP
KOGA!
SNRG
LET'S GO TO LADY KIKYO!
JWSH

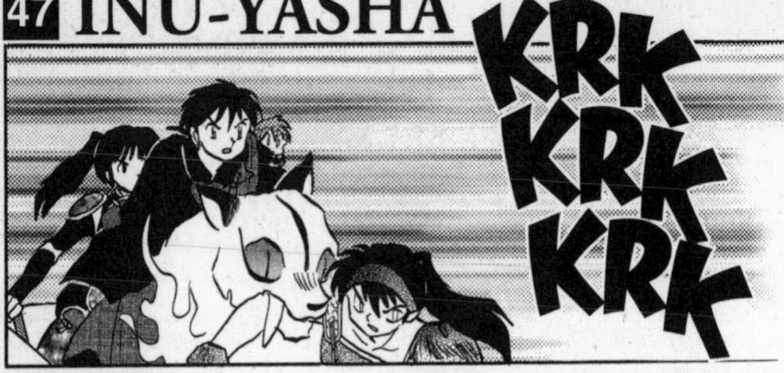
KRK
KRK
KRK

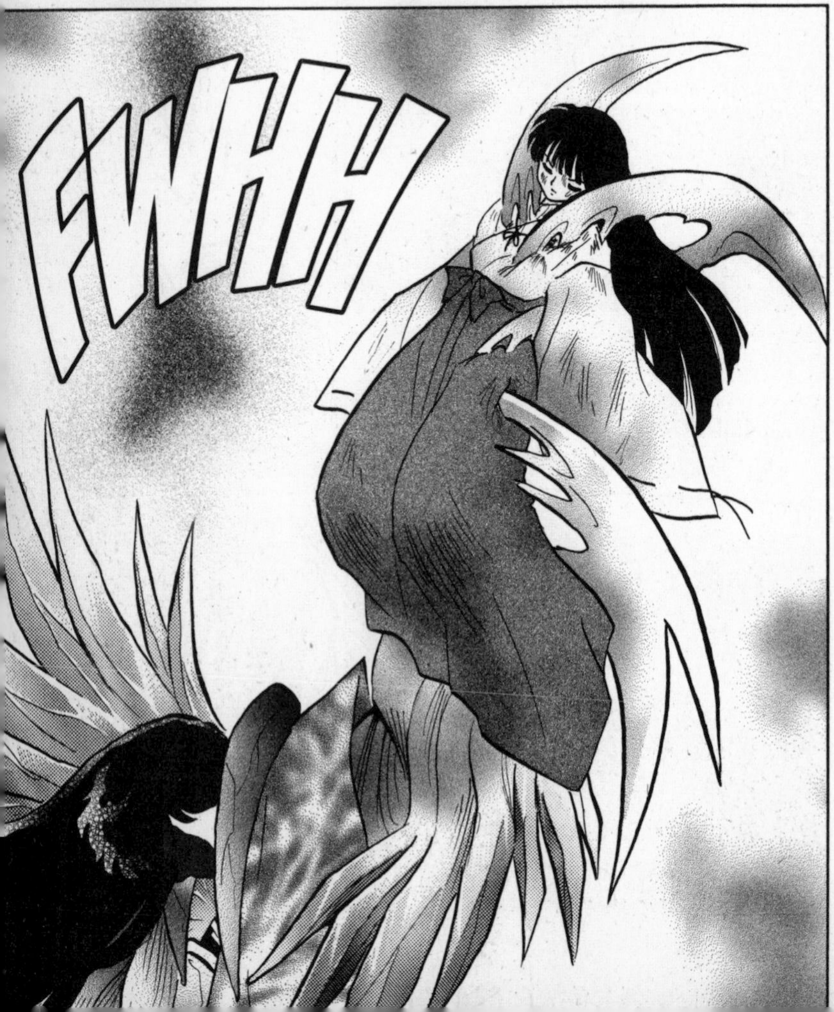
FWHH

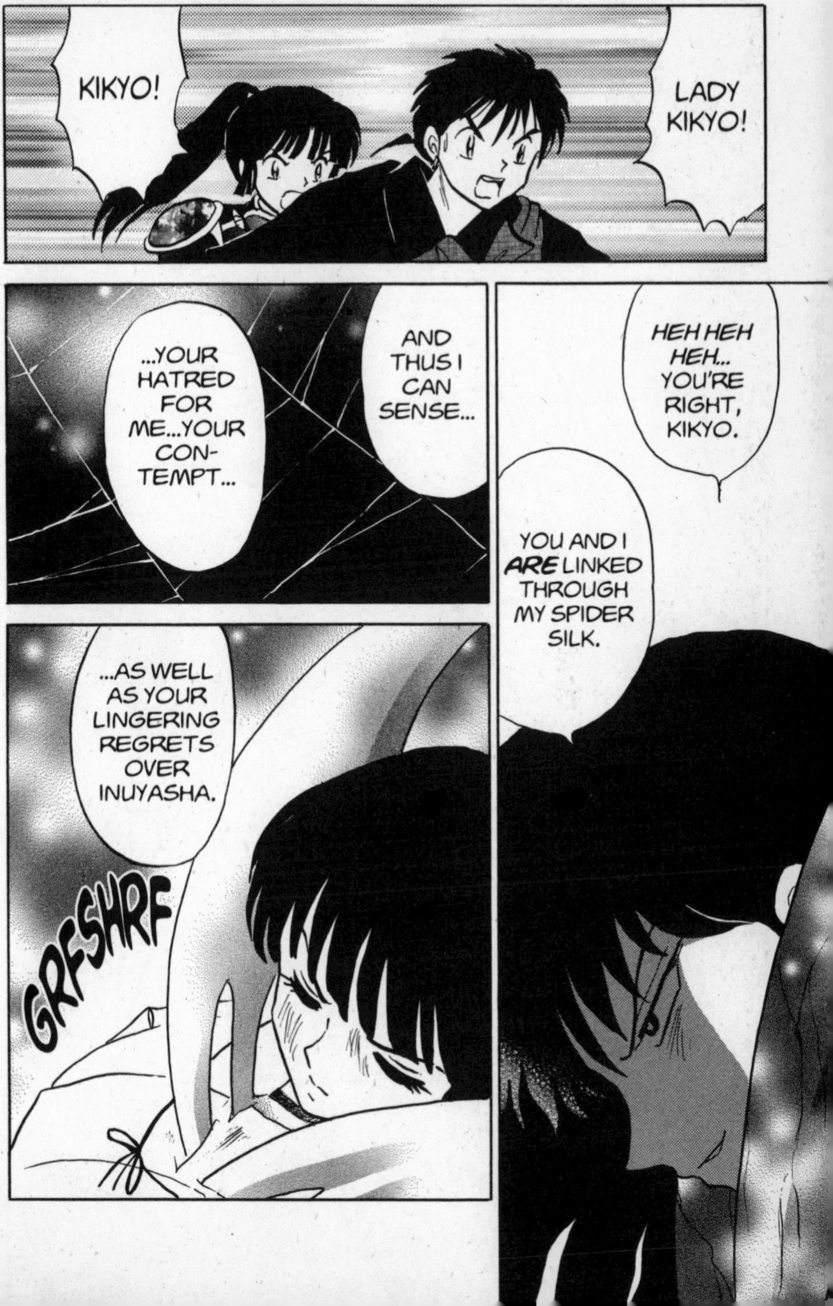
LADY KIKYO!
KIKYO!
HEH HEH HEH... YOU'RE RIGHT, KIKYO.
YOU AND I ARE LINKED THROUGH MY SPIDER SILK.
AND THUS I CAN SENSE...
...YOUR HATRED FOR ME...YOUR CONTEMPT...
...AS WELL AS YOUR LINGERING REGRETS OVER INUYASHA.
GRFSHRF

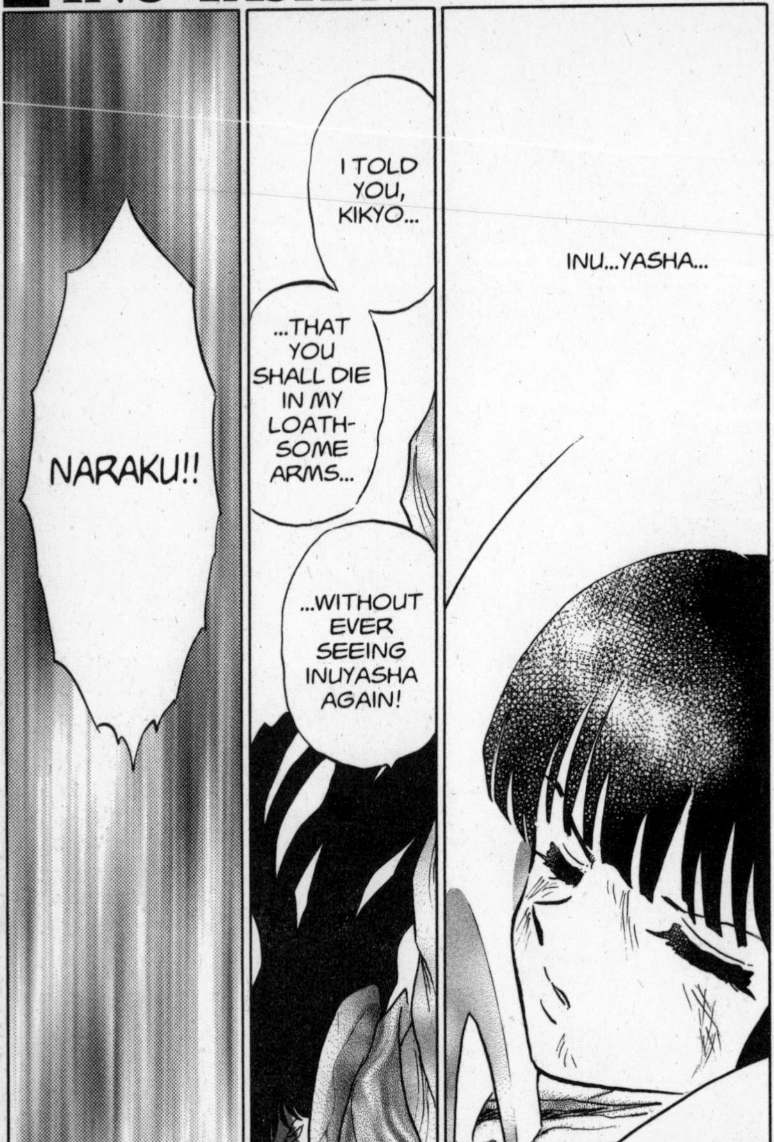
INU...YASHA...
I TOLD YOU, KIKYO...
...THAT YOU SHALL DIE IN MY LOATH-SOME ARMS...
...WITHOUT EVER SEEING INUYASHA AGAIN!
NARAKU!!

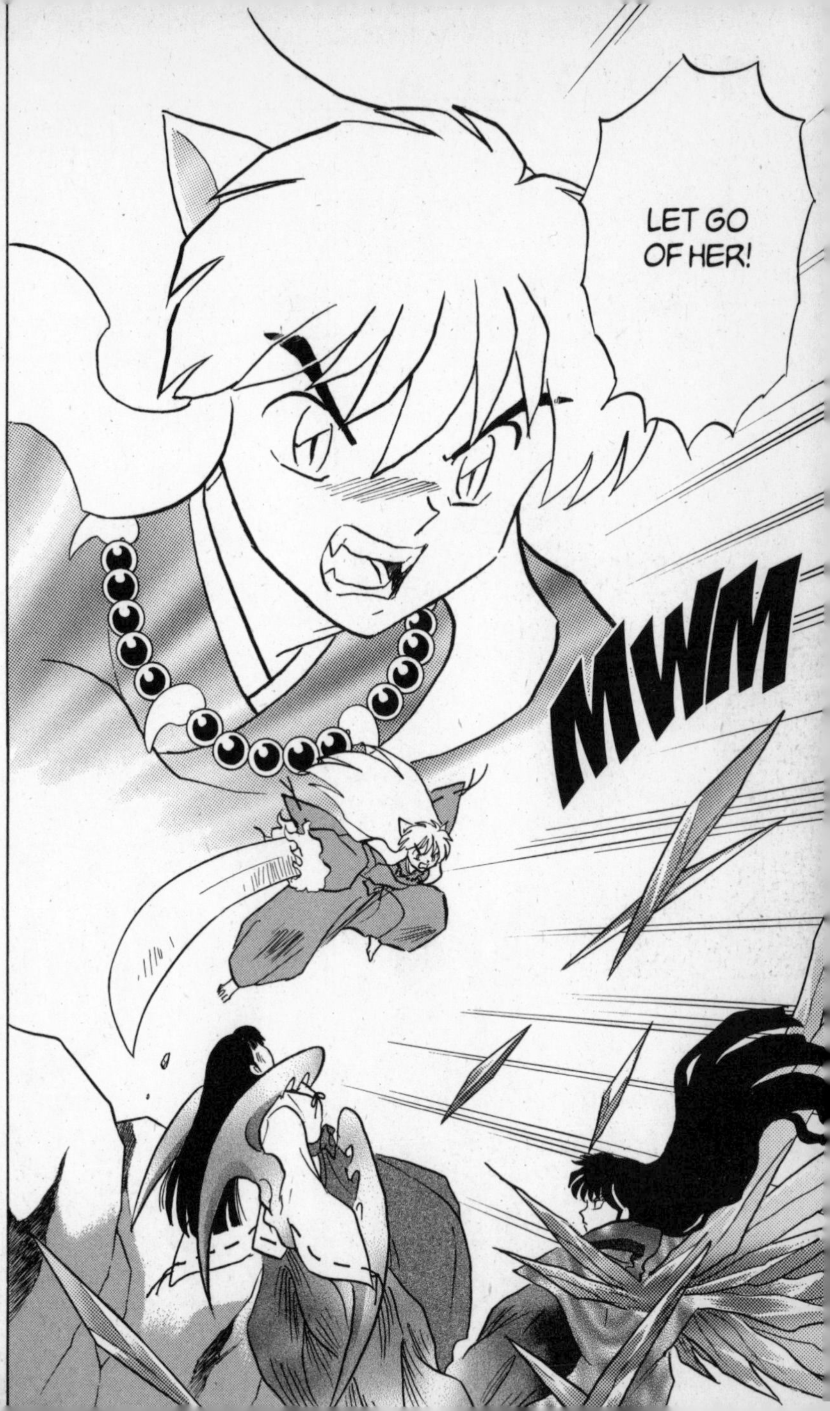
LET GO OF HER!
MWM

SCROLL 3

THE OPENED BODY

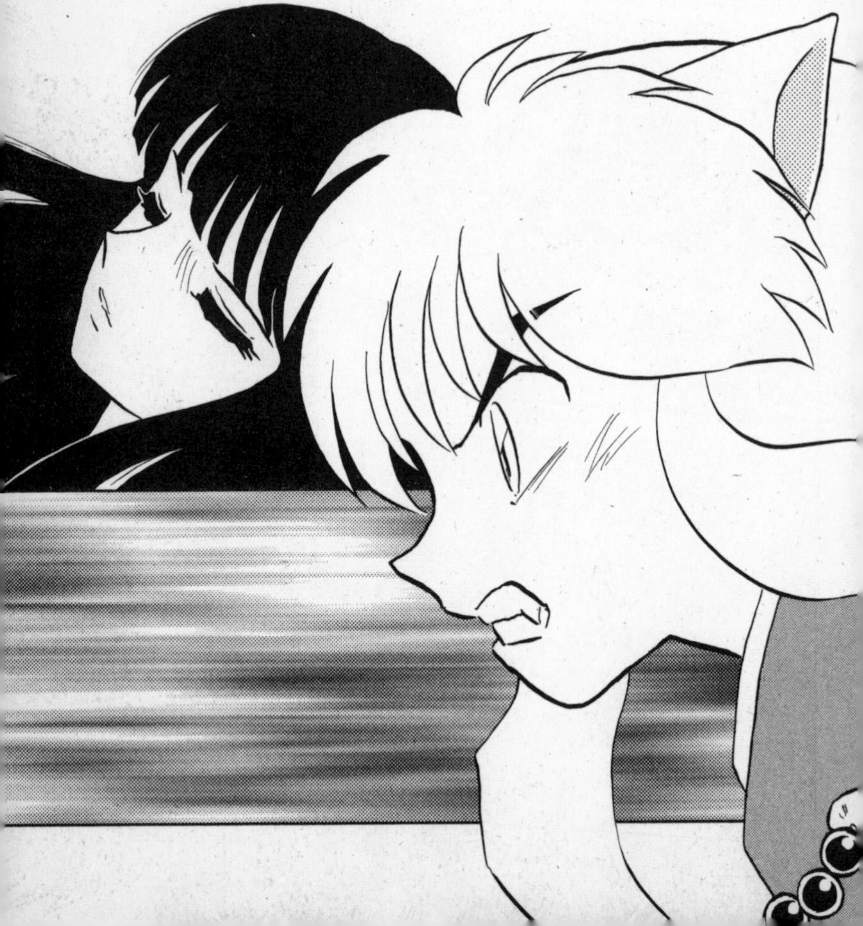

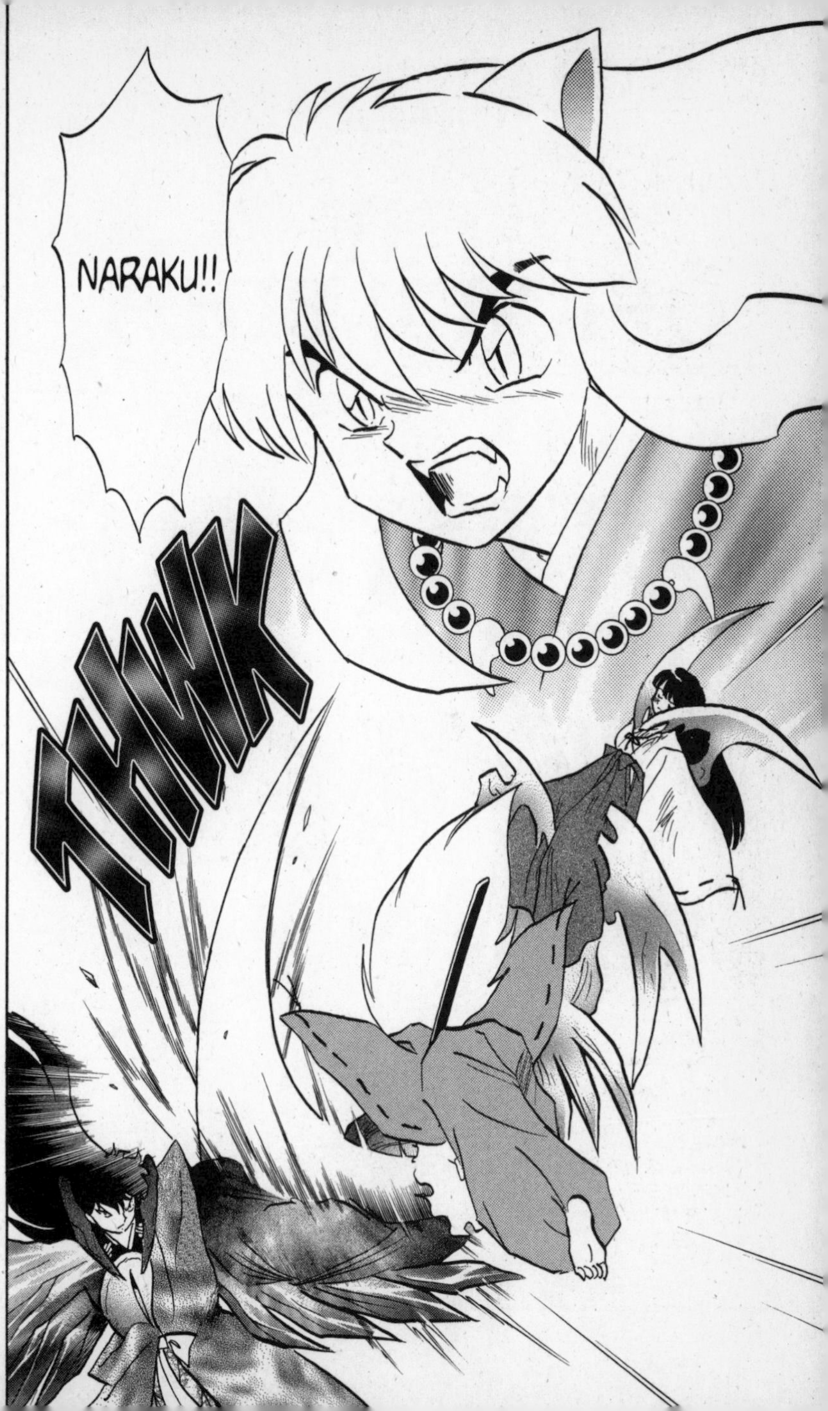
NARAKU!!
THWK

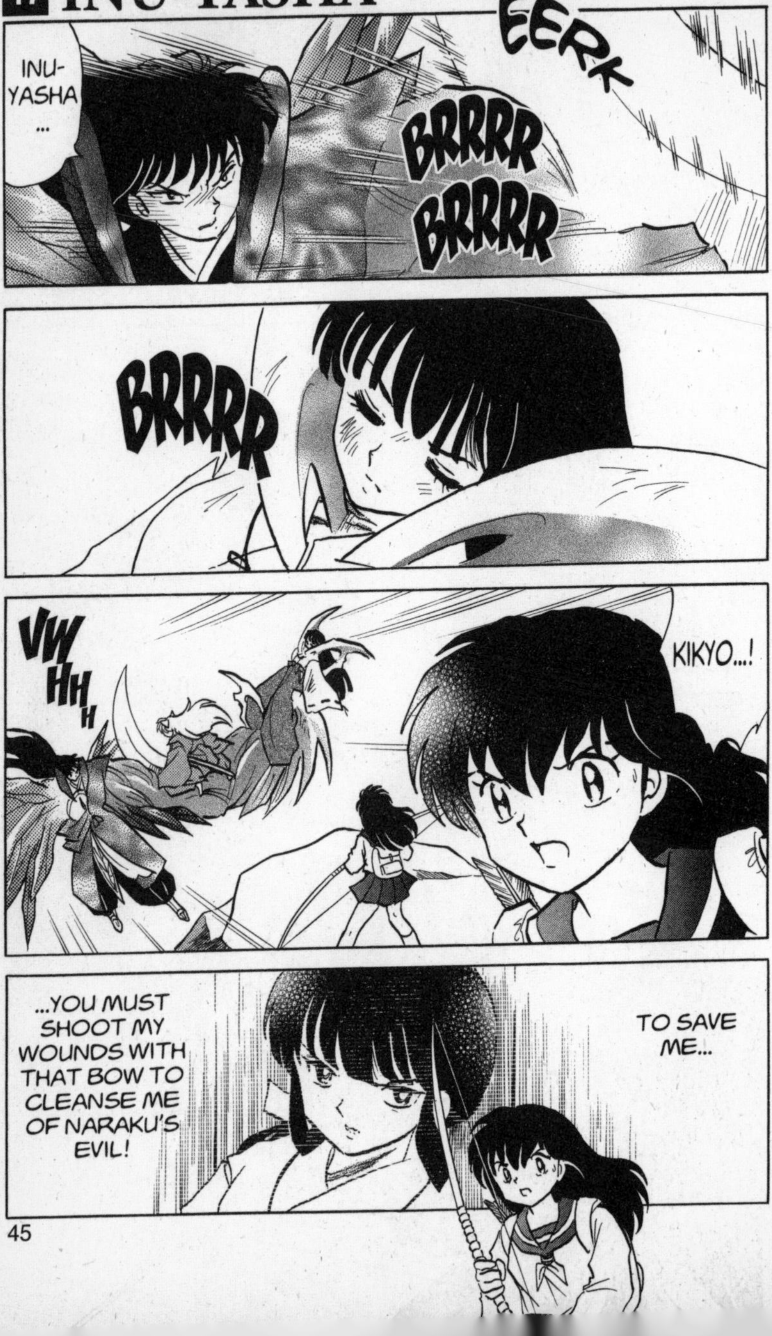
EERK
BRRRR
BRRRR
INU-YASHA ...
BRRRR
KIKYO...!
VWHHH
TO SAVE ME...
...YOU MUST SHOOT MY WOUNDS WITH THAT BOW TO CLEANSE ME OF NARAKU'S EVIL!

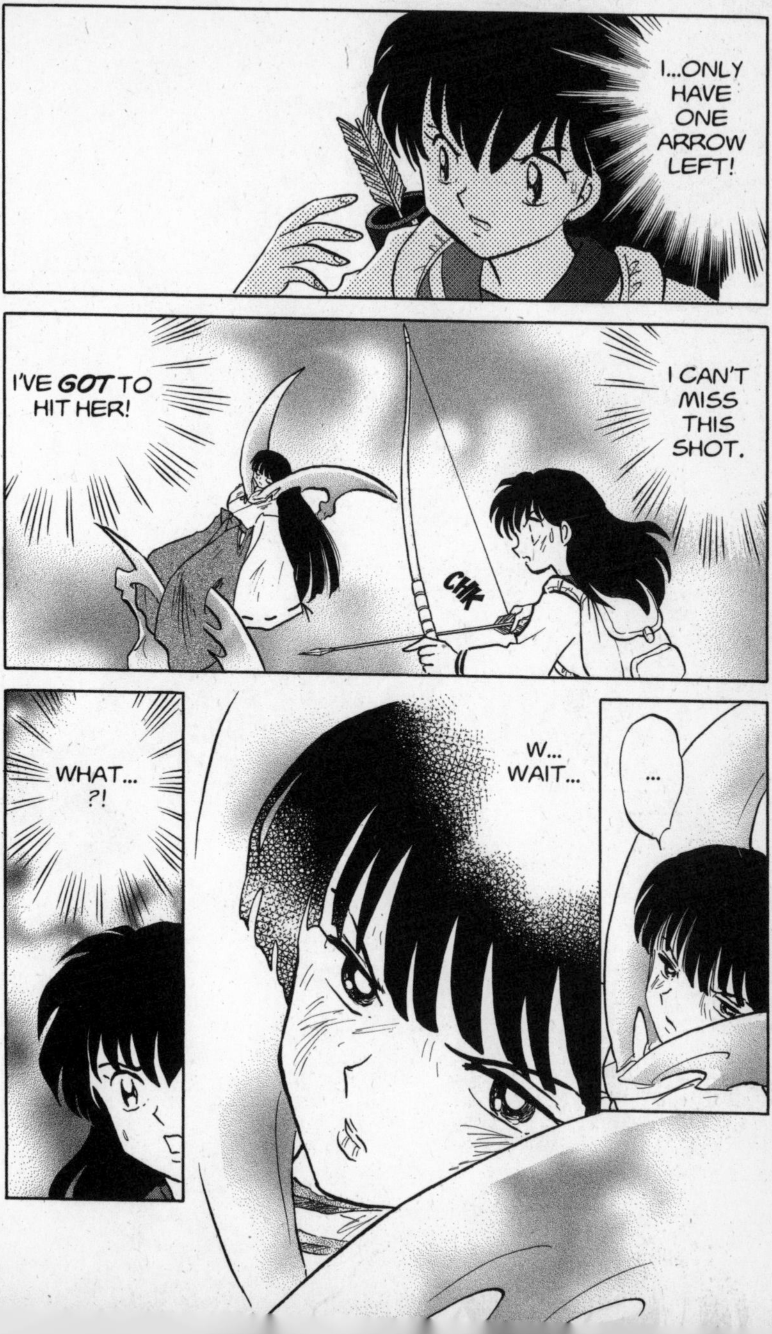
I...ONLY HAVE ONE ARROW LEFT!
I CAN'T MISS THIS SHOT.
I'VE **GOT** TO HIT HER!
CHK
...
W... WAIT...
WHAT... ?!

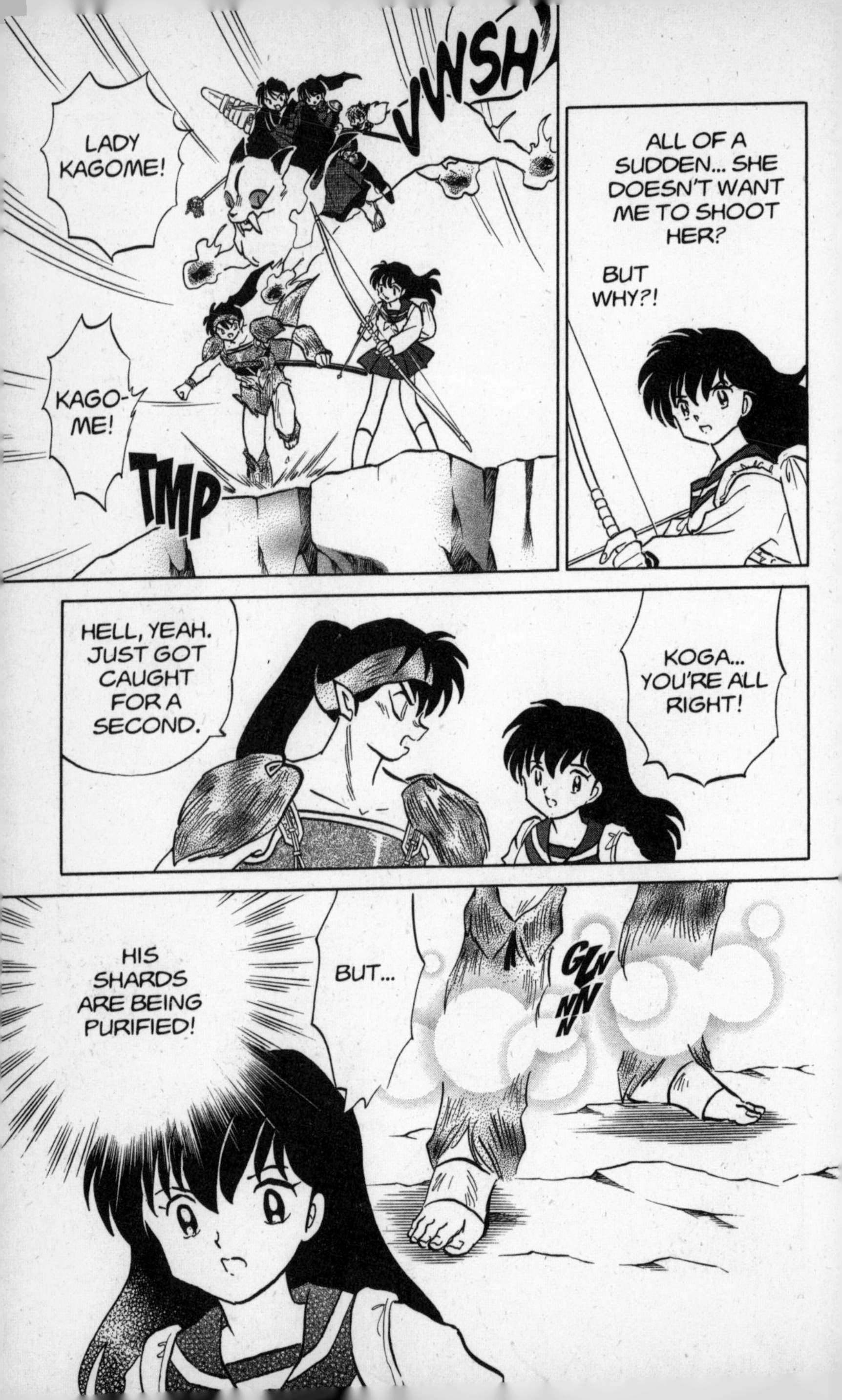
ALL OF A SUDDEN... SHE DOESN'T WANT ME TO SHOOT HER?
BUT WHY?!
VWSH
LADY KAGOME!
KAGO-ME!
TMP
KOGA... YOU'RE ALL RIGHT!
HELL, YEAH. JUST GOT CAUGHT FOR A SECOND.
GLNNNN
BUT...
HIS SHARDS ARE BEING PURIFIED!

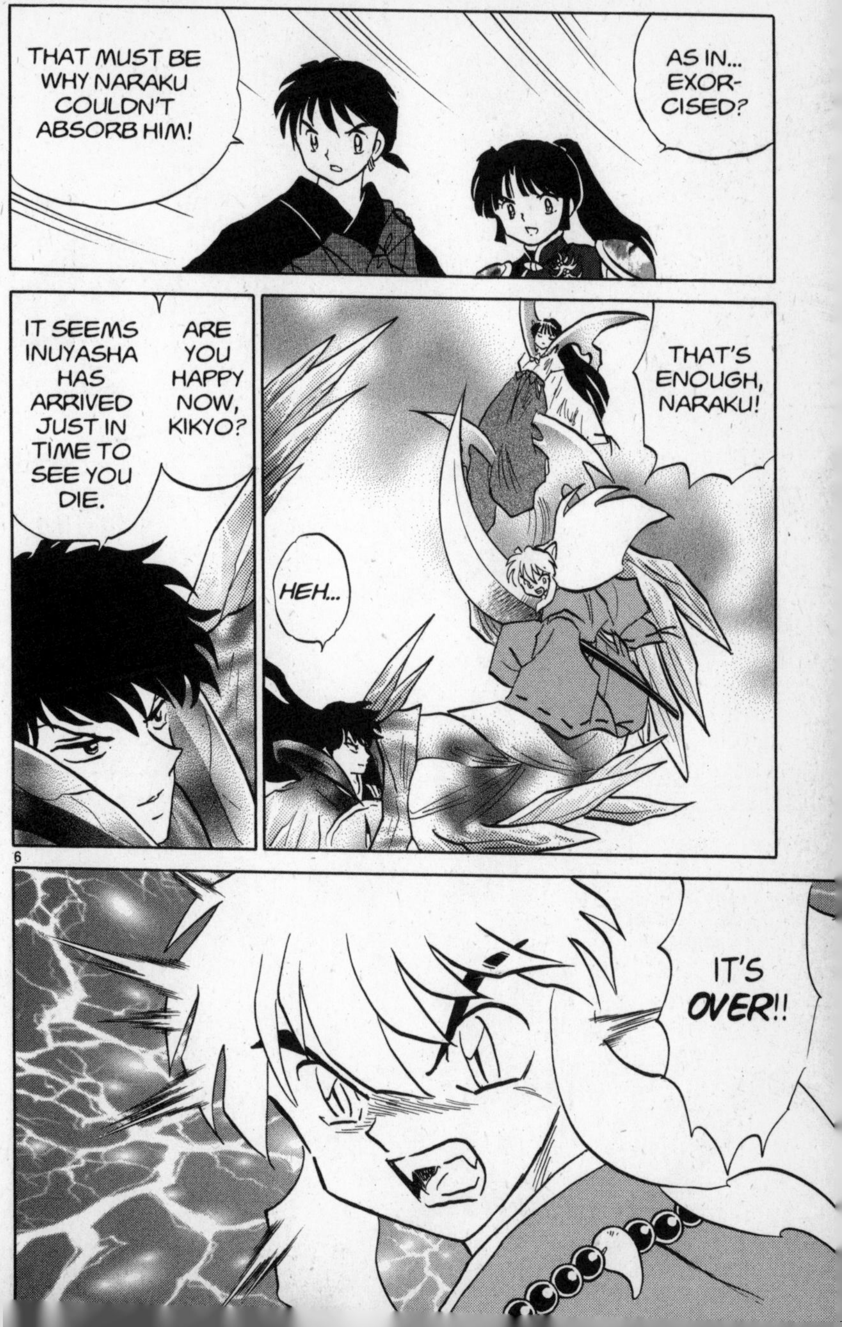
AS IN... EXOR-CISED?
THAT MUST BE WHY NARAKU COULDN'T ABSORB HIM!
THAT'S ENOUGH, NARAKU!
HEH...
ARE YOU HAPPY NOW, KIKYO?
IT SEEMS INUYASHA HAS ARRIVED JUST IN TIME TO SEE YOU DIE.
IT'S *OVER*!!

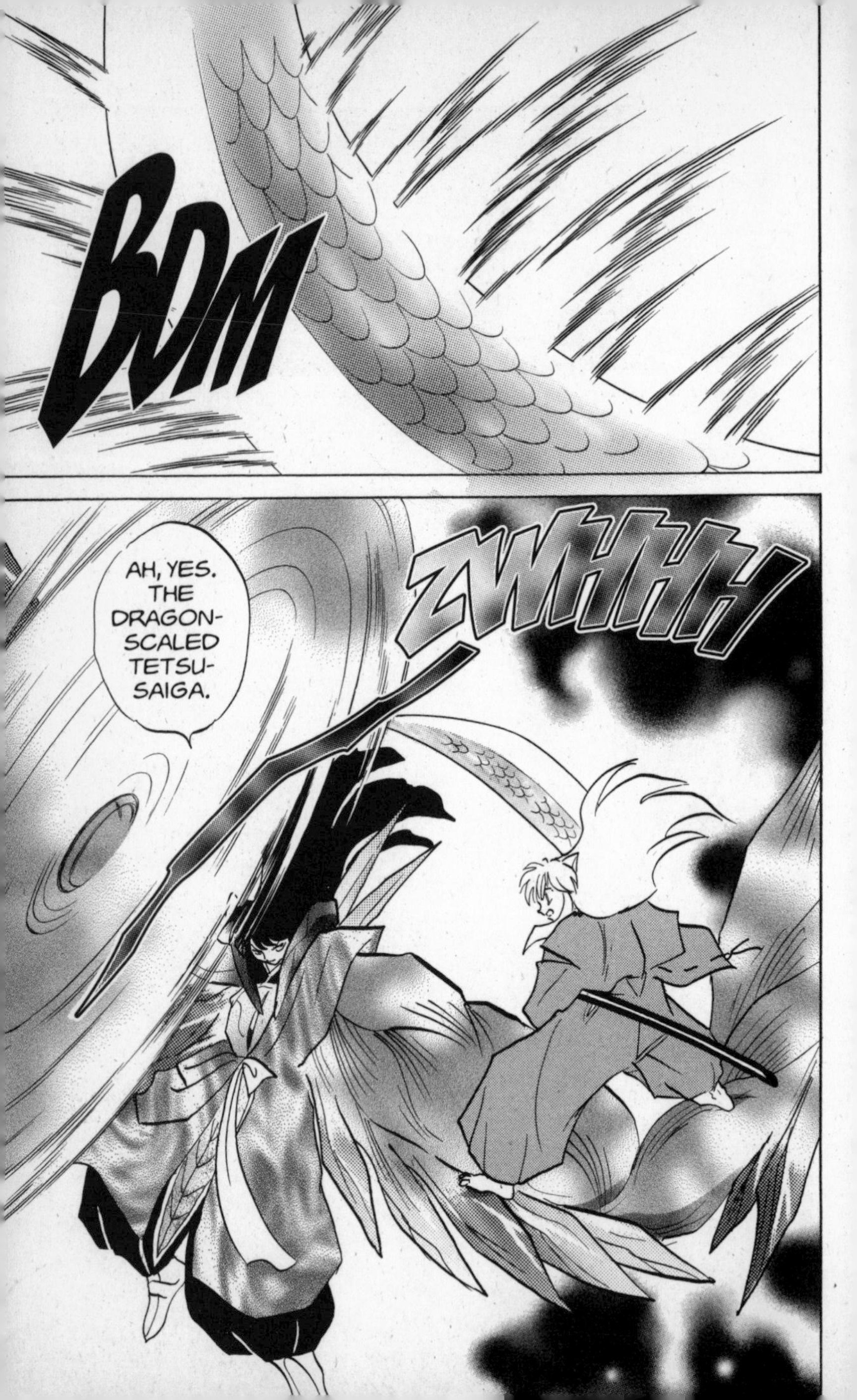
BOM
ZWHHHH
AH, YES. THE DRAGON-SCALED TETSU-SAIGA.

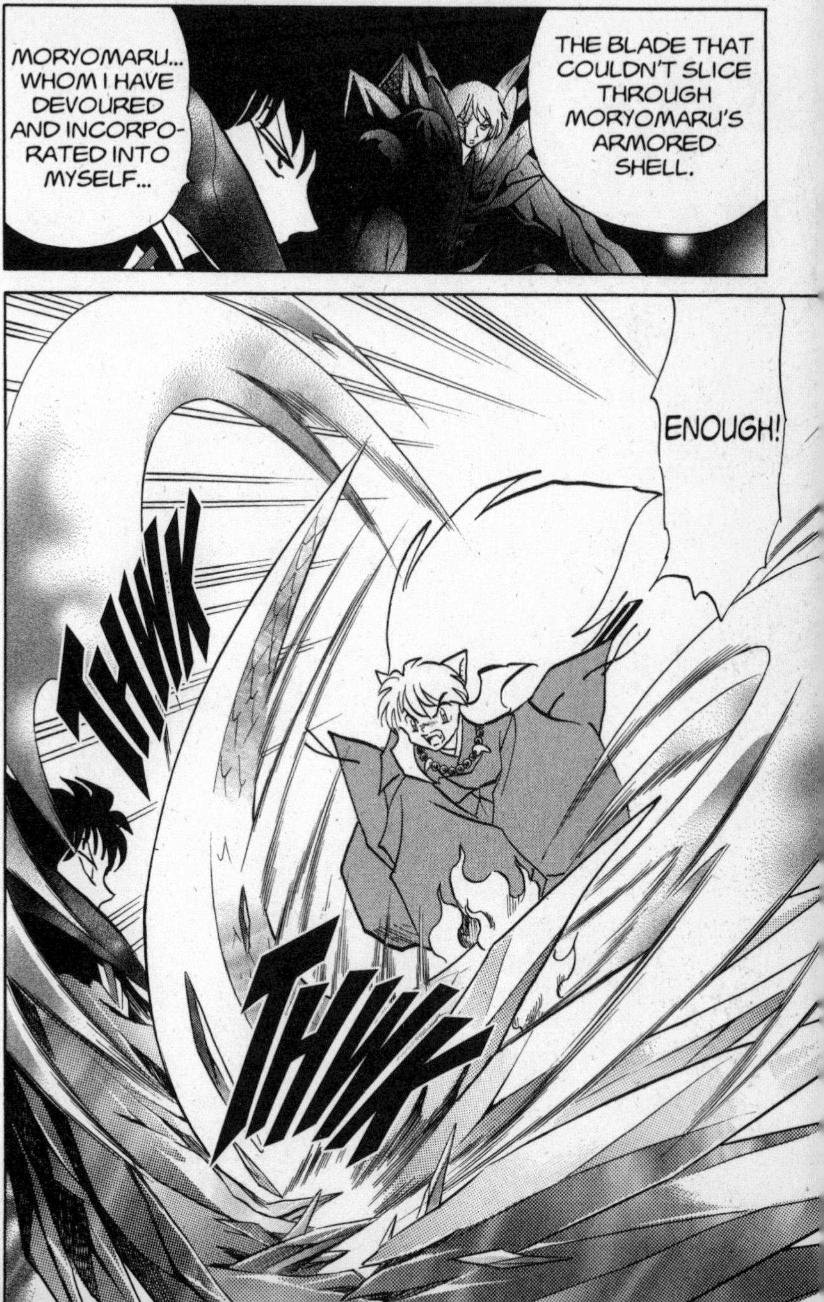
THE BLADE THAT COULDN'T SLICE THROUGH MORYOMARU'S ARMORED SHELL.
MORYOMARU... WHOM I HAVE DEVOURED AND INCORPORATED INTO MYSELF...
ENOUGH!
THUNK
THUNK

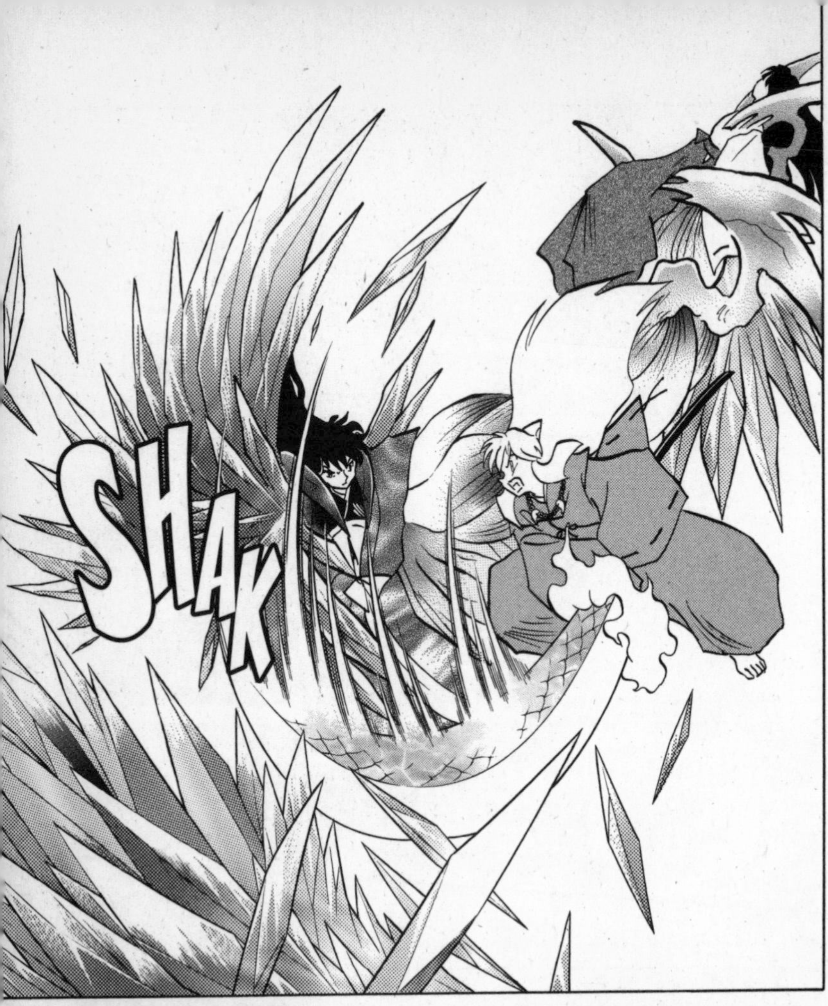
SHAK

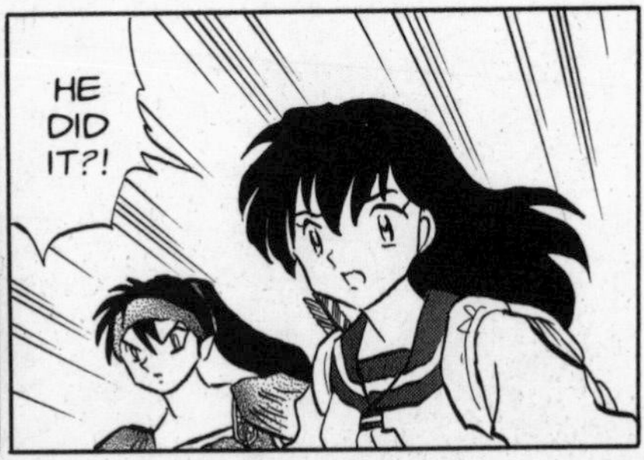
HE DID IT?!

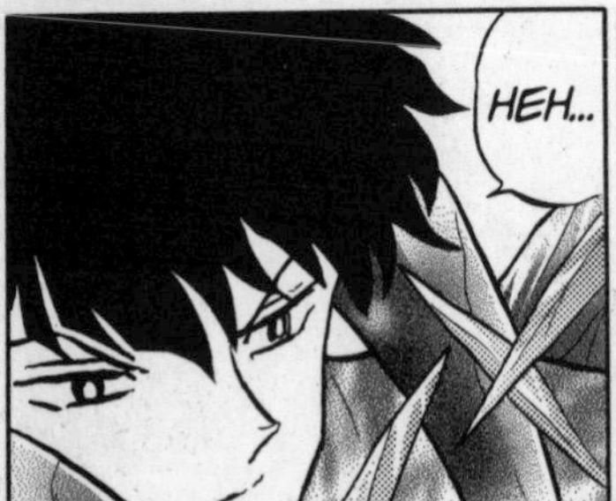
HEH...

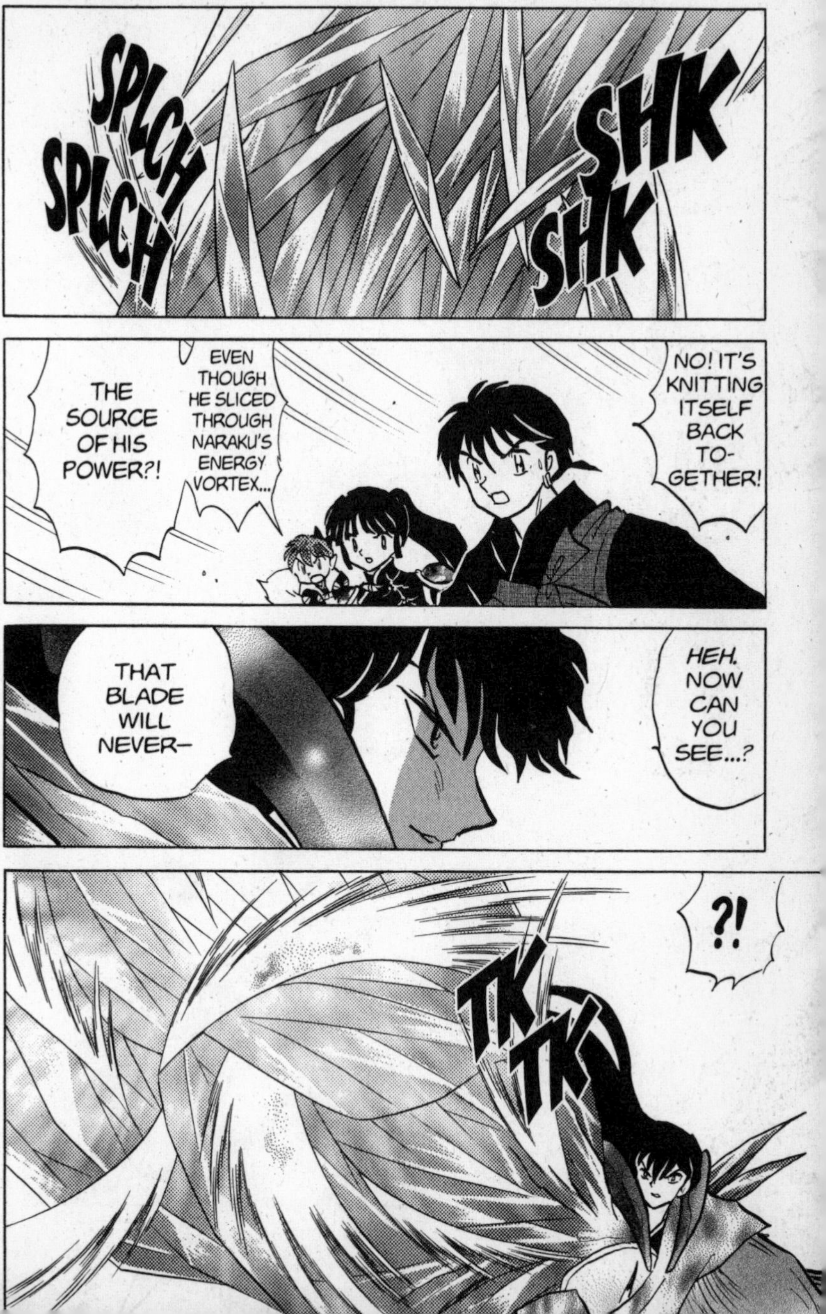
SHK SHK
SPLCH SPLCH
NO! IT'S KNITTING ITSELF BACK TO-GETHER!
EVEN THOUGH HE SLICED THROUGH NARAKU'S ENERGY VORTEX...
THE SOURCE OF HIS POWER?!
HEH. NOW CAN YOU SEE...?
THAT BLADE WILL NEVER–
?!
TK TK

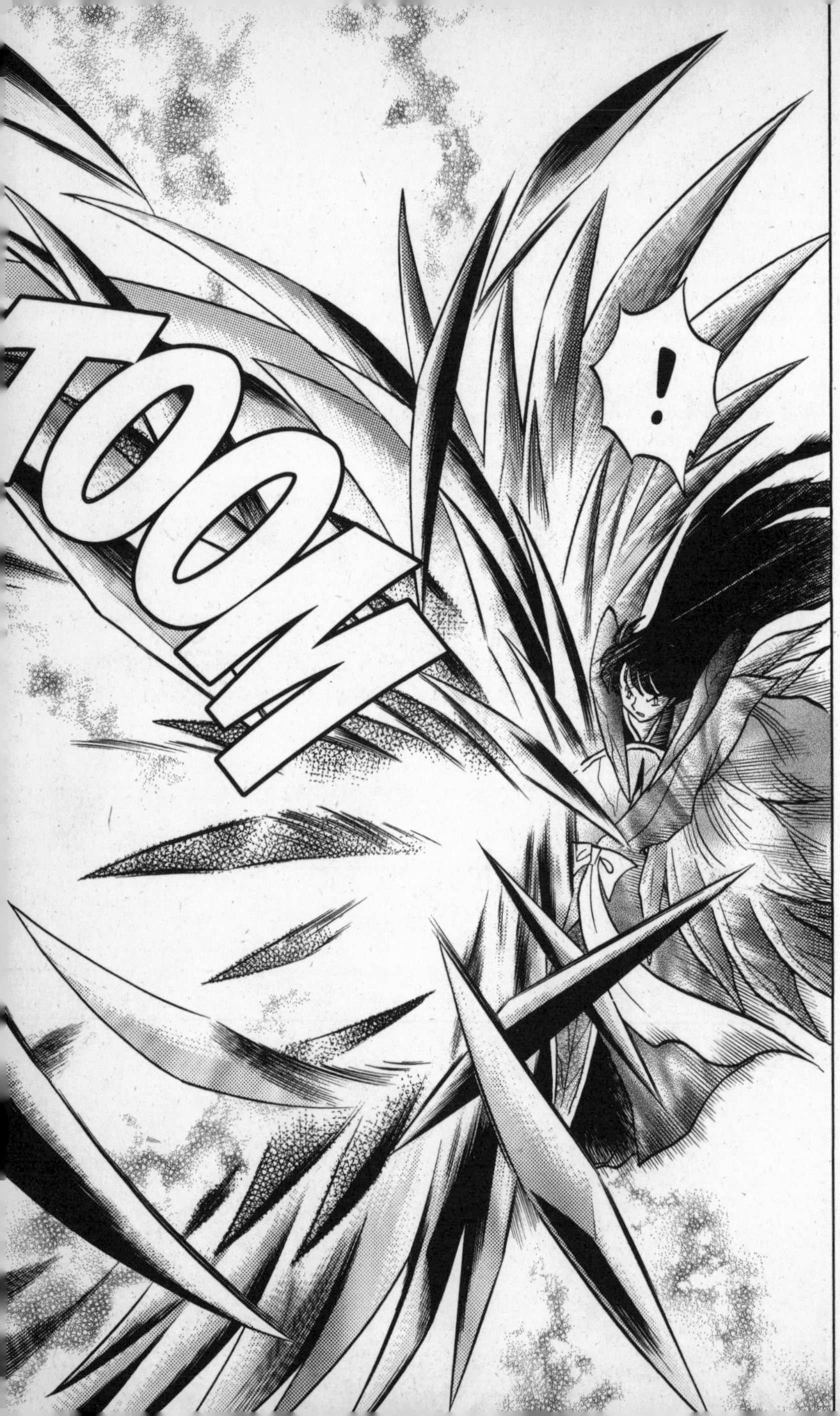

ZOOM
!

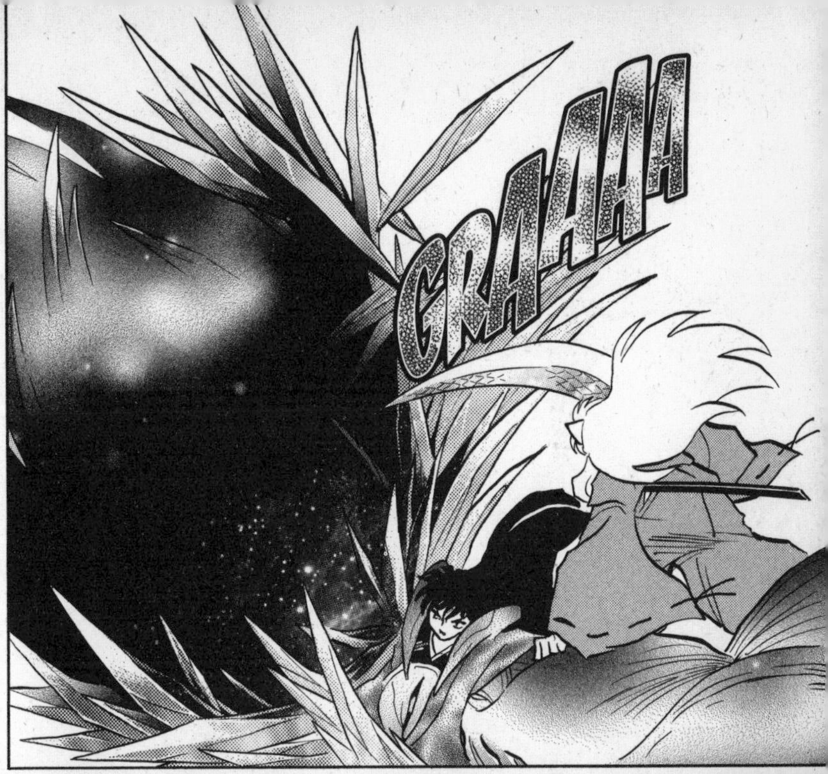
CRAAAA

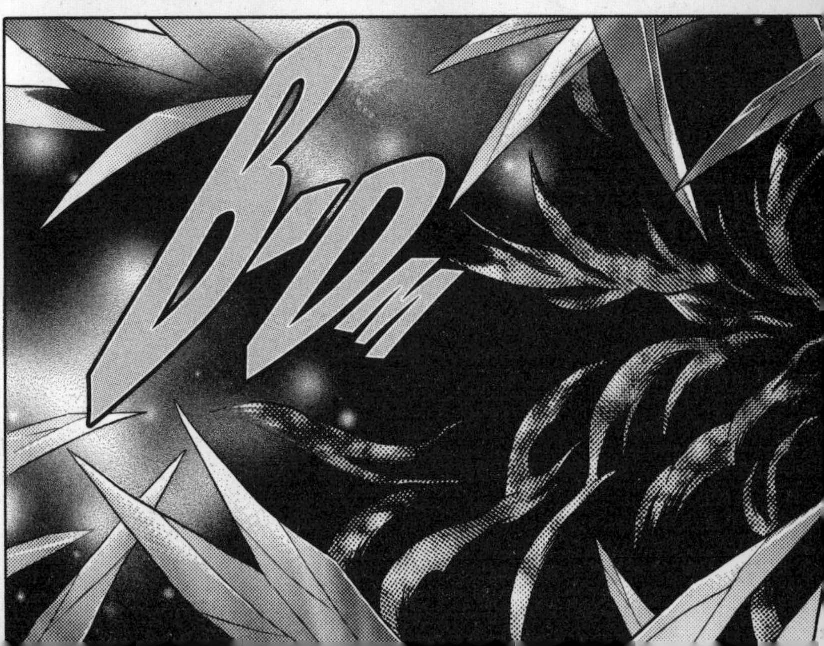
BOM

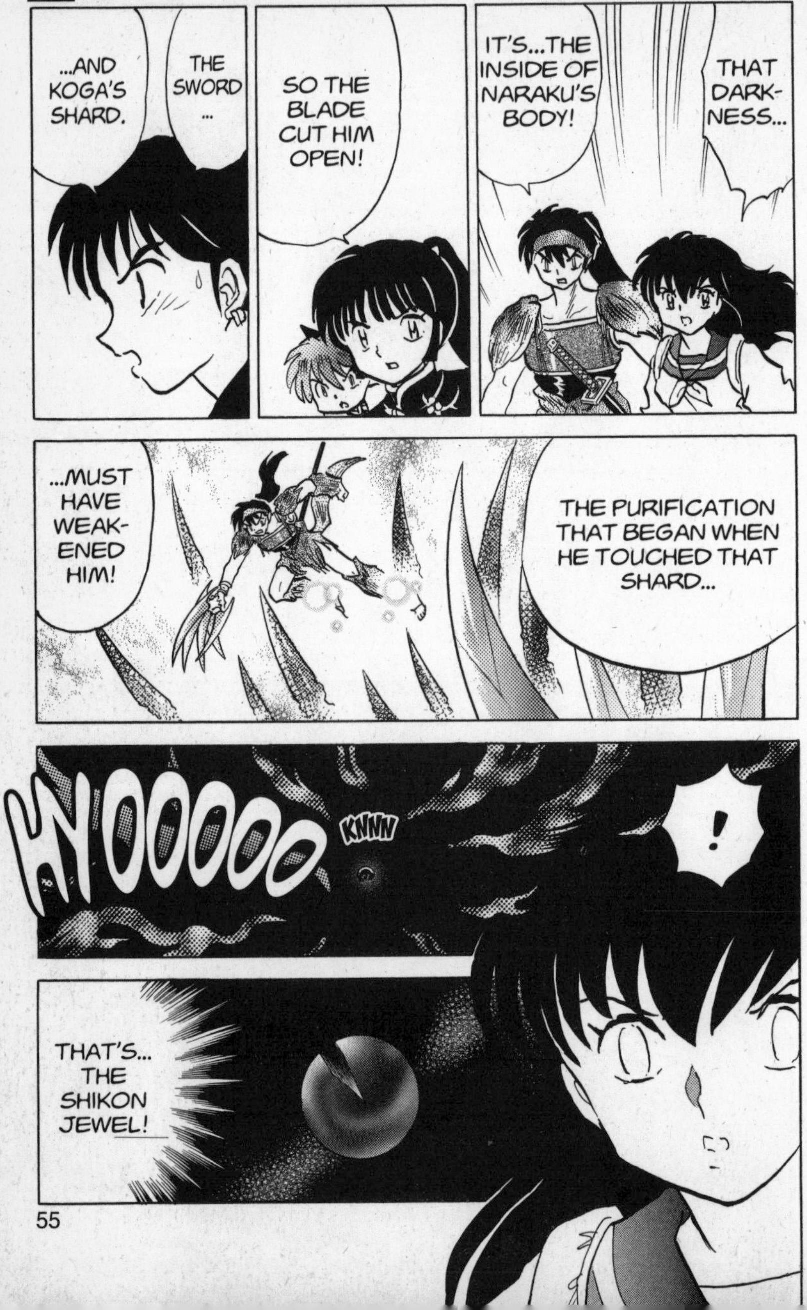
THAT DARKNESS...
IT'S...THE INSIDE OF NARAKU'S BODY!
SO THE BLADE CUT HIM OPEN!
THE SWORD...
...AND KOGA'S SHARD.
THE PURIFICATION THAT BEGAN WHEN HE TOUCHED THAT SHARD...
...MUST HAVE WEAKENED HIM!
!
HYOOOOO
KNNN
THAT'S... THE SHIKON JEWEL!

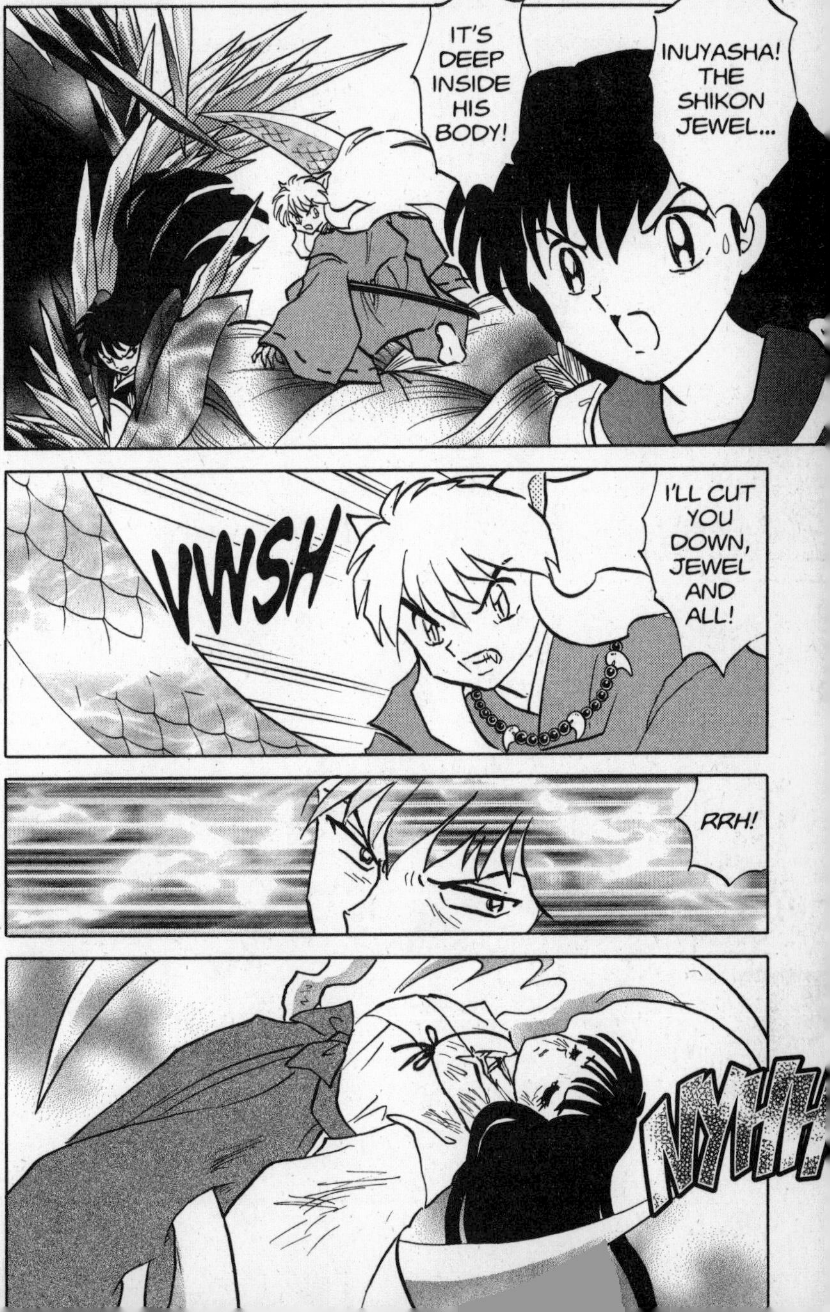
INUYASHA! THE SHIKON JEWEL...
IT'S DEEP INSIDE HIS BODY!
I'LL CUT YOU DOWN, JEWEL AND ALL!
VWSH
RRH!
NYHH

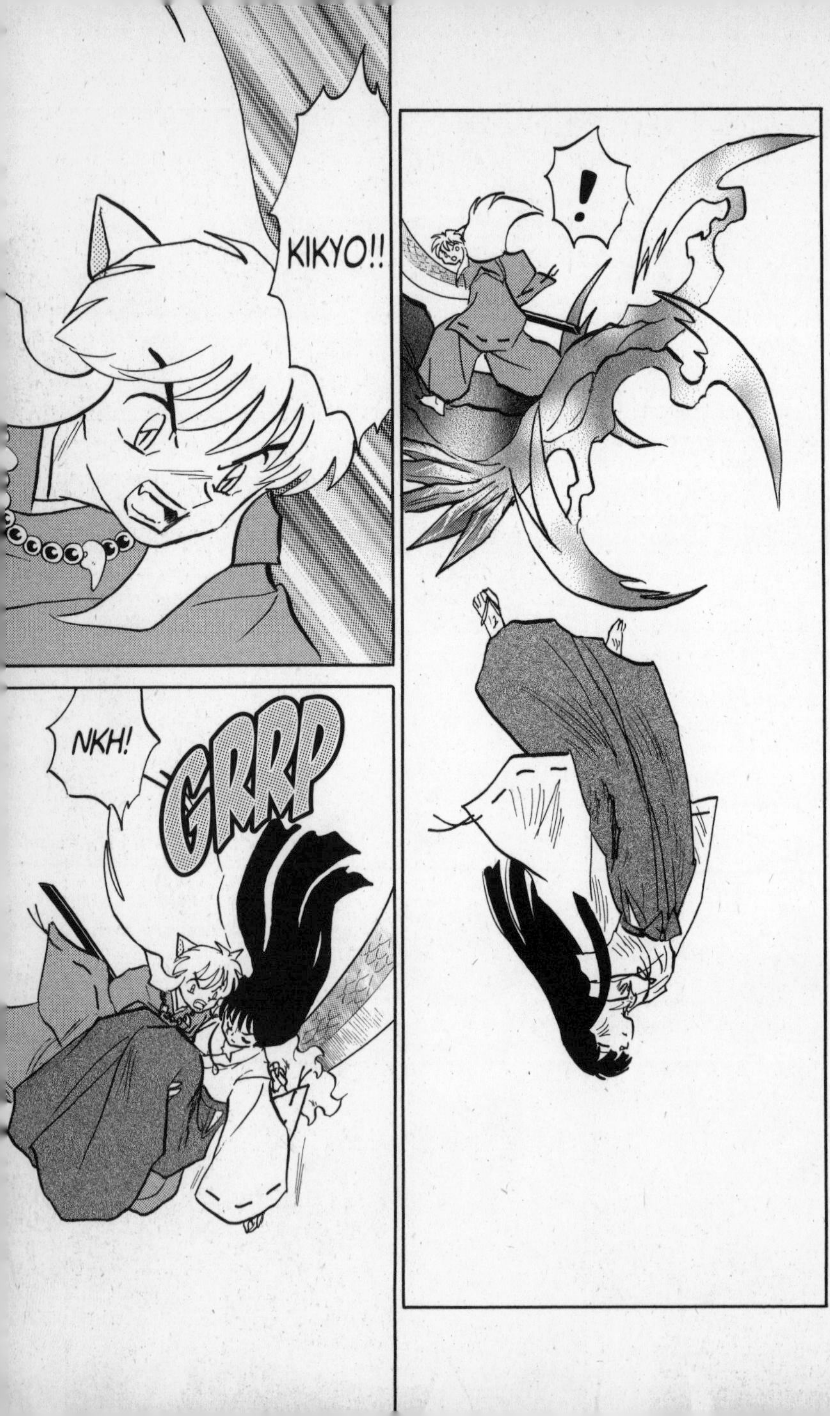
!
KIKYO!!
NKH!
GRRP

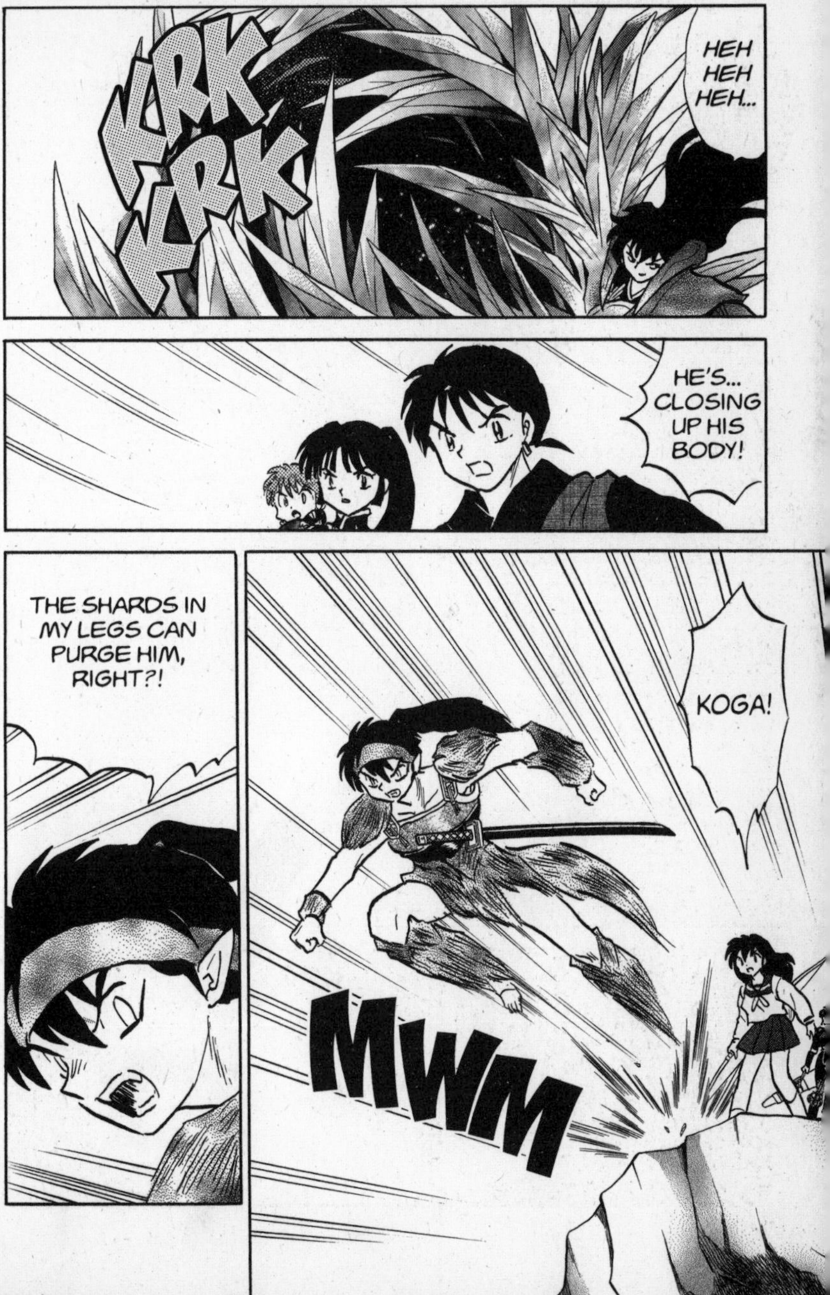
HEH HEH HEH...
KRK KRK
HE'S... CLOSING UP HIS BODY!
KOGA!
MWM
THE SHARDS IN MY LEGS CAN PURGE HIM, RIGHT?!

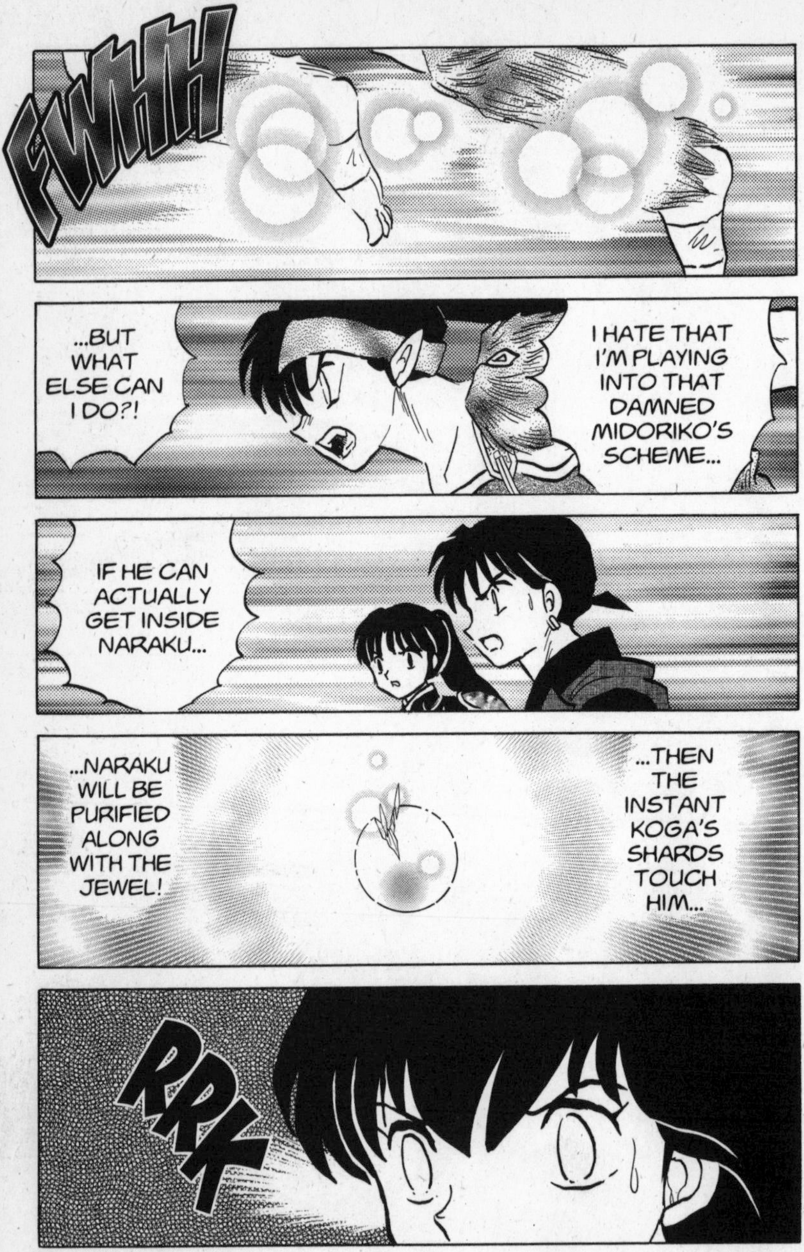
FWHH
I HATE THAT I'M PLAYING INTO THAT DAMNED MIDORIKO'S SCHEME...
...BUT WHAT ELSE CAN I DO?!
IF HE CAN ACTUALLY GET INSIDE NARAKU...
...THEN THE INSTANT KOGA'S SHARDS TOUCH HIM...
...NARAKU WILL BE PURIFIED ALONG WITH THE JEWEL!
RRK

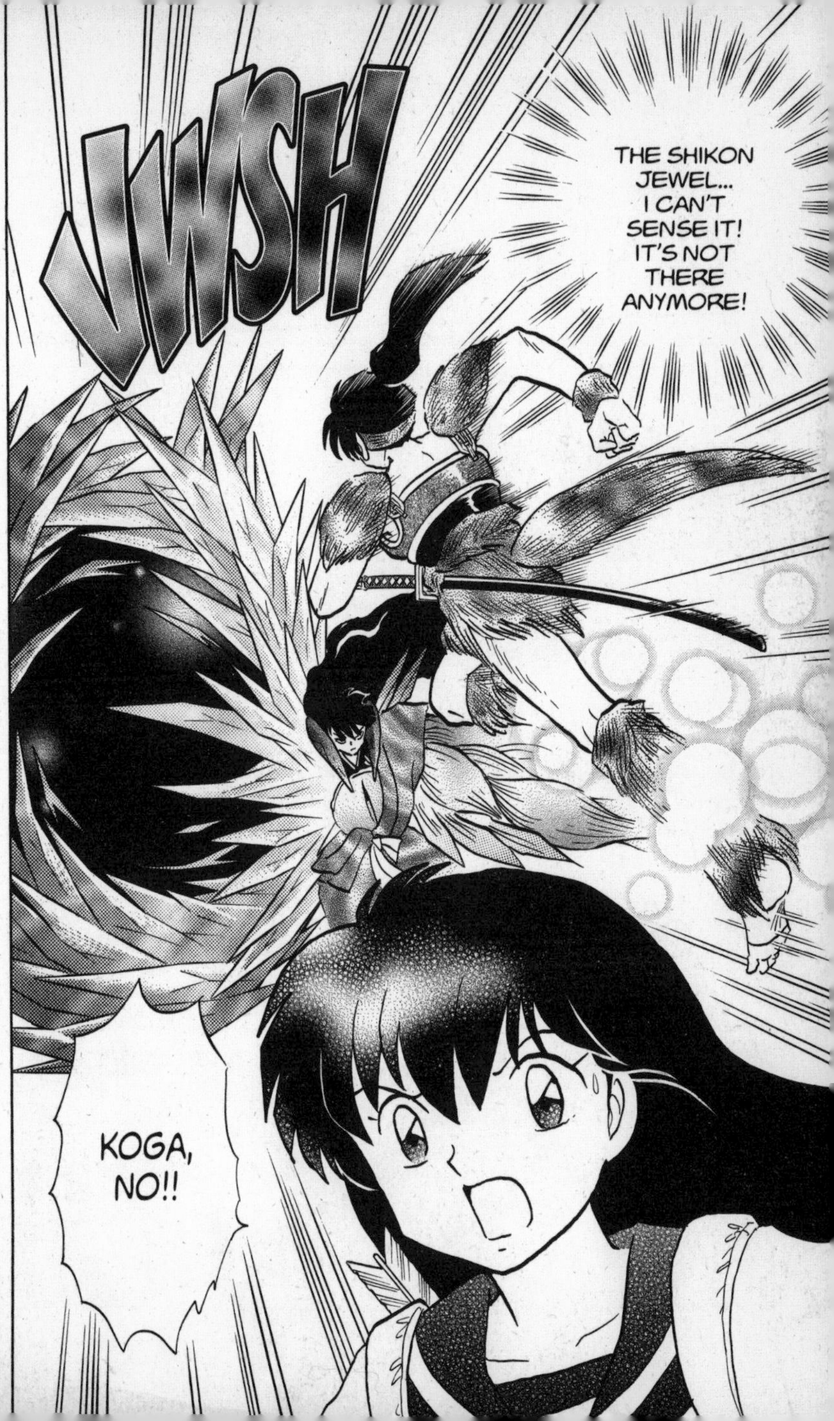
THE SHIKON JEWEL... I CAN'T SENSE IT! IT'S NOT THERE ANYMORE!
VWSH
KOGA, NO!!

SCROLL 4

THE VANISHED JEWEL

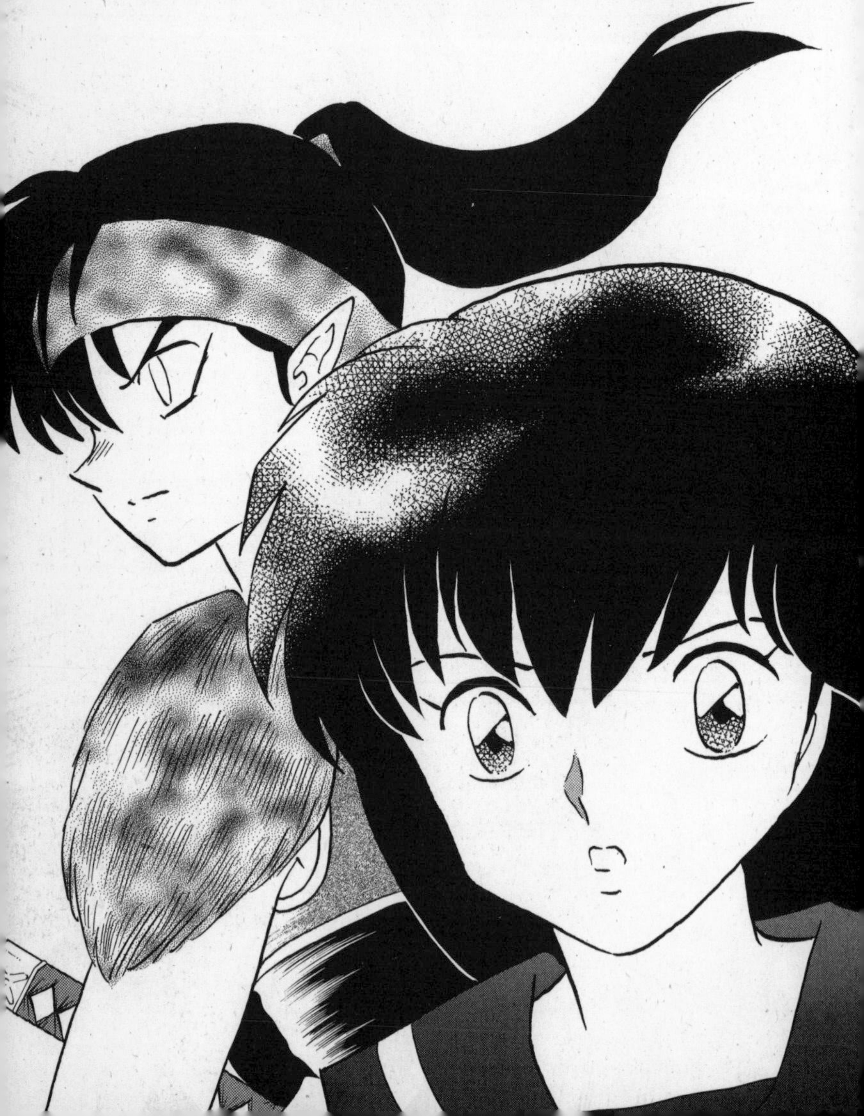

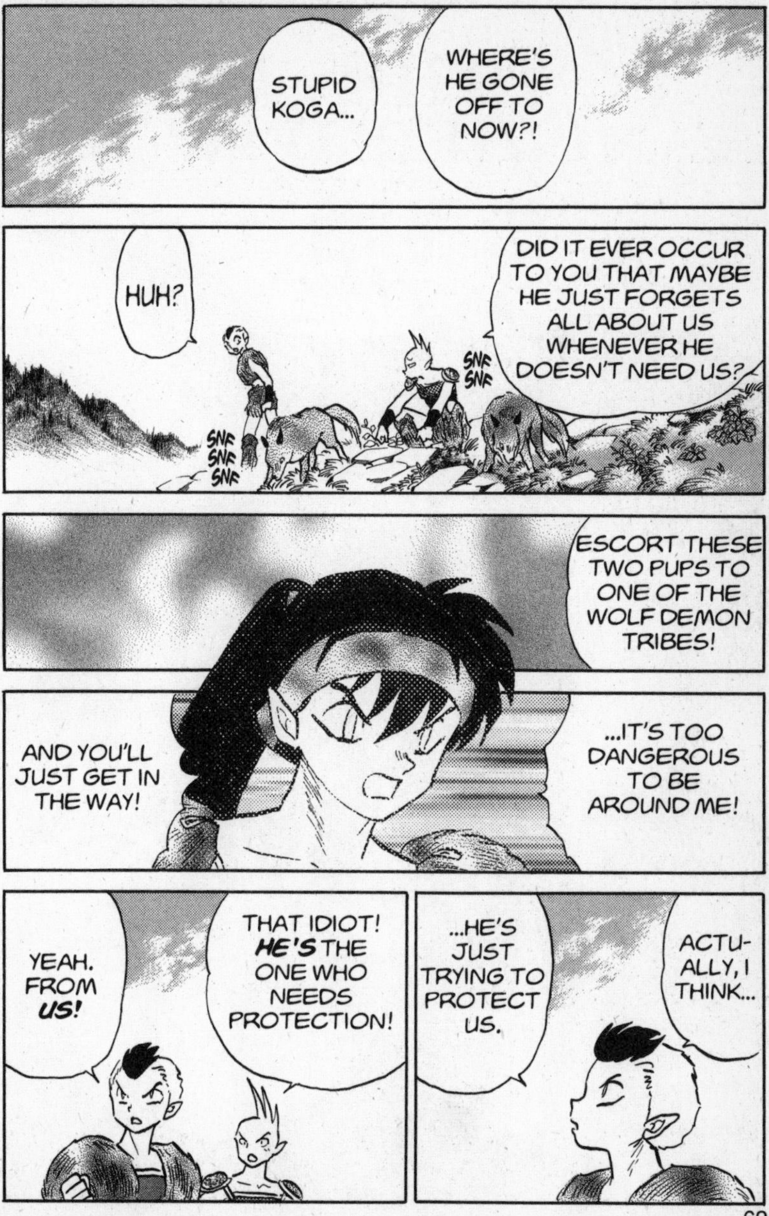
WHERE'S HE GONE OFF TO NOW?!
STUPID KOGA...
DID IT EVER OCCUR TO YOU THAT MAYBE HE JUST FORGETS ALL ABOUT US WHENEVER HE DOESN'T NEED US?
SNF SNF
HUH?
SNF SNF SNF
ESCORT THESE TWO PUPS TO ONE OF THE WOLF DEMON TRIBES!
...IT'S TOO DANGEROUS TO BE AROUND ME!
AND YOU'LL JUST GET IN THE WAY!
ACTU-ALLY, I THINK...
...HE'S JUST TRYING TO PROTECT US.
THAT IDIOT! *HE'S* THE ONE WHO NEEDS PROTECTION!
YEAH. FROM *US!*

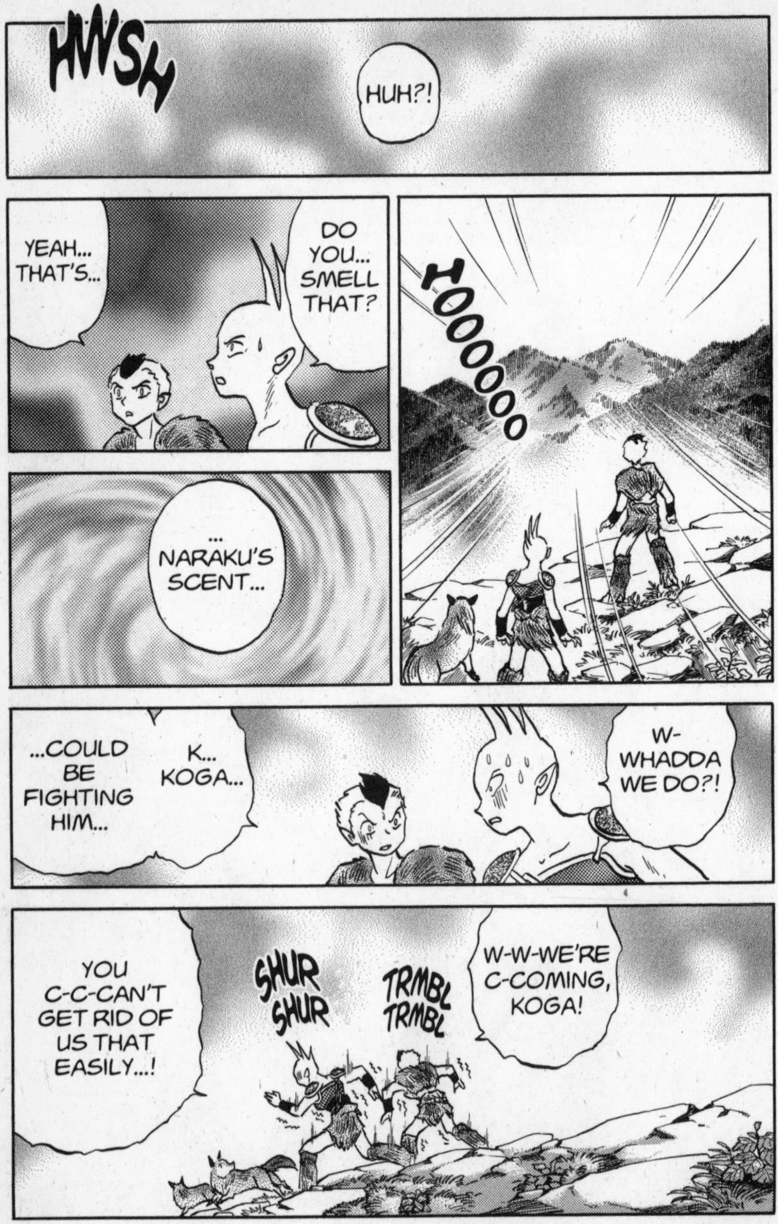
HUH?!
HWSH
HOOOOOOO
DO YOU... SMELL THAT?
YEAH... THAT'S...
... NARAKU'S SCENT...
W- WHADDA WE DO?!
K... KOGA...
...COULD BE FIGHTING HIM...
W-W-WE'RE C-COMING, KOGA!
TRMBL TRMBL
SHUR SHUR
YOU C-C-CAN'T GET RID OF US THAT EASILY...!

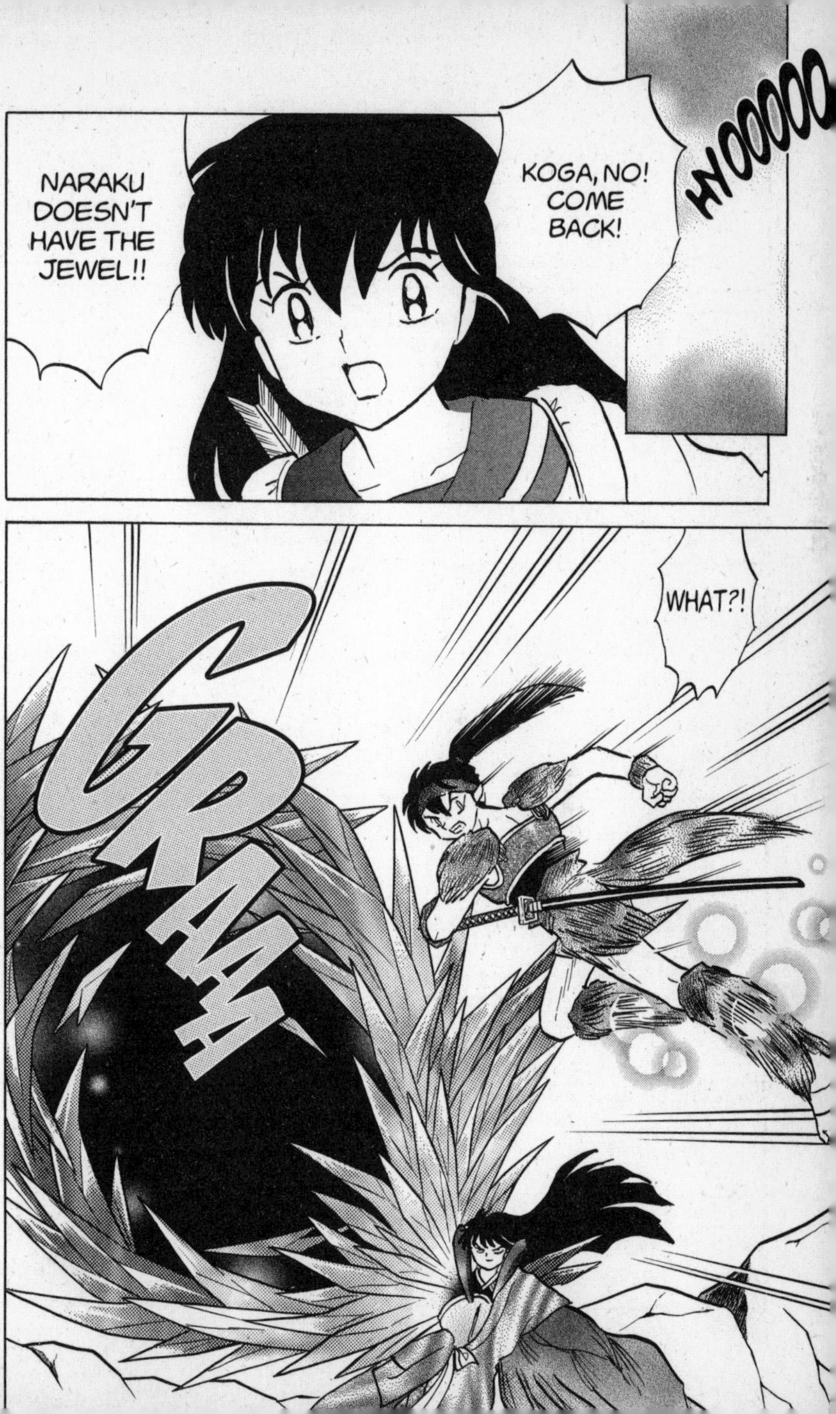
HYOOOOO
KOGA, NO! COME BACK!
NARAKU DOESN'T HAVE THE JEWEL!!
WHAT?!

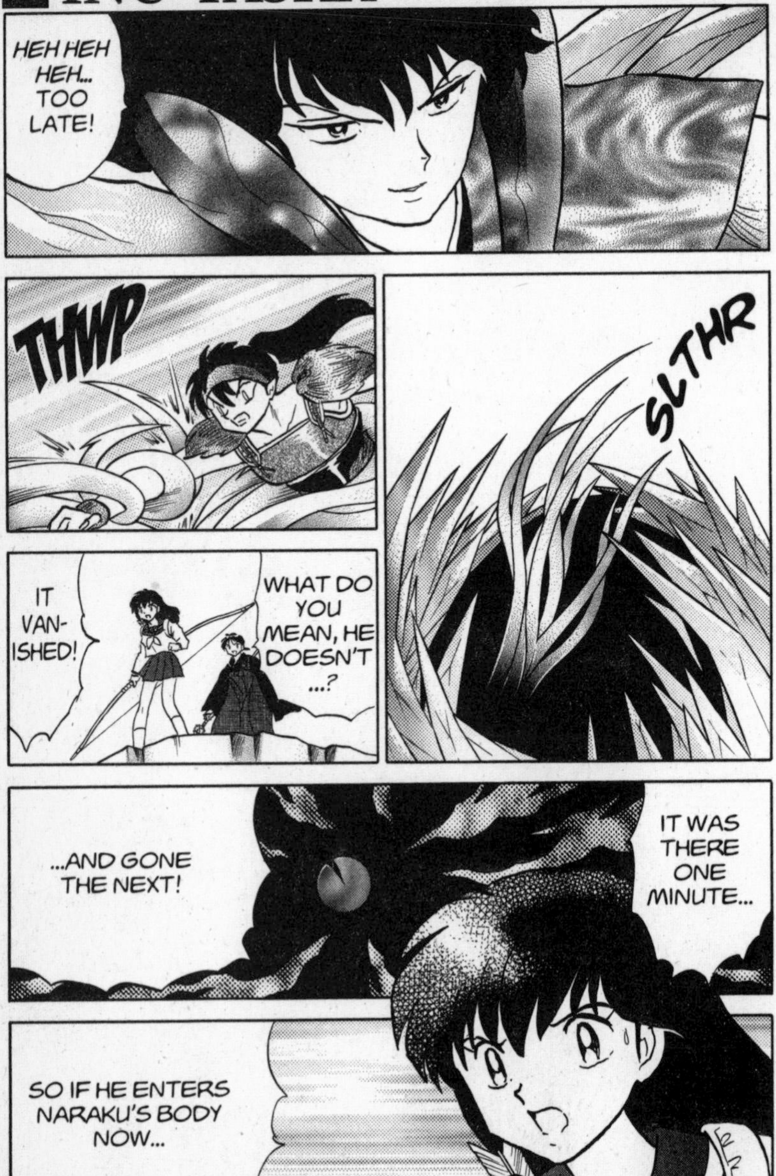
HEH HEH HEH... TOO LATE!
SLTHR
THWP
WHAT DO YOU MEAN, HE DOESN'T ...?
IT VAN-ISHED!
IT WAS THERE ONE MINUTE...
...AND GONE THE NEXT!
SO IF HE ENTERS NARAKU'S BODY NOW...

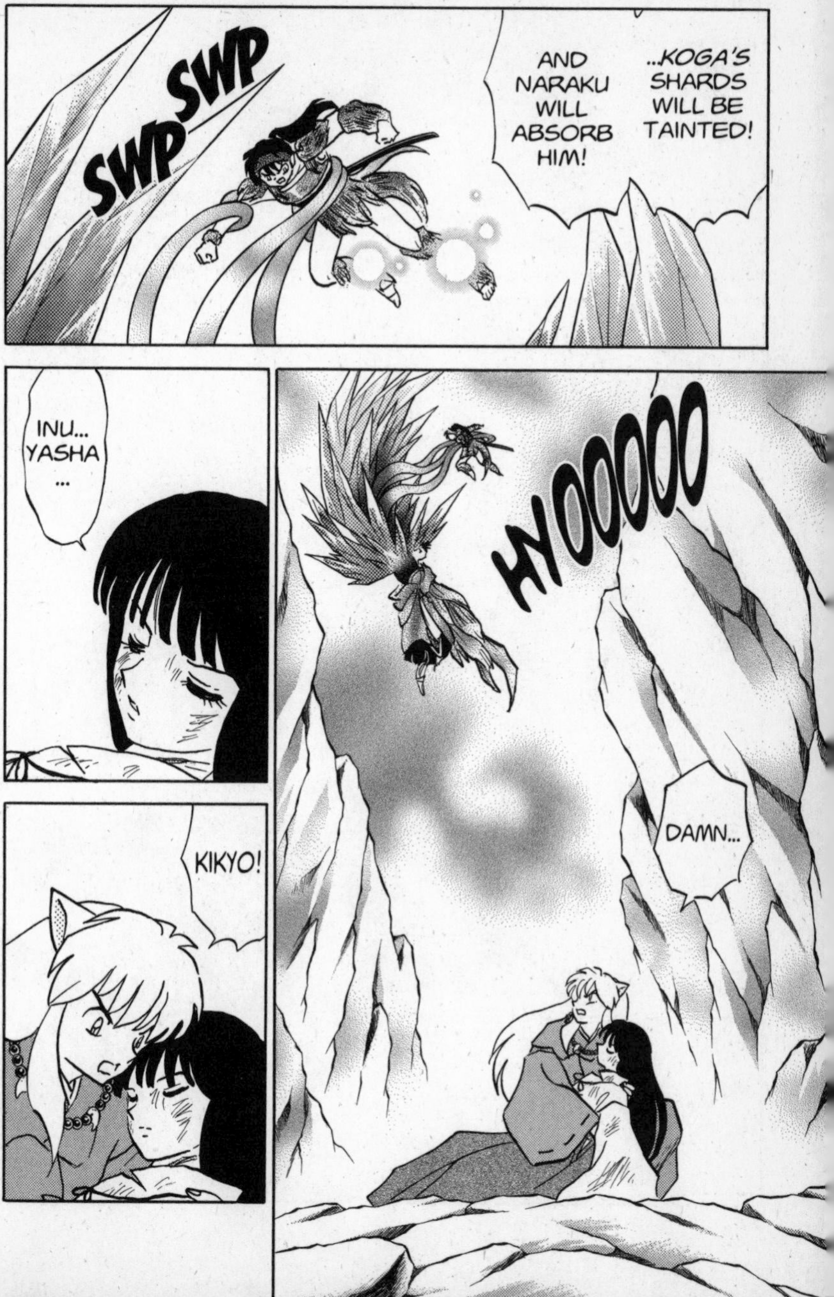
...KOGA'S SHARDS WILL BE TAINTED!
AND NARAKU WILL ABSORB HIM!
SWP SWP
HYOOOOO
DAMN...
INU... YASHA ...
KIKYO!

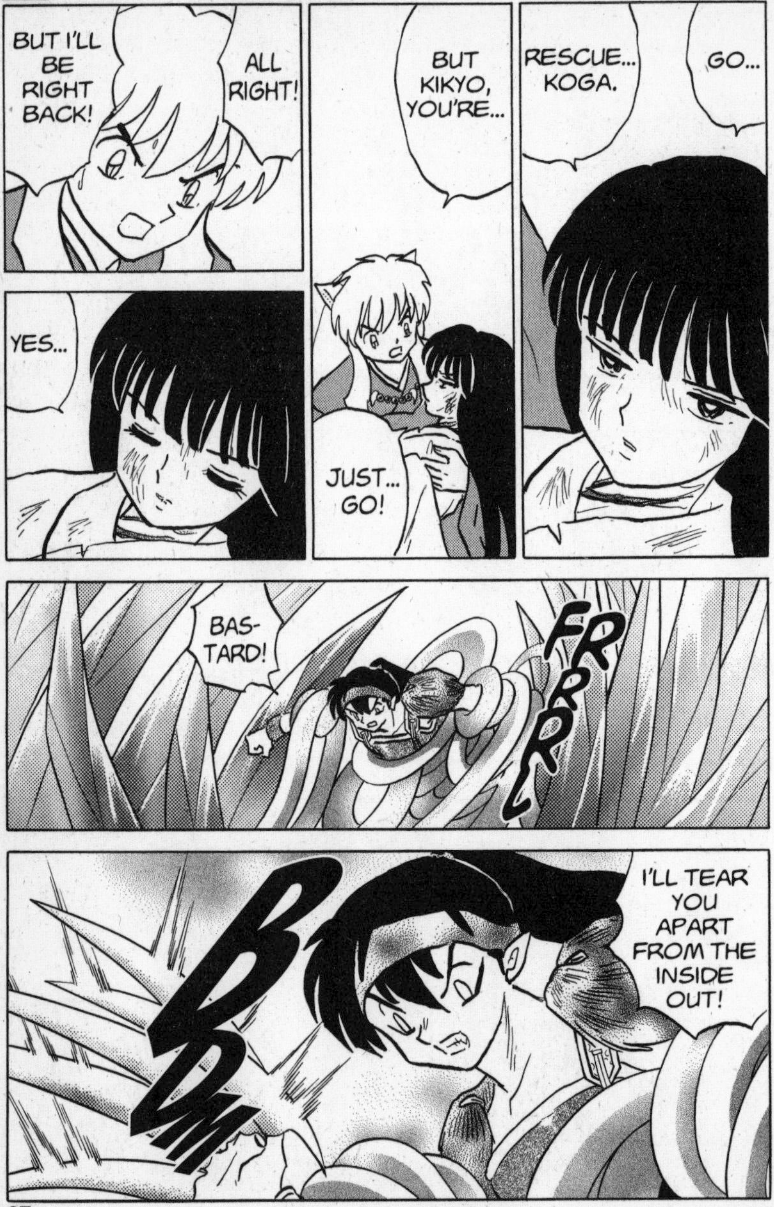
GO...
RESCUE... KOGA.
BUT KIKYO, YOU'RE...
JUST... GO!
ALL RIGHT!
BUT I'LL BE RIGHT BACK!
YES...
FRRRL
BAS-TARD!
I'LL TEAR YOU APART FROM THE INSIDE OUT!
BM

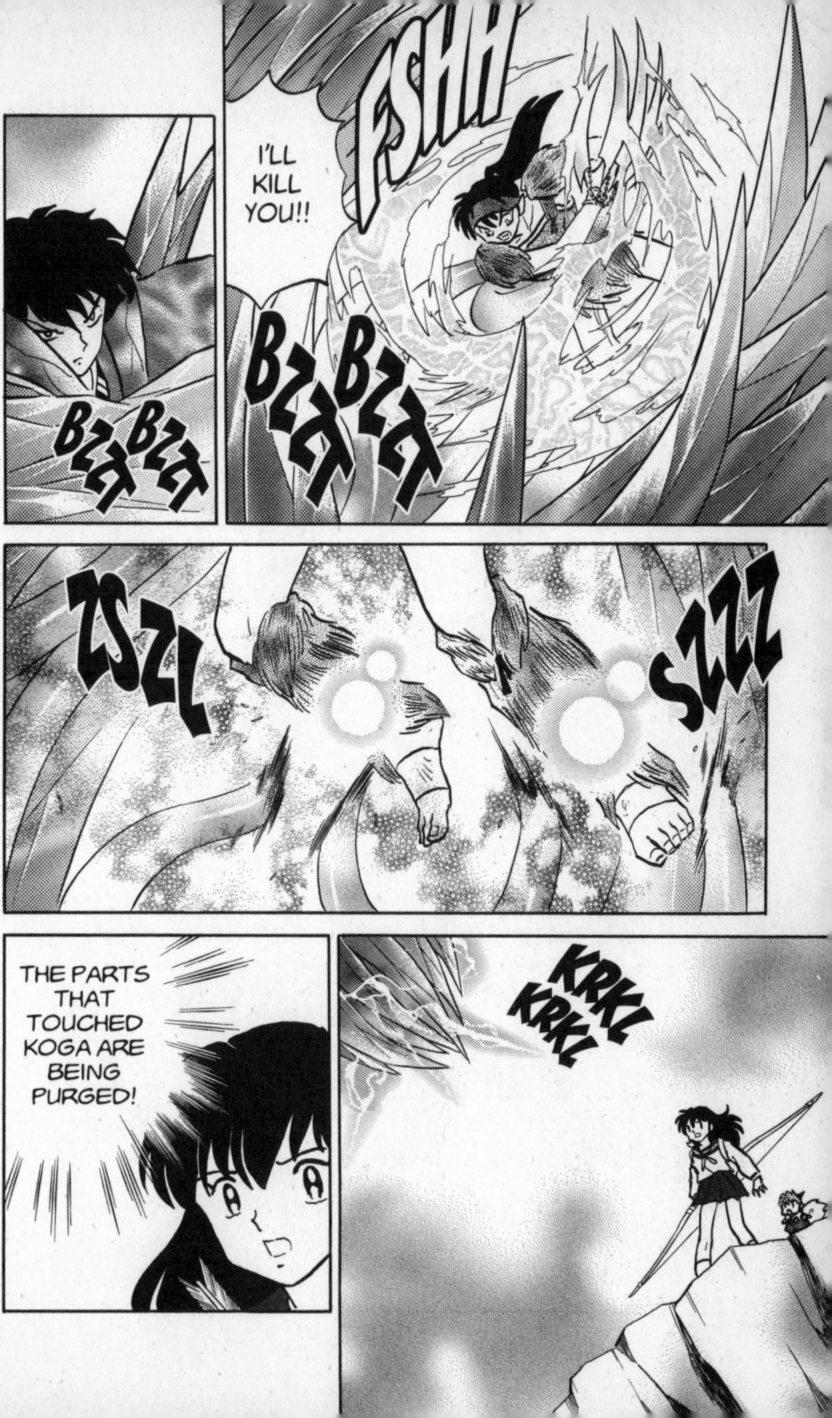
FSHH
I'LL KILL YOU!!
BZZT BZZT
BZZT BZZT
SZZZ
ZSZL
KRKL KRKL
THE PARTS THAT TOUCHED KOGA ARE BEING PURGED!

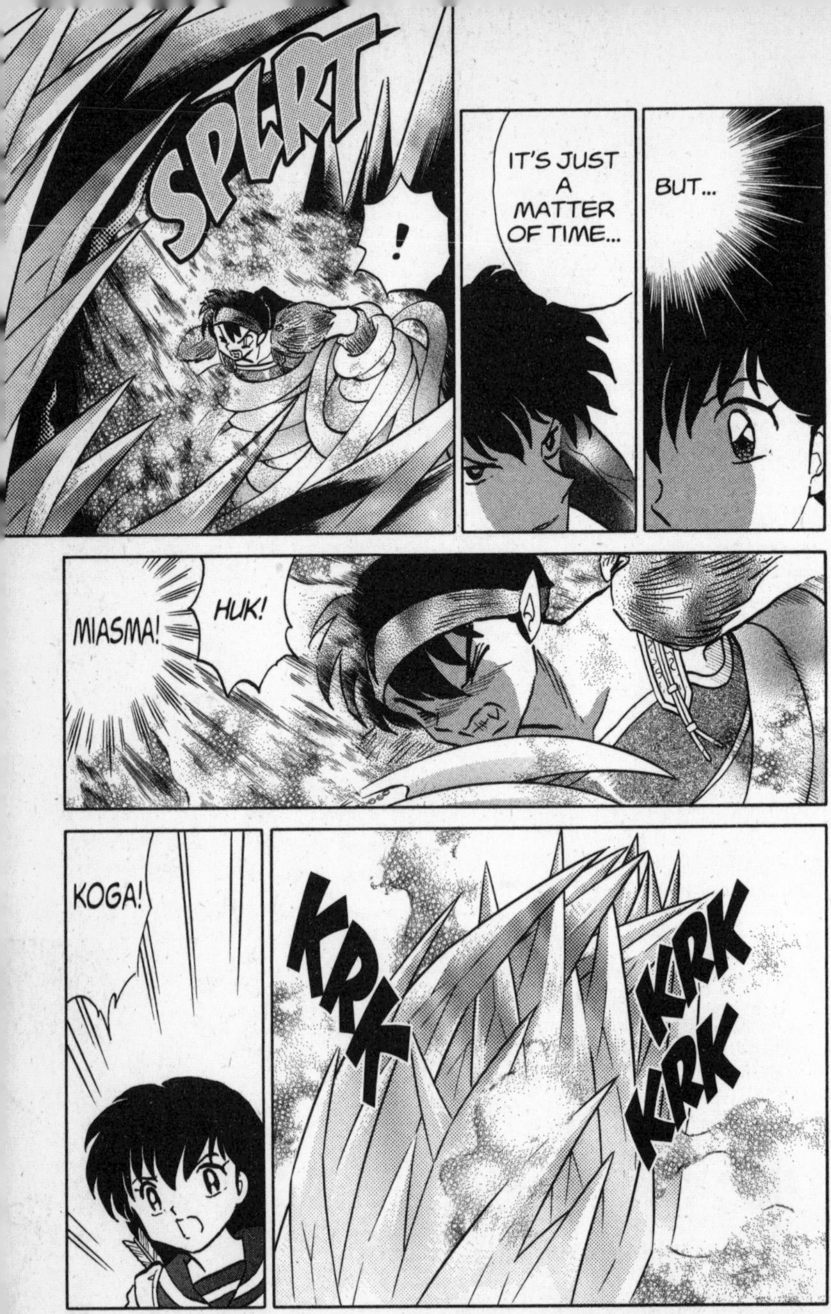
BUT...
IT'S JUST A MATTER OF TIME...
SPLRT
!
HUK!
MIASMA!
KRK
KRK KRK
KOGA!

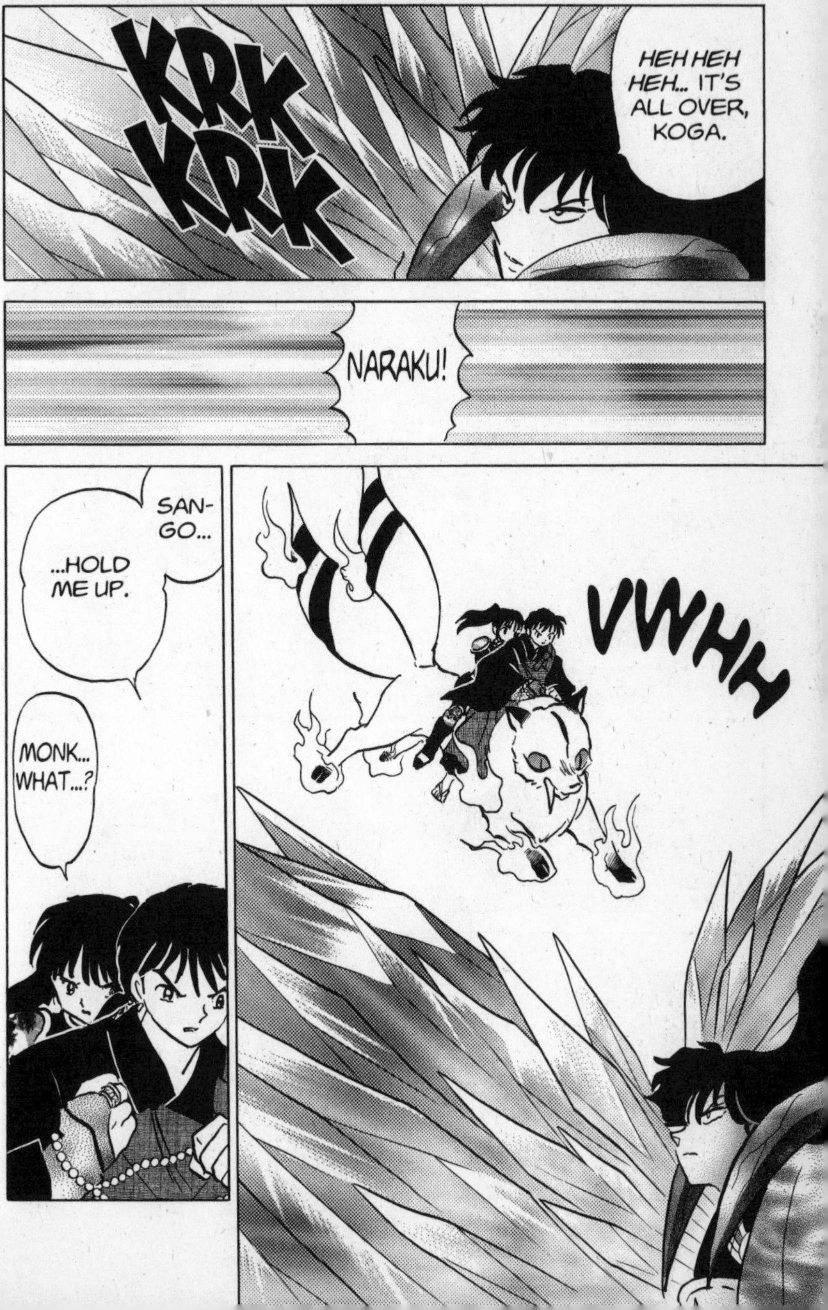
HEH HEH HEH... IT'S ALL OVER, KOGA.
KRK KRK
NARAKU!
VWHH
SAN-GO...
...HOLD ME UP.
MONK... WHAT...?

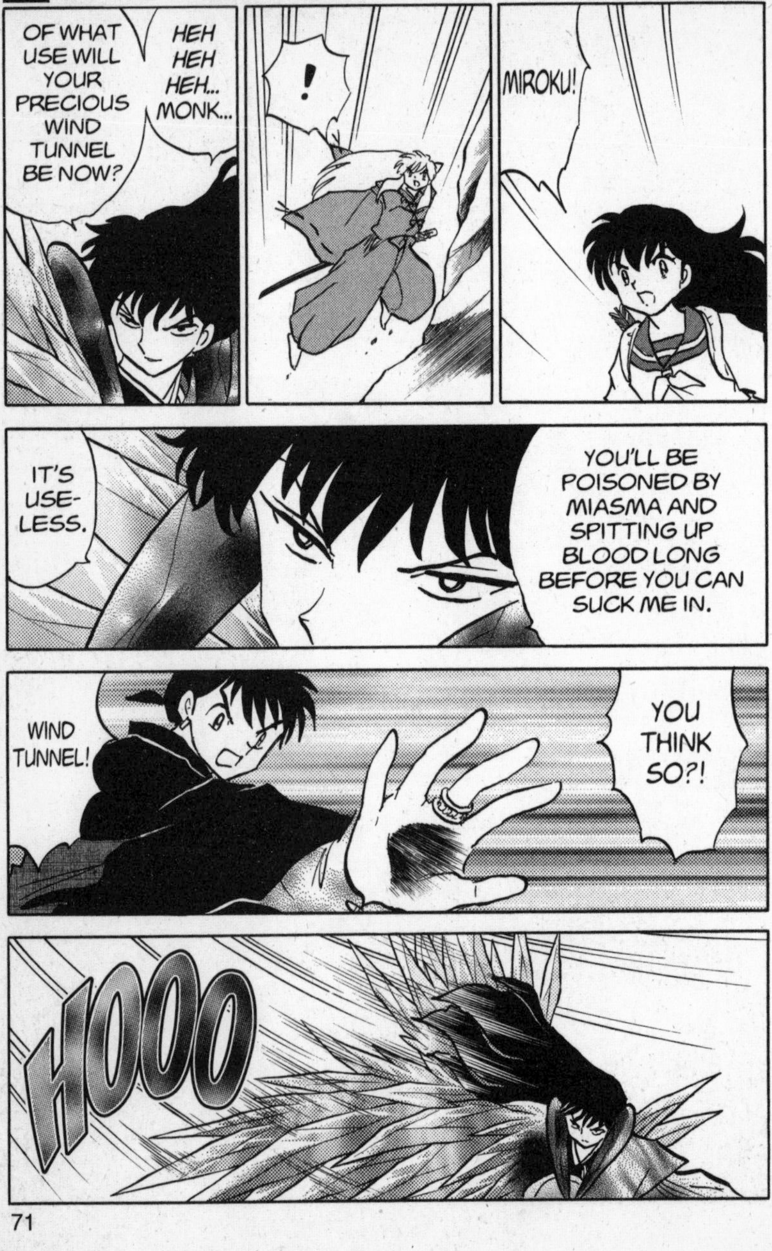
MIROKU!
!
HEH HEH HEH... MONK...
OF WHAT USE WILL YOUR PRECIOUS WIND TUNNEL BE NOW?
YOU'LL BE POISONED BY MIASMA AND SPITTING UP BLOOD LONG BEFORE YOU CAN SUCK ME IN.
IT'S USE-LESS.
YOU THINK SO?!
WIND TUNNEL!
HOOO

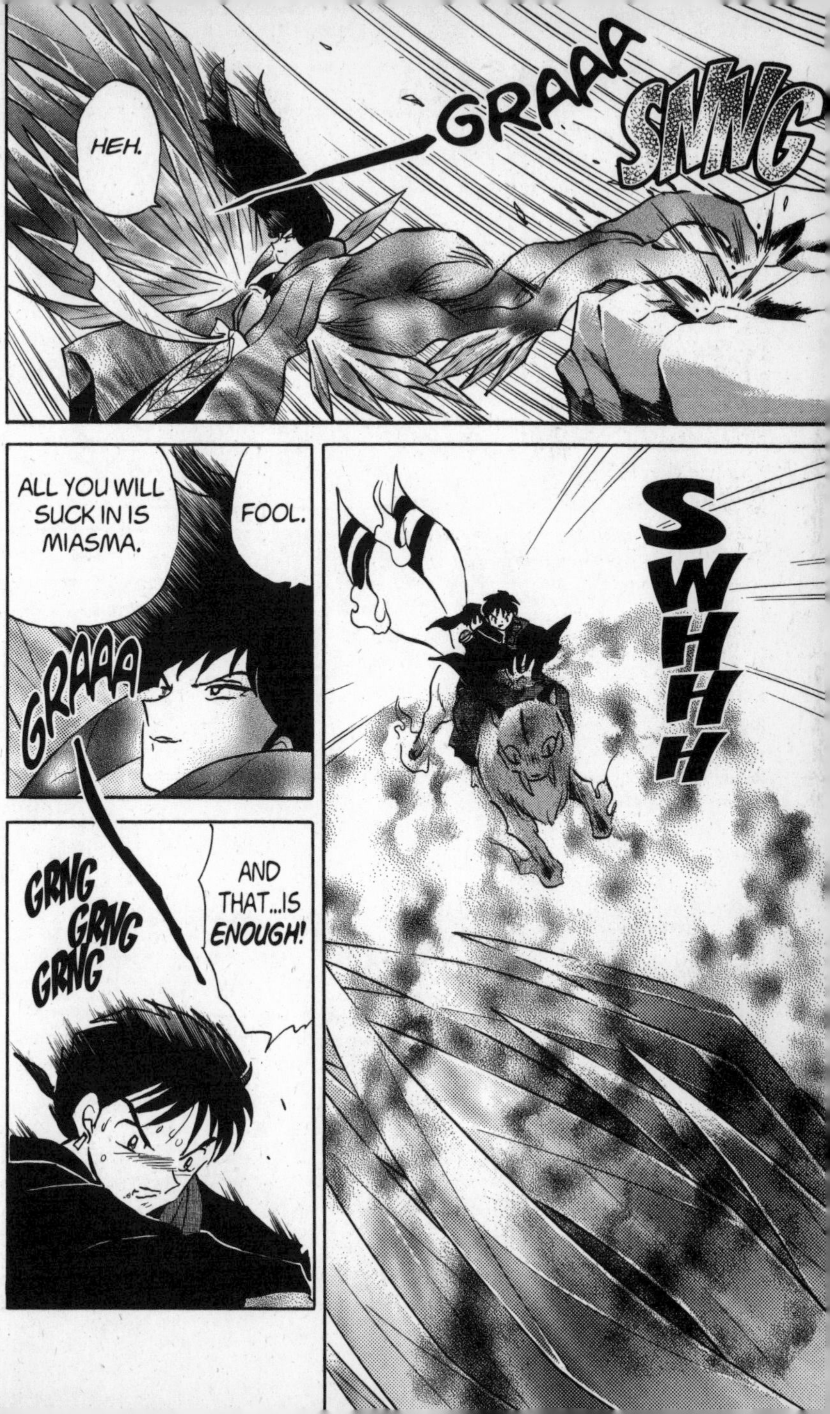
SNNG
GRAAA
HEH.
SWHHH
FOOL.
ALL YOU WILL SUCK IN IS MIASMA.
GRAAA
AND THAT...IS ENOUGH!
GRNG GRNG GRNG

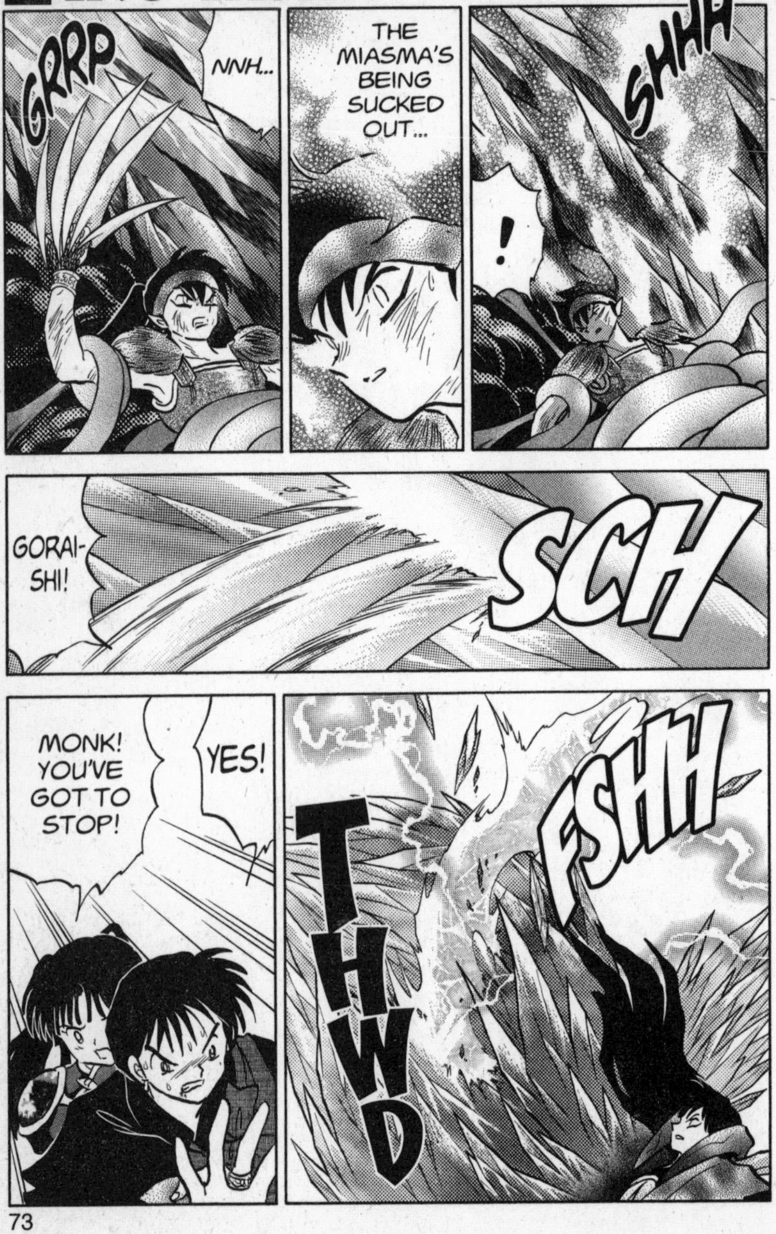
SHHH
!
THE MIASMA'S BEING SUCKED OUT...
NNH...
GRRP
SCH
GORAI-SHI!
FSHH
THWD
YES!
MONK! YOU'VE GOT TO STOP!

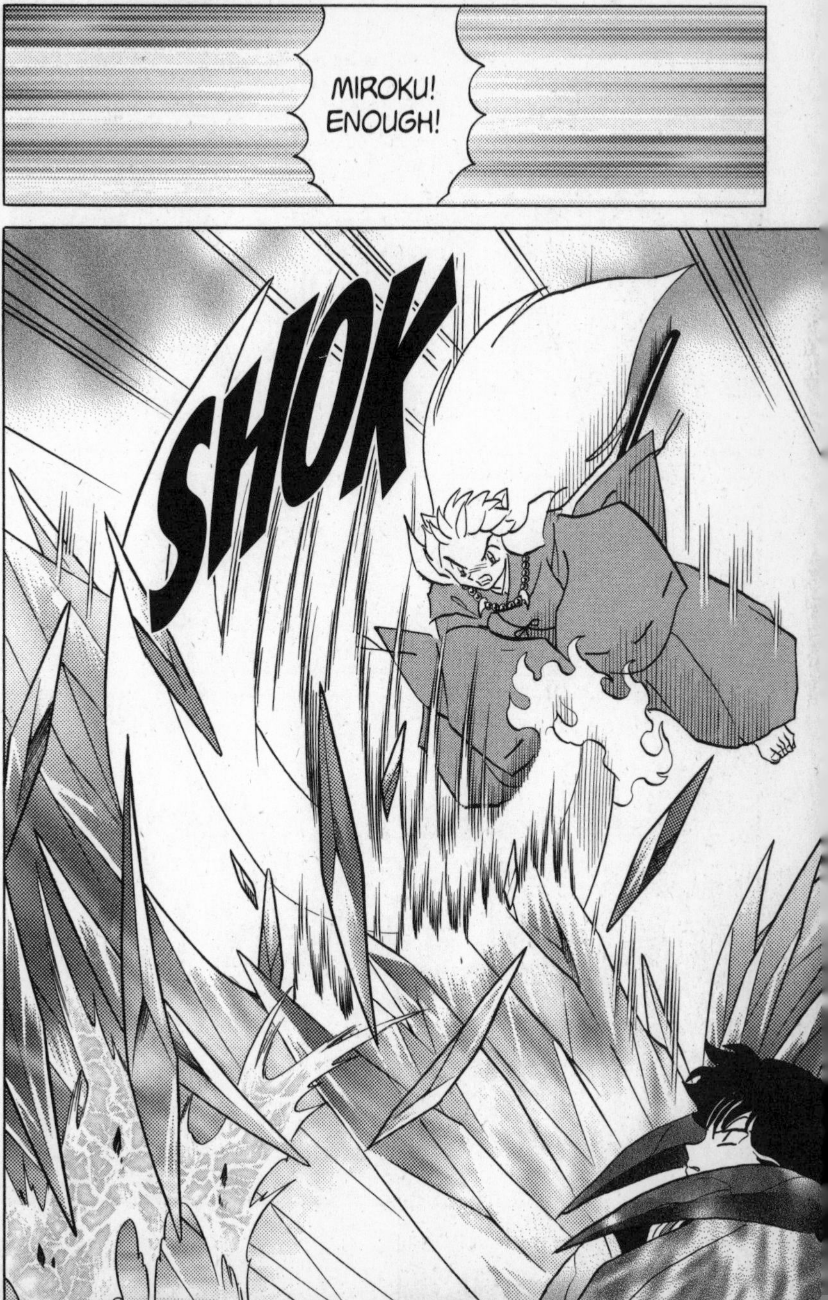
MIROKU!
ENOUGH!
SHOK

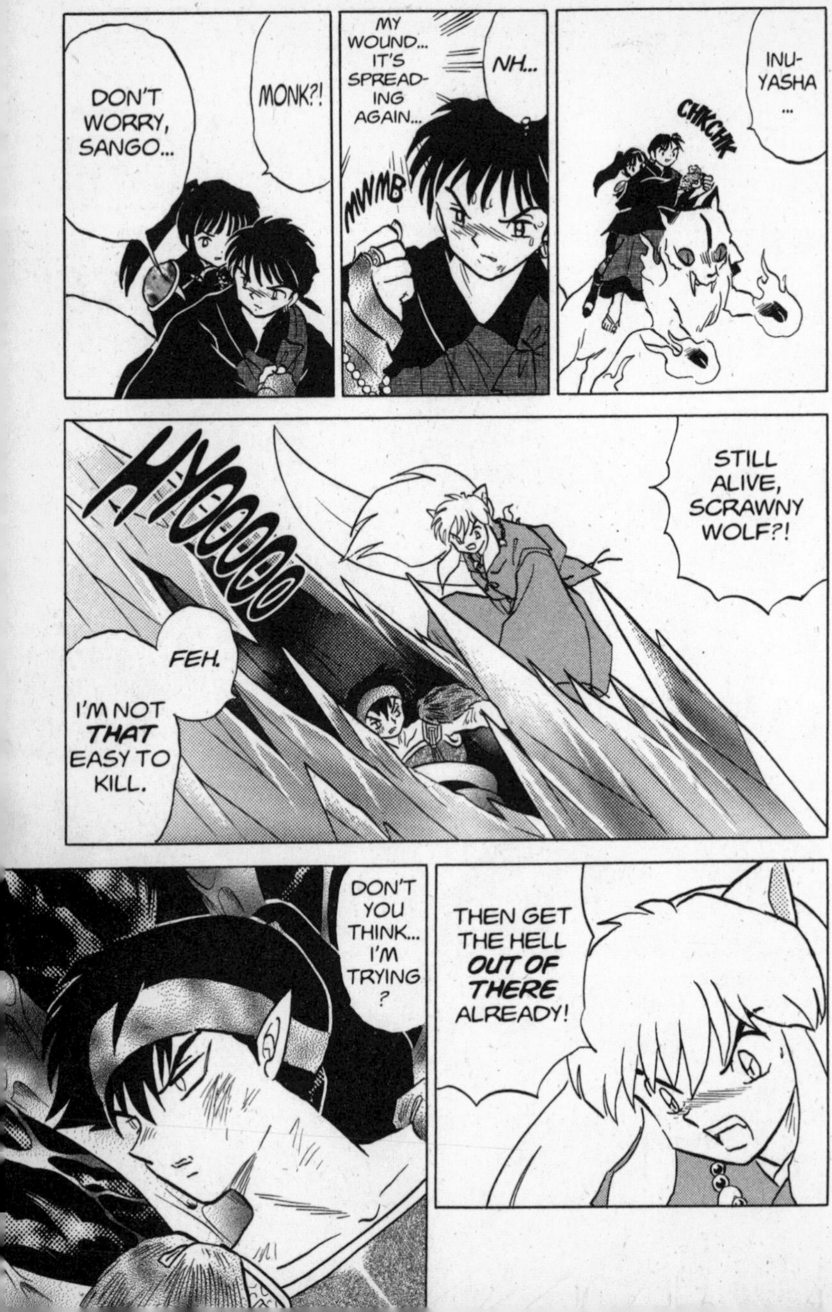
INU-YASHA ...
CHKCHK
NH...
MY WOUND... IT'S SPREAD-ING AGAIN...
MWMB
MONK?!
DON'T WORRY, SANGO...
STILL ALIVE, SCRAWNY WOLF?!
HYOOOO
FEH.
I'M NOT THAT EASY TO KILL.
THEN GET THE HELL OUT OF THERE ALREADY!
DON'T YOU THINK... I'M TRYING ?

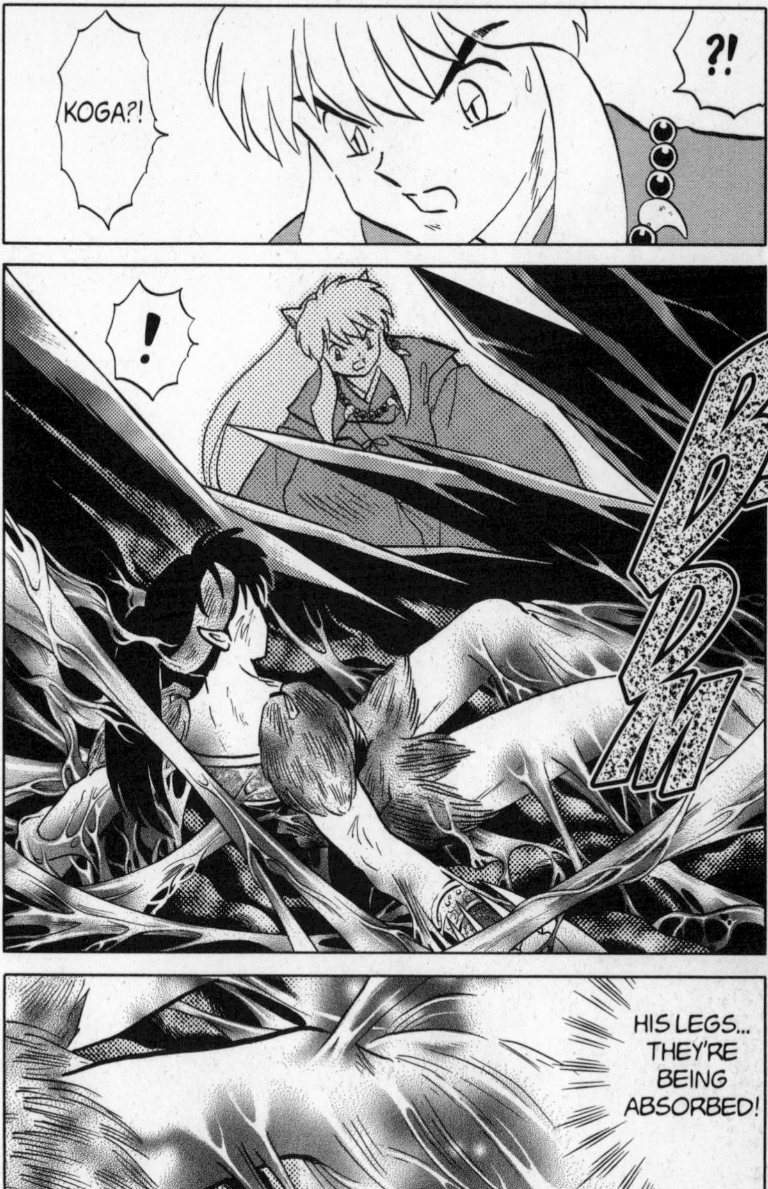
?!
KOGA?!
!
HIS LEGS... THEY'RE BEING ABSORBED!

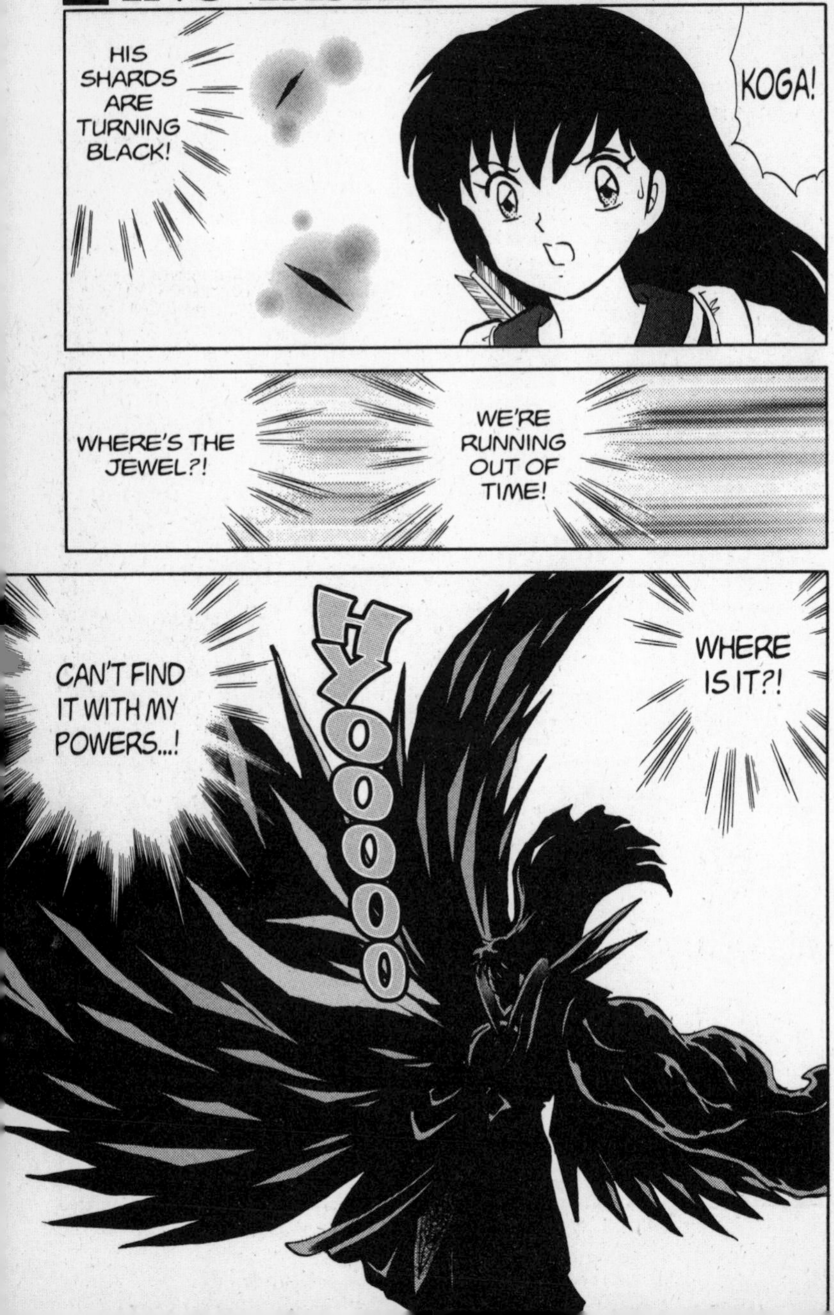
KOGA!
HIS SHARDS ARE TURNING BLACK!
WE'RE RUNNING OUT OF TIME!
WHERE'S THE JEWEL?!
WHERE IS IT?!
HYOOOOOO
CAN'T FIND IT WITH MY POWERS...!

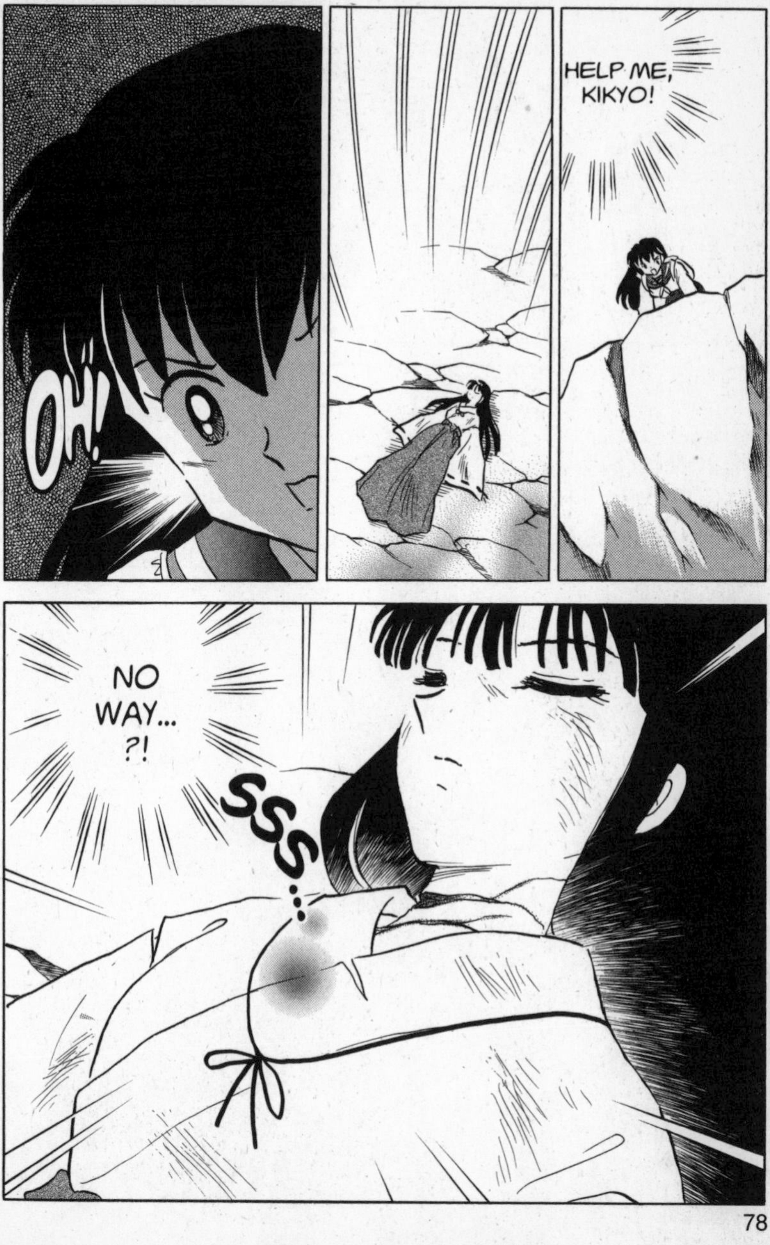
HELP ME, KIKYO!
OH!
NO WAY...?!
SSS...

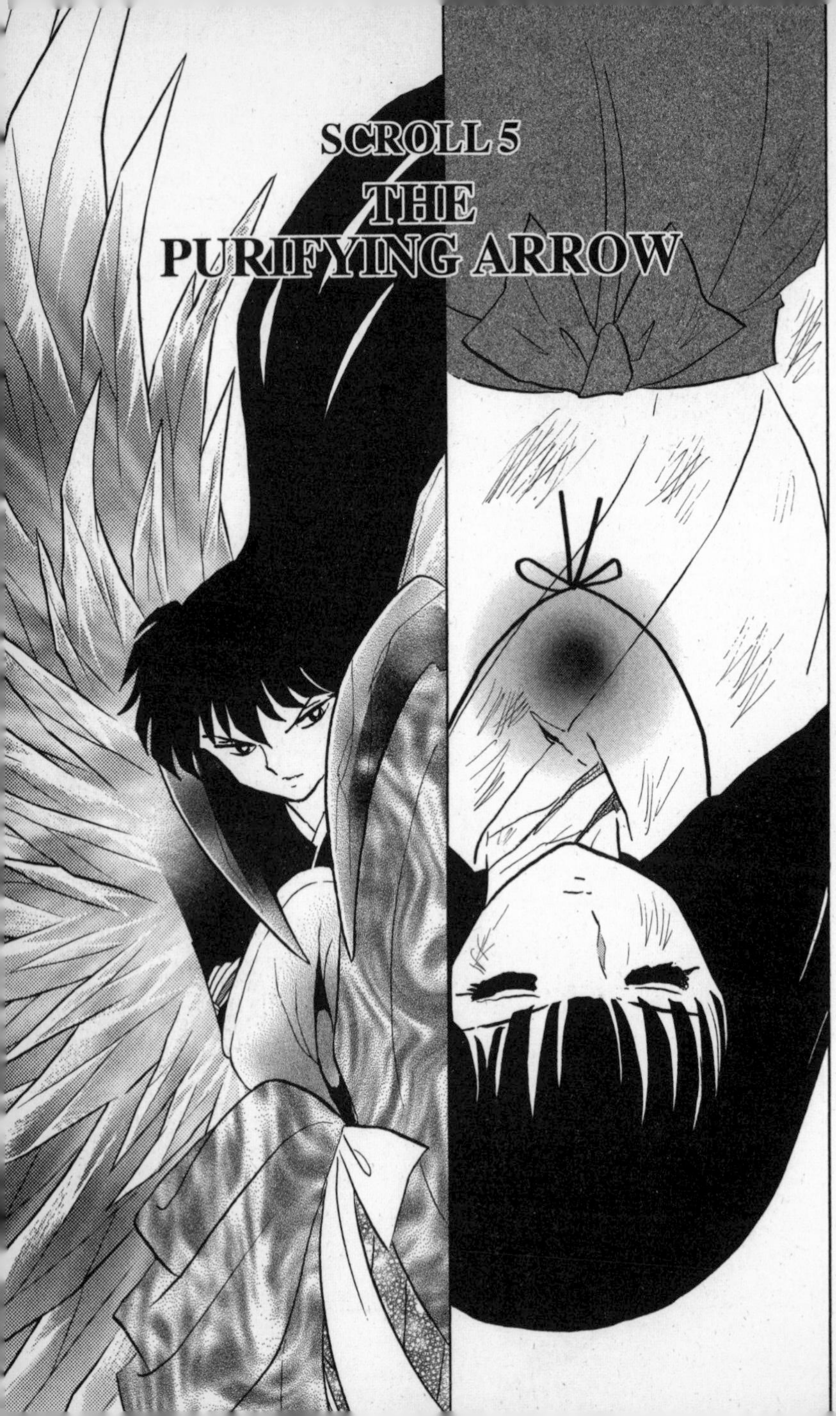
SCROLL 5
THE
PURIFYING ARROW

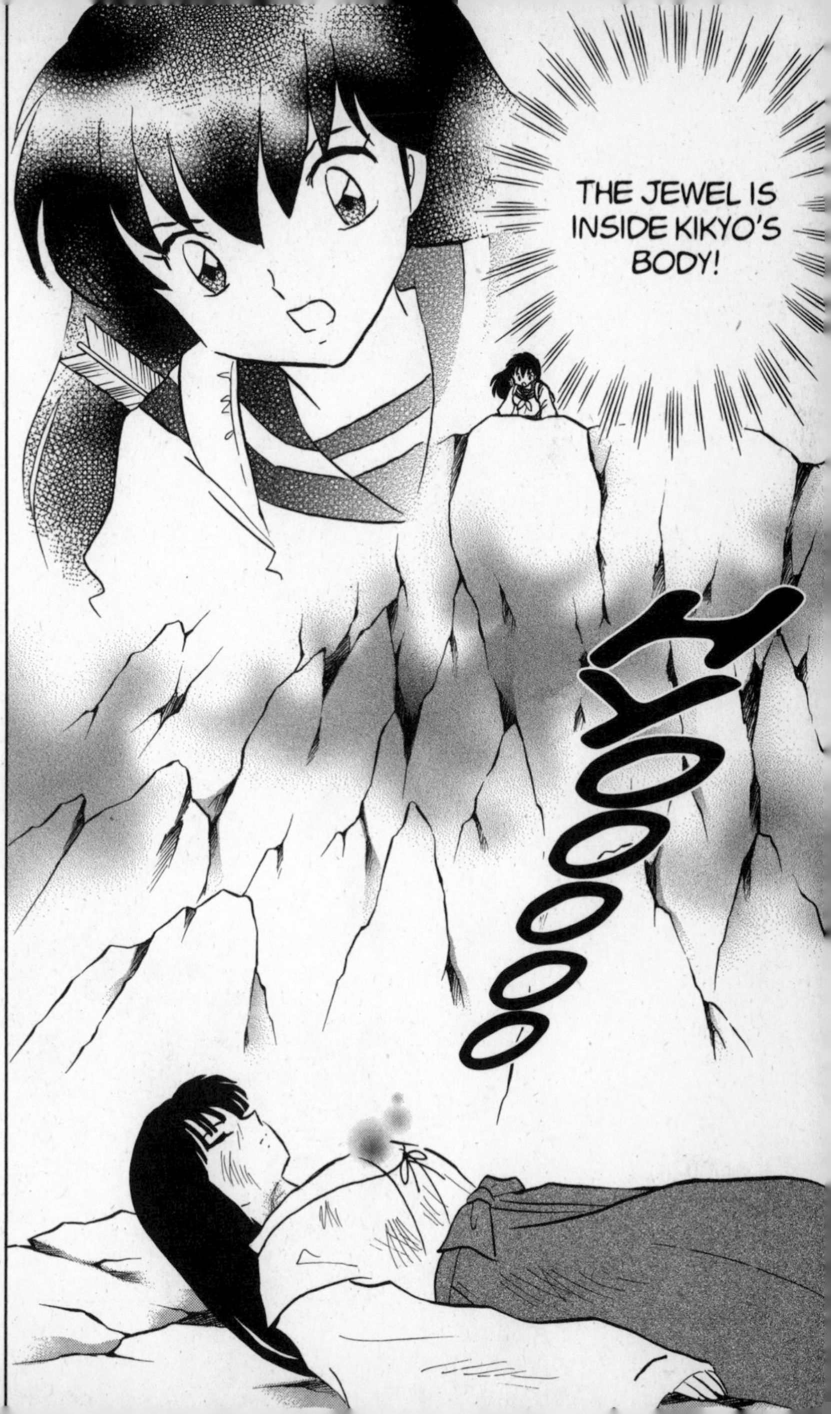
THE JEWEL IS INSIDE KIKYO'S BODY!
HOOOOOO

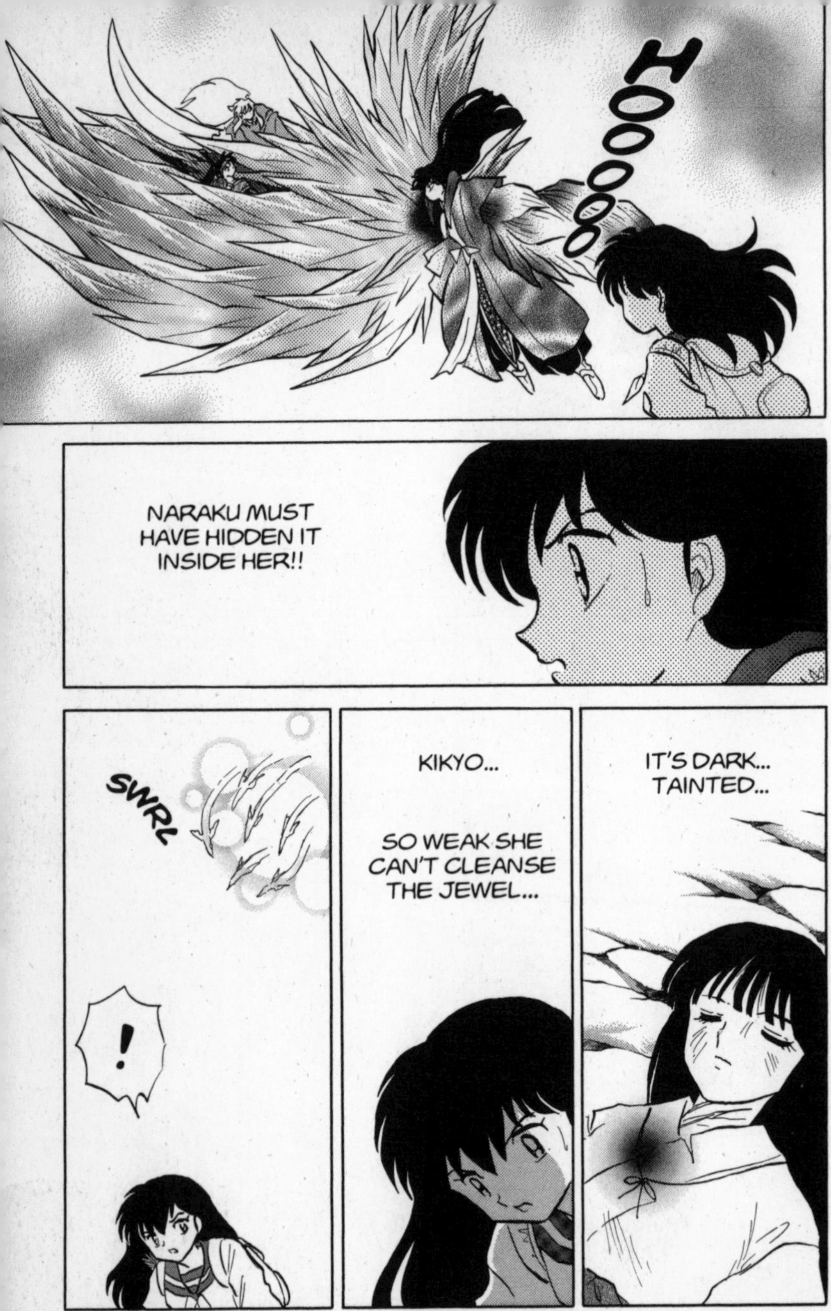
HOOOOOO
NARAKU MUST HAVE HIDDEN IT INSIDE HER!!
IT'S DARK... TAINTED...
KIKYO...
SO WEAK SHE CAN'T CLEANSE THE JEWEL...
SWRL
!

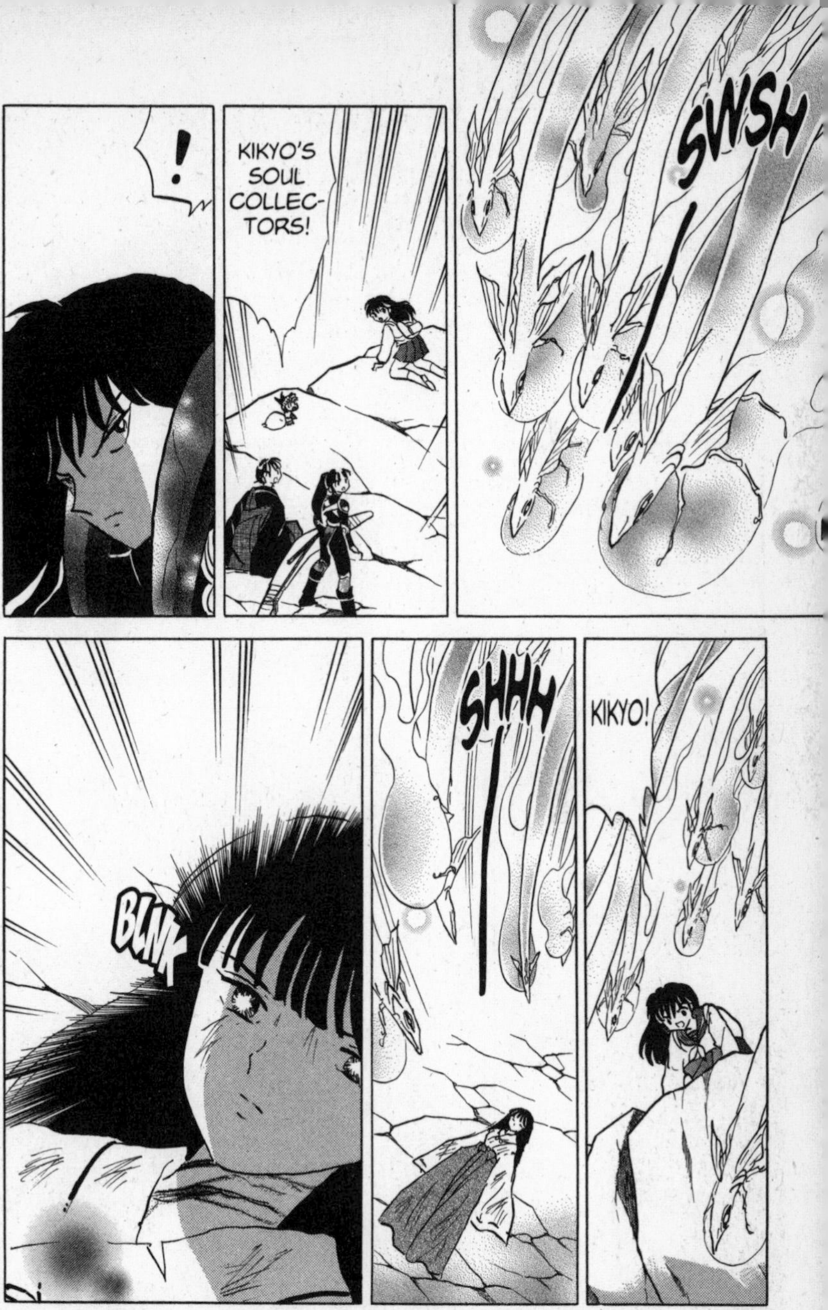
SWSH
KIKYO'S SOUL COLLEC- TORS!
!
KIKYO!
SHHH
BLINK

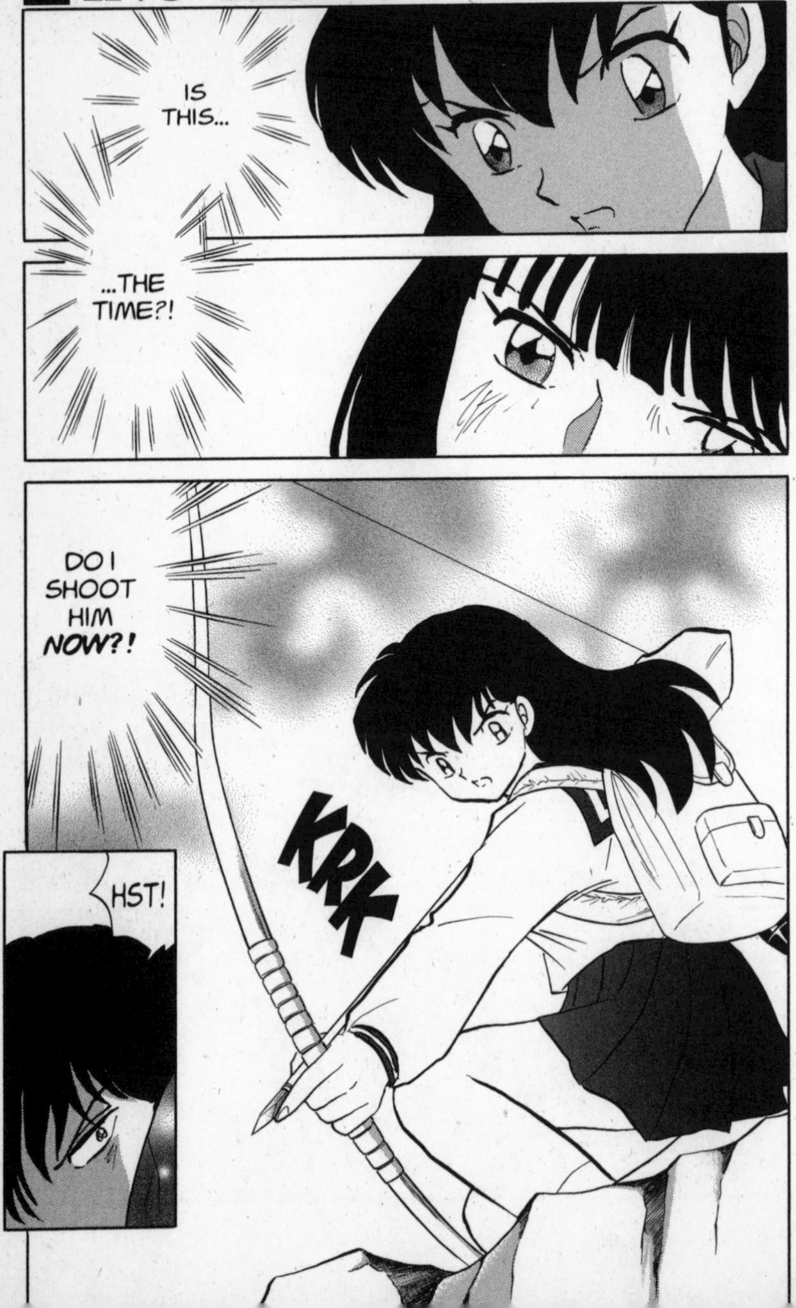
IS THIS...
...THE TIME?!
DO I SHOOT HIM *NOW?!*
KRK
HST!

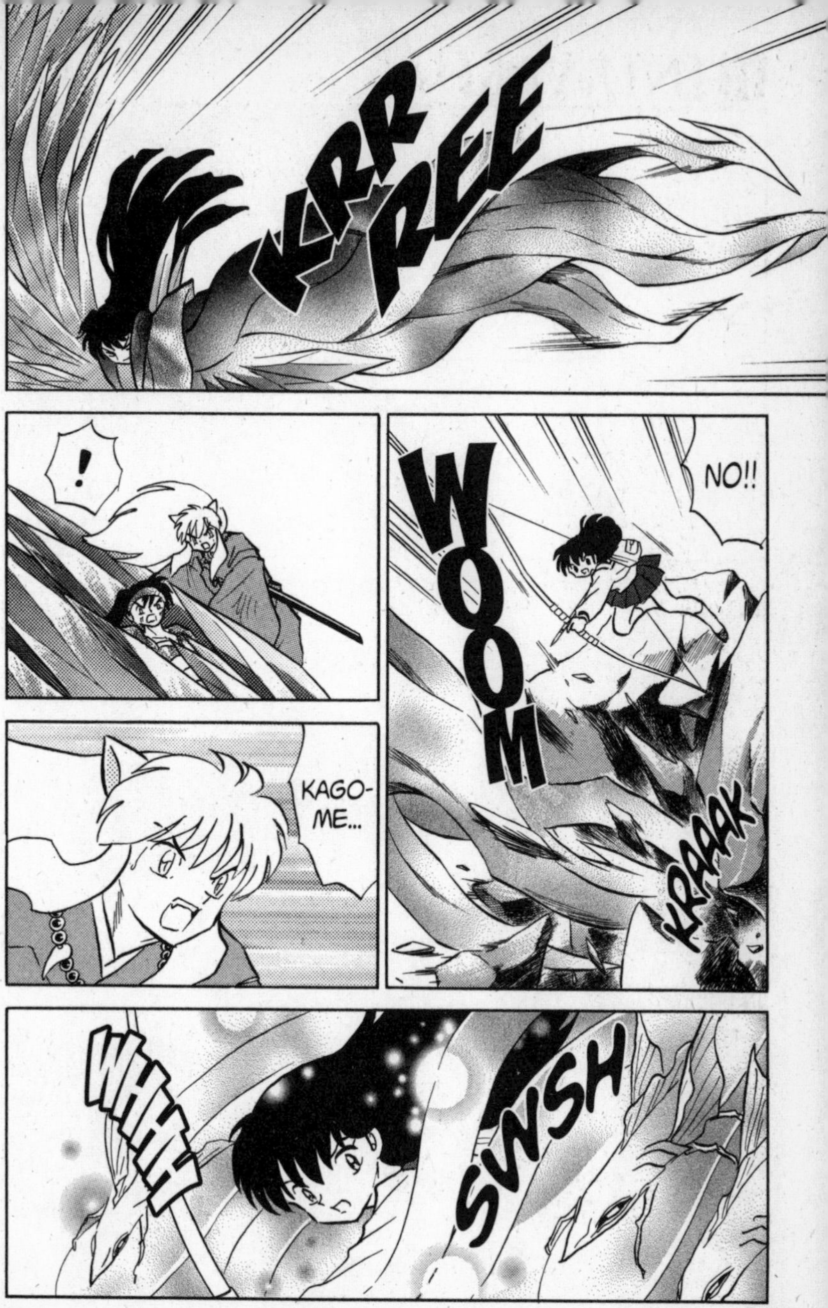
KRR
REE
NO!!
WOOM
KRAAAK
!
KAGO-
ME...
SWSH
WHHH

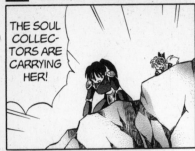

THE SOUL COLLECTORS ARE CARRYING HER!

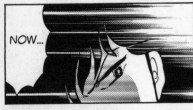

NOW...

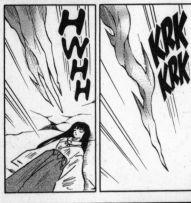

HWHH

KRK KRK

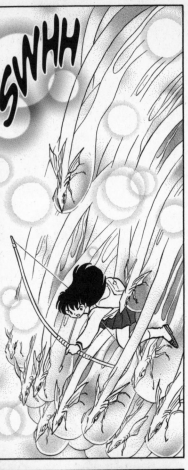

SWHH

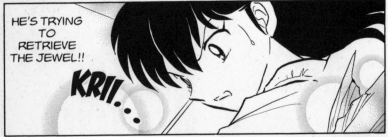

HE'S TRYING TO RETRIEVE THE JEWEL!!

KRII...

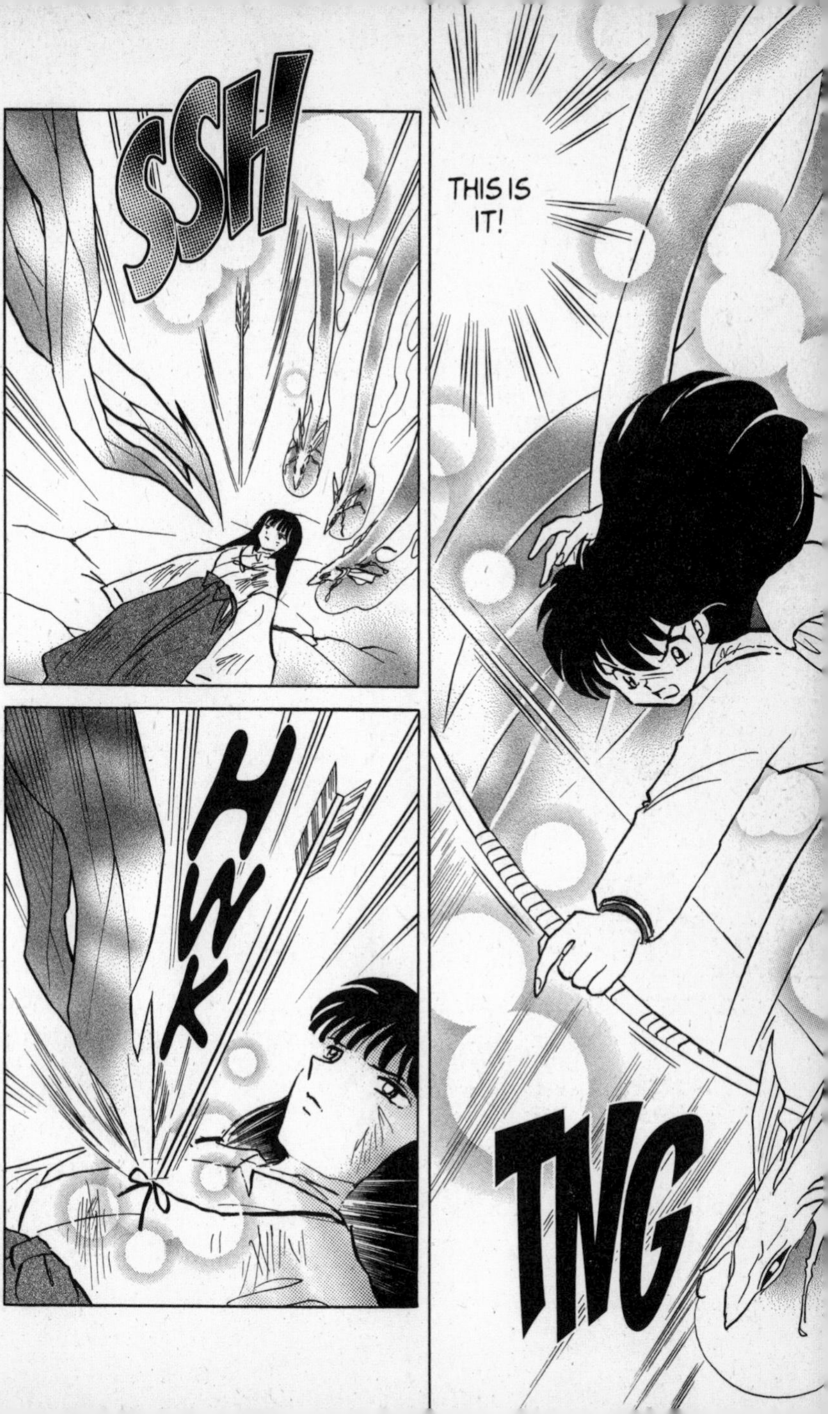
THIS IS IT!
TNG
SSH
HWK

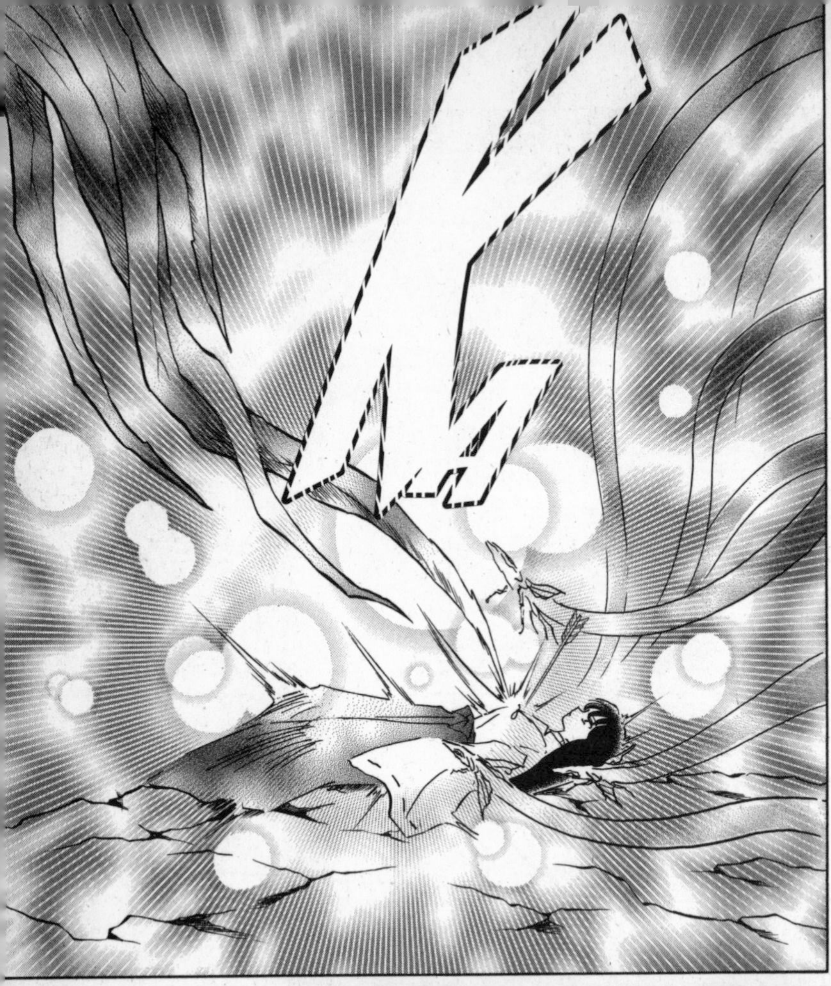
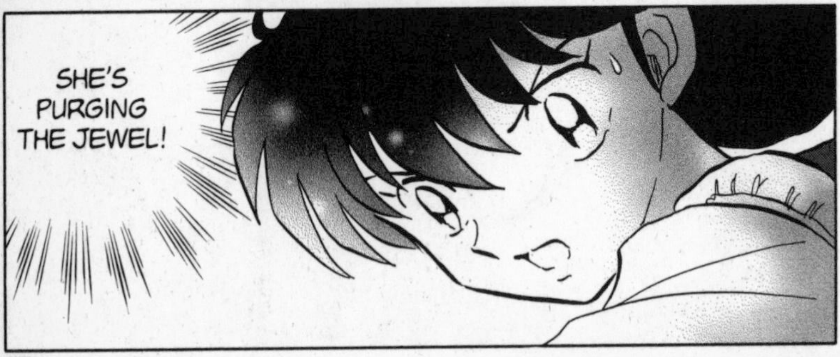
SHE'S PURGING THE JEWEL!

UHH...
BZP BZP BZP BZP
...
KIKYO ...!
SZZZ
PPP

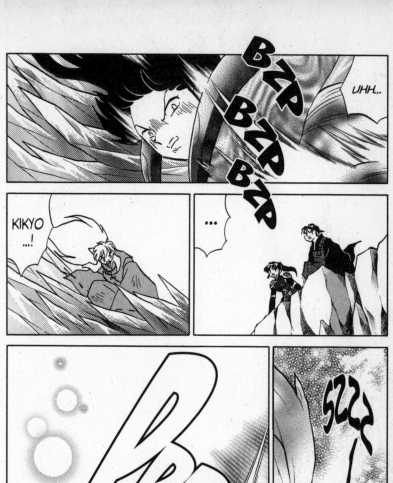

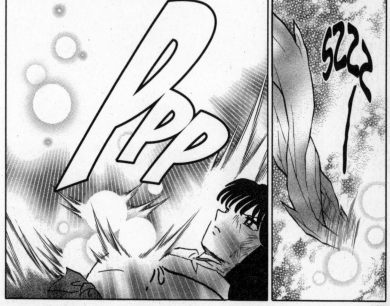

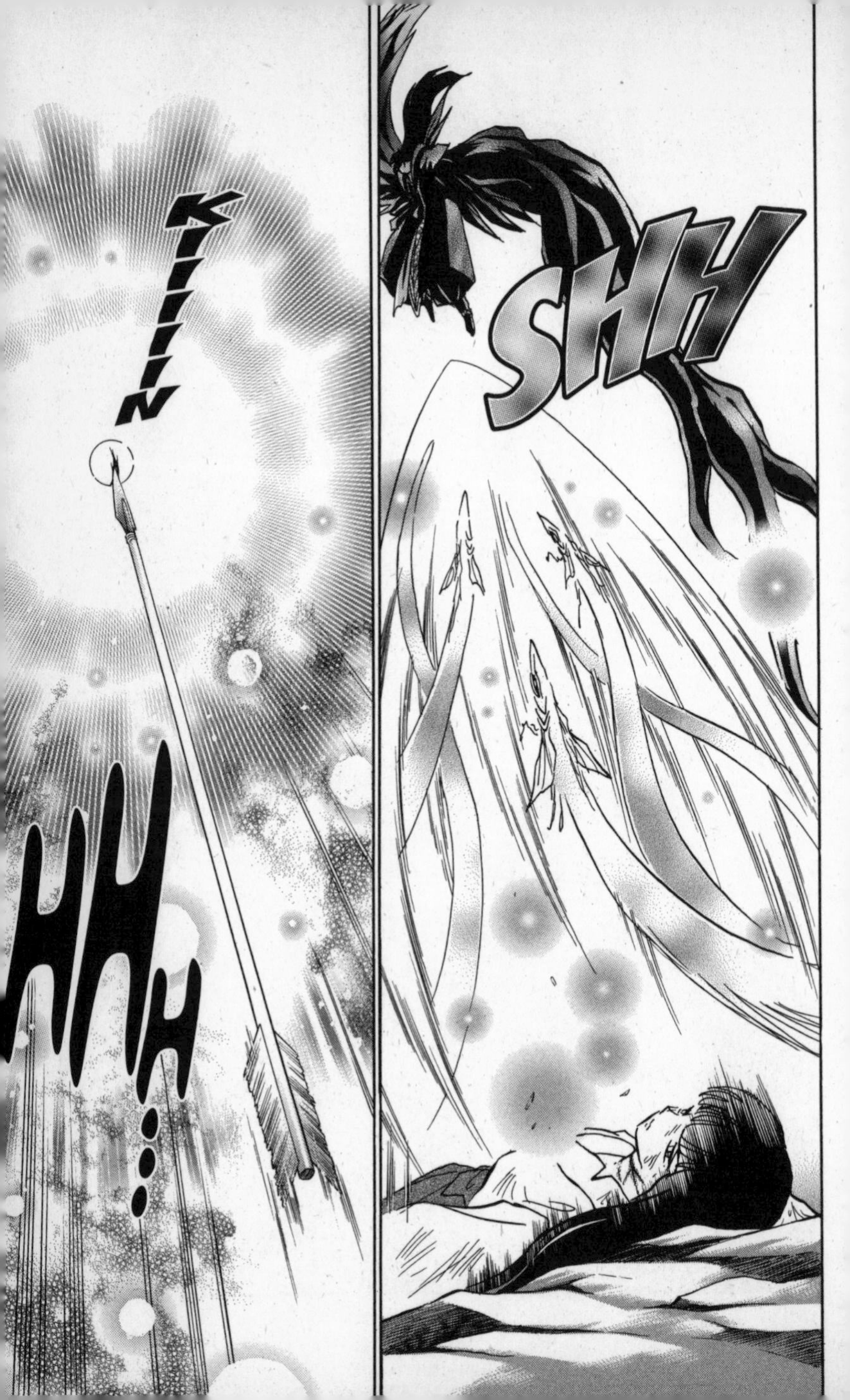
SHH
KIIIIN
HHH...

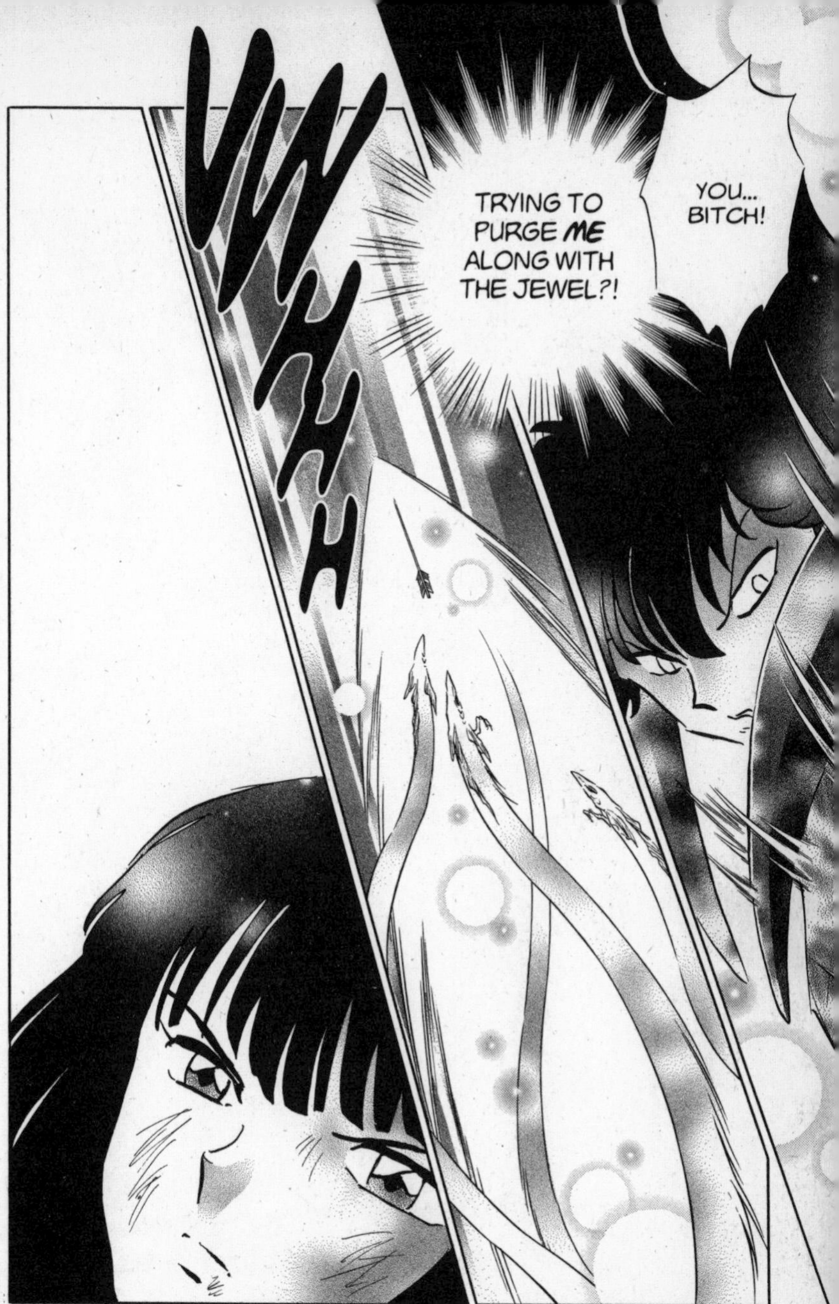
YOU... BITCH!
TRYING TO PURGE *ME* ALONG WITH THE JEWEL?!

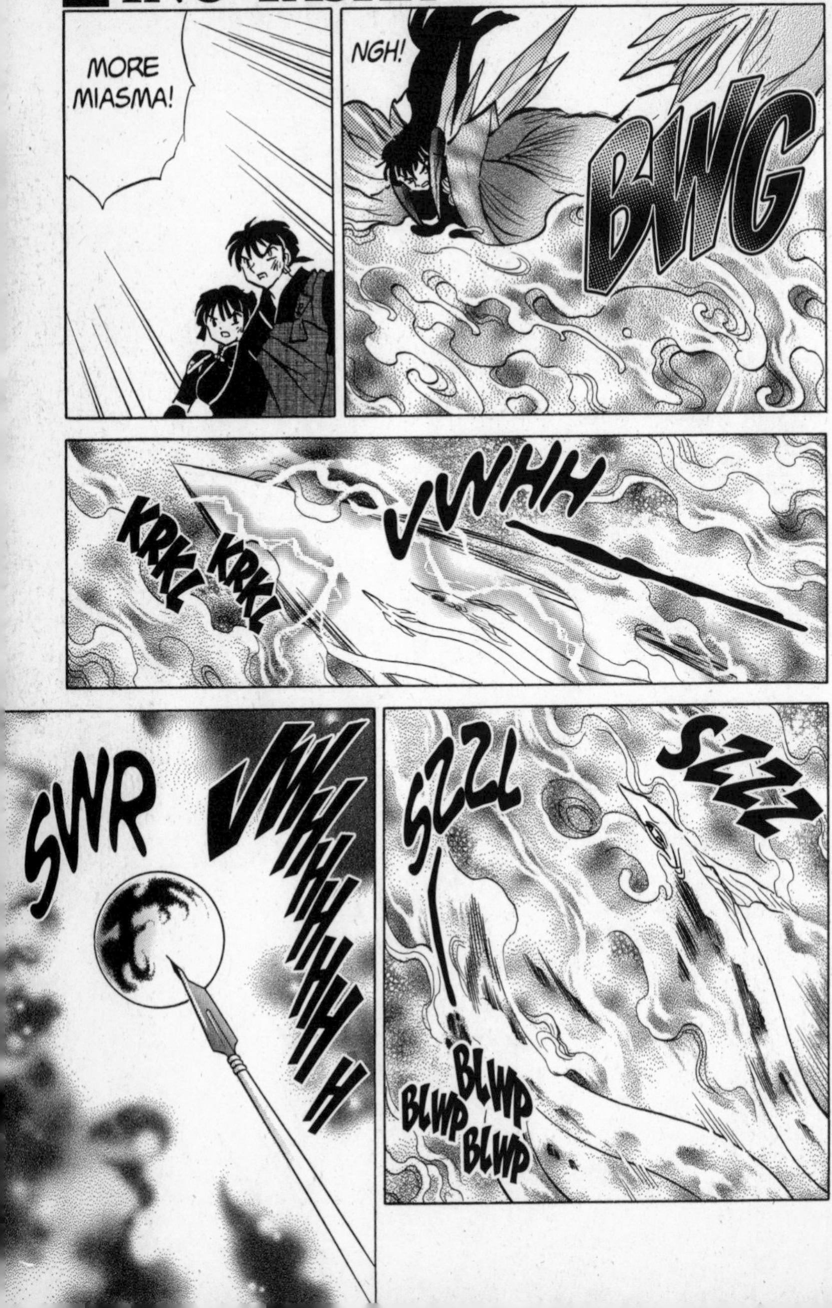
NGH!
BWG
MORE MIASMA!
VVNHH
KRKL KRKL
SZZZ
SZZZ
BLWP BLWP
BLWP BLWP
VVNHHHHH H
SWR

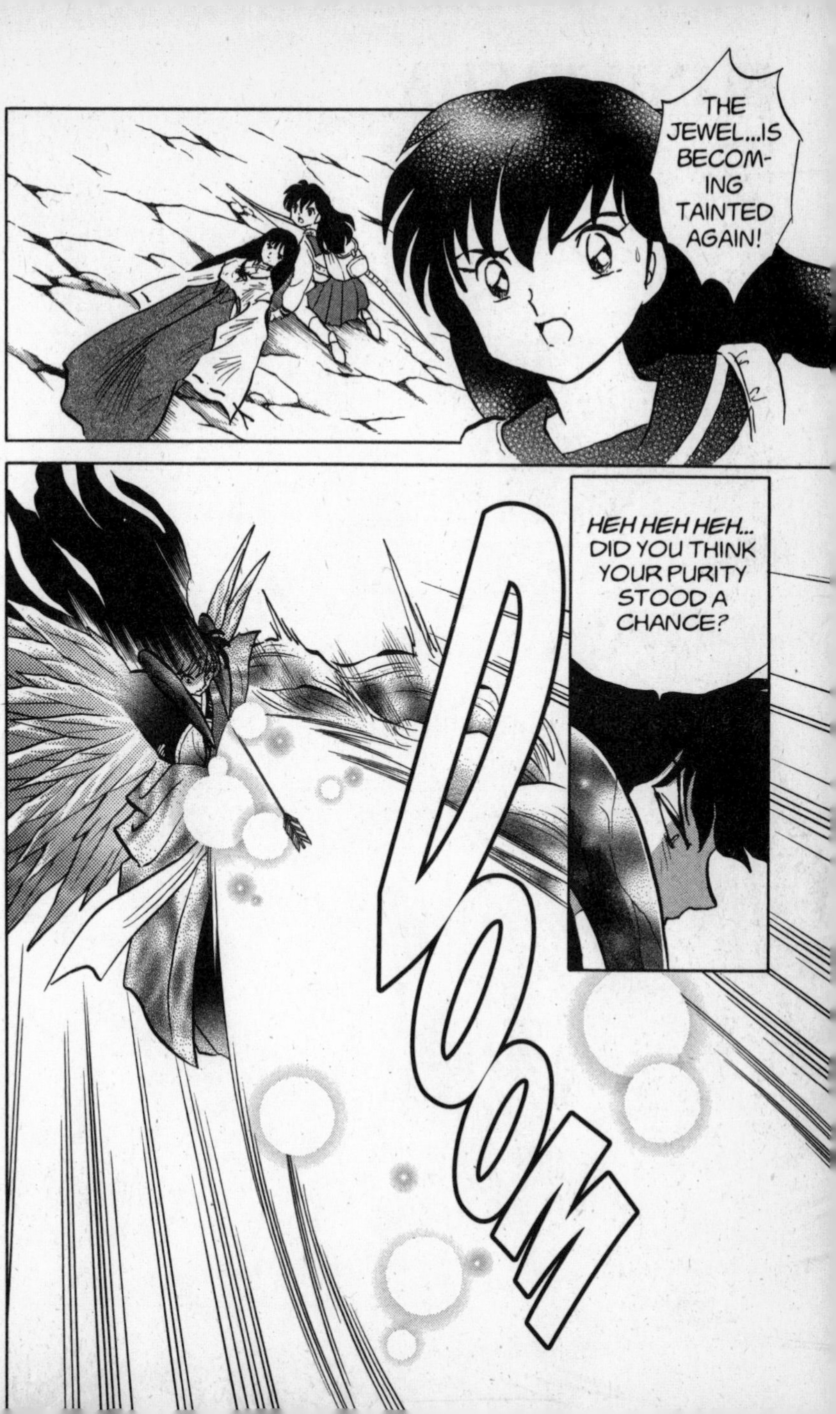
THE JEWEL...IS BECOMING TAINTED AGAIN!
HEH HEH HEH... DID YOU THINK YOUR PURITY STOOD A CHANCE?
VOOOM

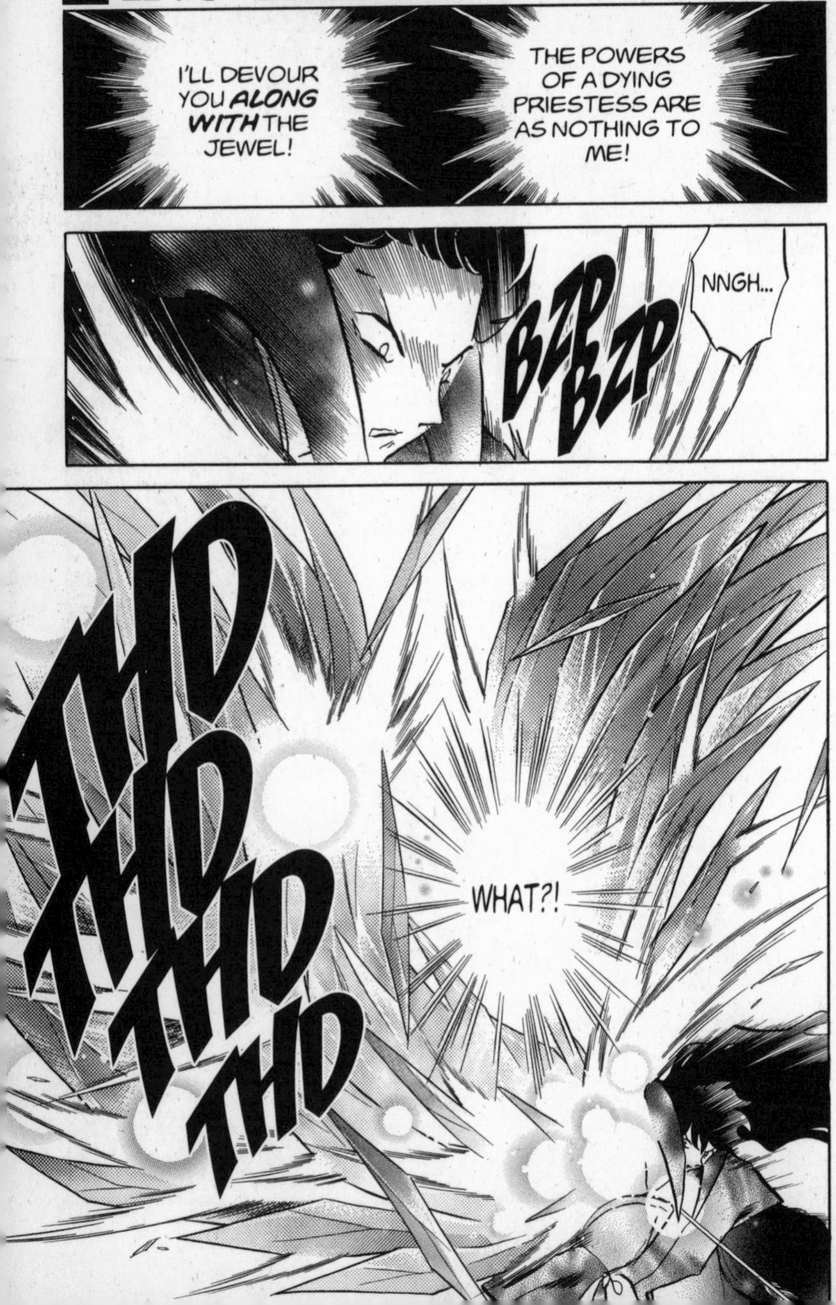
THE POWERS OF A DYING PRIESTESS ARE AS NOTHING TO ME!
I'LL DEVOUR YOU ALONG WITH THE JEWEL!
NNGH...
BZP BZP
WHAT?!
THD THD THD THD

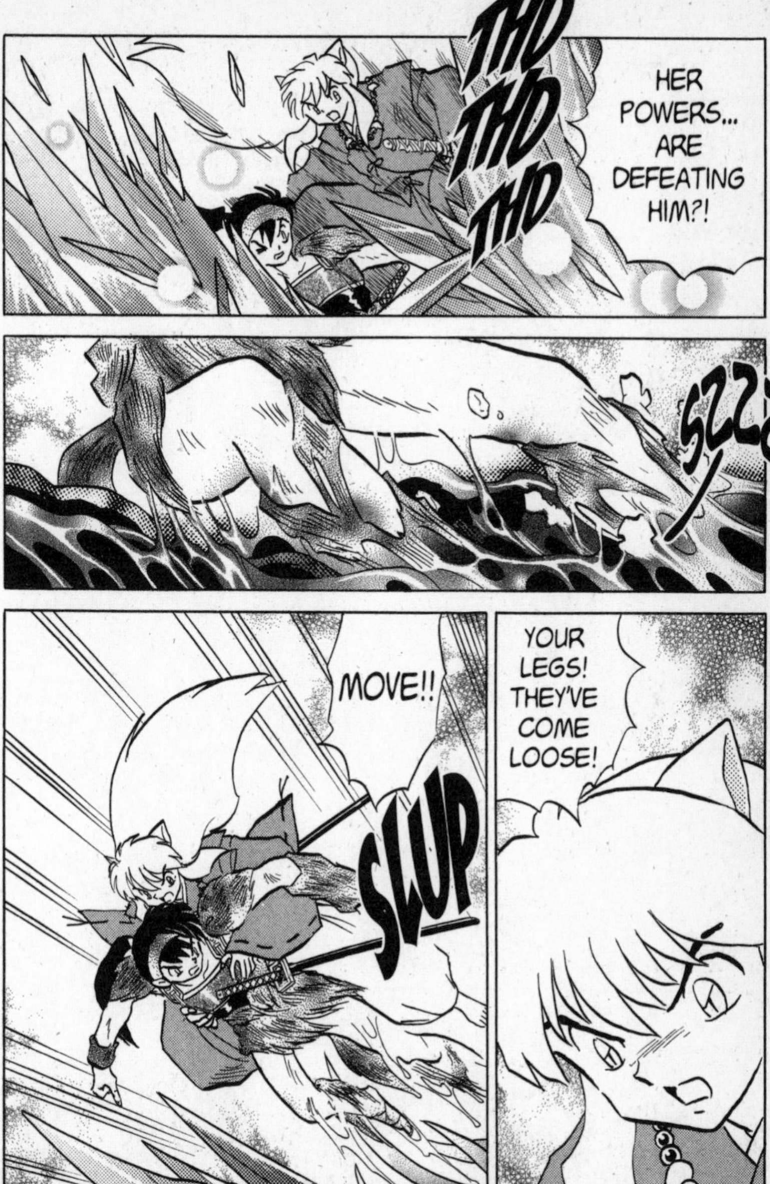
HER POWERS... ARE DEFEATING HIM?!
THD THD THD
SZZZ
YOUR LEGS! THEY'VE COME LOOSE!
MOVE!!
SLUP

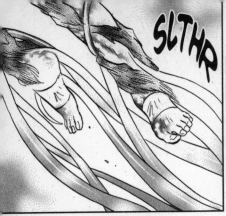

SLTHR

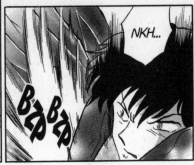

NKH...

BZP BZP

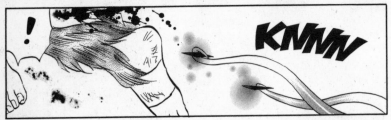

!

KMM

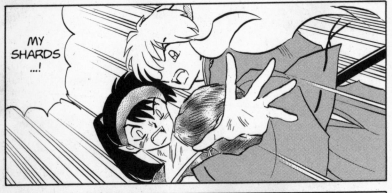

MY
SHARDS
...!

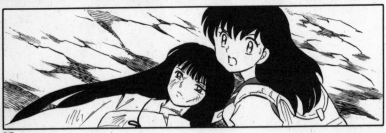

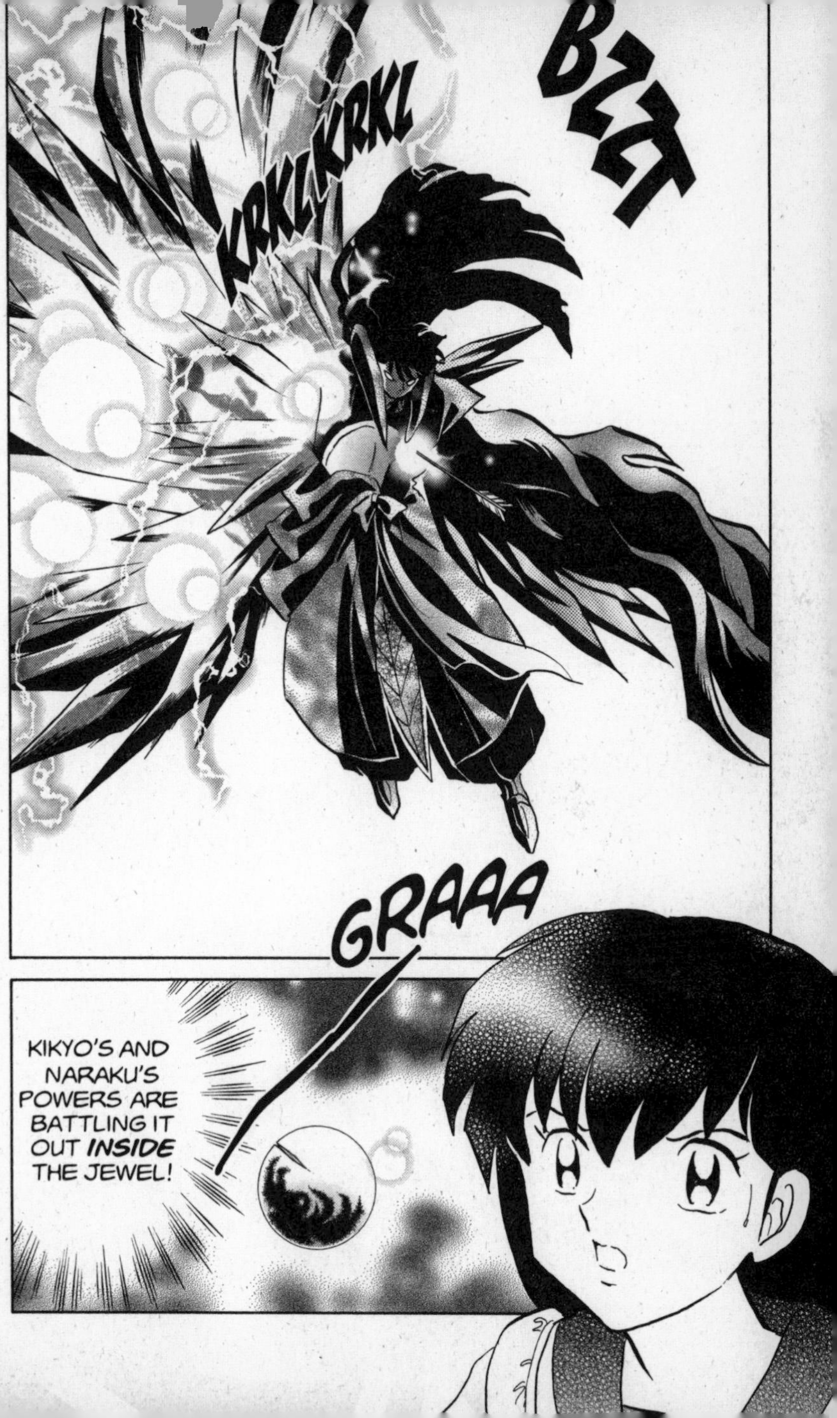
BZZT
KRKLKRKL
GRAAA
KIKYO'S AND NARAKU'S POWERS ARE BATTLING IT OUT *INSIDE* THE JEWEL!

SCROLL 6
SUNSET

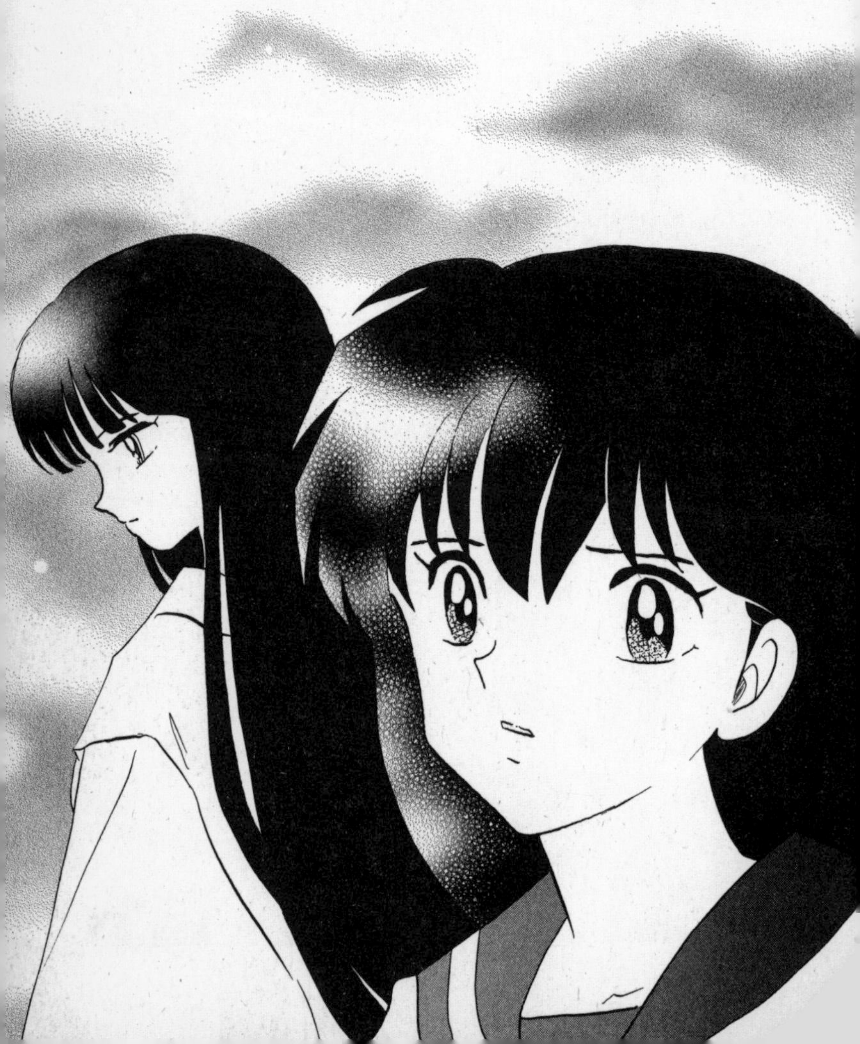

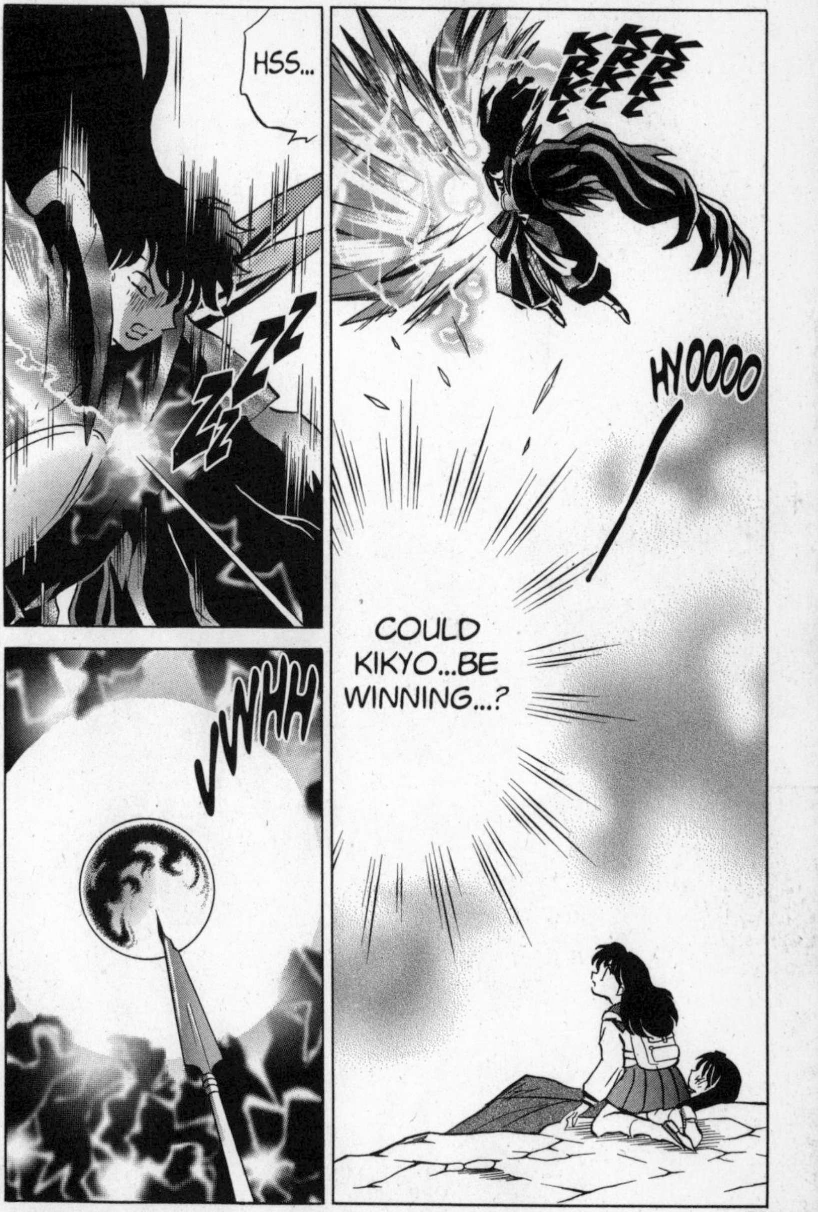
KRKL KRKL KRKL
HYOOOO
COULD KIKYO...BE WINNING...?
HSS...
ZZZZZ
VWHH

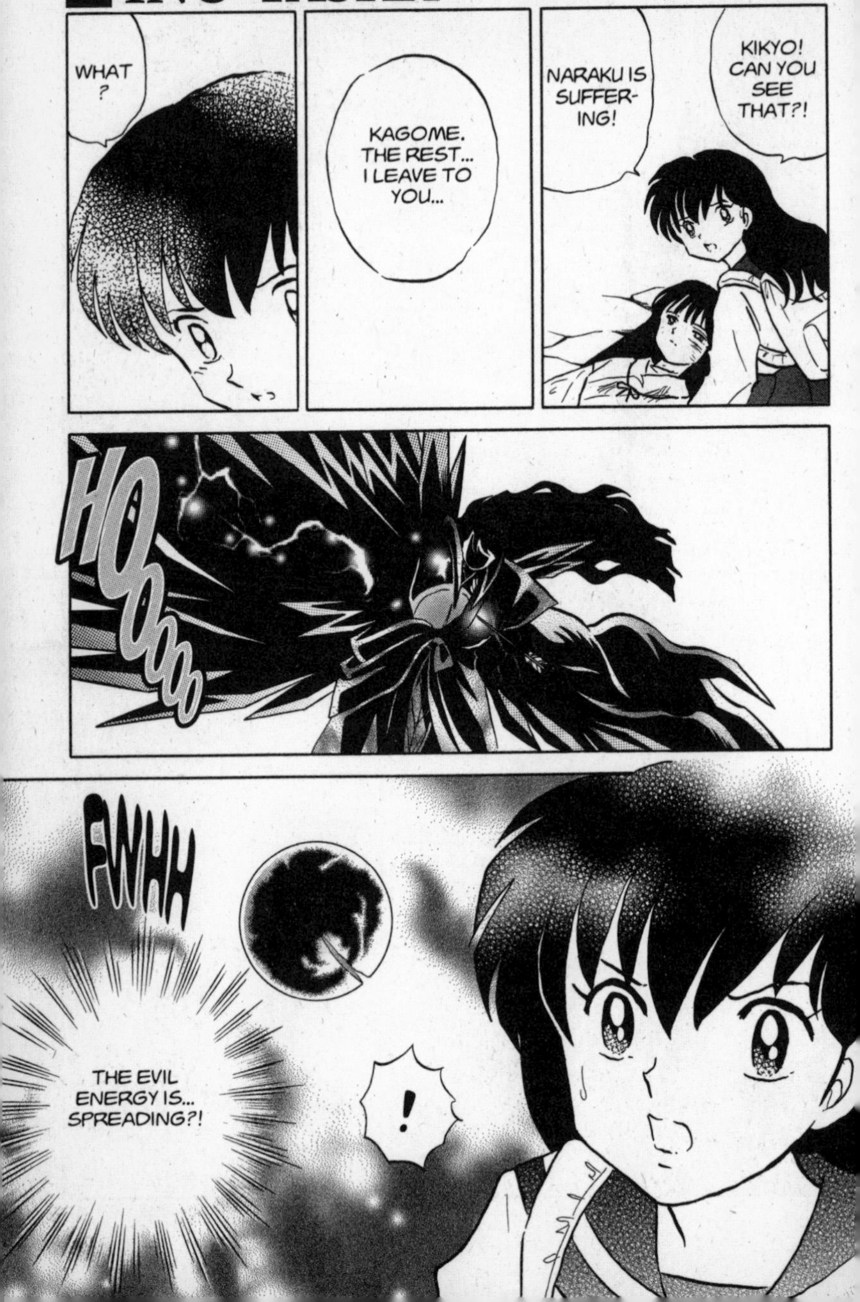
KIKYO! CAN YOU SEE THAT?!
NARAKU IS SUFFER-ING!
KAGOME. THE REST... I LEAVE TO YOU...
WHAT ?
HOOOOOO
FWHH
!
THE EVIL ENERGY IS... SPREADING?!

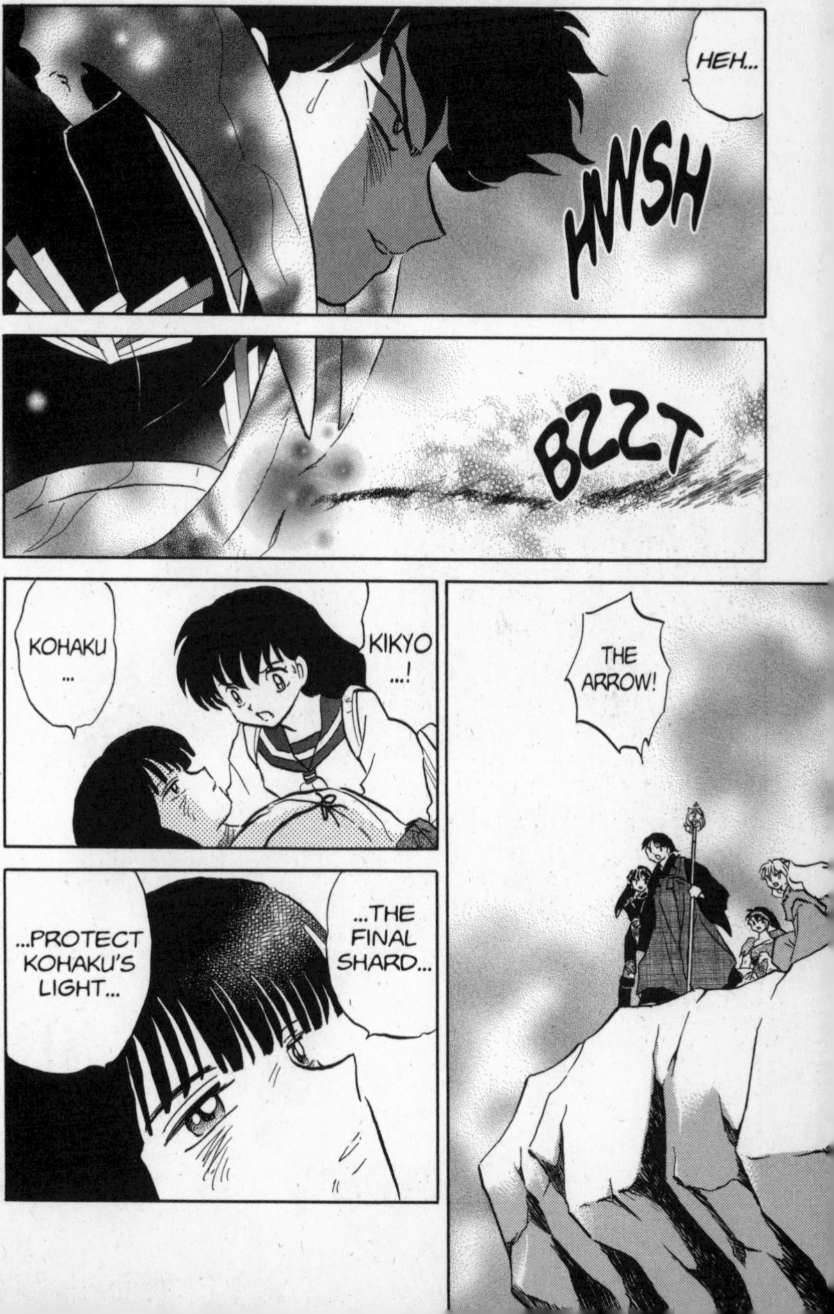

HEH...
HWSH
BZZT
THE ARROW!
KIKYO ...!
KOHAKU ...
...THE FINAL SHARD...
...PROTECT KOHAKU'S LIGHT...

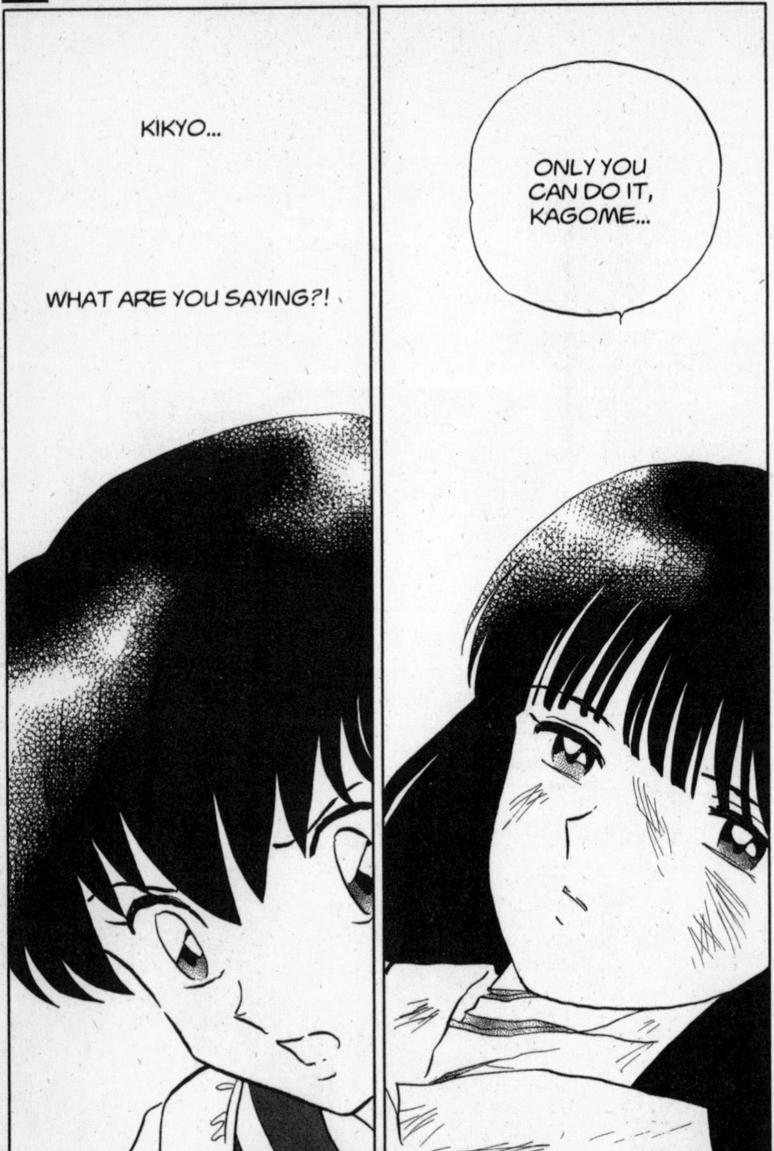
ONLY YOU CAN DO IT, KAGOME...
KIKYO...
WHAT ARE YOU SAYING?!

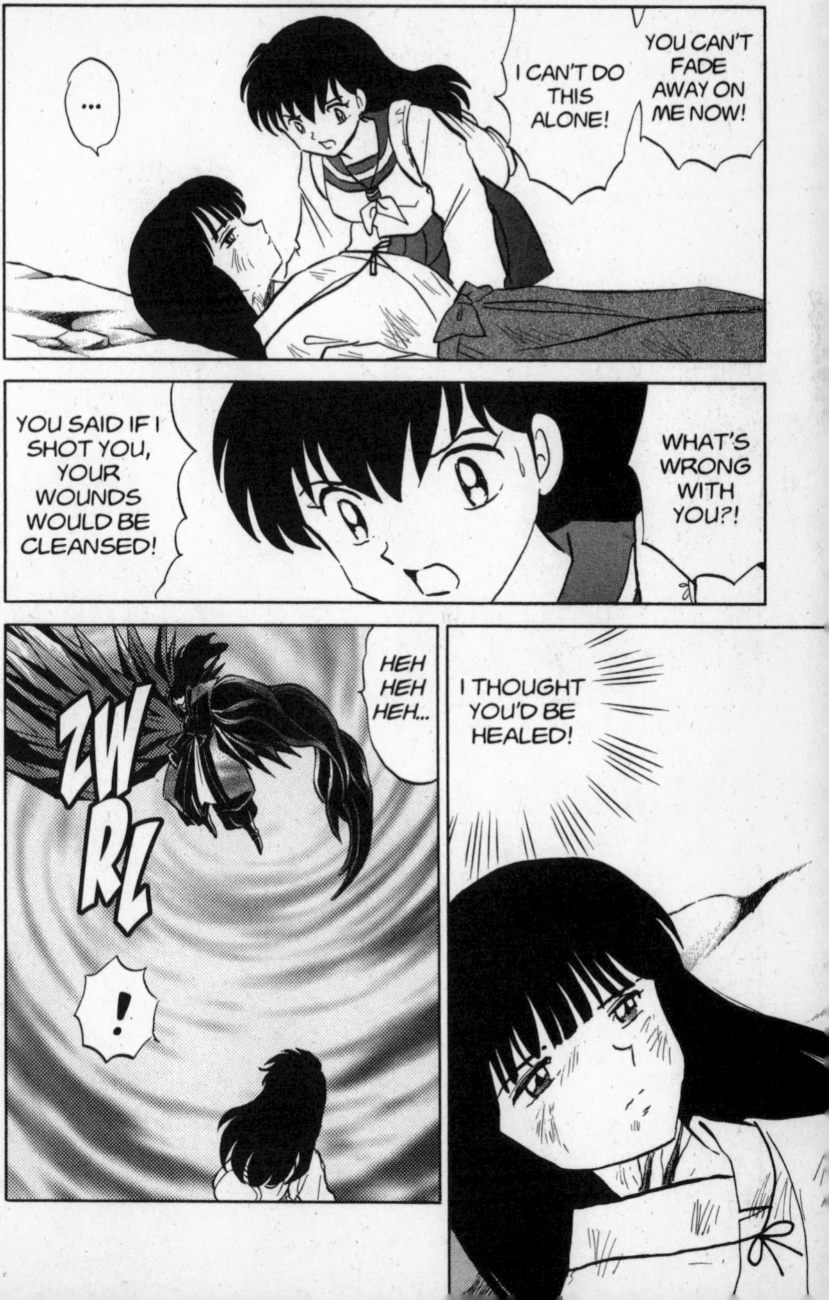
YOU CAN'T FADE AWAY ON ME NOW!
I CAN'T DO THIS ALONE!
...
WHAT'S WRONG WITH YOU?!
YOU SAID IF I SHOT YOU, YOUR WOUNDS WOULD BE CLEANSED!
I THOUGHT YOU'D BE HEALED!
HEH HEH HEH...
ZWRL
!

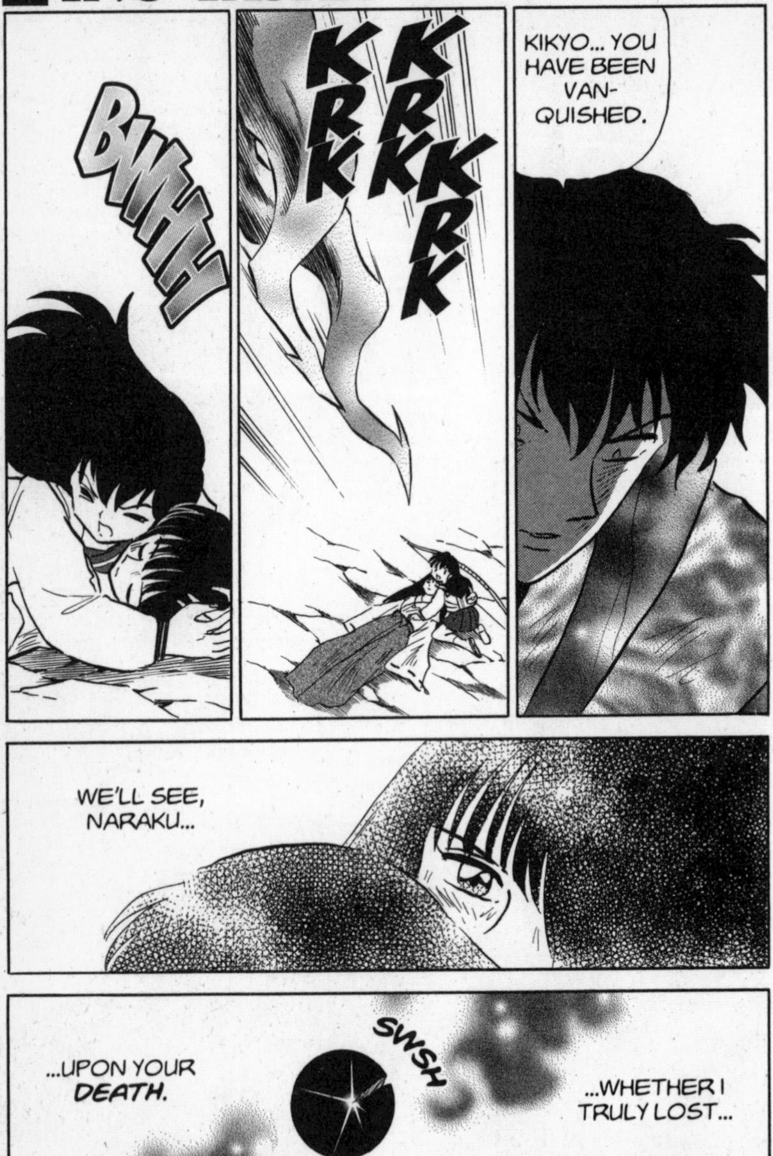
KIKYO... YOU HAVE BEEN VAN-QUISHED.
KRK KRKRK
BWHH
WE'LL SEE, NARAKU...
...WHETHER I TRULY LOST...
SWSH
...UPON YOUR DEATH.

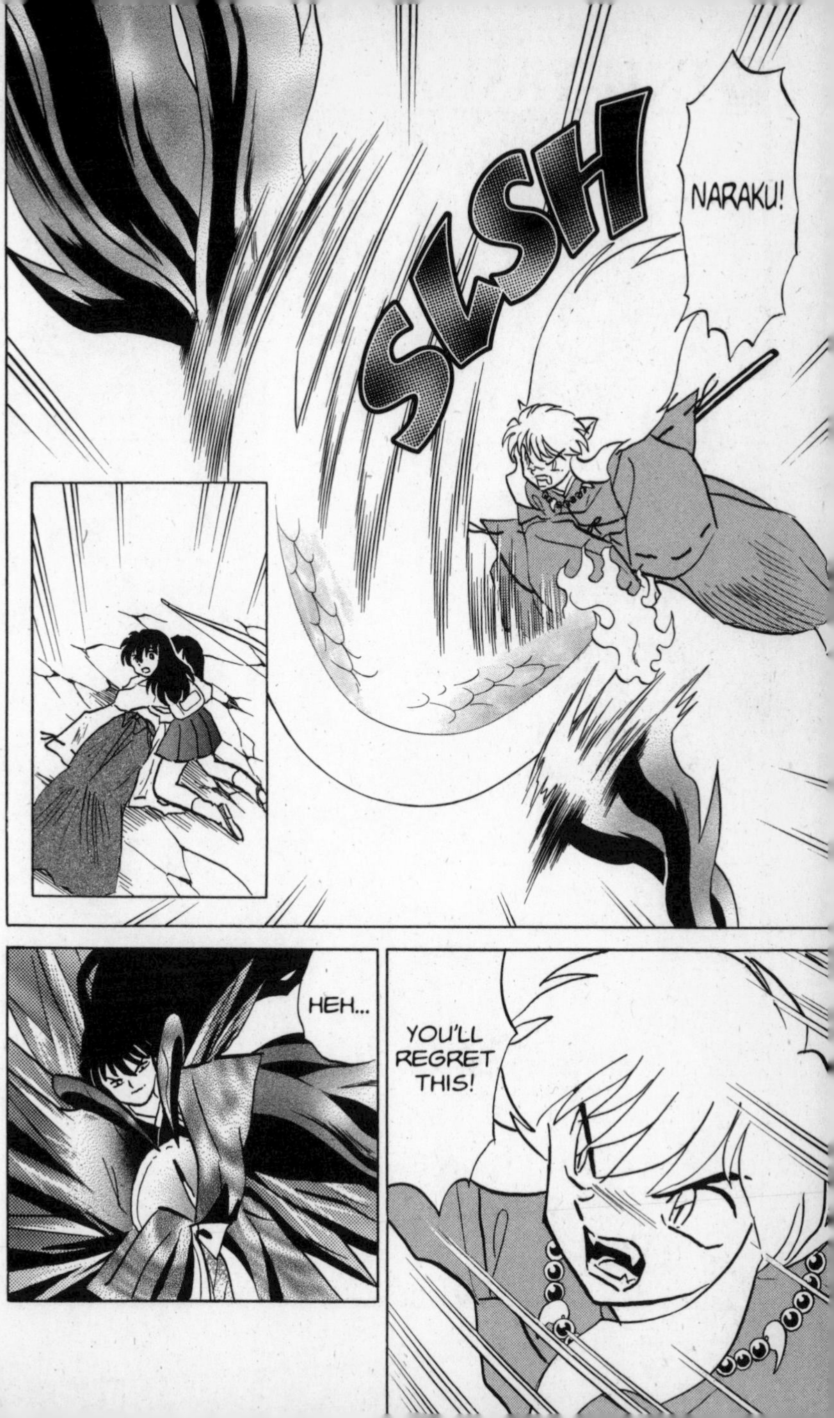
NARAKU!
SLSH
YOU'LL REGRET THIS!
HEH...

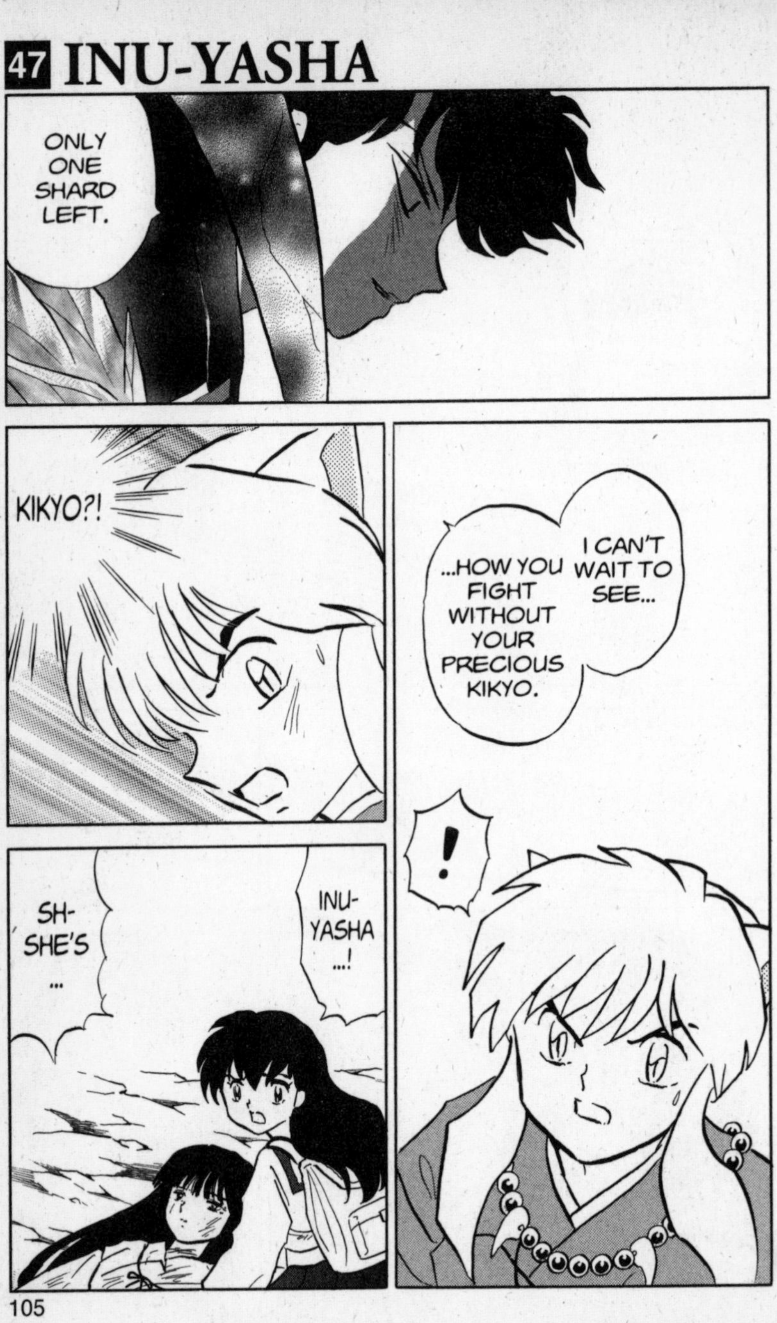
ONLY ONE SHARD LEFT.
I CAN'T WAIT TO SEE...
...HOW YOU FIGHT WITHOUT YOUR PRECIOUS KIKYO.
!
KIKYO?!
INU-YASHA ...!
SH-SHE'S ...

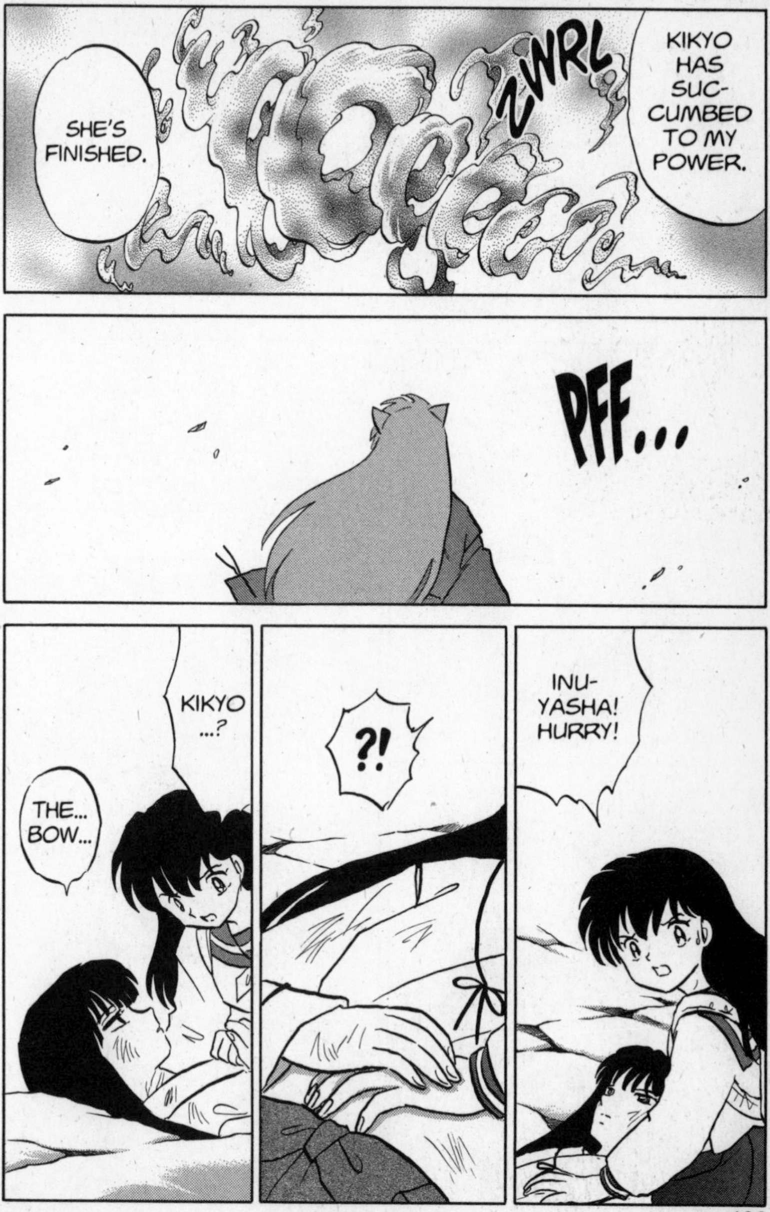
KIKYO HAS SUC-CUMBED TO MY POWER.
ZWRL
SHE'S FINISHED.
PFF...
INU-YASHA! HURRY!
?!
KIKYO ...?
THE... BOW...

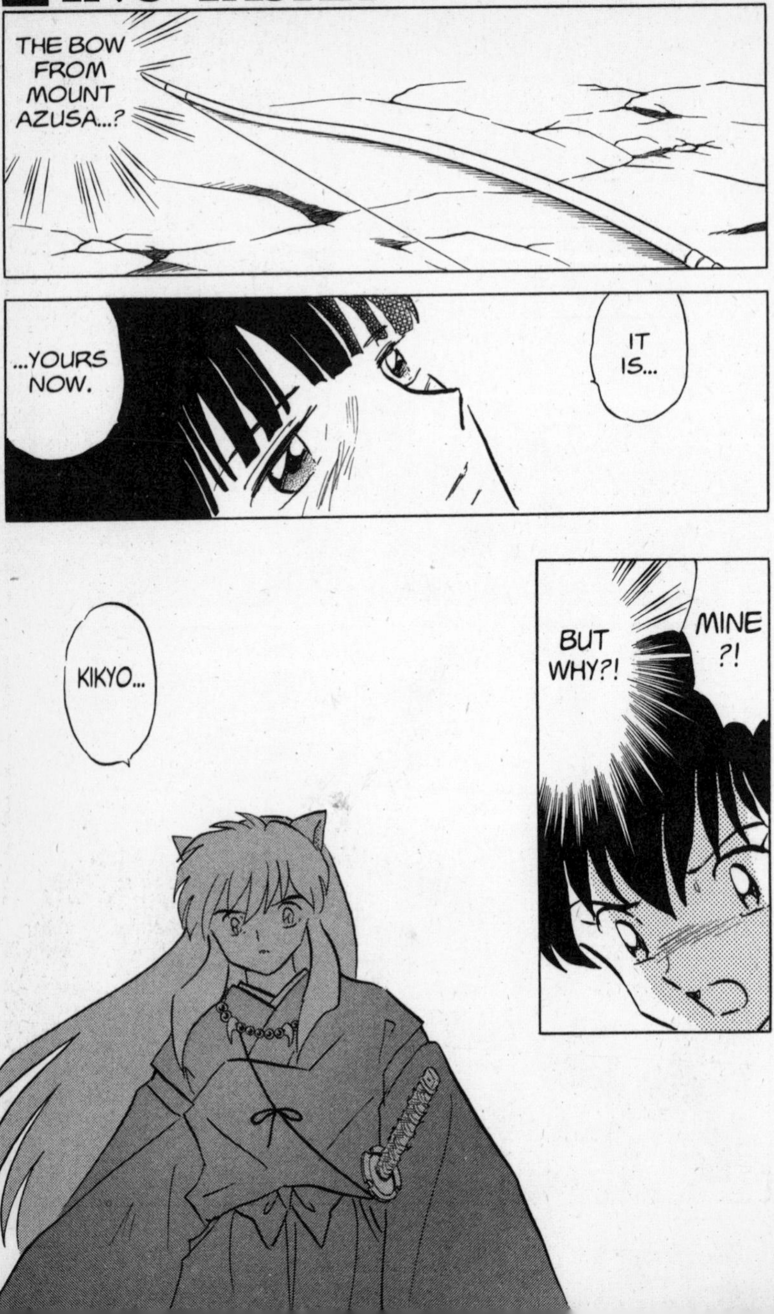
THE BOW FROM MOUNT AZUSA...?
IT IS...
...YOURS NOW.
MINE?!
BUT WHY?!
KIKYO...

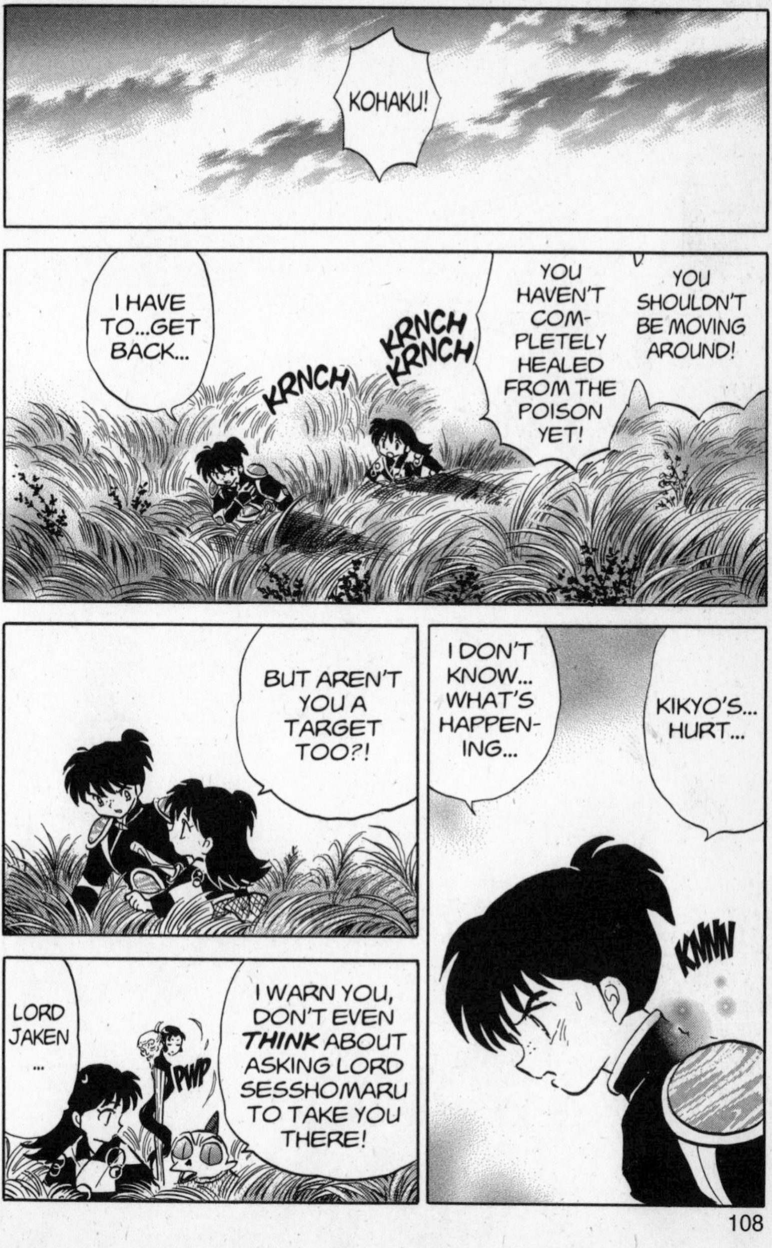
KOHAKU!
YOU SHOULDN'T BE MOVING AROUND!
YOU HAVEN'T COMPLETELY HEALED FROM THE POISON YET!
KRNCH KRNCH
KRNCH
I HAVE TO...GET BACK...
KIKYO'S... HURT...
I DON'T KNOW... WHAT'S HAPPENING...
KNNN
BUT AREN'T YOU A TARGET TOO?!
I WARN YOU, DON'T EVEN THINK ABOUT ASKING LORD SESSHOMARU TO TAKE YOU THERE!
PWP
LORD JAKEN ...

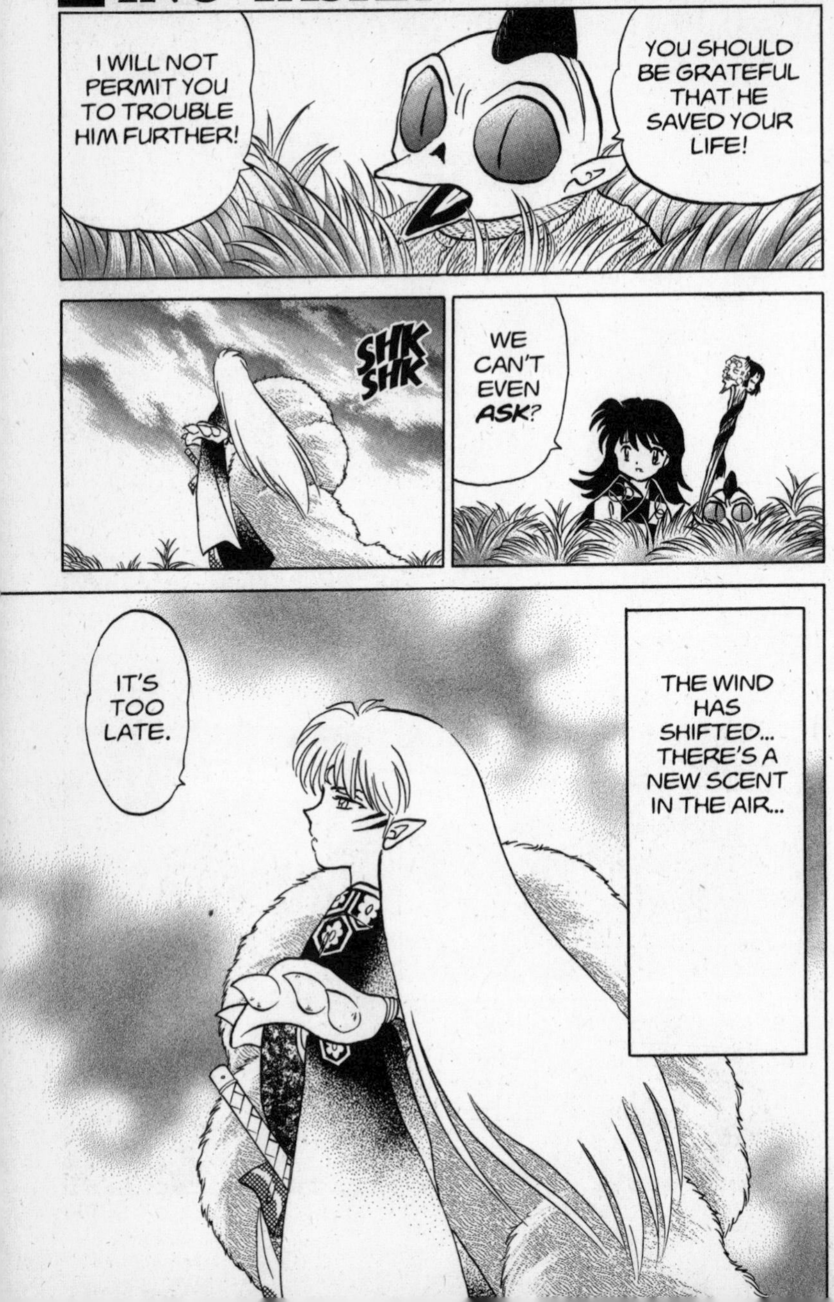
YOU SHOULD BE GRATEFUL THAT HE SAVED YOUR LIFE!
I WILL NOT PERMIT YOU TO TROUBLE HIM FURTHER!
WE CAN'T EVEN *ASK*?
SHK SHK
THE WIND HAS SHIFTED... THERE'S A NEW SCENT IN THE AIR...
IT'S TOO LATE.

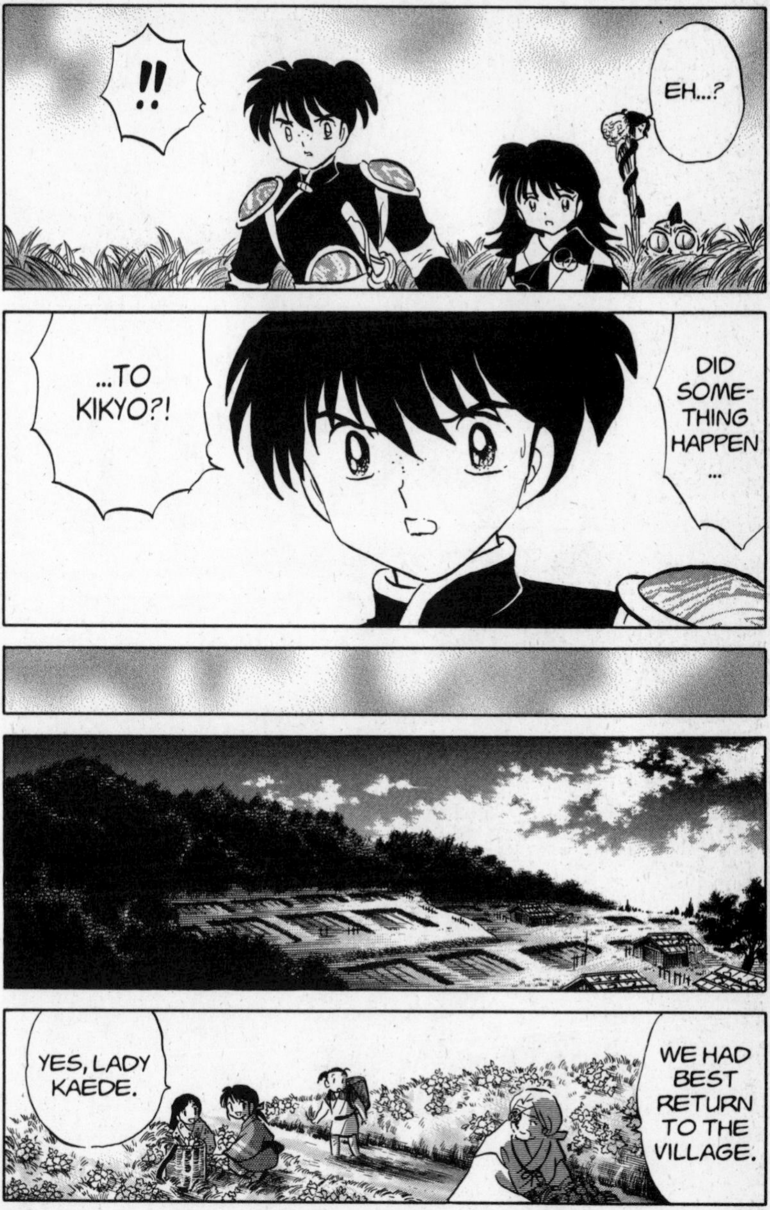
EH...?
!!
DID SOME-THING HAPPEN...
...TO KIKYO?!
WE HAD BEST RETURN TO THE VILLAGE.
YES, LADY KAEDE.

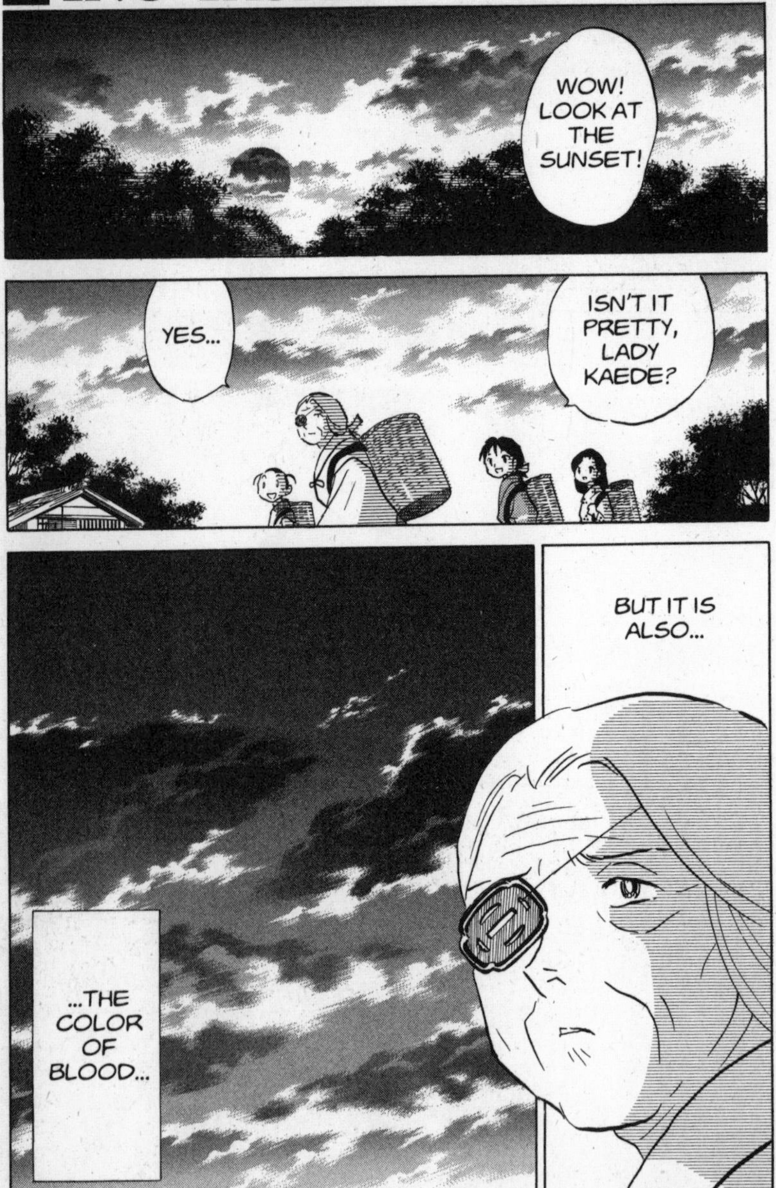
WOW! LOOK AT THE SUNSET!
ISN'T IT PRETTY, LADY KAEDE?
YES...
BUT IT IS ALSO...
...THE COLOR OF BLOOD...

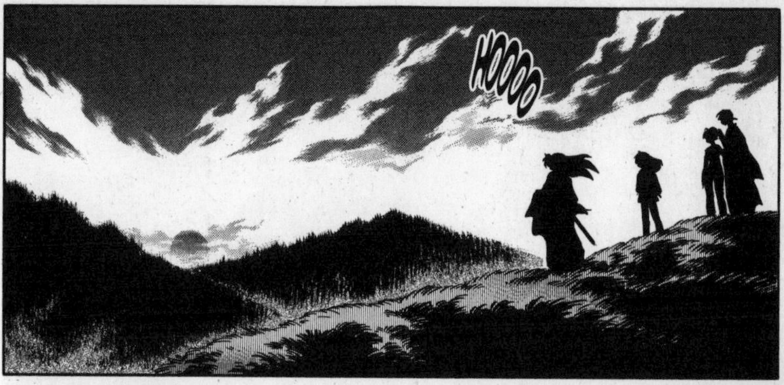
HOOOO
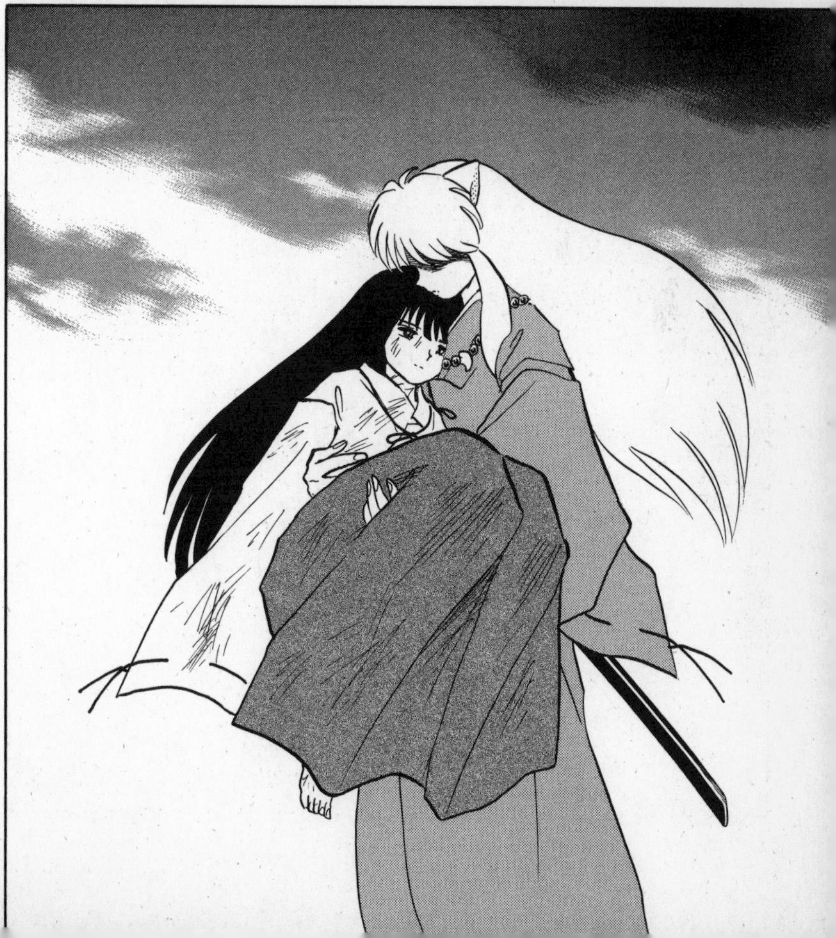

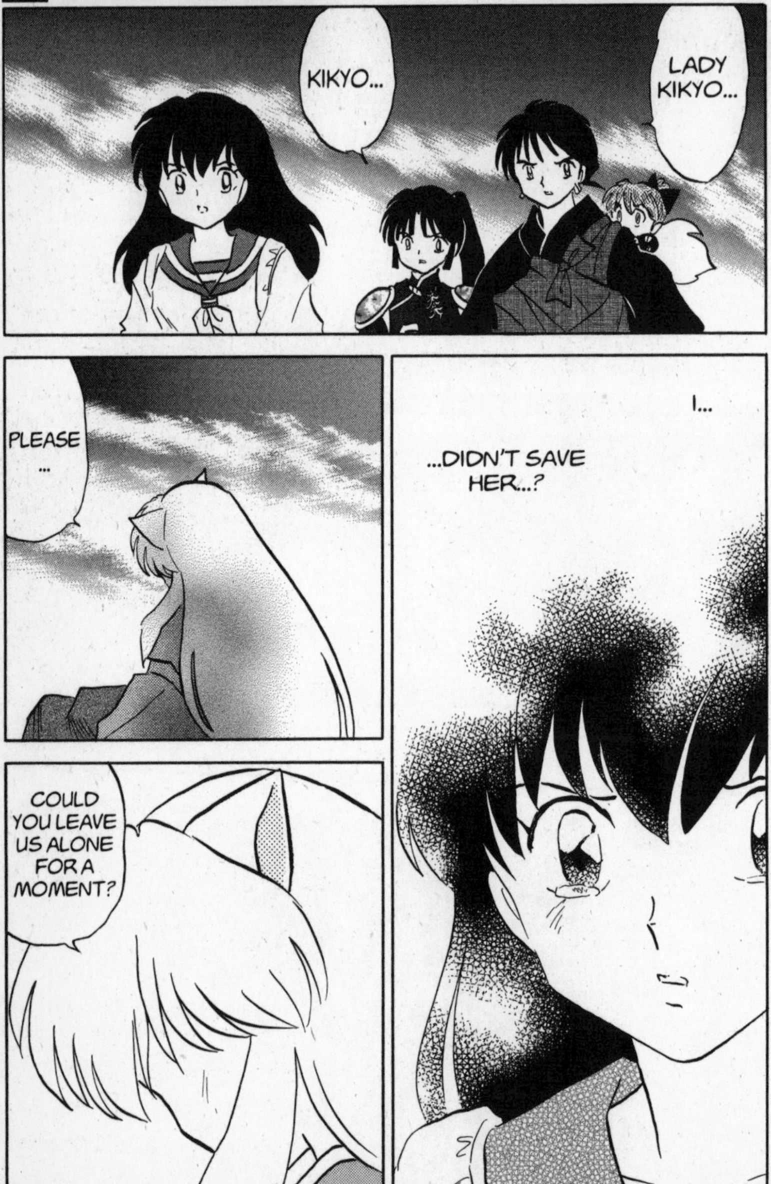
LADY KIKYO...
KIKYO...
I...
...DIDN'T SAVE HER...?
PLEASE ...
COULD YOU LEAVE US ALONE FOR A MOMENT?

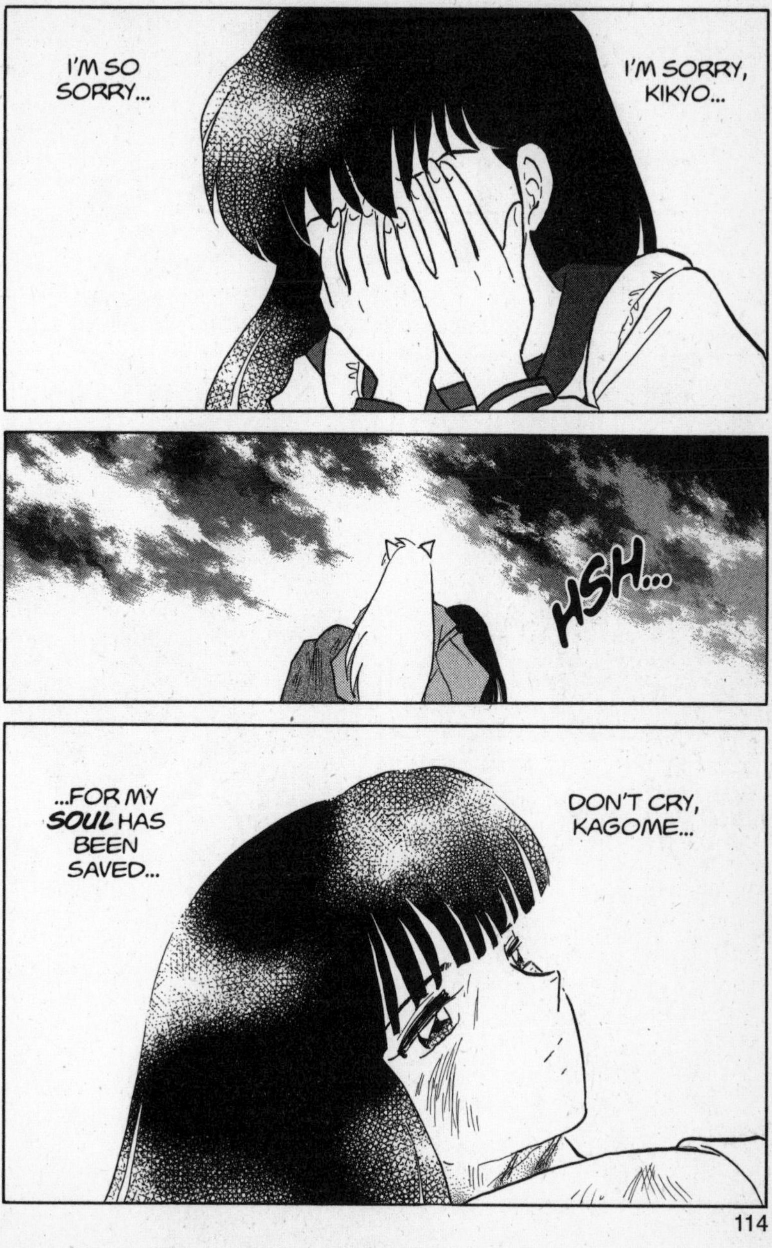
I'M SORRY, KIKYO...
I'M SO SORRY...
HSH...
DON'T CRY, KAGOME...
...FOR MY SOUL HAS BEEN SAVED...

SCROLL 7

THE LIGHTS

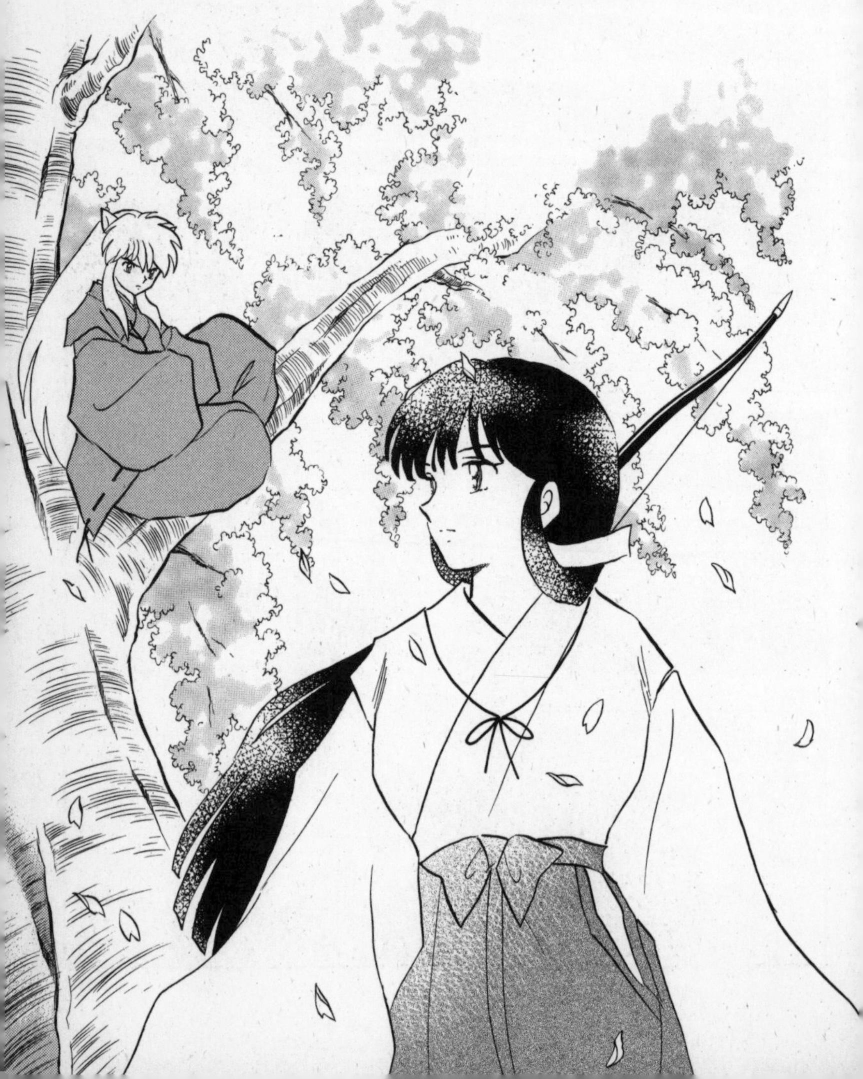

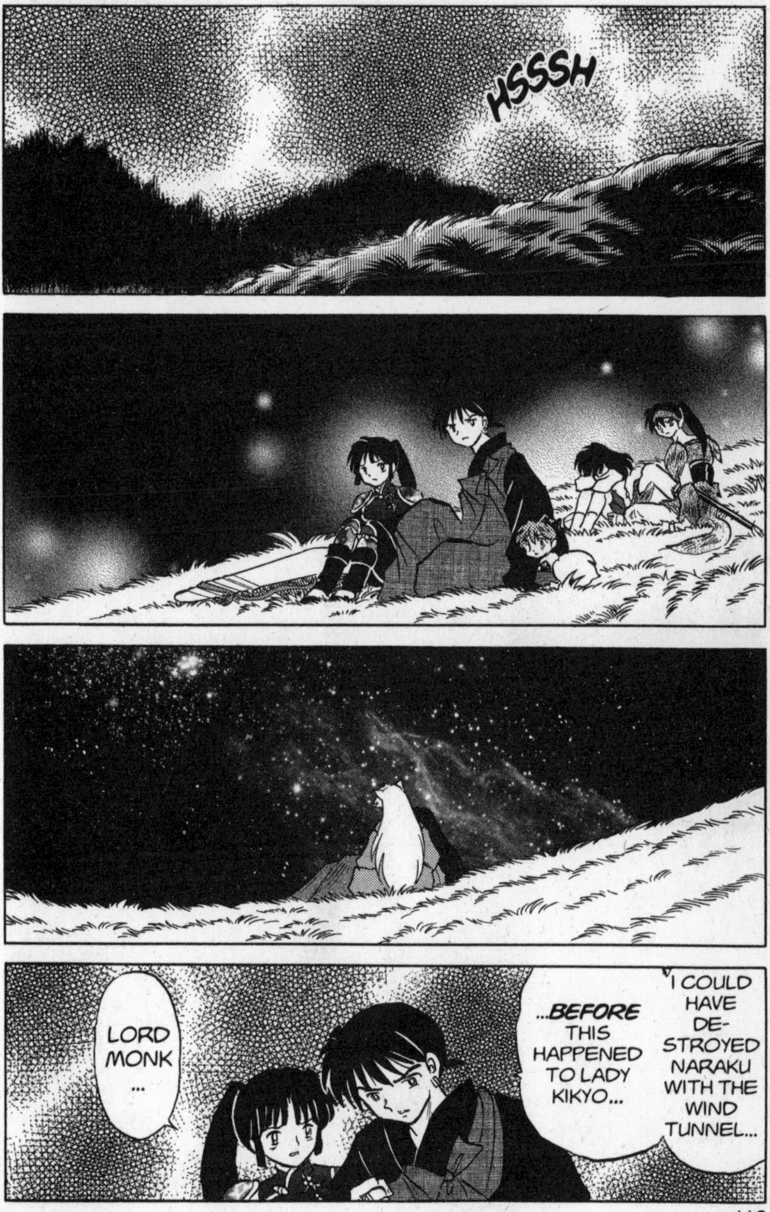
HSSSH
I COULD HAVE DE-STROYED NARAKU WITH THE WIND TUNNEL...
...BEFORE THIS HAPPENED TO LADY KIKYO...
LORD MONK...

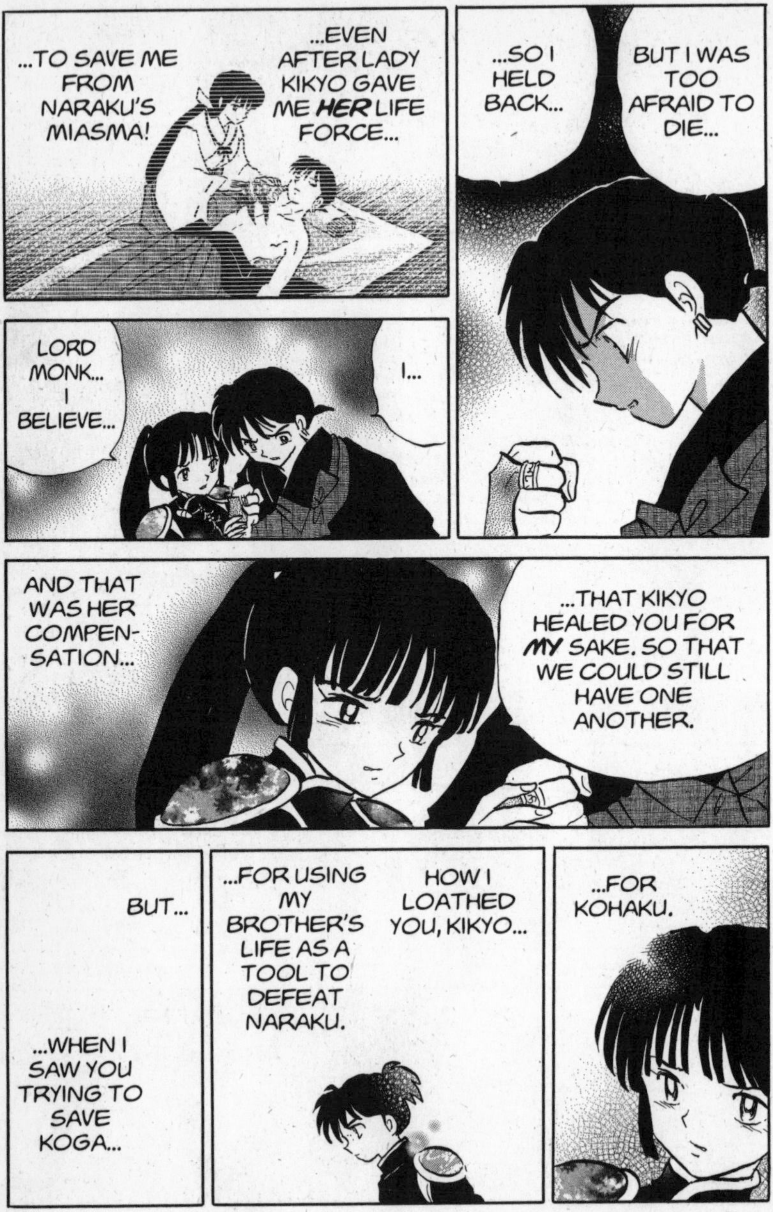
...TO SAVE ME FROM NARAKU'S MIASMA!
...EVEN AFTER LADY KIKYO GAVE ME HER LIFE FORCE...
BUT I WAS TOO AFRAID TO DIE...
...SO I HELD BACK...
I...
LORD MONK... I BELIEVE...
...THAT KIKYO HEALED YOU FOR MY SAKE. SO THAT WE COULD STILL HAVE ONE ANOTHER.
AND THAT WAS HER COMPENSATION...
BUT...
...WHEN I SAW YOU TRYING TO SAVE KOGA...
HOW I LOATHED YOU, KIKYO...
...FOR USING MY BROTHER'S LIFE AS A TOOL TO DEFEAT NARAKU.
...FOR KOHAKU.

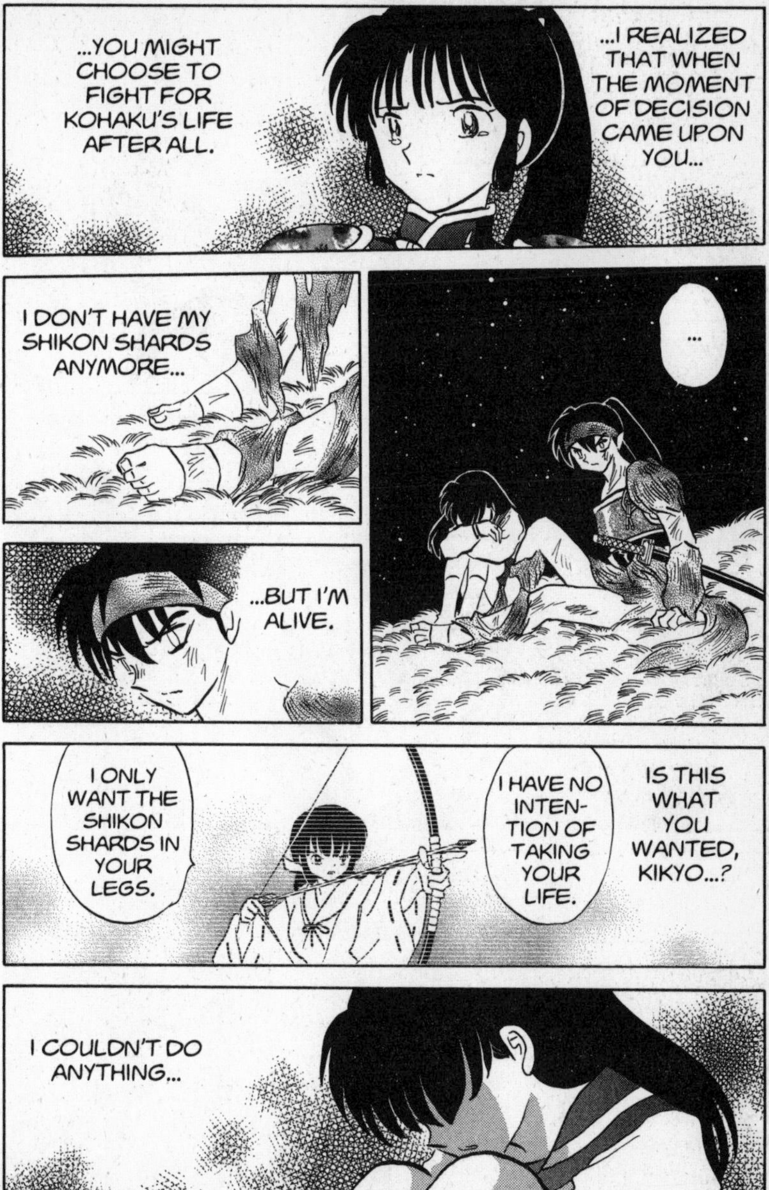
...I REALIZED THAT WHEN THE MOMENT OF DECISION CAME UPON YOU...
...YOU MIGHT CHOOSE TO FIGHT FOR KOHAKU'S LIFE AFTER ALL.
...
I DON'T HAVE MY SHIKON SHARDS ANYMORE...
...BUT I'M ALIVE.
IS THIS WHAT YOU WANTED, KIKYO...?
I HAVE NO INTEN-TION OF TAKING YOUR LIFE.
I ONLY WANT THE SHIKON SHARDS IN YOUR LEGS.
I COULDN'T DO ANYTHING...

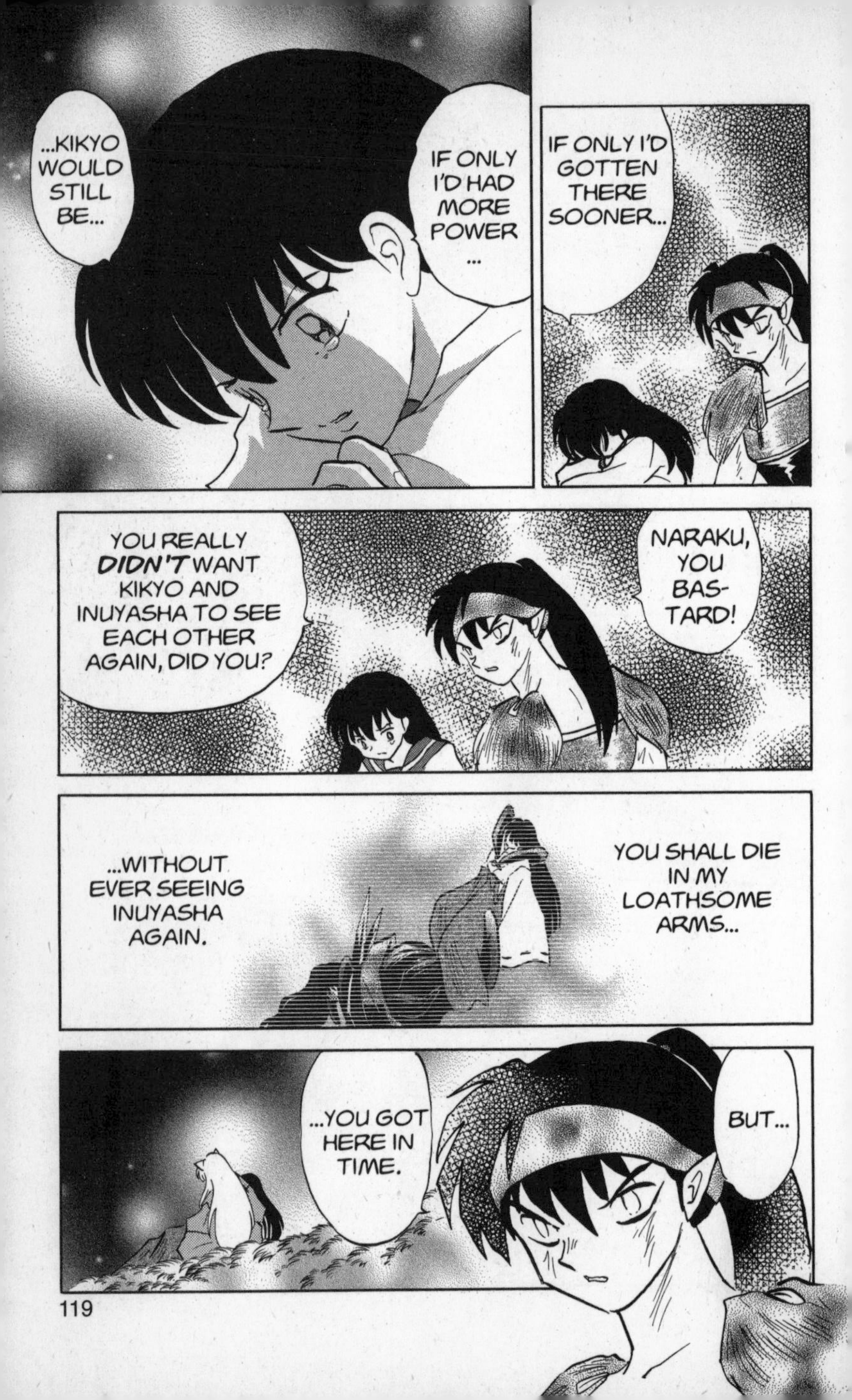
IF ONLY I'D GOTTEN THERE SOONER...
IF ONLY I'D HAD MORE POWER...
...KIKYO WOULD STILL BE...
NARAKU, YOU BAS-TARD!
YOU REALLY **DIDN'T** WANT KIKYO AND INUYASHA TO SEE EACH OTHER AGAIN, DID YOU?
YOU SHALL DIE IN MY LOATHSOME ARMS...
...WITHOUT EVER SEEING INUYASHA AGAIN.
BUT...
...YOU GOT HERE IN TIME.

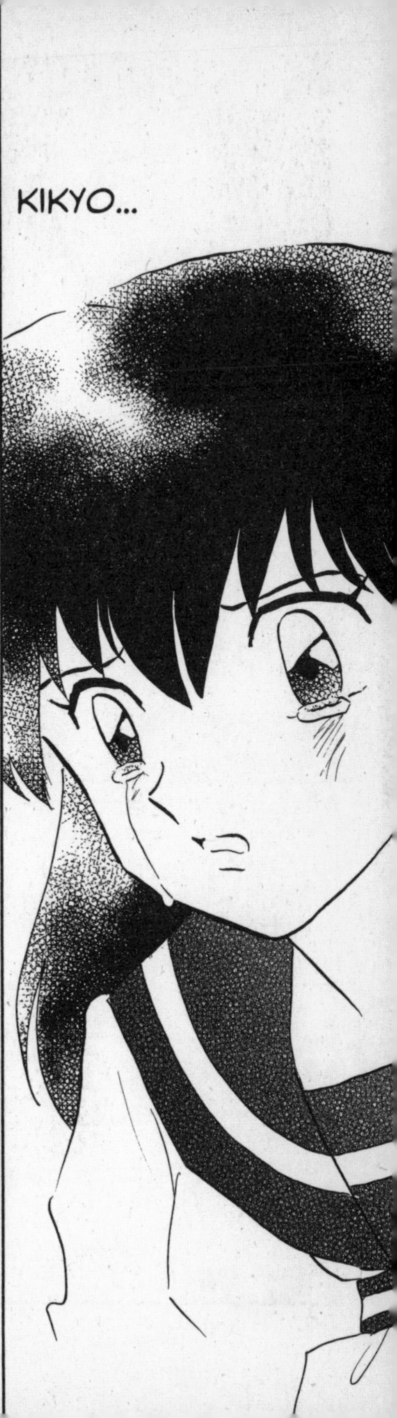
KIKYO...

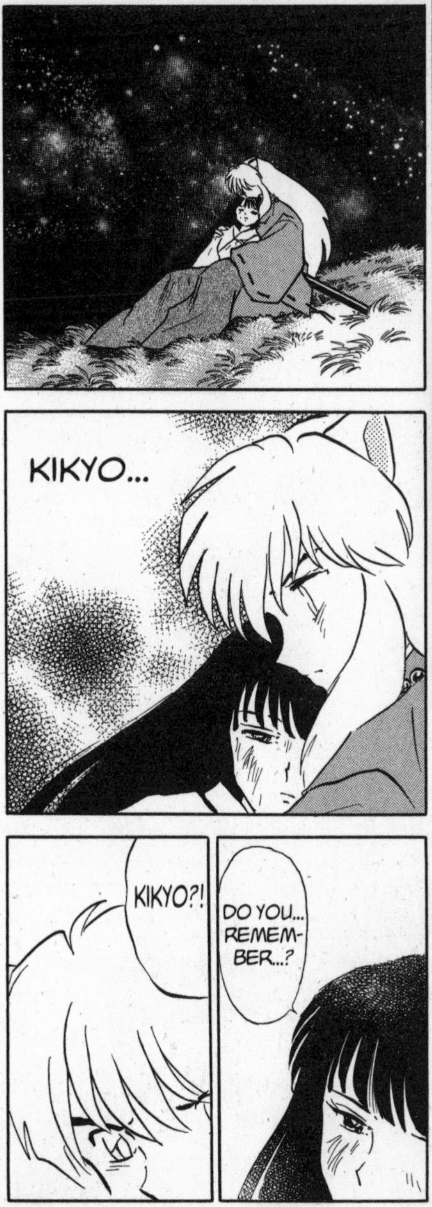
KIKYO...
DO YOU... REMEM-BER...?
KIKYO?!

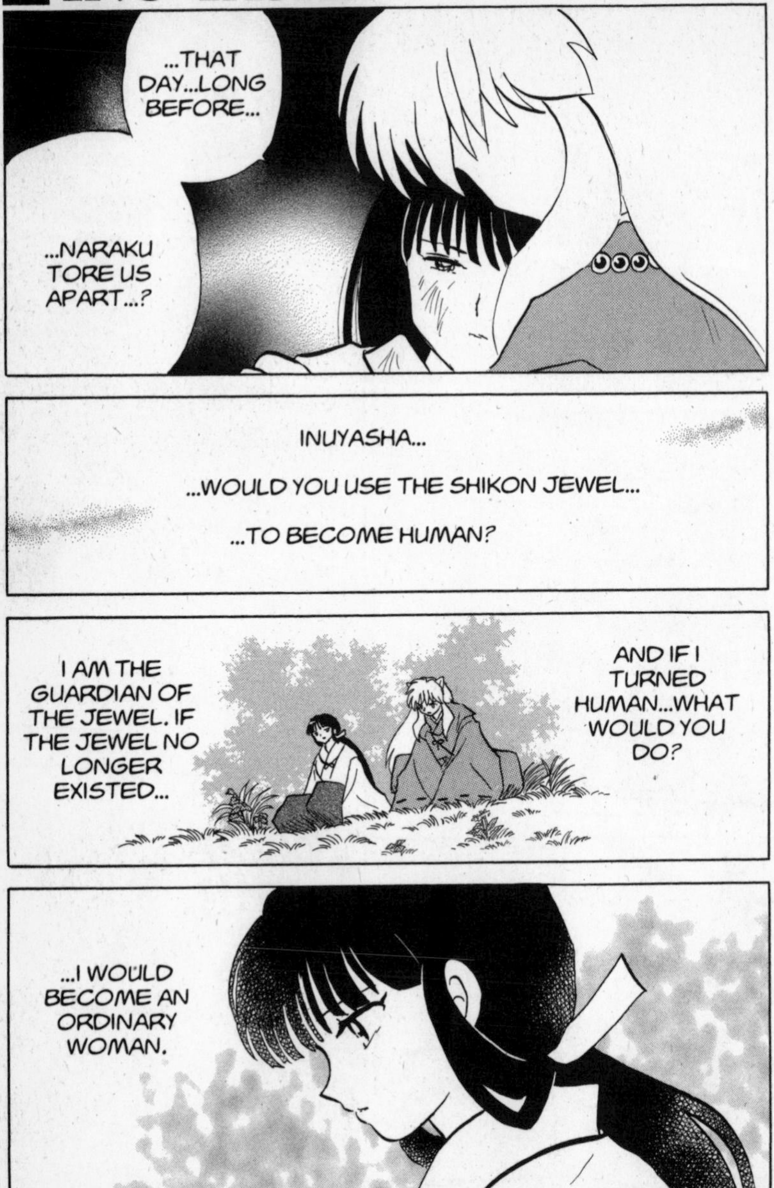
...THAT DAY...LONG BEFORE...
...NARAKU TORE US APART...?
INUYASHA...
...WOULD YOU USE THE SHIKON JEWEL...
...TO BECOME HUMAN?
AND IF I TURNED HUMAN...WHAT WOULD YOU DO?
I AM THE GUARDIAN OF THE JEWEL. IF THE JEWEL NO LONGER EXISTED...
...I WOULD BECOME AN ORDINARY WOMAN.

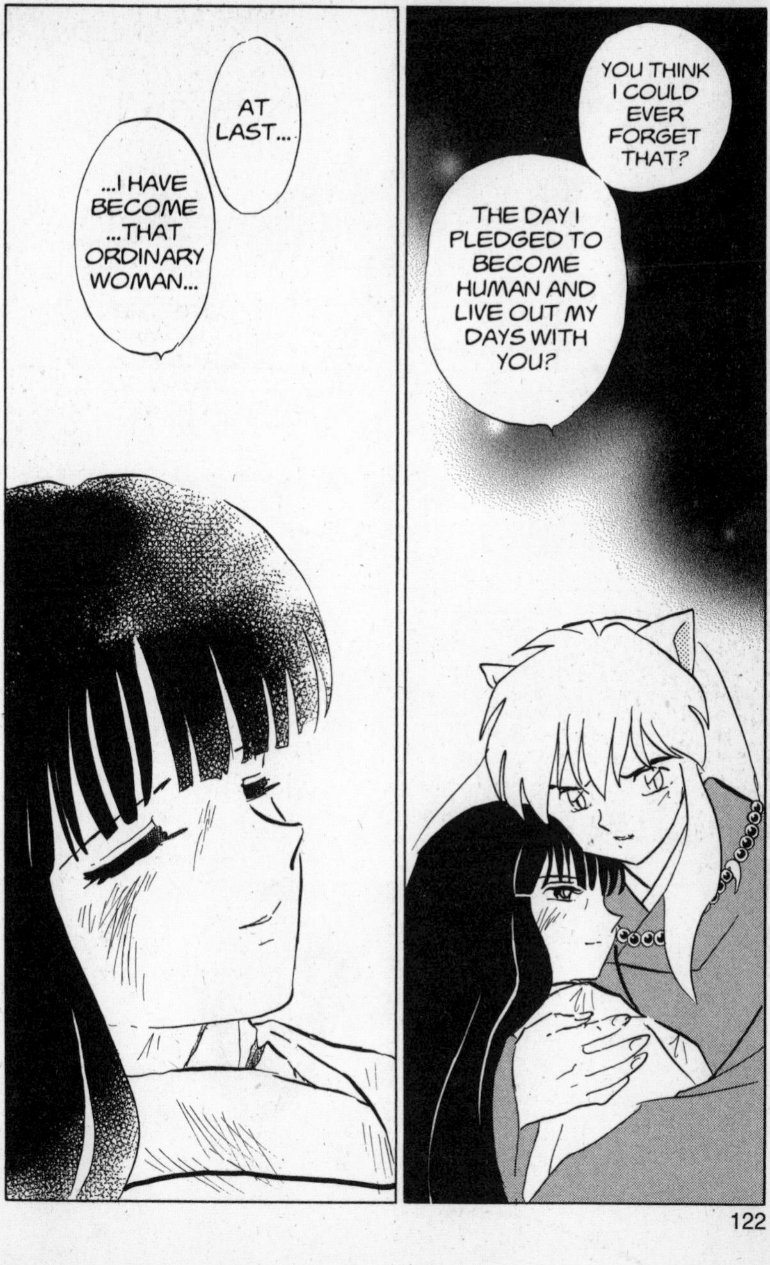
YOU THINK I COULD EVER FORGET THAT?
THE DAY I PLEDGED TO BECOME HUMAN AND LIVE OUT MY DAYS WITH YOU?
AT LAST...
...I HAVE BECOME ...THAT ORDINARY WOMAN...

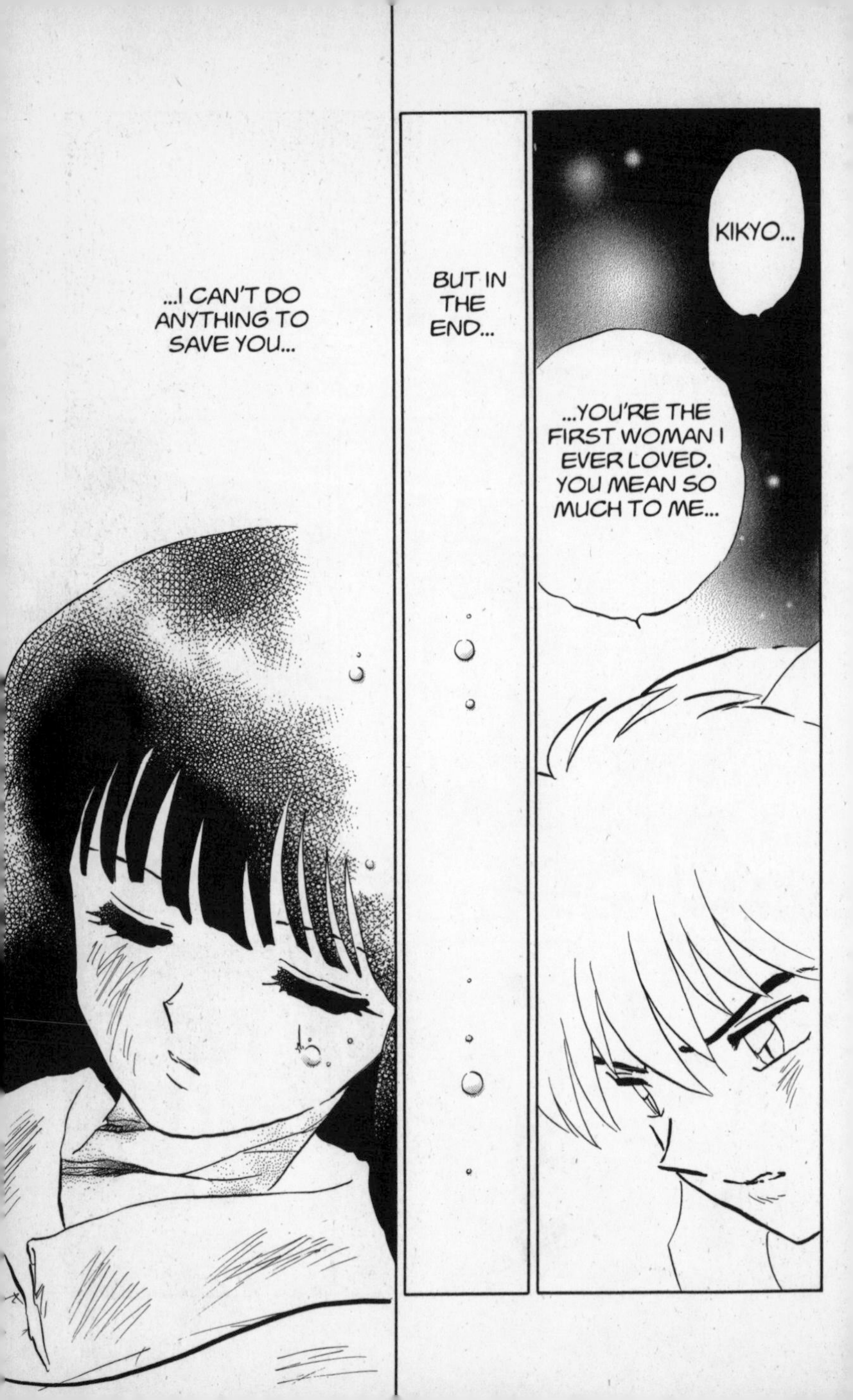
KIKYO...
...YOU'RE THE FIRST WOMAN I EVER LOVED. YOU MEAN SO MUCH TO ME...
BUT IN THE END...
...I CAN'T DO ANYTHING TO SAVE YOU...

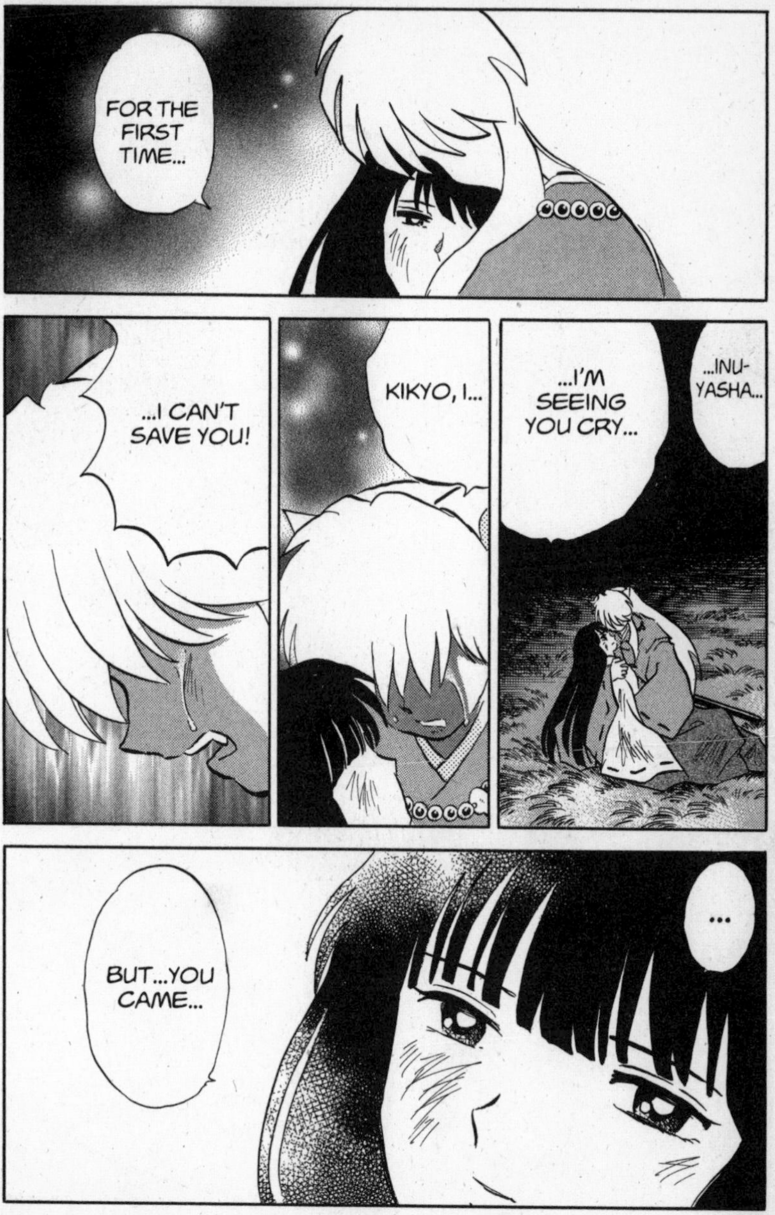
FOR THE FIRST TIME...
...INU-YASHA...
...I'M SEEING YOU CRY...
KIKYO, I...
...I CAN'T SAVE YOU!
...
BUT...YOU CAME...

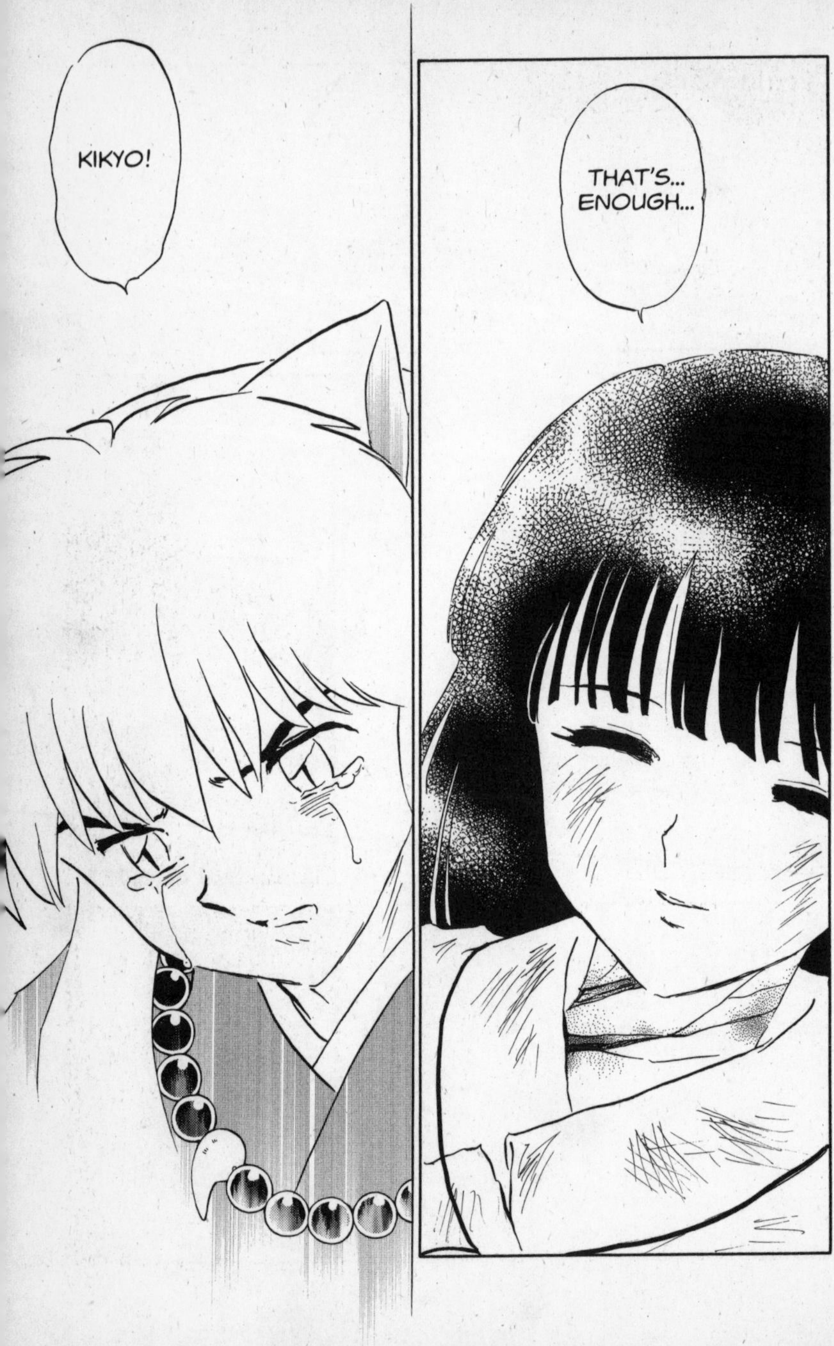
THAT'S...
ENOUGH...
KIKYO!

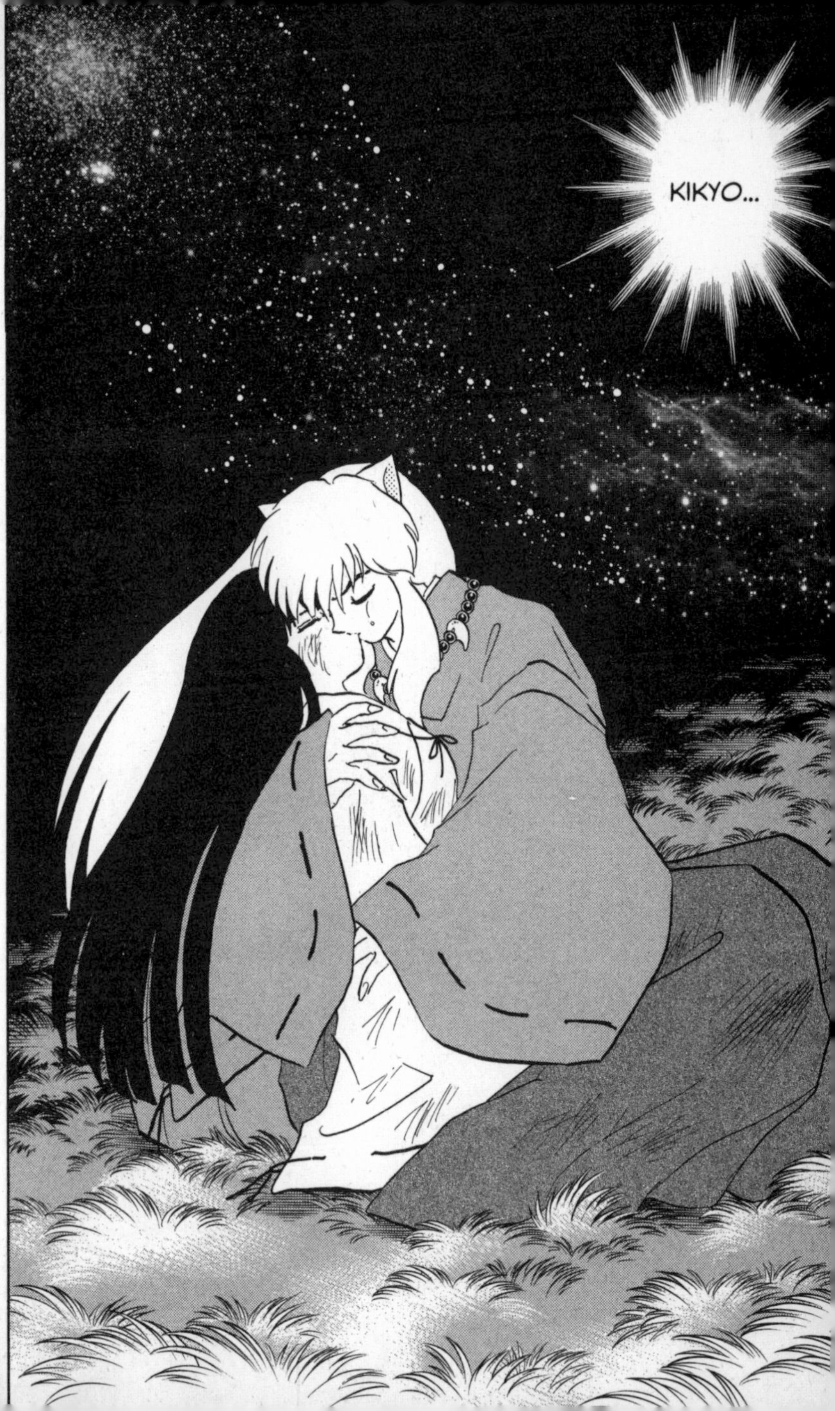
KIKYO...

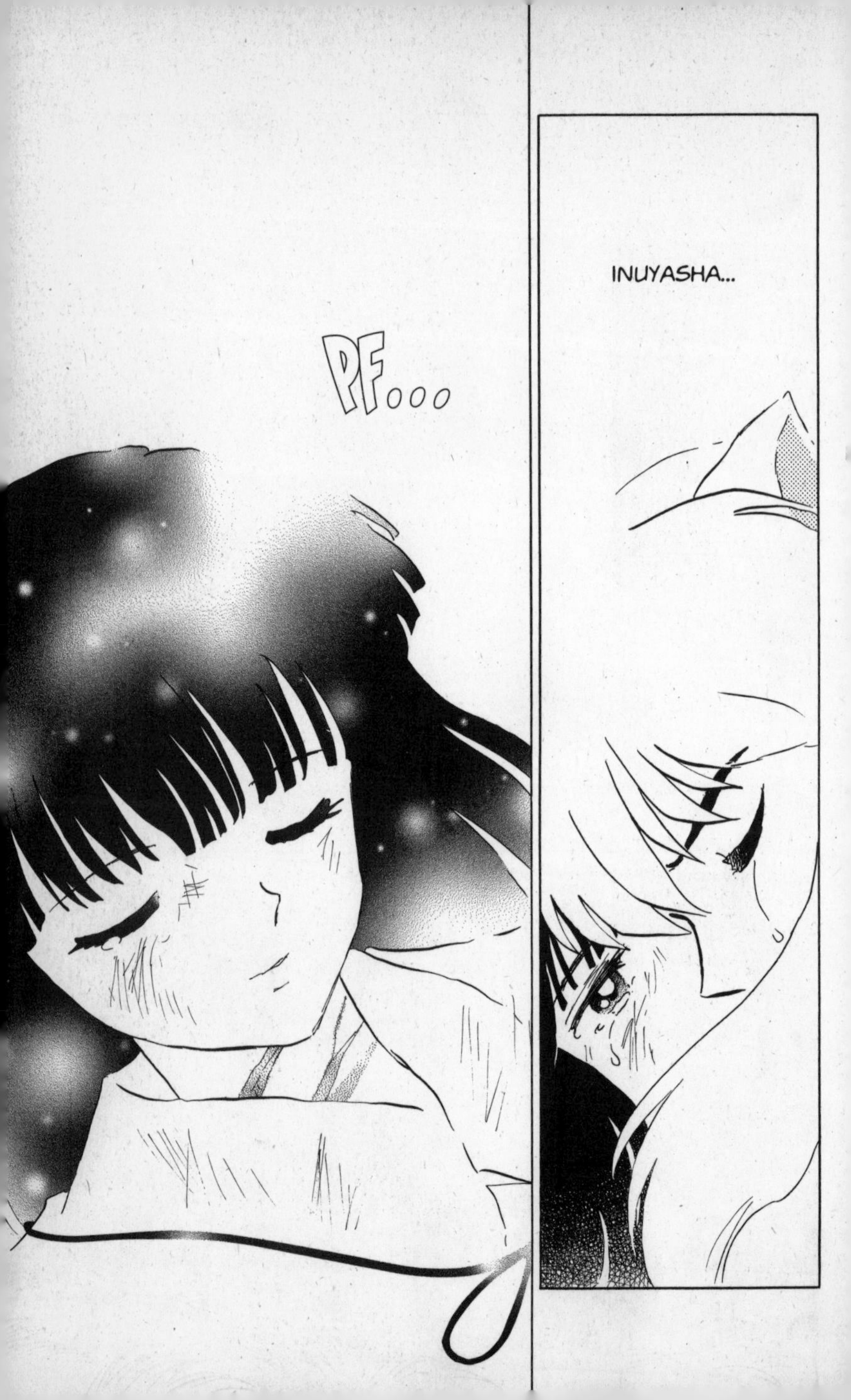
INUYASHA...
PF...

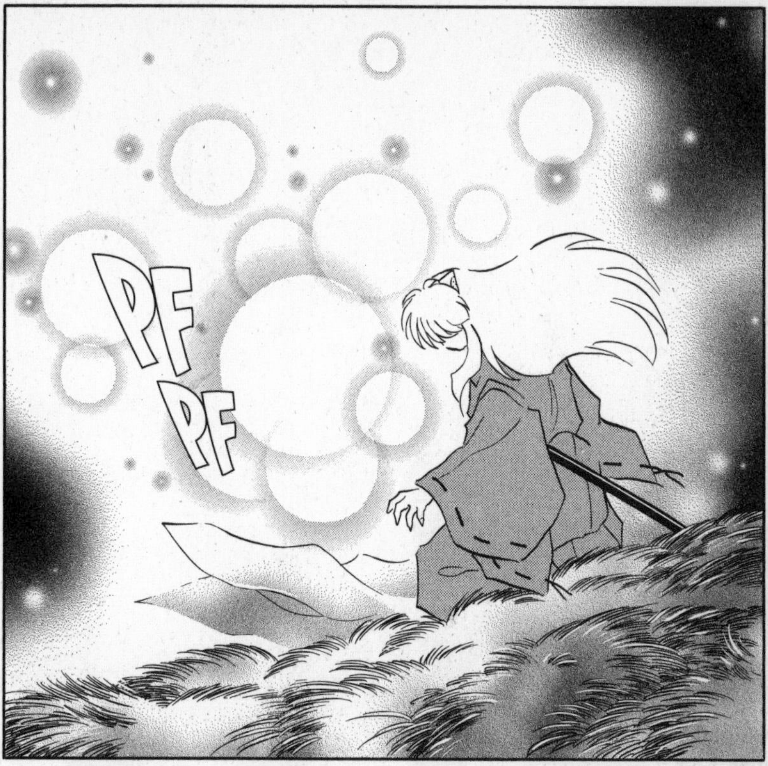
PF
PF
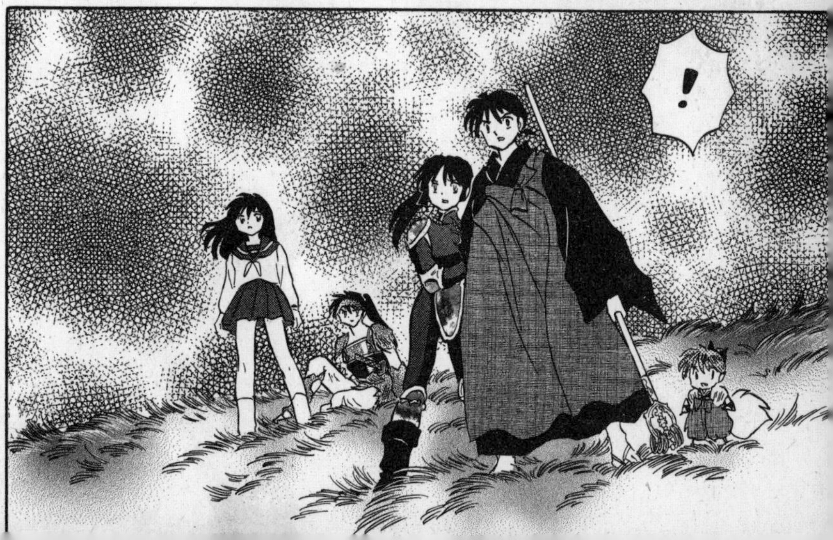
!

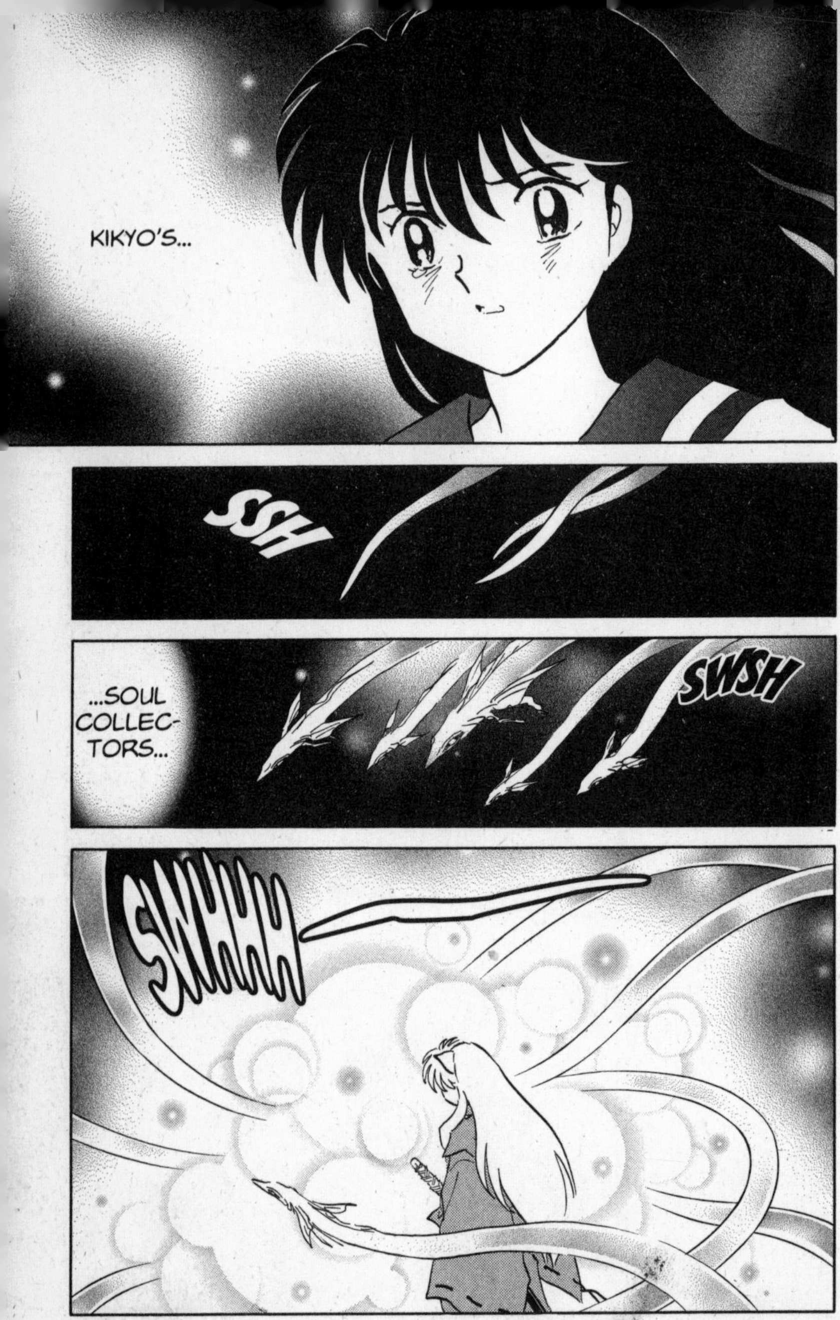
KIKYO'S...
SSH
SWSH
...SOUL COLLEC-TORS...
SWHHH

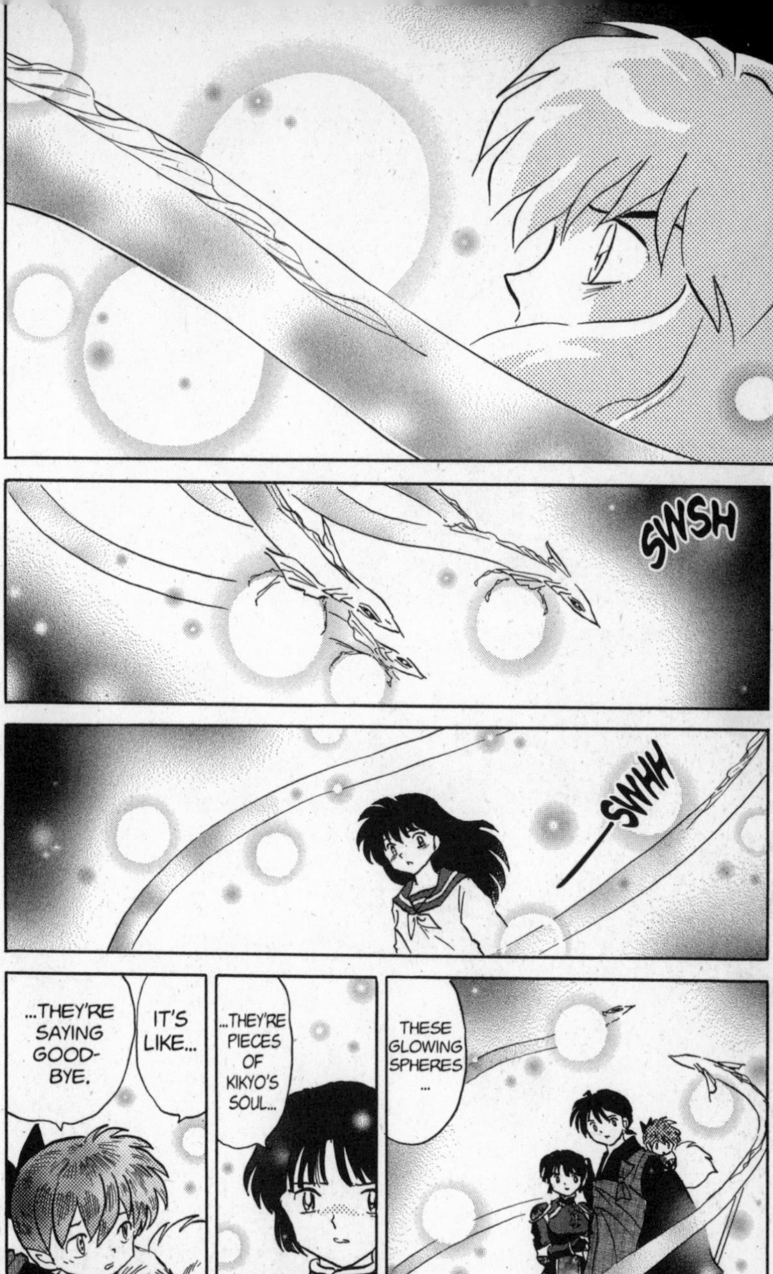
SWSH
SWHH
THESE GLOWING SPHERES ...
...THEY'RE PIECES OF KIKYO'S SOUL...
IT'S LIKE...
...THEY'RE SAYING GOOD-BYE.

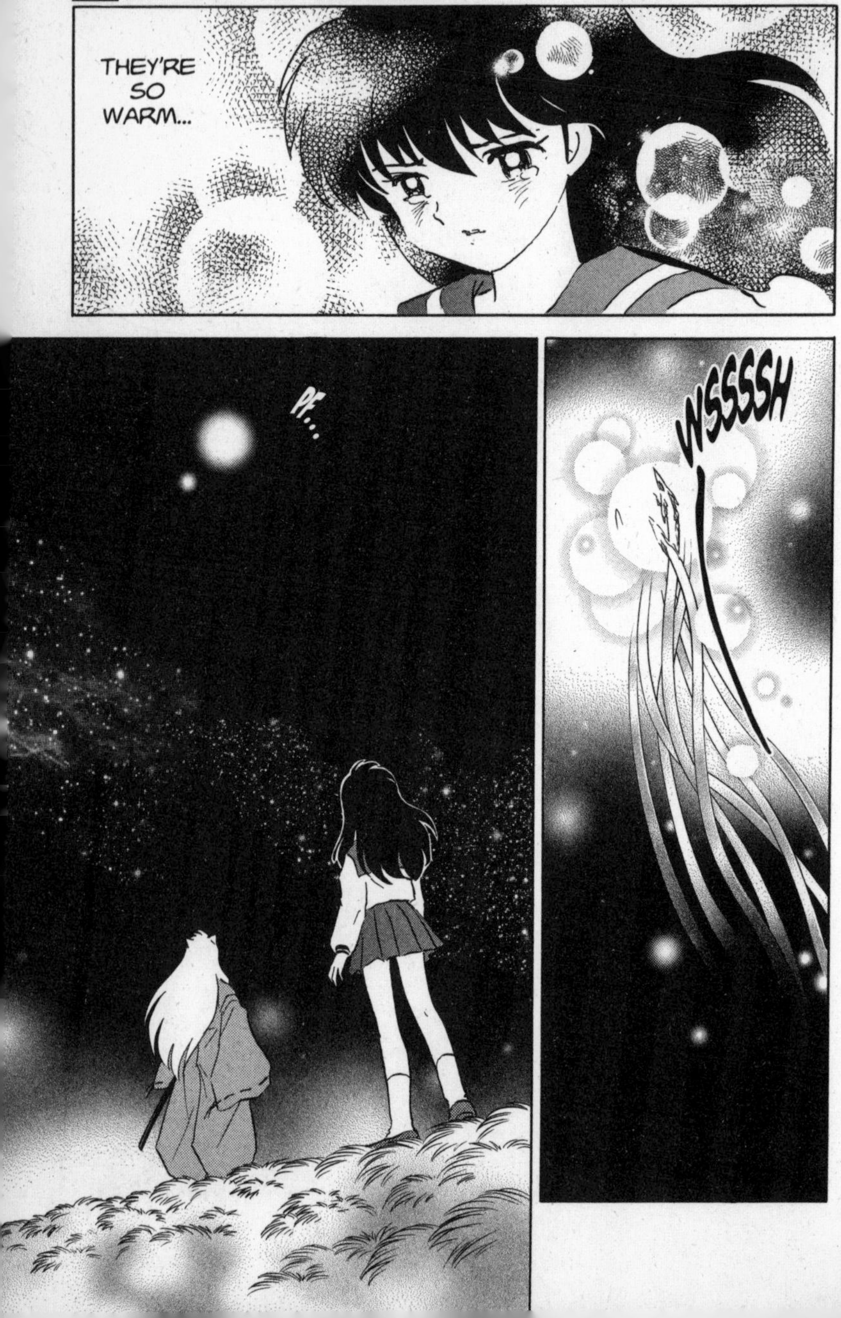
THEY'RE SO WARM...
WSSSSH
PF...

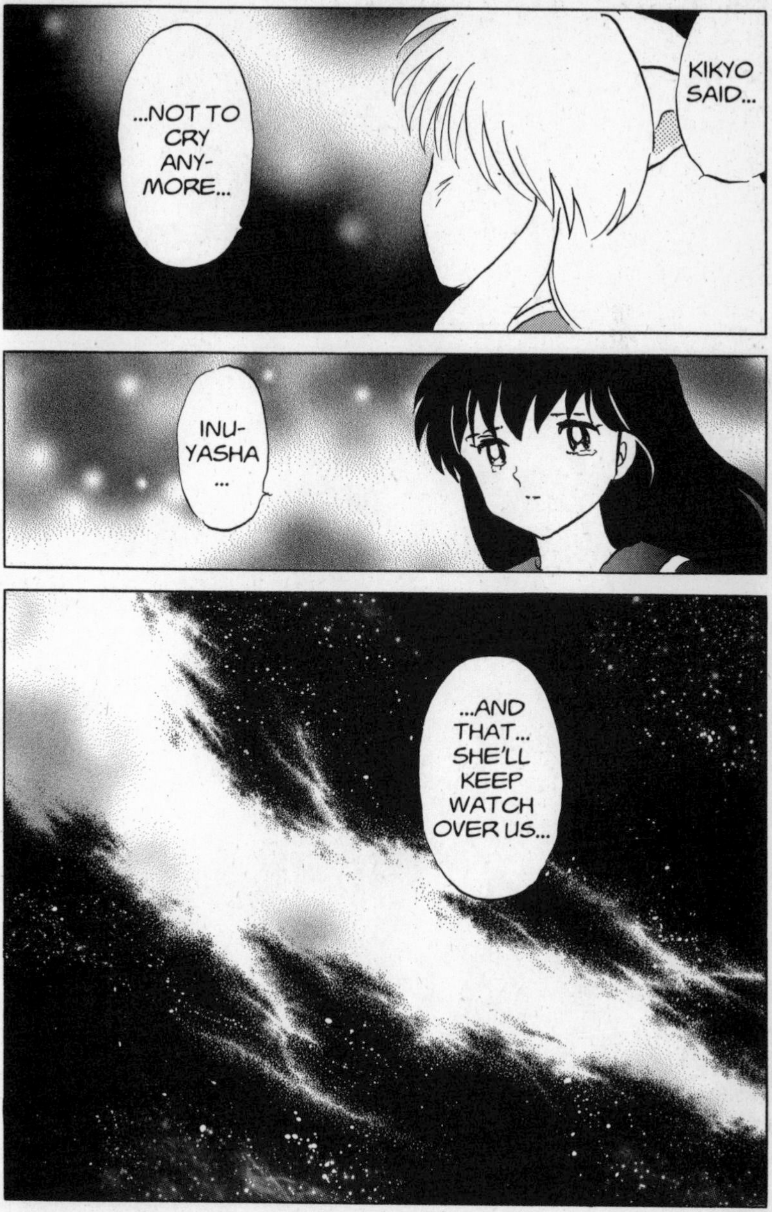
KIKYO SAID...
...NOT TO CRY ANY-MORE...
INU-YASHA ...
...AND THAT... SHE'LL KEEP WATCH OVER US...

SCROLL 8
PARTING THOUGHTS

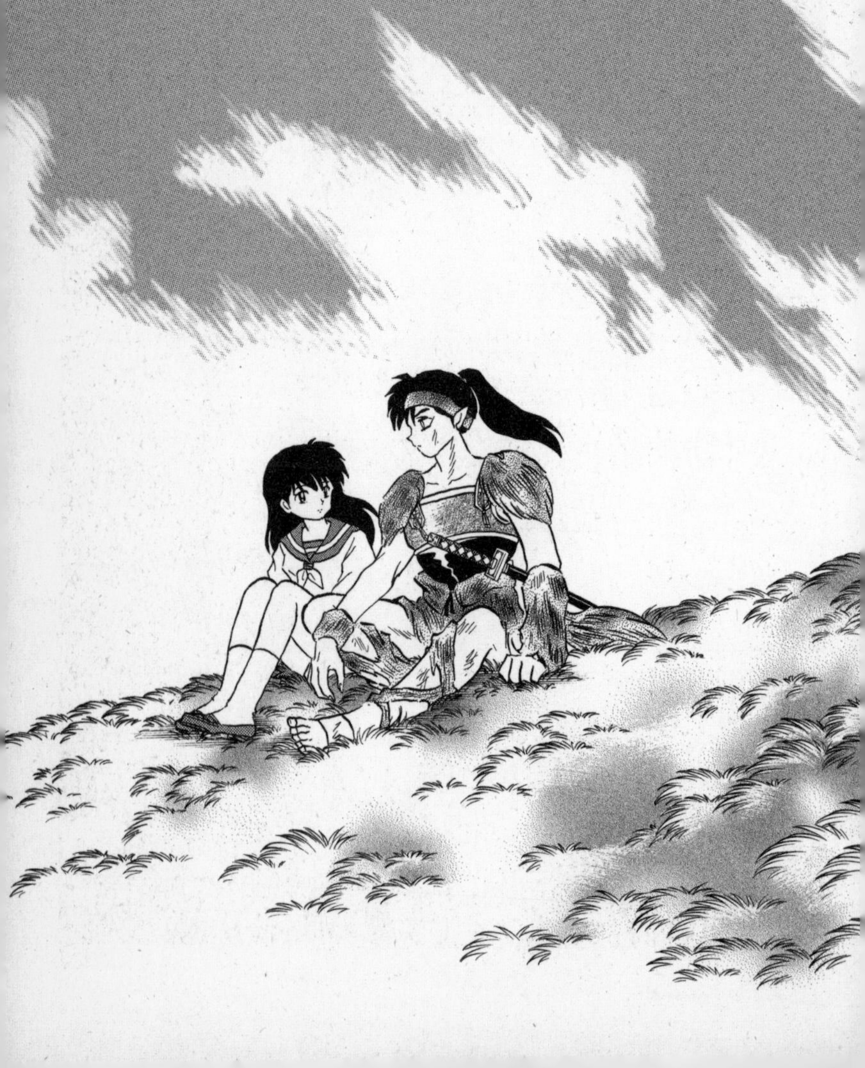

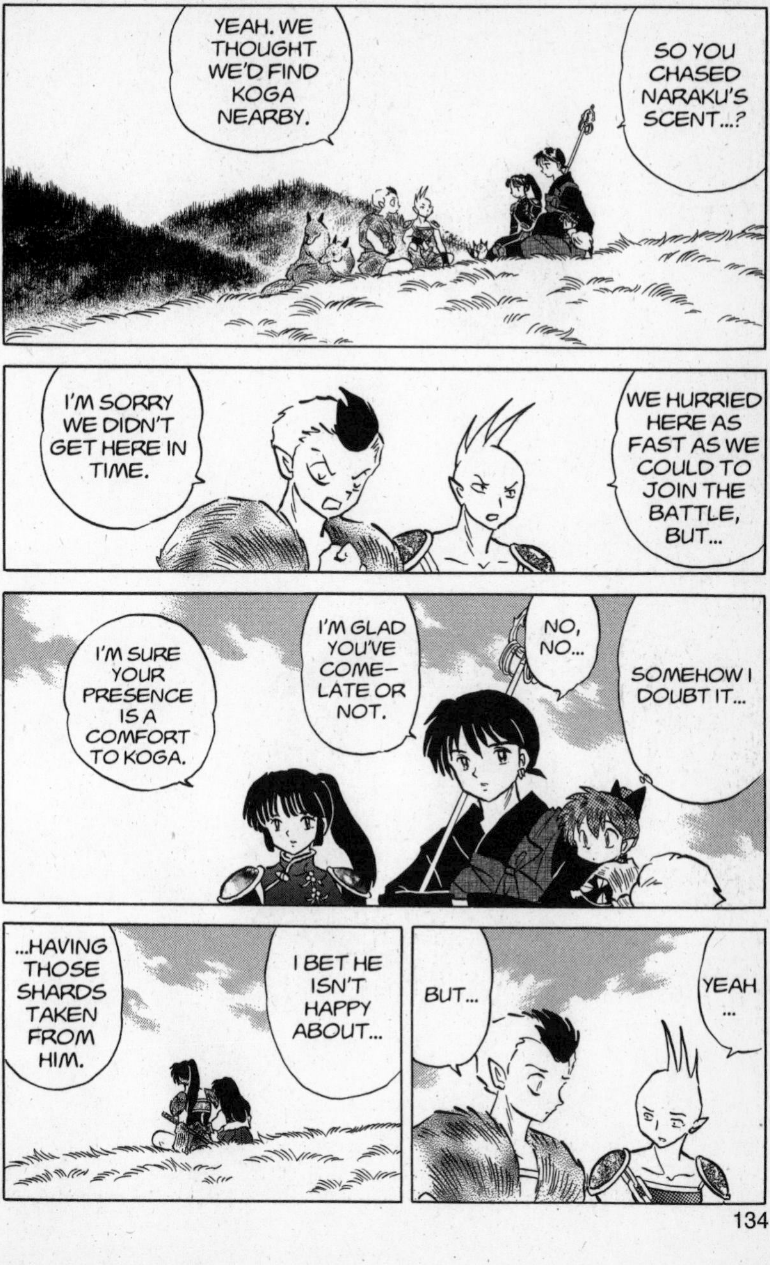
SO YOU CHASED NARAKU'S SCENT...?
YEAH. WE THOUGHT WE'D FIND KOGA NEARBY.
WE HURRIED HERE AS FAST AS WE COULD TO JOIN THE BATTLE, BUT...
I'M SORRY WE DIDN'T GET HERE IN TIME.
I'M SURE YOUR PRESENCE IS A COMFORT TO KOGA.
I'M GLAD YOU'VE COME— LATE OR NOT.
NO, NO...
SOMEHOW I DOUBT IT...
YEAH ...
BUT...
I BET HE ISN'T HAPPY ABOUT...
...HAVING THOSE SHARDS TAKEN FROM HIM.

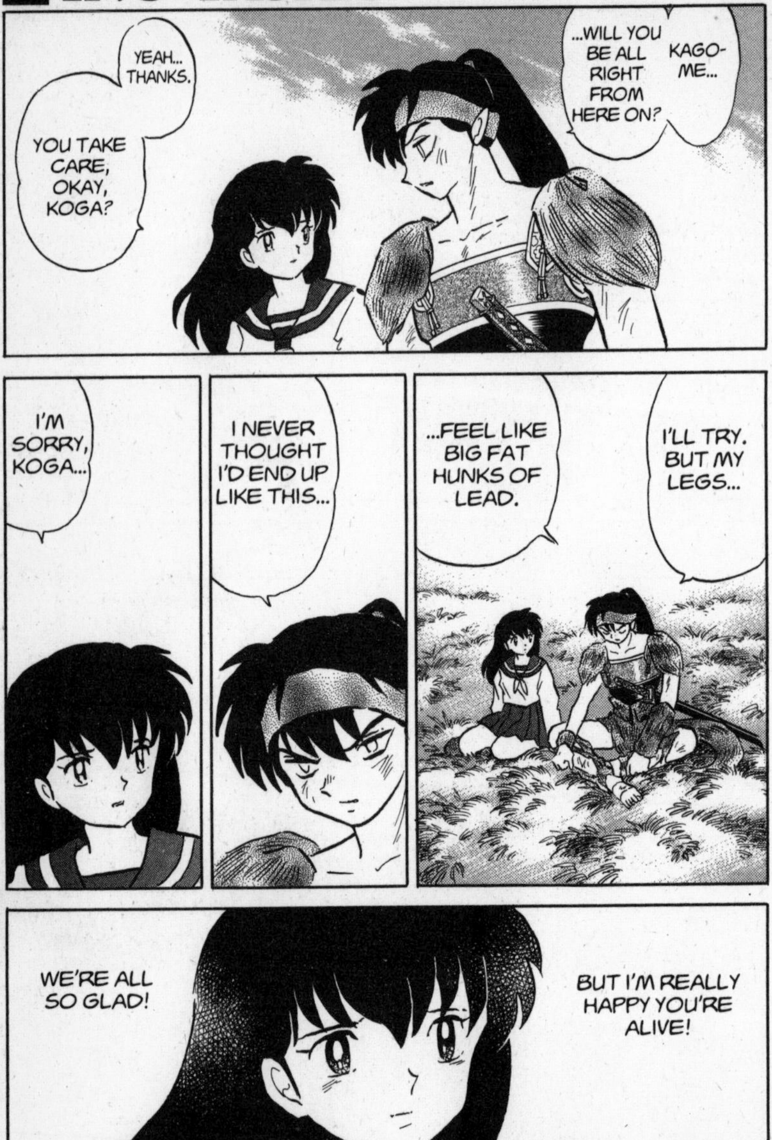
KAGO-ME...
...WILL YOU BE ALL RIGHT FROM HERE ON?
YEAH... THANKS.
YOU TAKE CARE, OKAY, KOGA?
I'LL TRY. BUT MY LEGS...
...FEEL LIKE BIG FAT HUNKS OF LEAD.
I NEVER THOUGHT I'D END UP LIKE THIS...
I'M SORRY, KOGA...
BUT I'M REALLY HAPPY YOU'RE ALIVE!
WE'RE ALL SO GLAD!

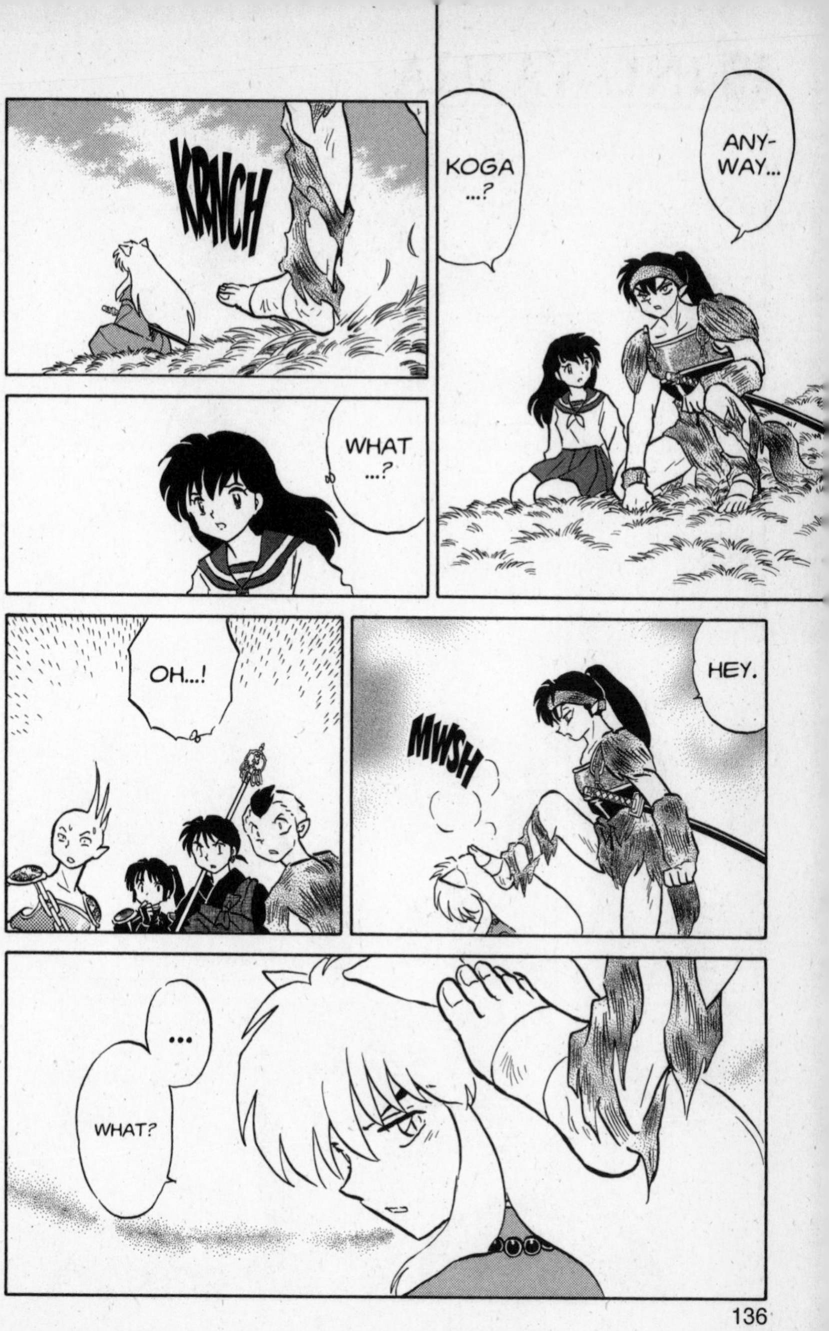
ANY-WAY...
KOGA ...?
KRNCH
WHAT ...?
HEY.
MWSH
OH...!
...
WHAT?

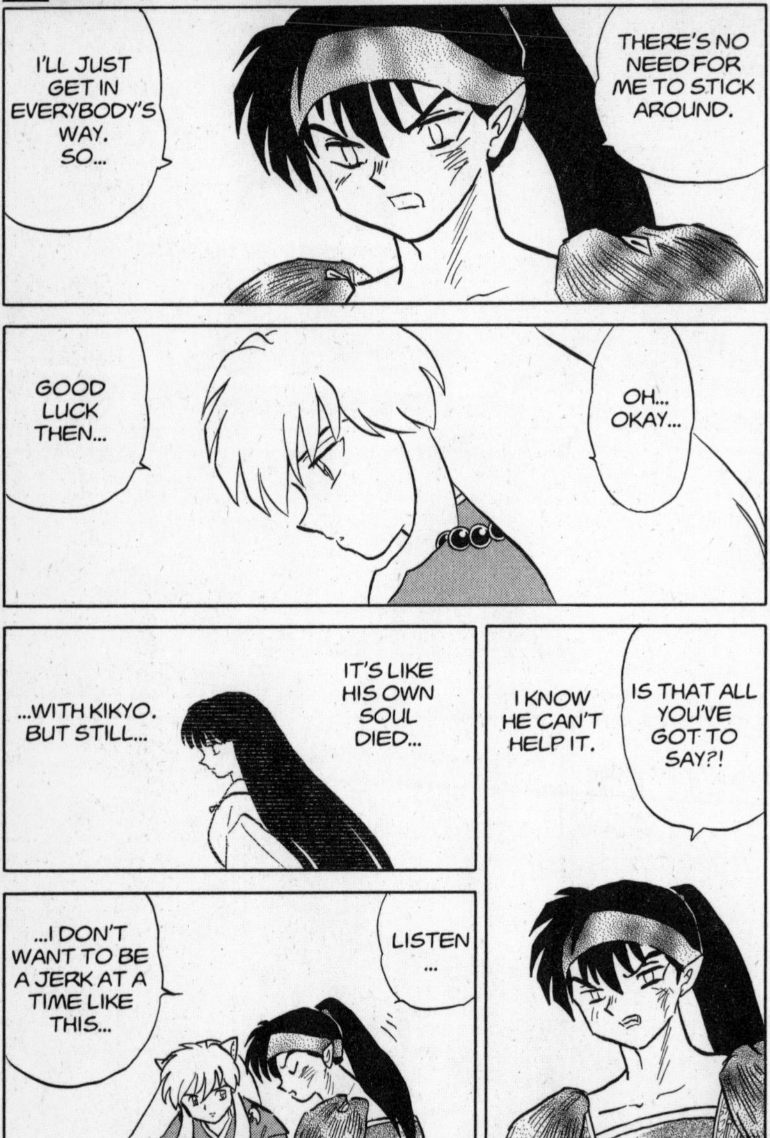
THERE'S NO NEED FOR ME TO STICK AROUND.
I'LL JUST GET IN EVERYBODY'S WAY. SO...
OH... OKAY...
GOOD LUCK THEN...
IS THAT ALL YOU'VE GOT TO SAY?!
I KNOW HE CAN'T HELP IT.
IT'S LIKE HIS OWN SOUL DIED...
...WITH KIKYO. BUT STILL...
LISTEN ...
...I DON'T WANT TO BE A JERK AT A TIME LIKE THIS...

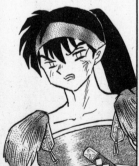

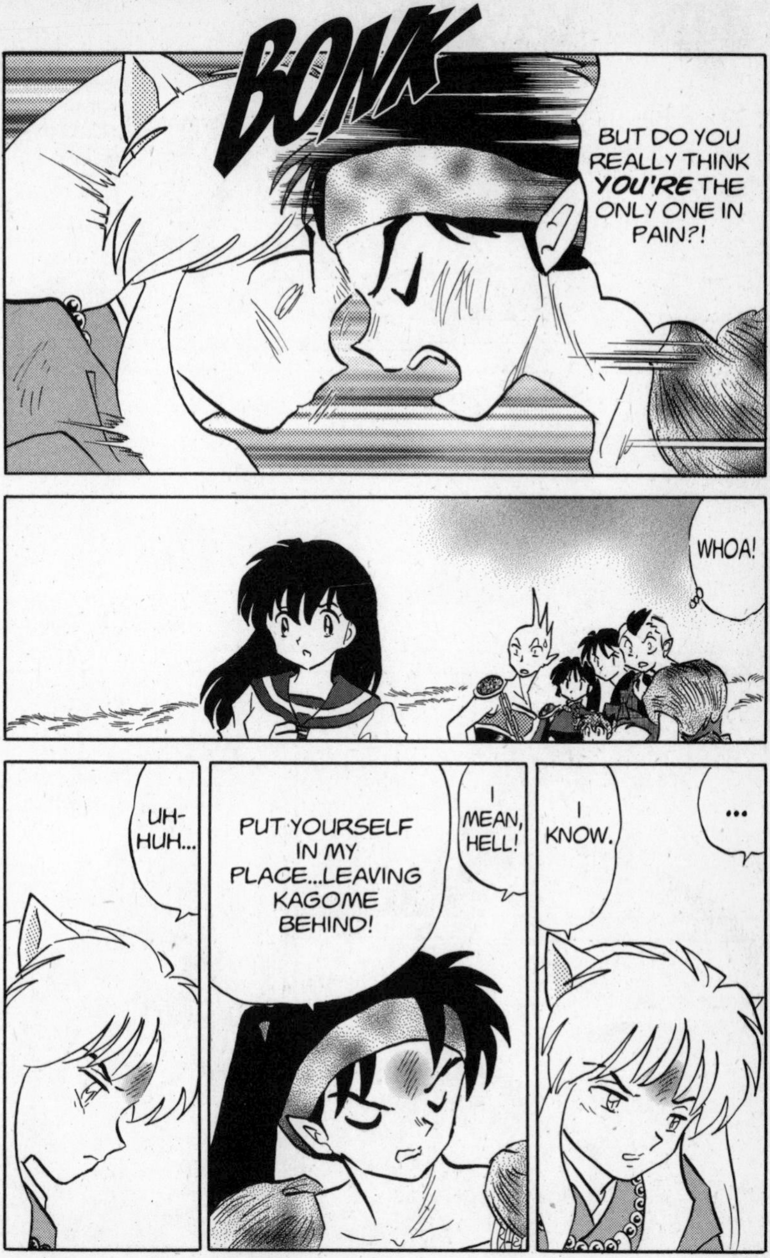
BONK
BUT DO YOU REALLY THINK ***YOU'RE*** THE ONLY ONE IN PAIN?!
WHOA!
...
I KNOW.
I MEAN, HELL!
PUT YOURSELF IN MY PLACE...LEAVING KAGOME BEHIND!
UH-HUH...

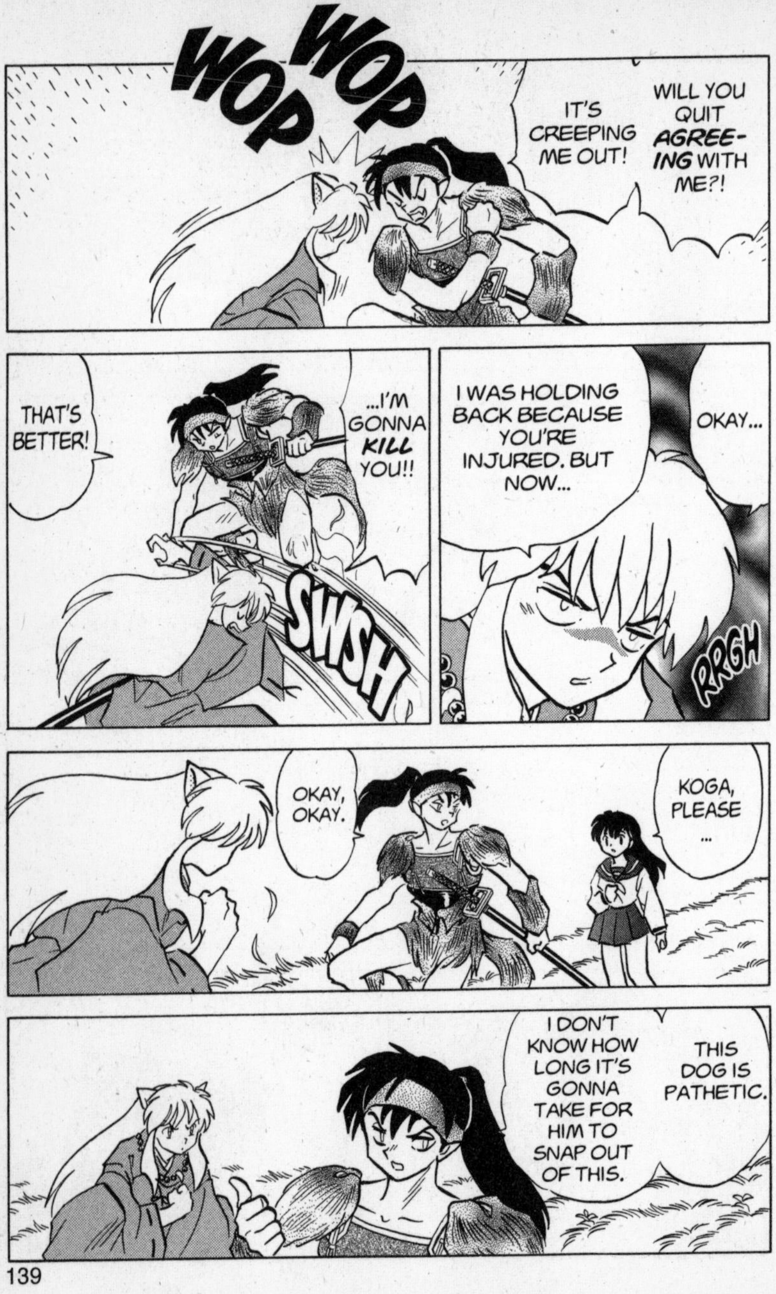
WOP WOP
WILL YOU QUIT AGREEING WITH ME?!
IT'S CREEPING ME OUT!
OKAY...
I WAS HOLDING BACK BECAUSE YOU'RE INJURED. BUT NOW...
RRGH
...I'M GONNA KILL YOU!!
THAT'S BETTER!
SWSH
KOGA, PLEASE ...
OKAY, OKAY.
THIS DOG IS PATHETIC.
I DON'T KNOW HOW LONG IT'S GONNA TAKE FOR HIM TO SNAP OUT OF THIS.

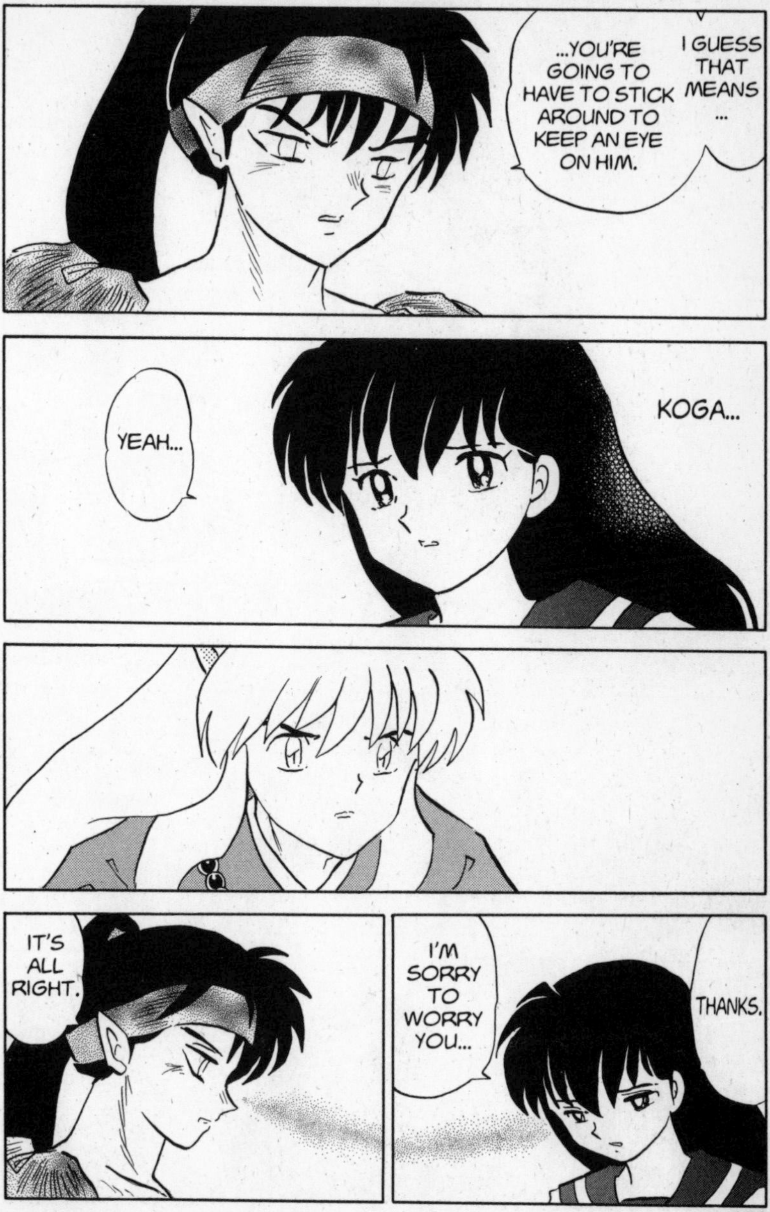
I GUESS THAT MEANS...
...YOU'RE GOING TO HAVE TO STICK AROUND TO KEEP AN EYE ON HIM.
KOGA...
YEAH...
THANKS.
I'M SORRY TO WORRY YOU...
IT'S ALL RIGHT.

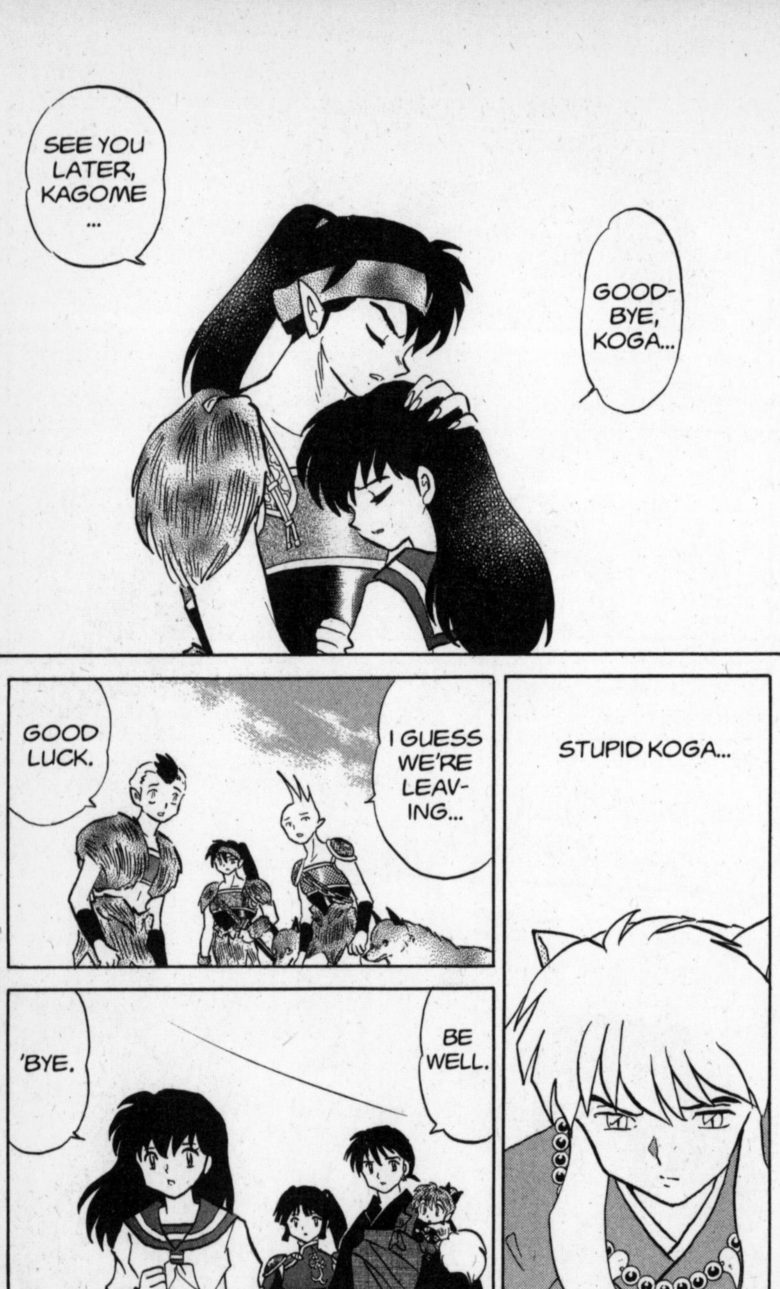
GOOD-BYE, KOGA...
SEE YOU LATER, KAGOME ...
STUPID KOGA...
I GUESS WE'RE LEAVING...
GOOD LUCK.
BE WELL.
'BYE.

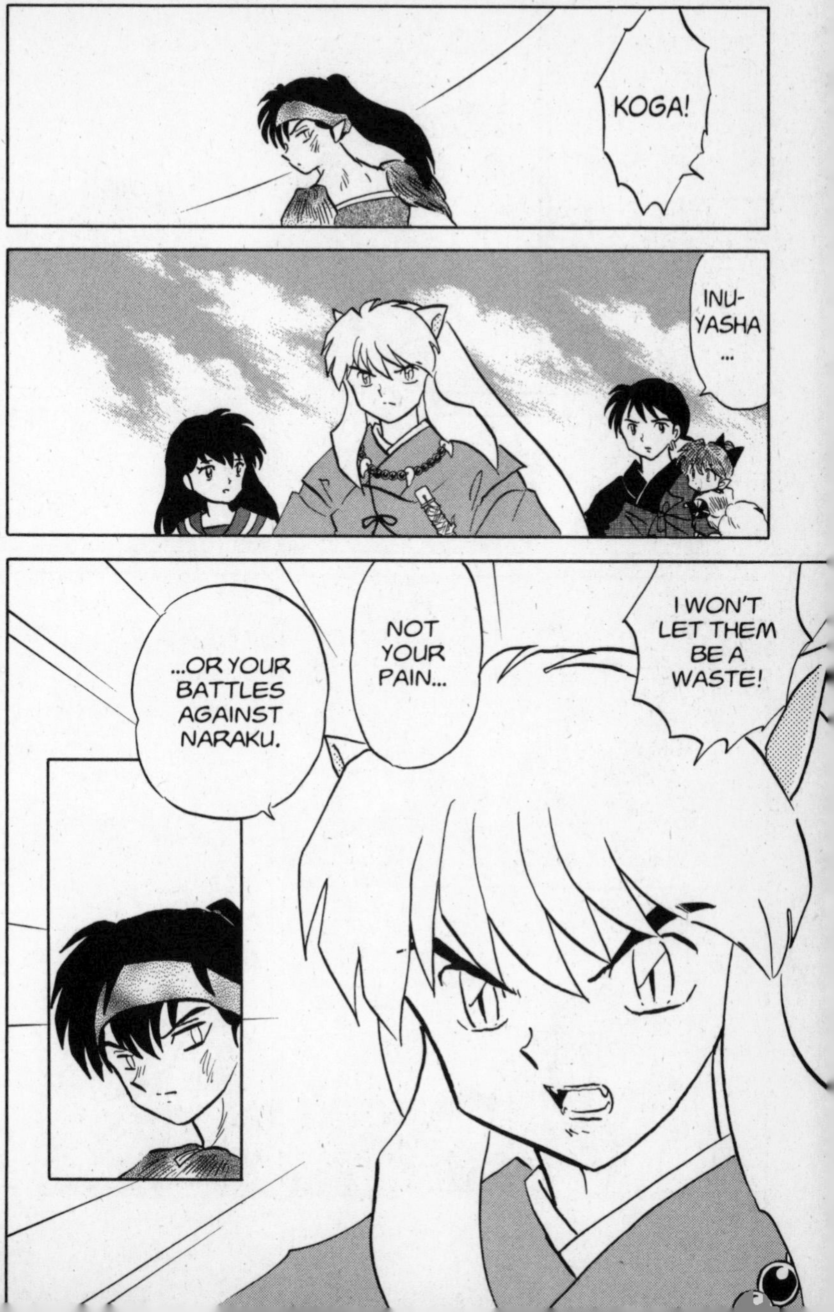
KOGA!
INU-YASHA ...
I WON'T LET THEM BE A WASTE!
NOT YOUR PAIN...
...OR YOUR BATTLES AGAINST NARAKU.

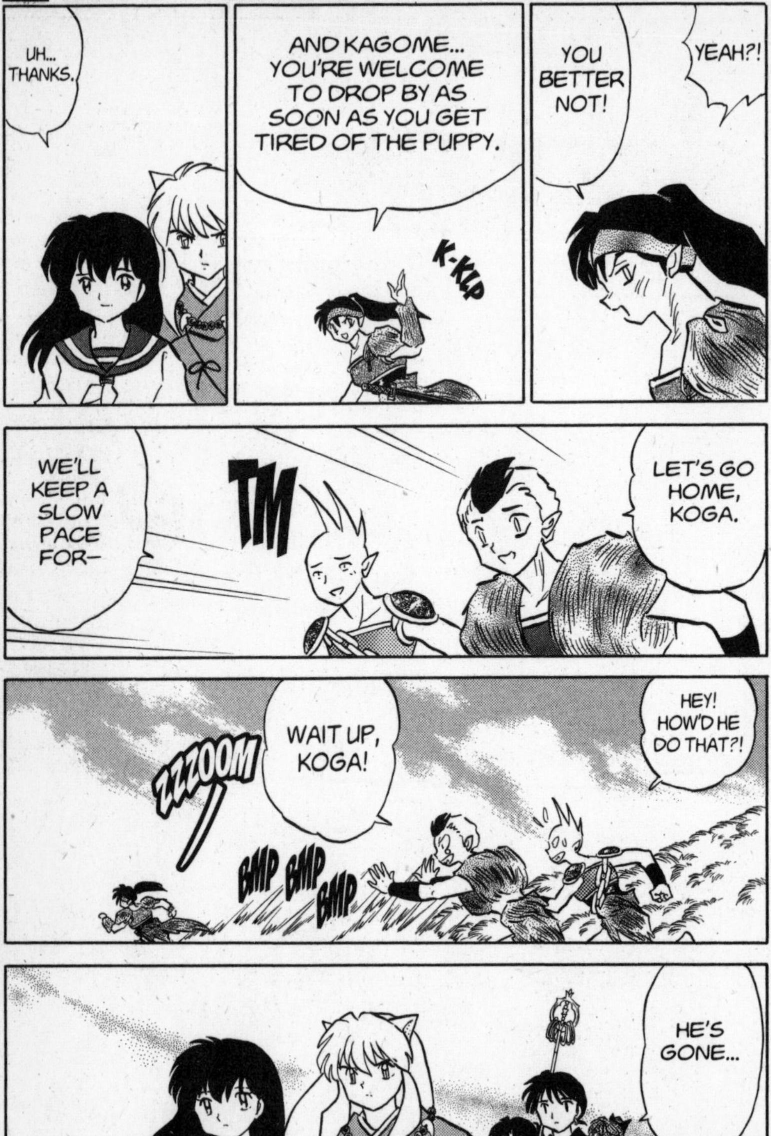
YEAH?!
YOU BETTER NOT!
AND KAGOME... YOU'RE WELCOME TO DROP BY AS SOON AS YOU GET TIRED OF THE PUPPY.
K-KLP
UH... THANKS.
LET'S GO HOME, KOGA.
TM
WE'LL KEEP A SLOW PACE FOR–
HEY! HOW'D HE DO THAT?!
WAIT UP, KOGA!
ZZZOOM
BMP BMP BMP
HE'S GONE...

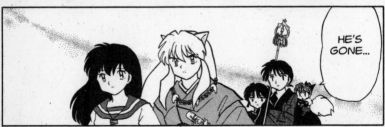

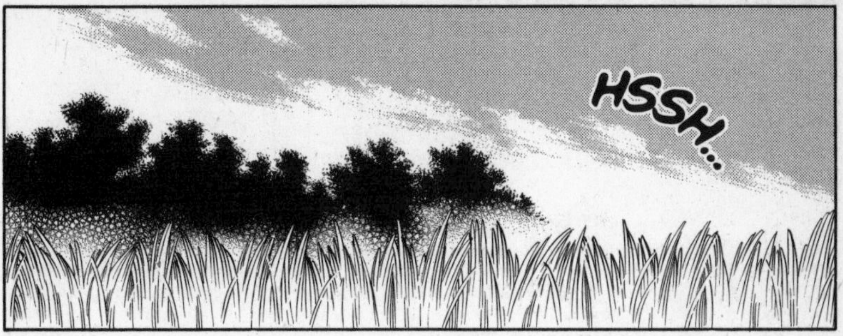
HSSH...
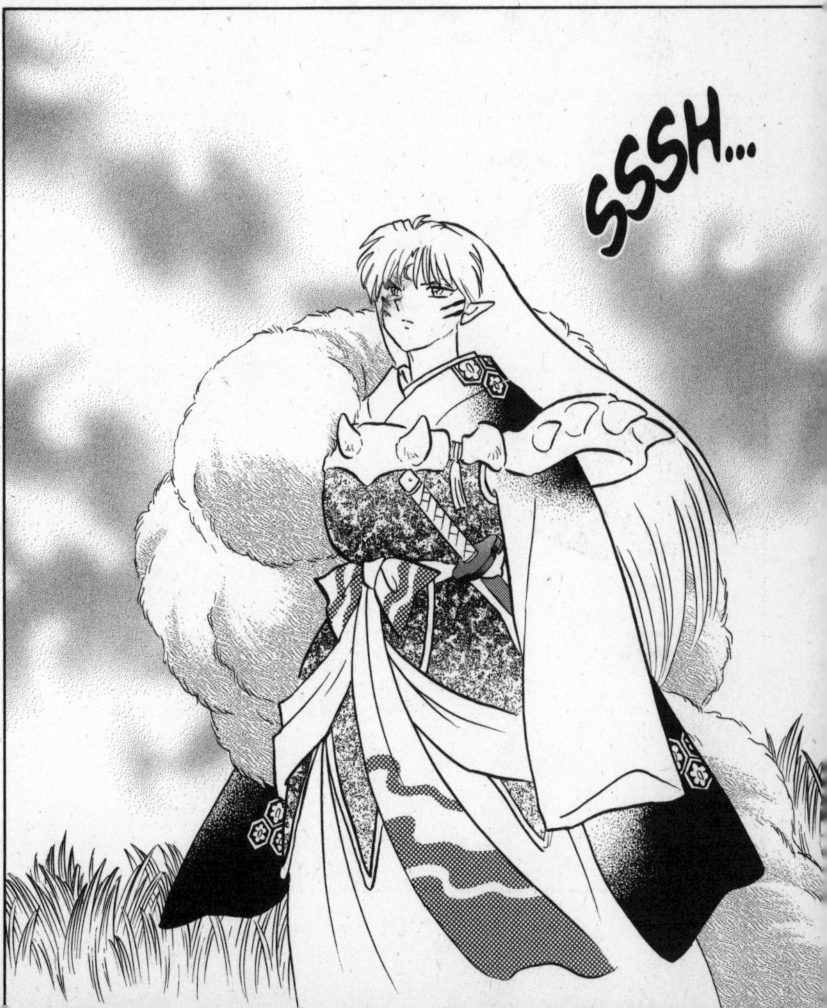
SSSH...

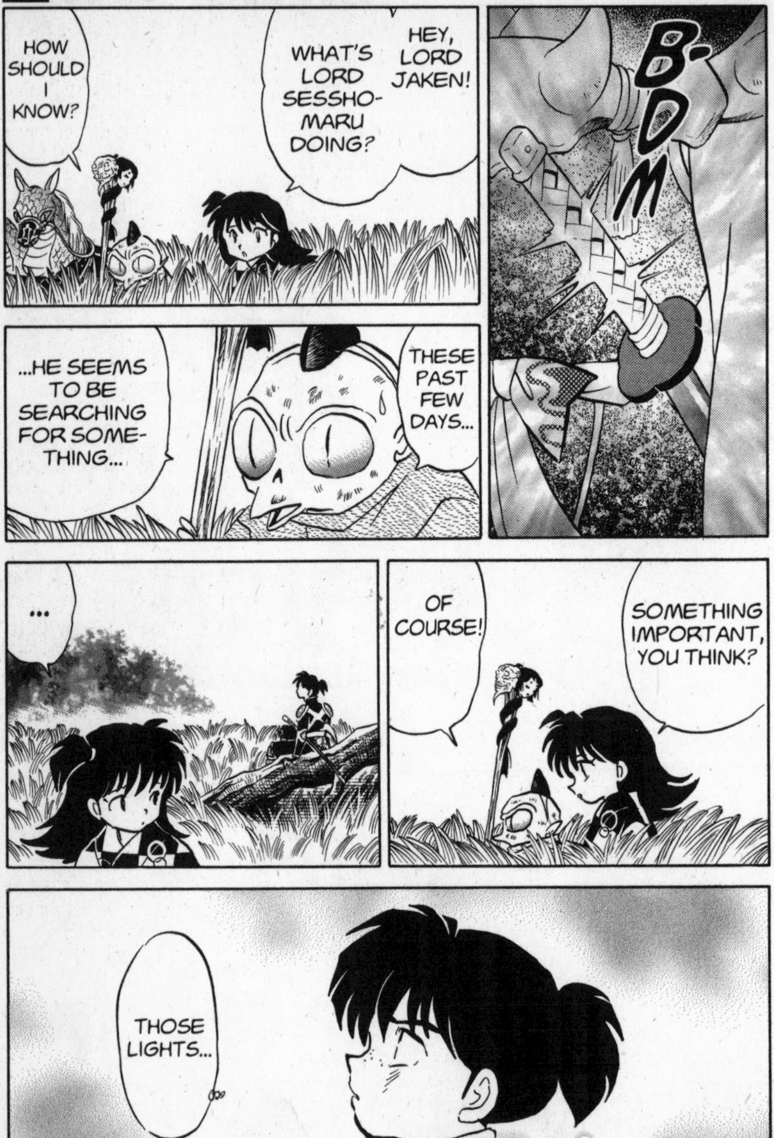
B-DOM
HEY, LORD JAKEN!
WHAT'S LORD SESSHO-MARU DOING?
HOW SHOULD I KNOW?
THESE PAST FEW DAYS...
...HE SEEMS TO BE SEARCHING FOR SOME-THING...
SOMETHING IMPORTANT, YOU THINK?
OF COURSE!
...
THOSE LIGHTS...

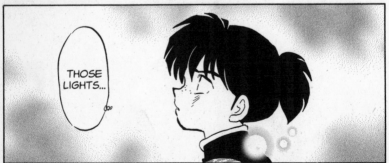

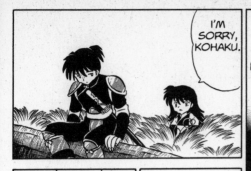

I'M SORRY, KOHAKU.

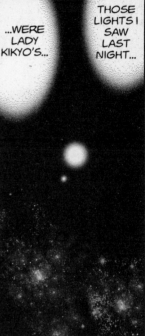

THOSE LIGHTS I SAW LAST NIGHT...

...WERE LADY KIKYO'S...

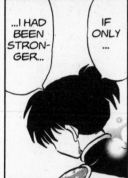

...I HAD BEEN STRONGER...

IF ONLY...

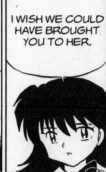

I WISH WE COULD HAVE BROUGHT YOU TO HER.

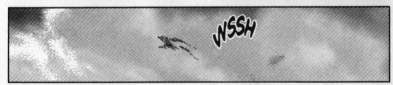

WSSH

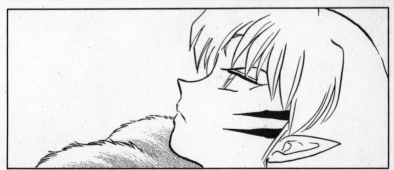

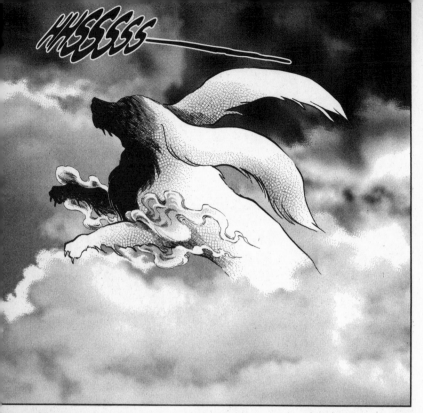

WSSSSS

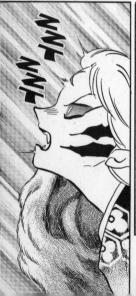

ZZT
ZZT

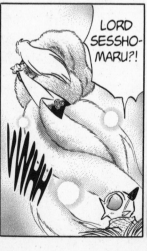

LORD
SESSHO-
MARU?!

VWHH

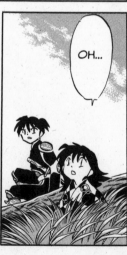

OH...

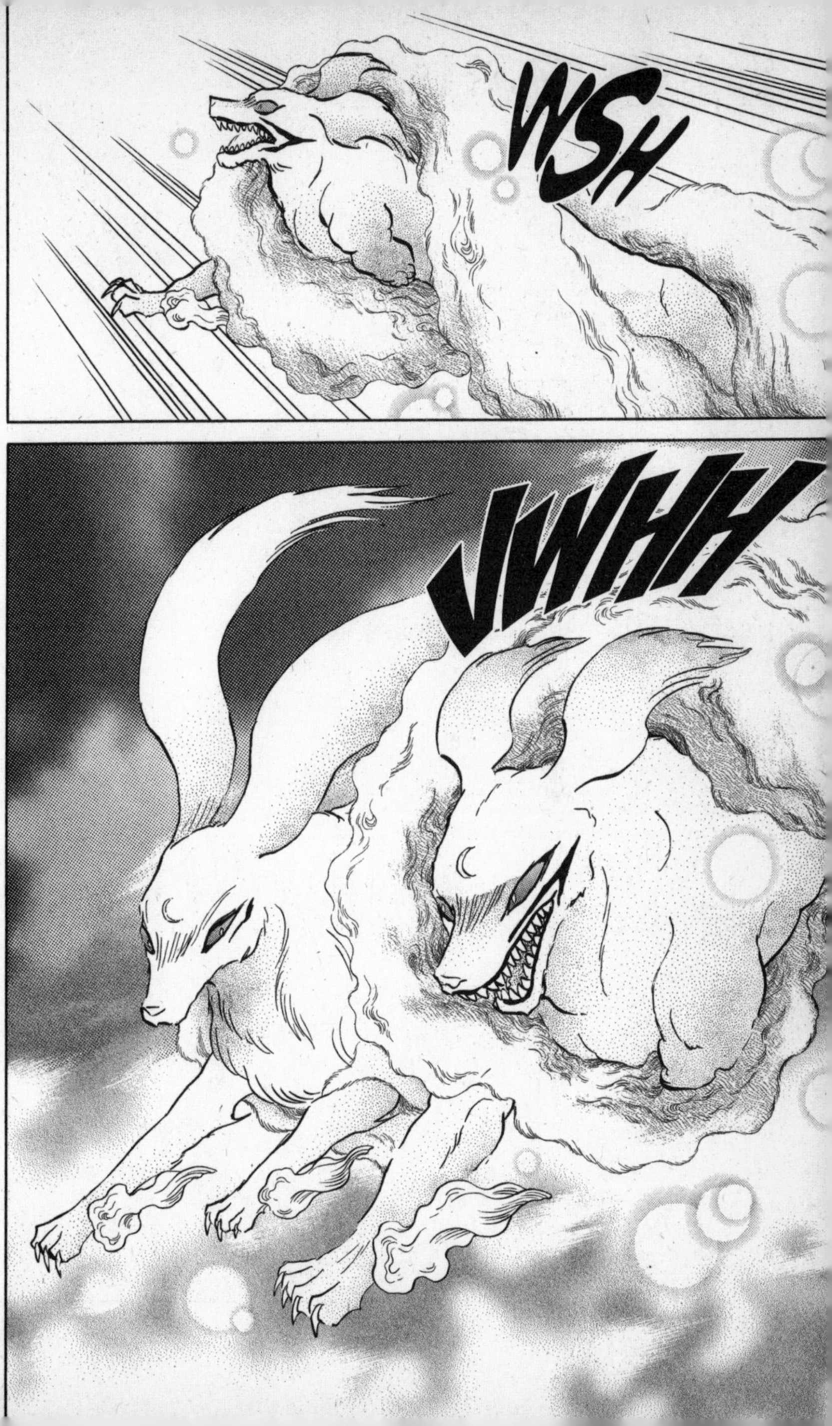
WSH
JWHH

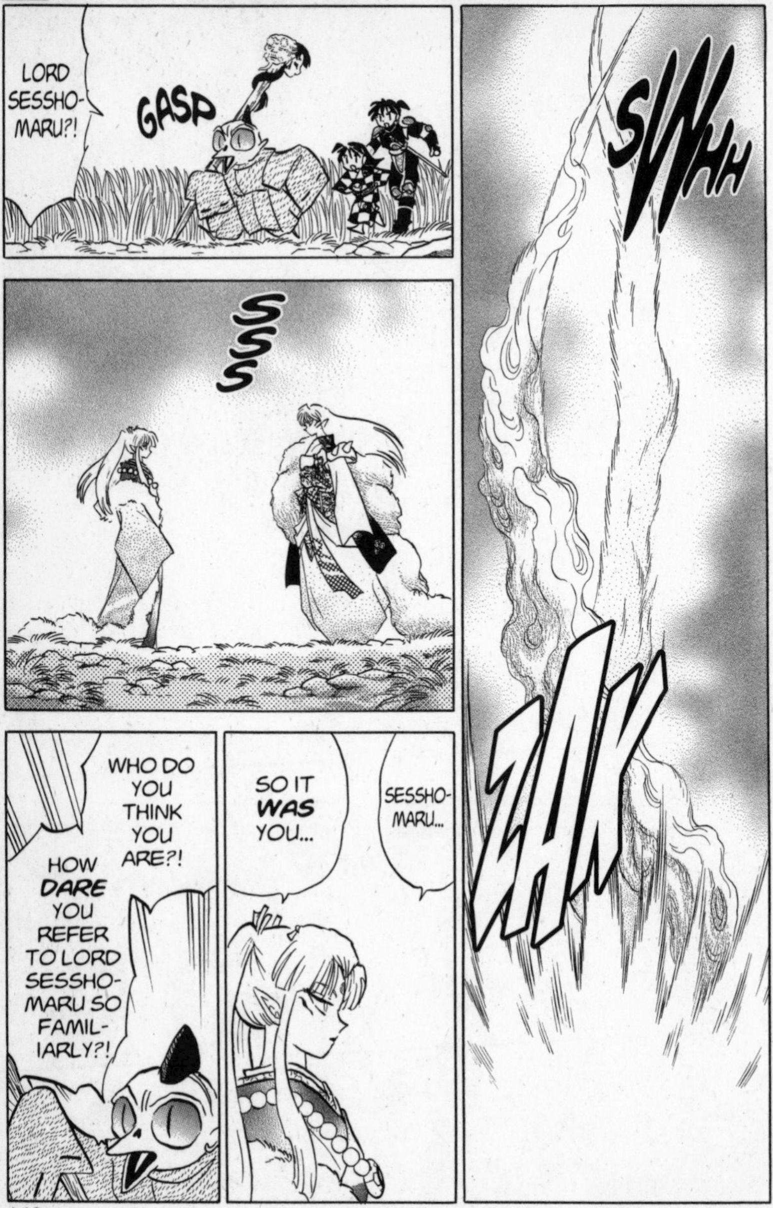
SWHH
ZAK
LORD SESSHO-MARU?!
GASP
SSS
SESSHO-MARU...
SO IT WAS YOU...
WHO DO YOU THINK YOU ARE?!
HOW DARE YOU REFER TO LORD SESSHO-MARU SO FAMIL-IARLY?!

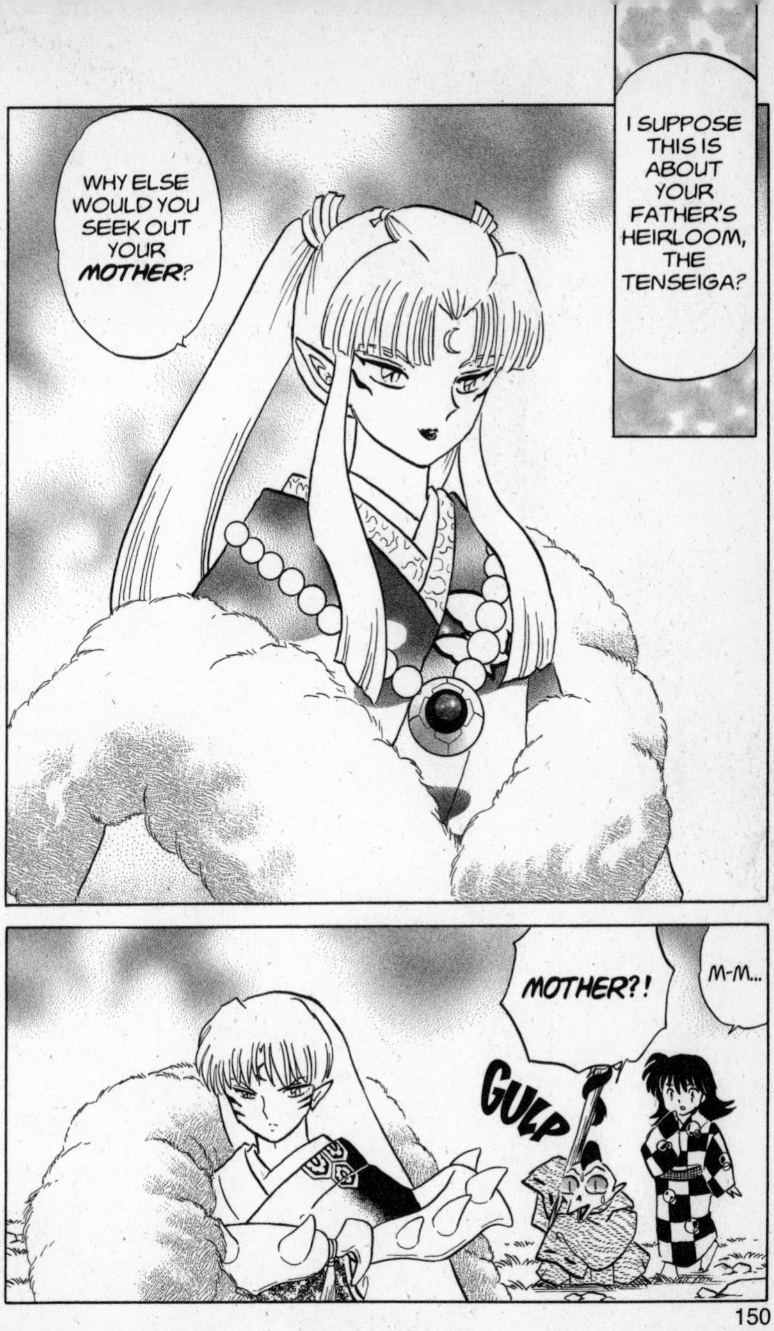
I SUPPOSE THIS IS ABOUT YOUR FATHER'S HEIRLOOM, THE TENSEIGA?
WHY ELSE WOULD YOU SEEK OUT YOUR *MOTHER*?
M-M...
MOTHER?!
GULP

SCROLL 9

THE MEIDO

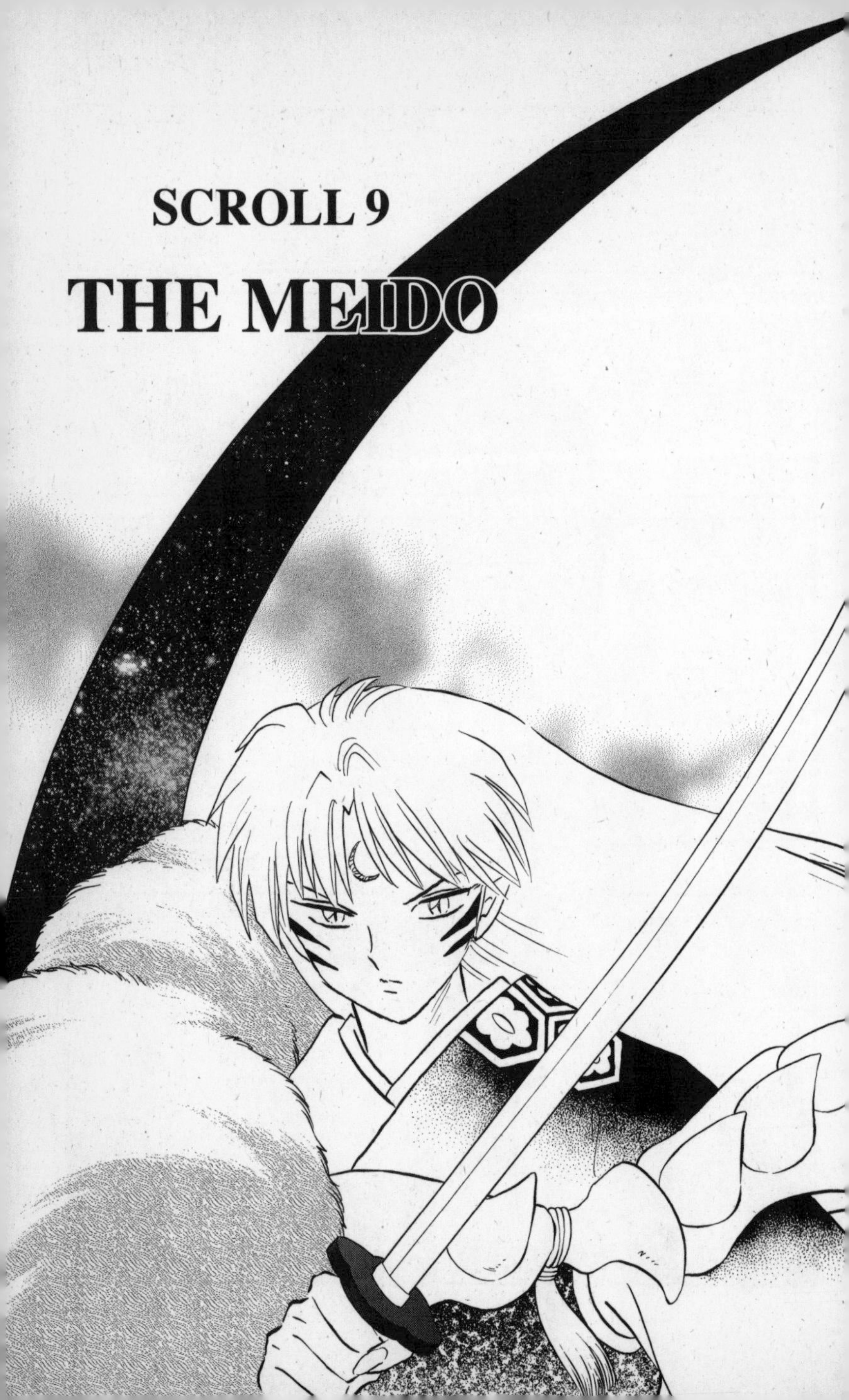

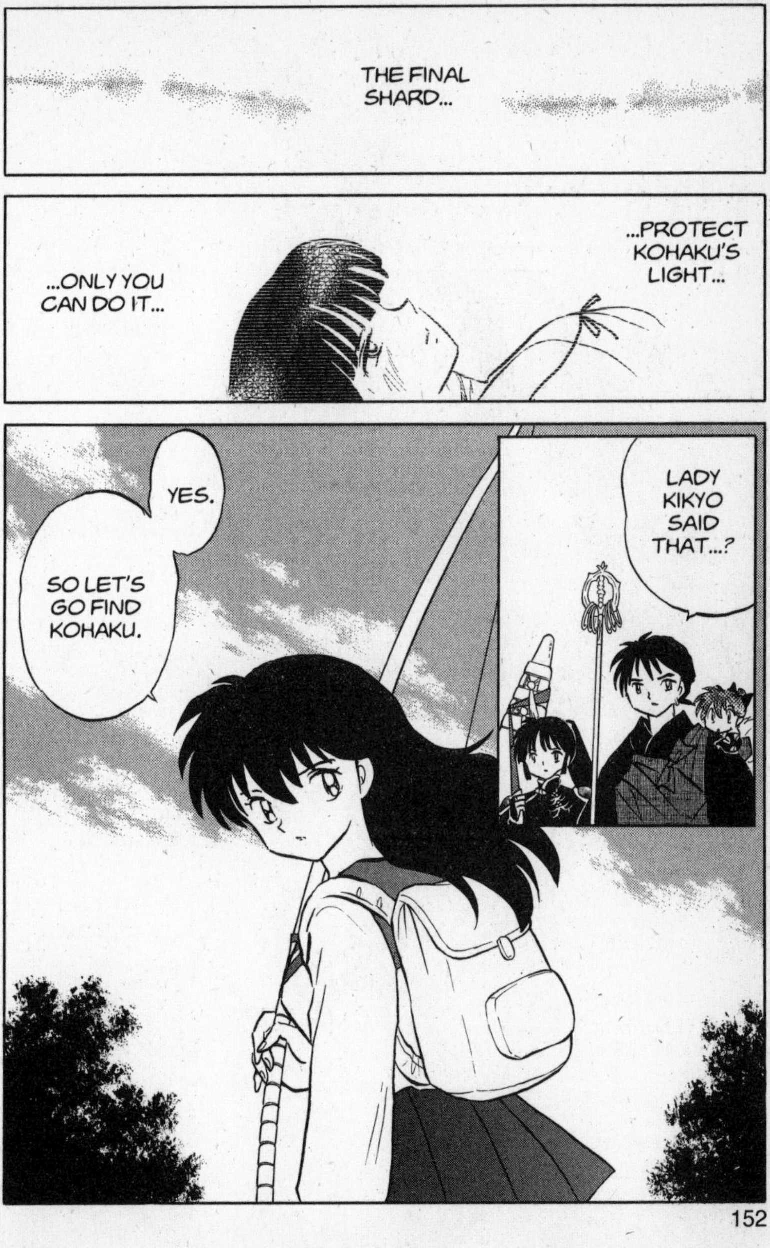
THE FINAL SHARD...
...PROTECT KOHAKU'S LIGHT...
...ONLY YOU CAN DO IT...
LADY KIKYO SAID THAT...?
YES.
SO LET'S GO FIND KOHAKU.

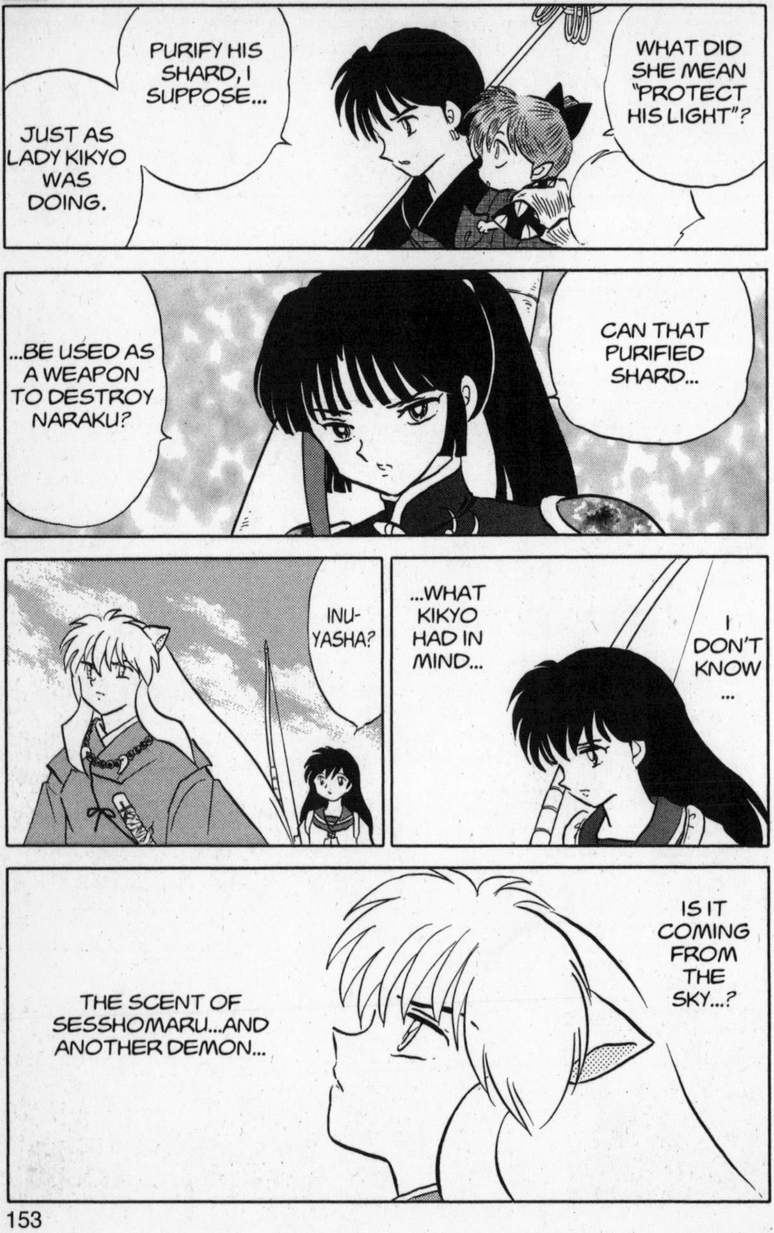
WHAT DID SHE MEAN "PROTECT HIS LIGHT"?
PURIFY HIS SHARD, I SUPPOSE...
JUST AS LADY KIKYO WAS DOING.
CAN THAT PURIFIED SHARD...
...BE USED AS A WEAPON TO DESTROY NARAKU?
I DON'T KNOW...
...WHAT KIKYO HAD IN MIND...
INU-YASHA?
IS IT COMING FROM THE SKY...?
THE SCENT OF SESSHOMARU...AND ANOTHER DEMON...

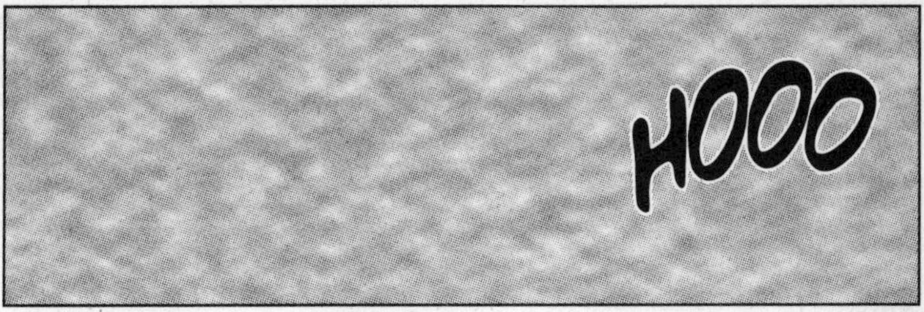
HOOO
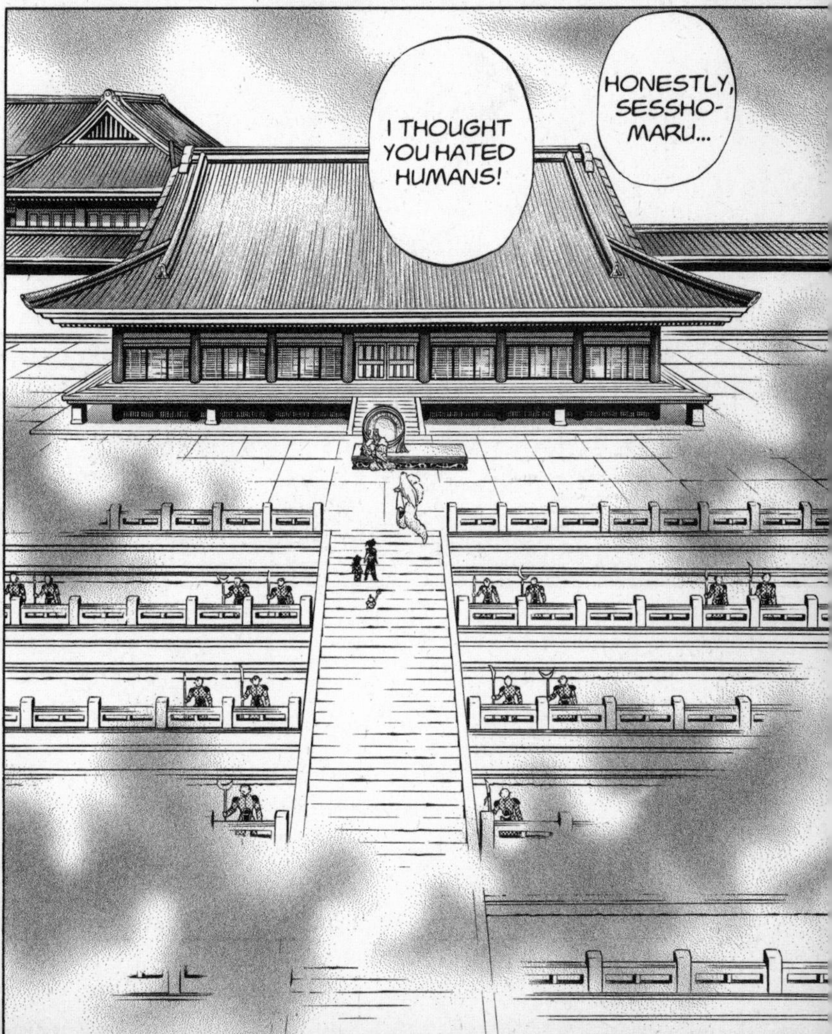
HONESTLY, SESSHO-MARU...
I THOUGHT YOU HATED HUMANS!

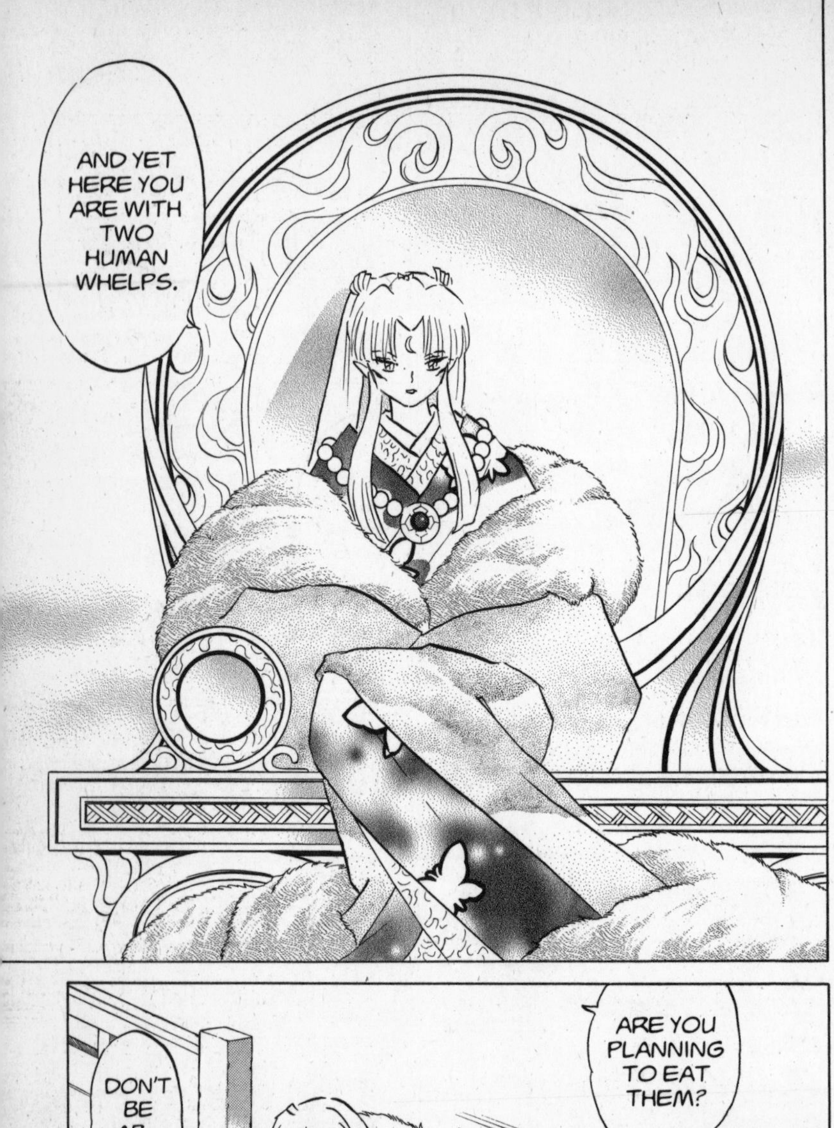
AND YET HERE YOU ARE WITH TWO HUMAN WHELPS.
ARE YOU PLANNING TO EAT THEM?
DON'T BE AB-SURD.

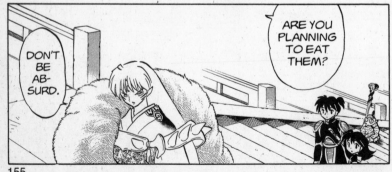

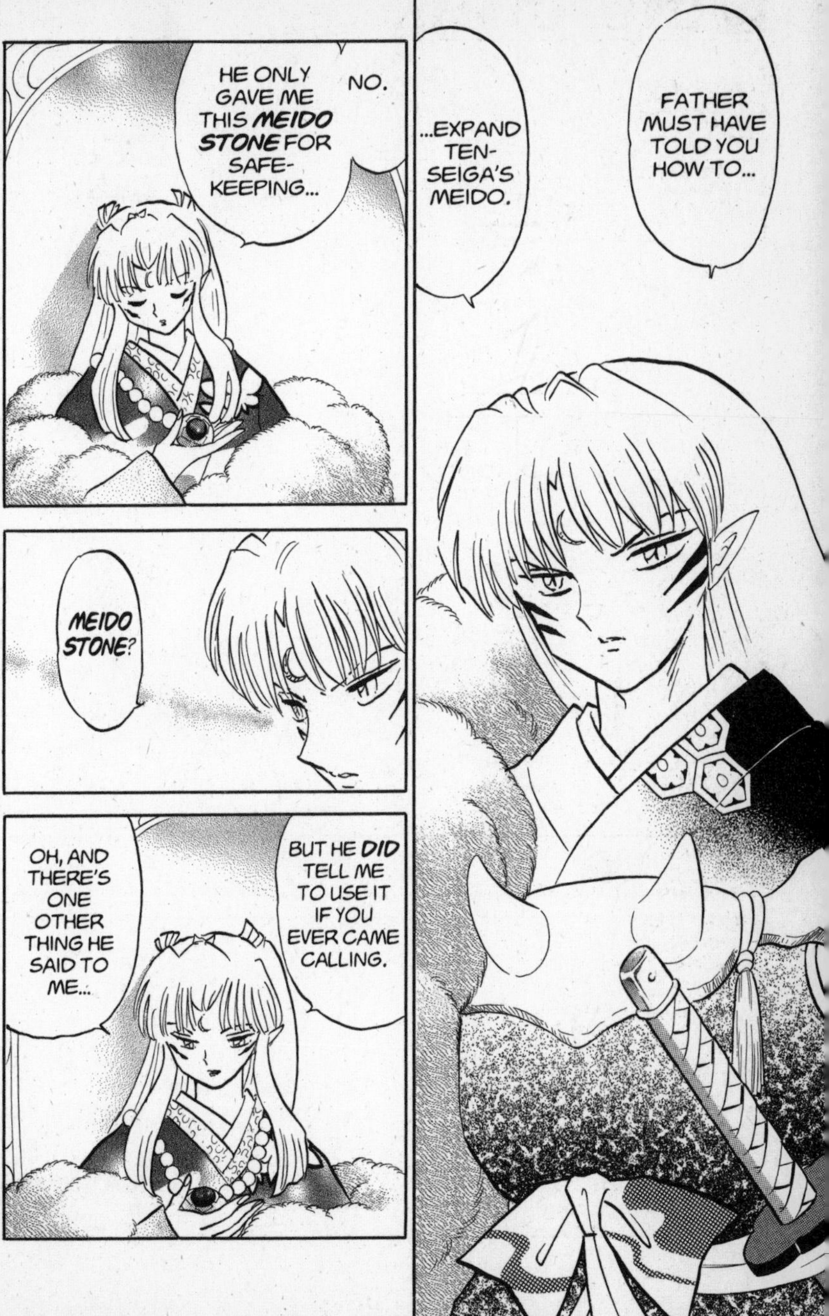
FATHER MUST HAVE TOLD YOU HOW TO...
...EXPAND TEN-SEIGA'S MEIDO.
NO.
HE ONLY GAVE ME THIS MEIDO STONE FOR SAFE-KEEPING...
MEIDO STONE?
BUT HE DID TELL ME TO USE IT IF YOU EVER CAME CALLING.
OH, AND THERE'S ONE OTHER THING HE SAID TO ME...

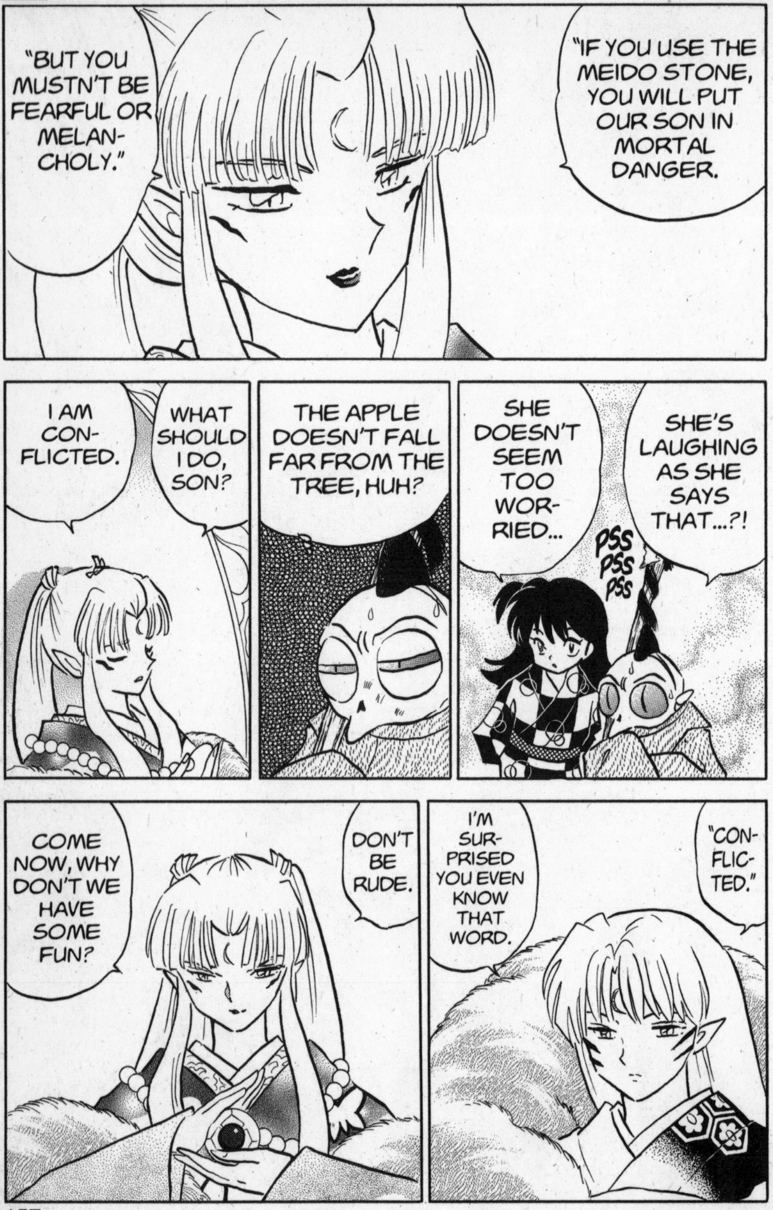
"IF YOU USE THE MEIDO STONE, YOU WILL PUT OUR SON IN MORTAL DANGER.
"BUT YOU MUSTN'T BE FEARFUL OR MELANCHOLY."
SHE'S LAUGHING AS SHE SAYS THAT...?!
SHE DOESN'T SEEM TOO WORRIED...
PSS PSS PSS
THE APPLE DOESN'T FALL FAR FROM THE TREE, HUH?
WHAT SHOULD I DO, SON?
I AM CONFLICTED.
"CONFLICTED."
I'M SURPRISED YOU EVEN KNOW THAT WORD.
DON'T BE RUDE.
COME NOW, WHY DON'T WE HAVE SOME FUN?

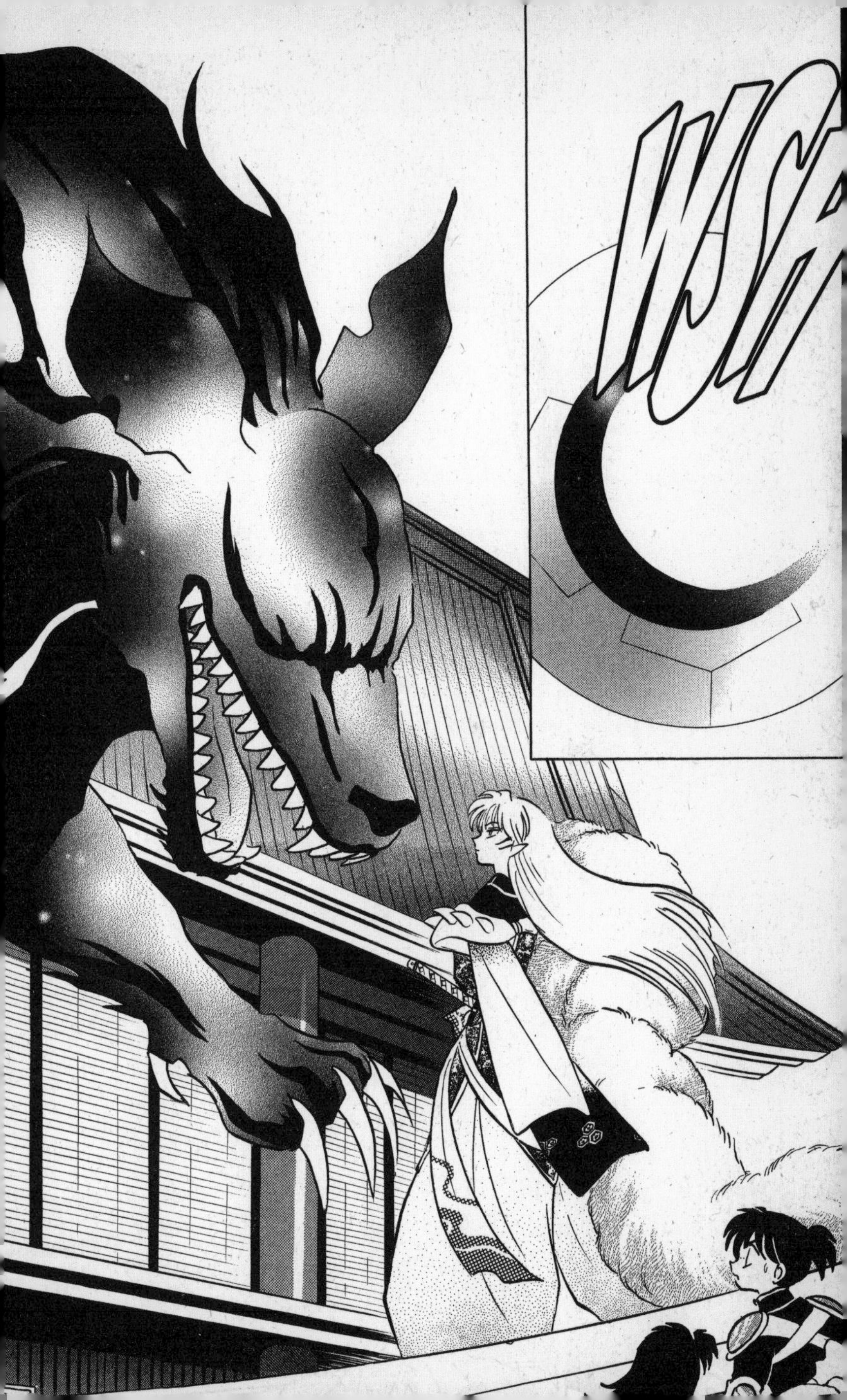

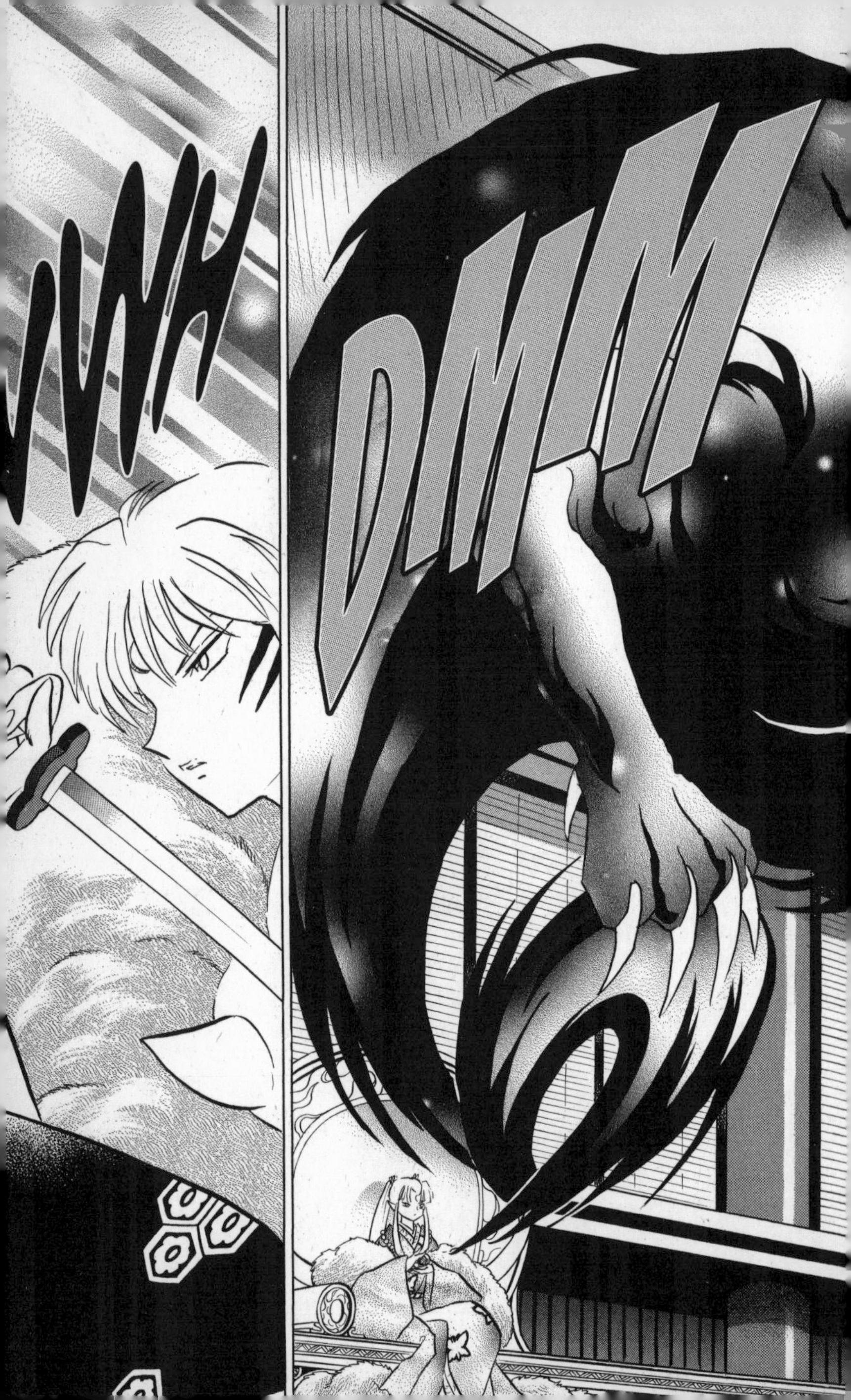
DMM
VWH

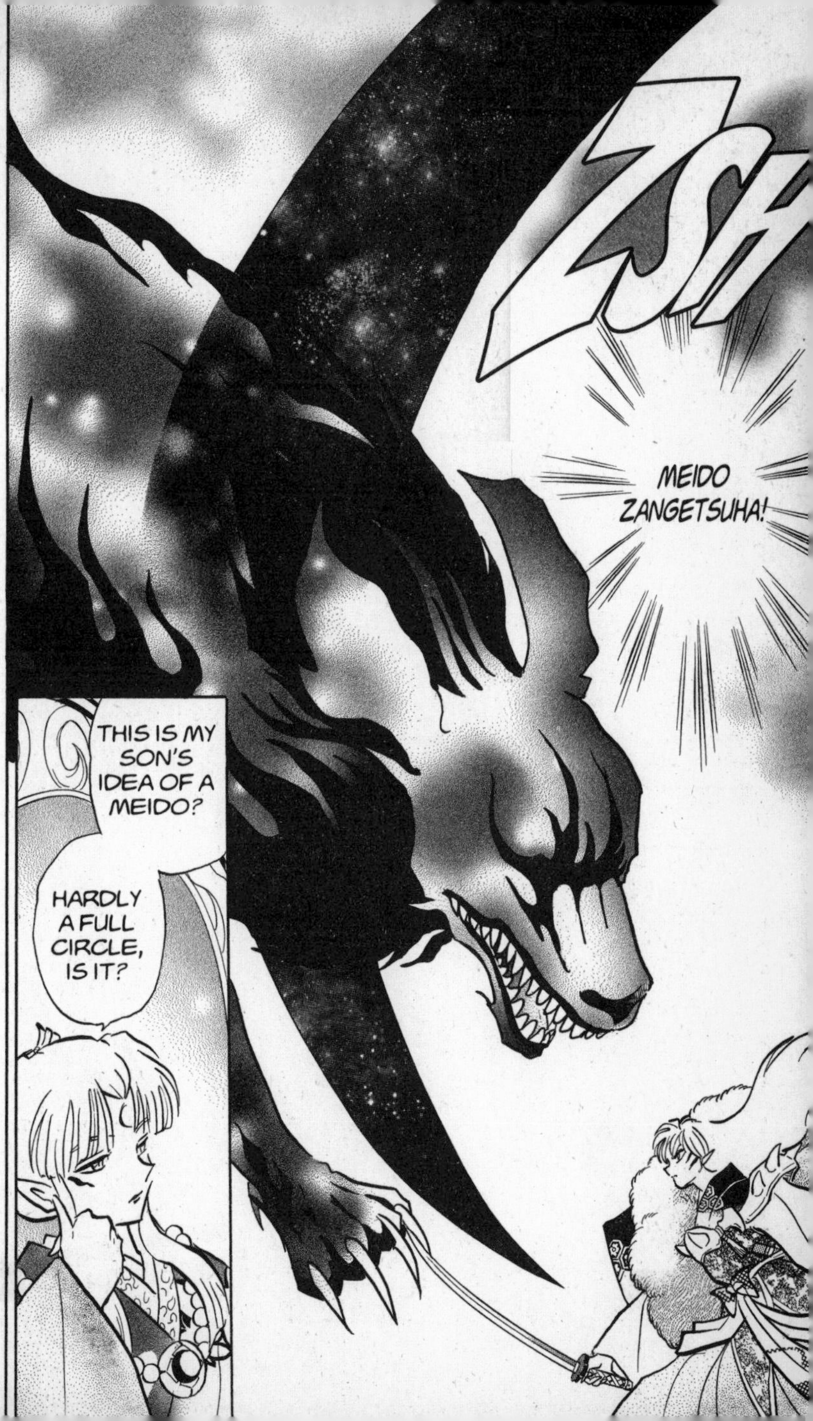
ZSH
MEIDO ZANGETSUHA!
THIS IS MY SON'S IDEA OF A MEIDO?
HARDLY A FULL CIRCLE, IS IT?

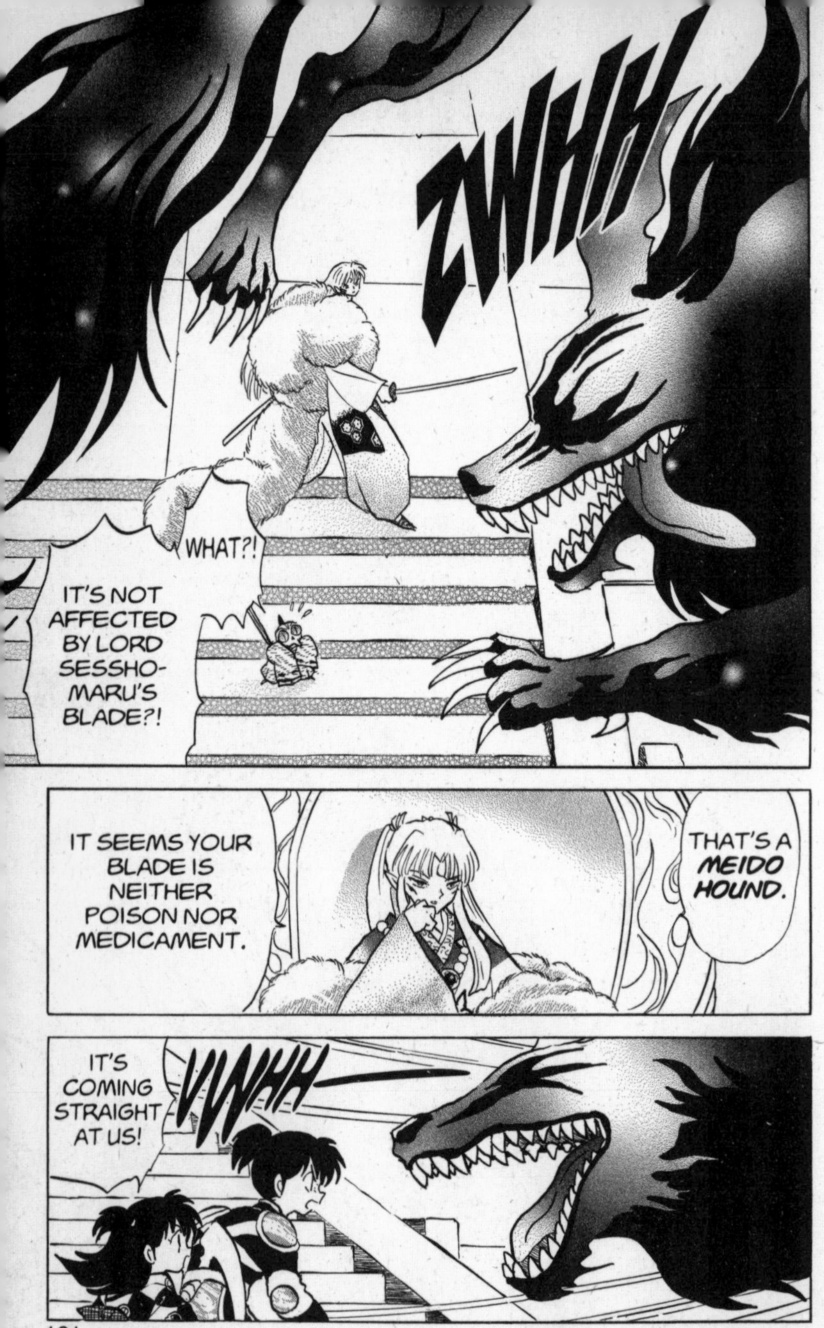
ZWHH
WHAT?!
IT'S NOT AFFECTED BY LORD SESSHO-MARU'S BLADE?!
THAT'S A *MEIDO* HOUND.
IT SEEMS YOUR BLADE IS NEITHER POISON NOR MEDICAMENT.
VWHH
IT'S COMING STRAIGHT AT US!

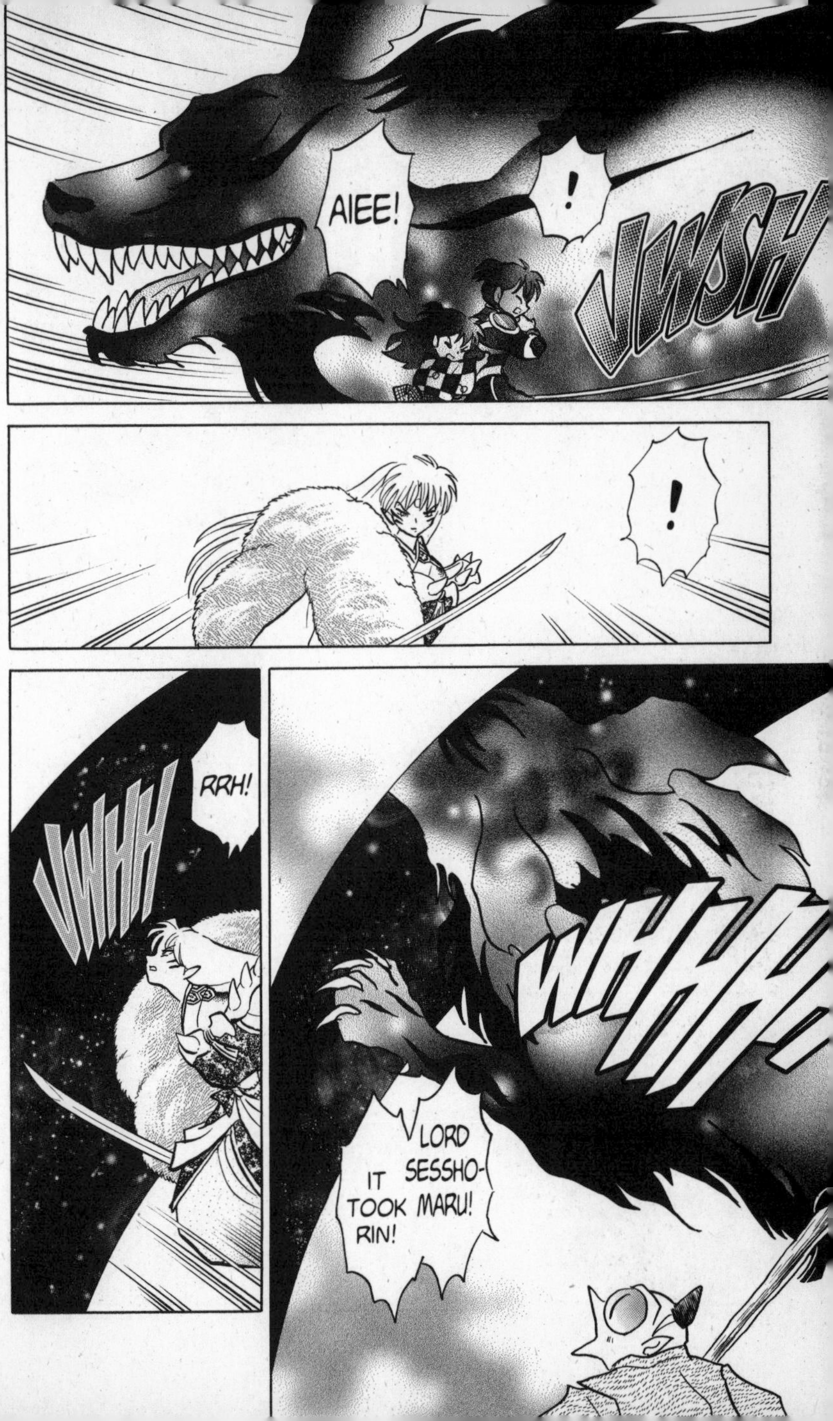
JWSH
!
AIEE!
!
WHHH-
LORD SESSHO-MARU! IT TOOK RIN!
RRH!
JWHH

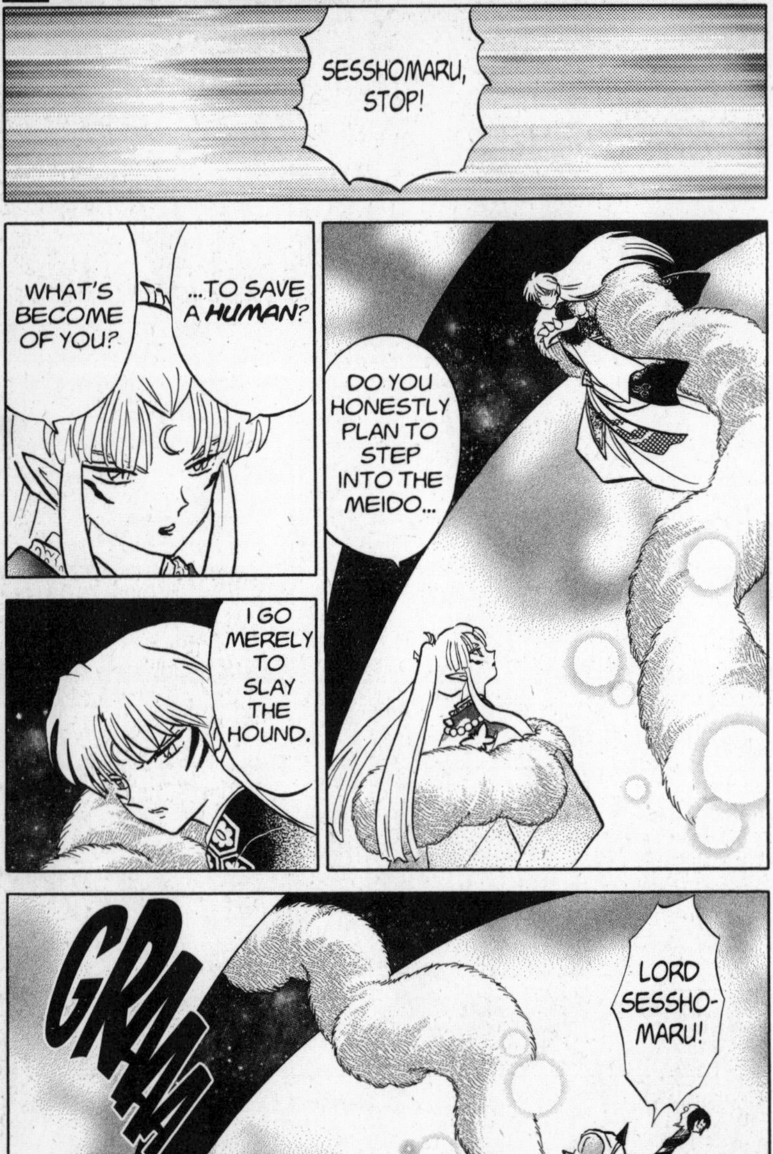
SESSHOMARU, STOP!
DO YOU HONESTLY PLAN TO STEP INTO THE MEIDO...
...TO SAVE A *HUMAN*?
WHAT'S BECOME OF YOU?
I GO MERELY TO SLAY THE HOUND.
LORD SESSHO-MARU!
GRAM

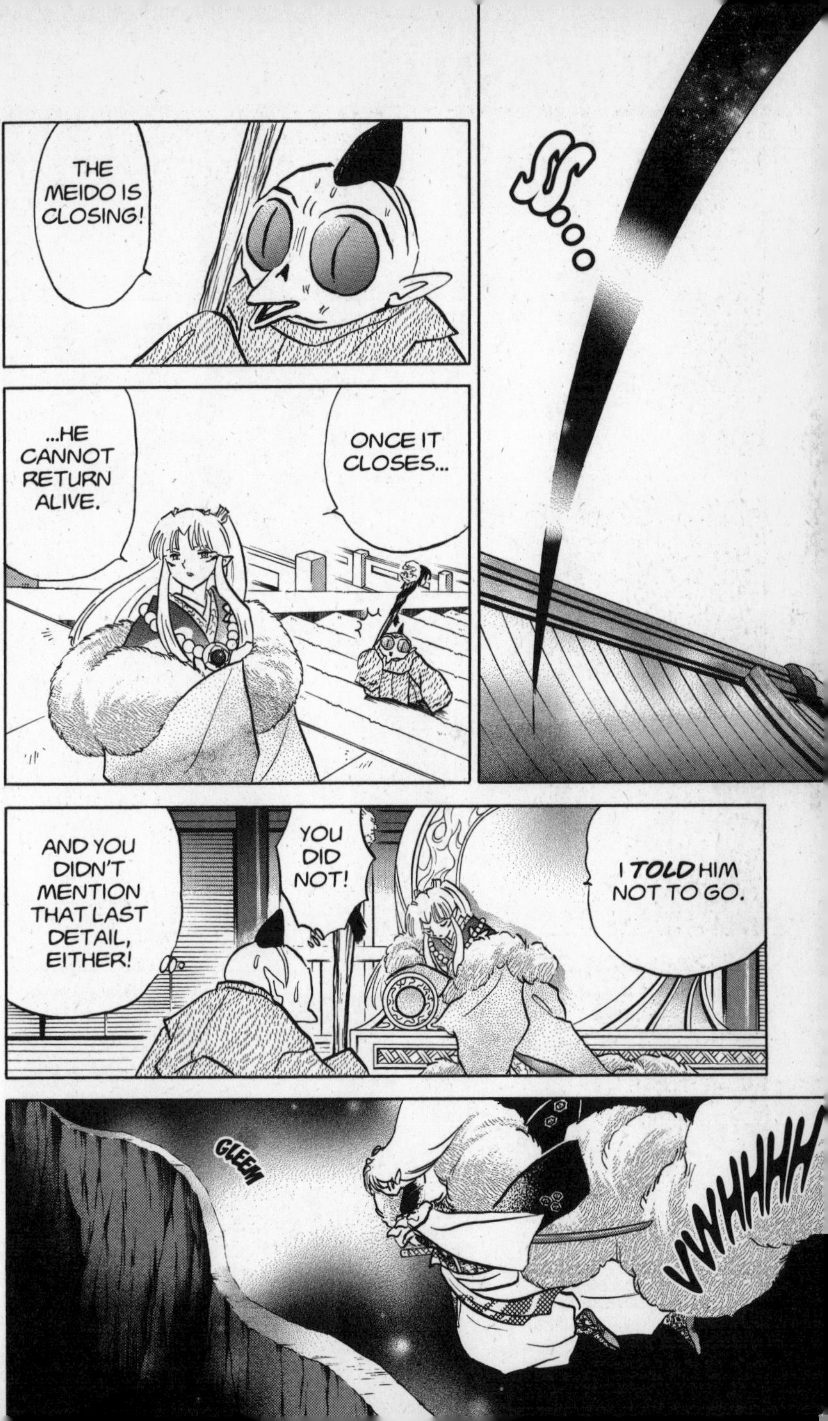
SSOOO
THE MEIDO IS CLOSING!
ONCE IT CLOSES...
...HE CANNOT RETURN ALIVE.
I *TOLD* HIM NOT TO GO.
YOU DID NOT!
AND YOU DIDN'T MENTION THAT LAST DETAIL, EITHER!
VWHHHH
GLEEM

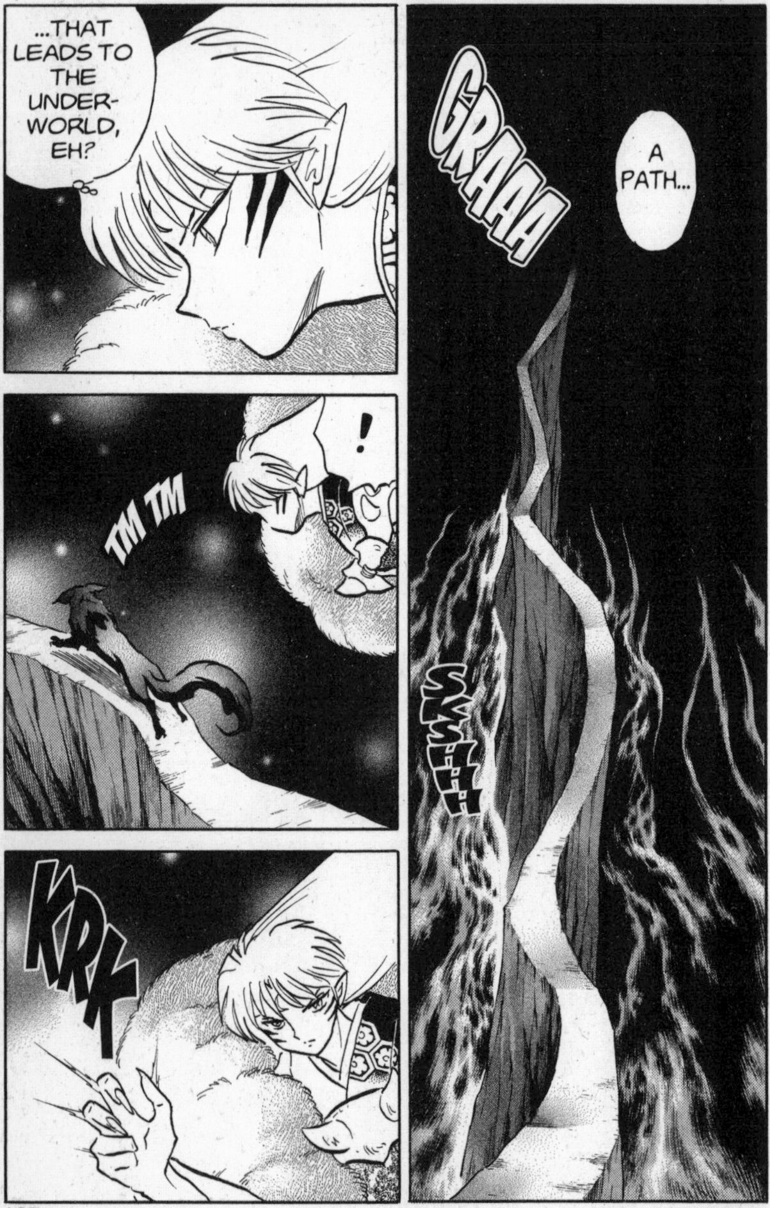
GRAAA
A PATH...
SWSHHH
...THAT LEADS TO THE UNDER-WORLD, EH?
!
TM TM
KRK

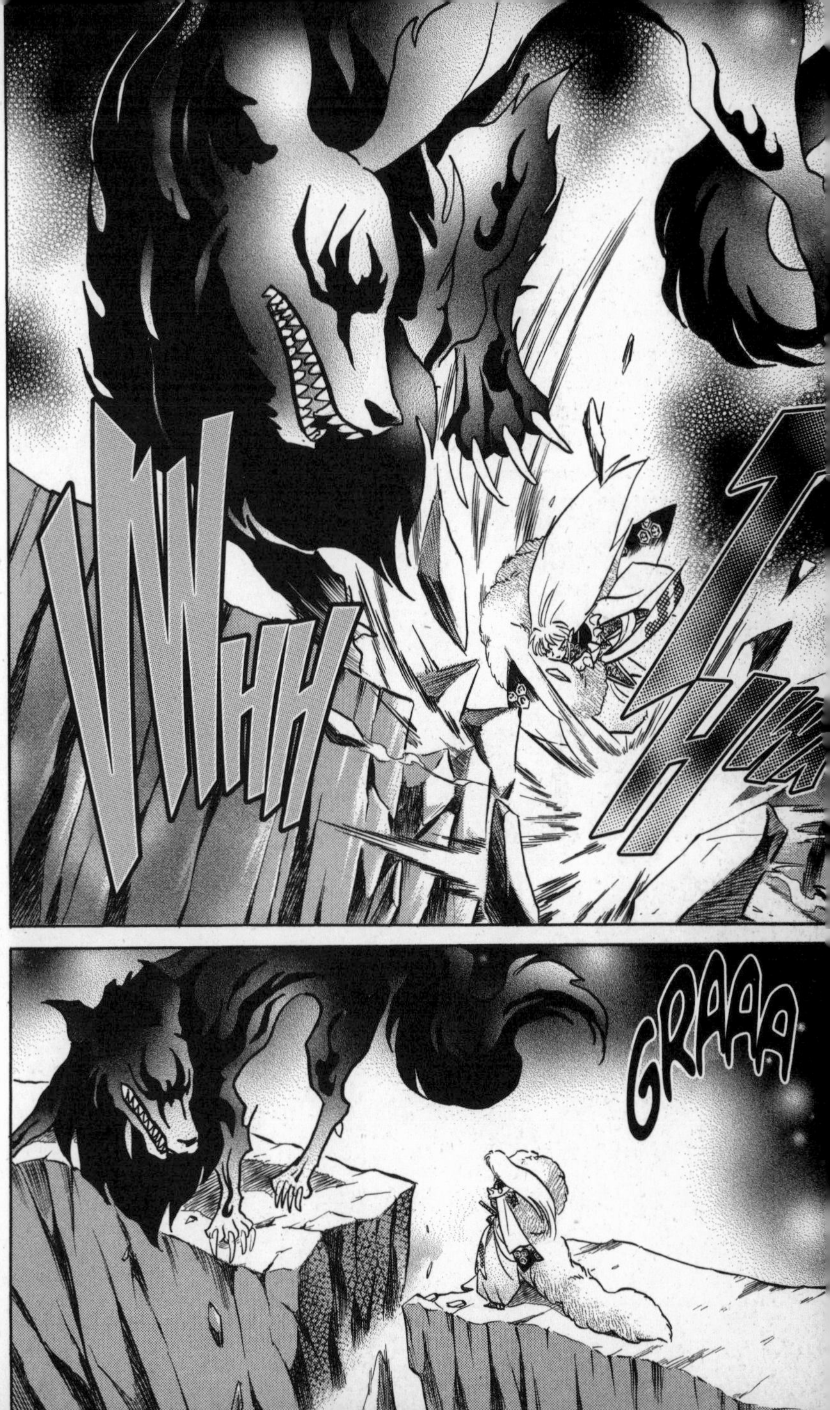
VWHH
GRAAA

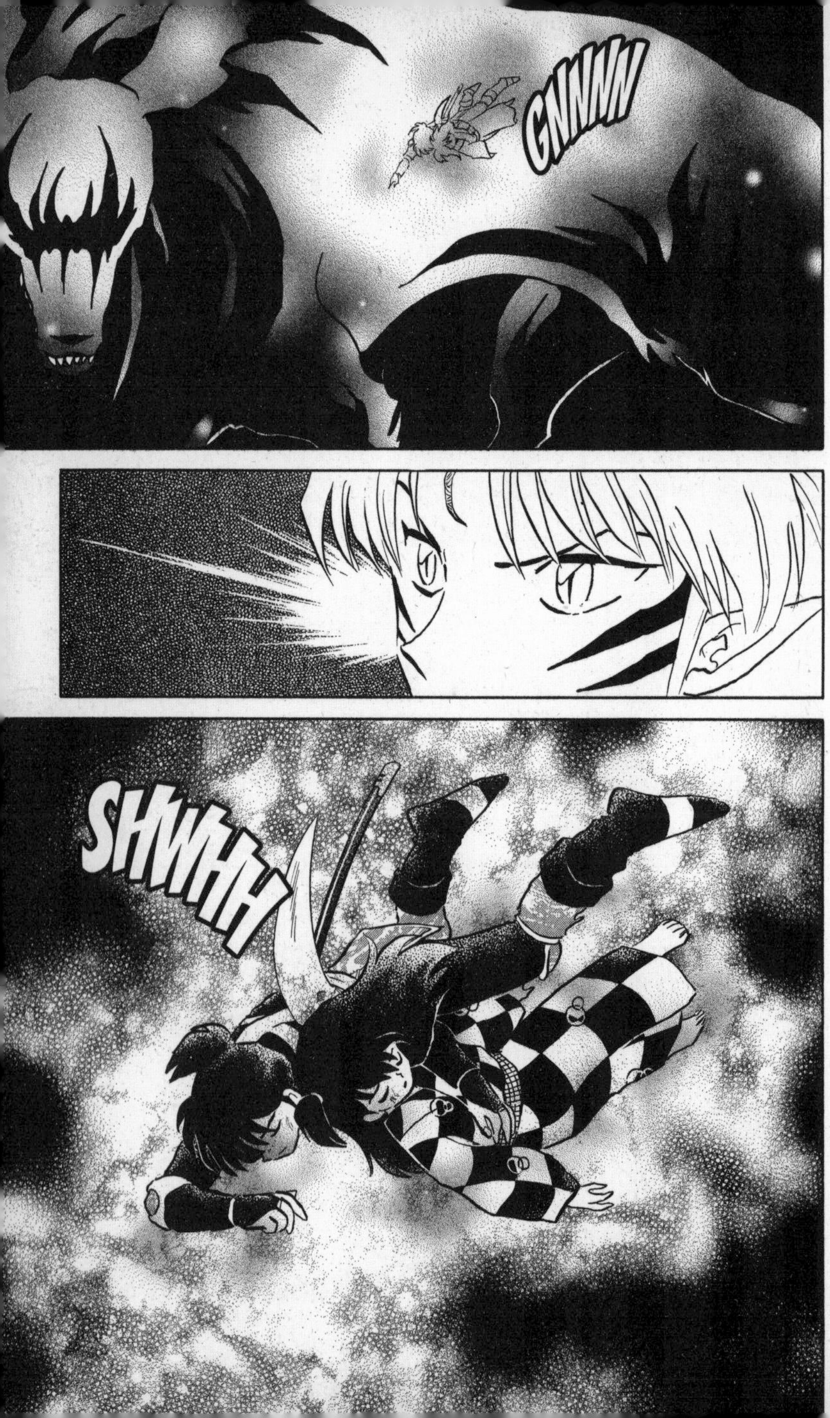
GNNNN
SHWHH

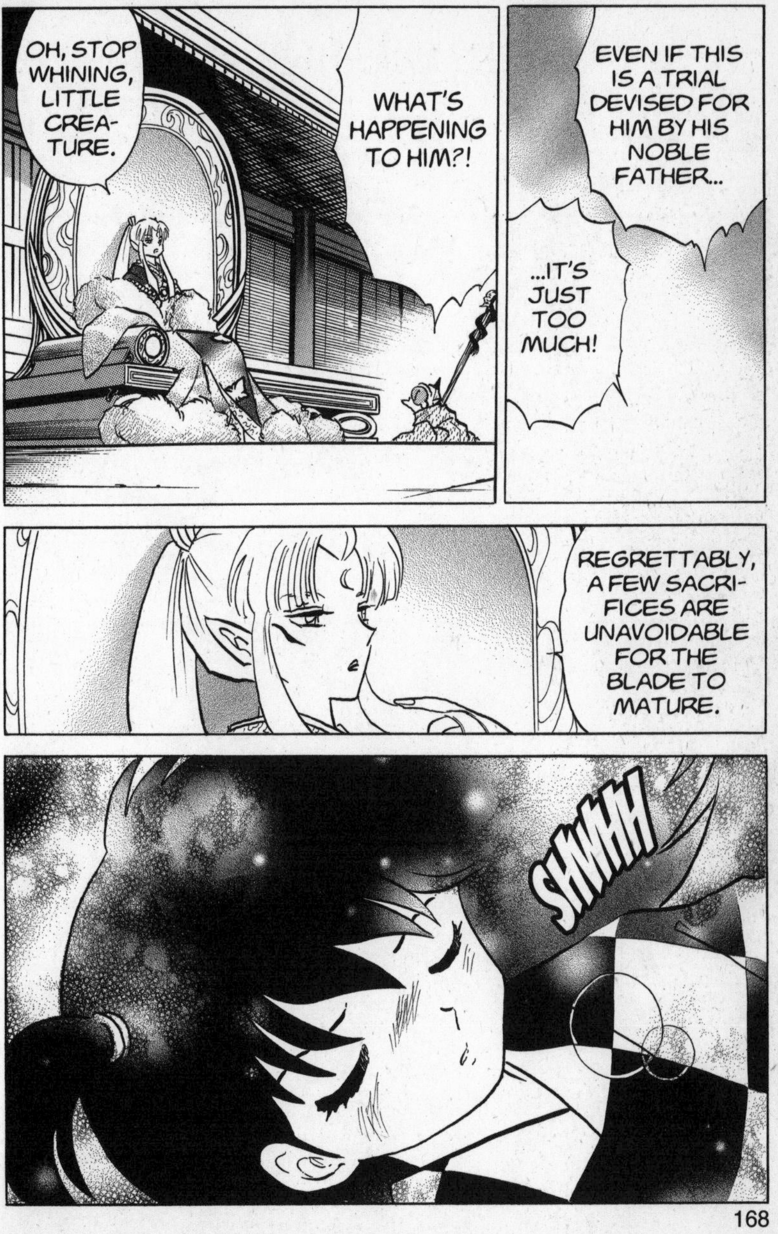
EVEN IF THIS IS A TRIAL DEVISED FOR HIM BY HIS NOBLE FATHER...
...IT'S JUST TOO MUCH!
WHAT'S HAPPENING TO HIM?!
OH, STOP WHINING, LITTLE CREA-TURE.
REGRETTABLY, A FEW SACRI-FICES ARE UNAVOIDABLE FOR THE BLADE TO MATURE.
SHWHH

SCROLL 10
THE GREAT DARKNESS

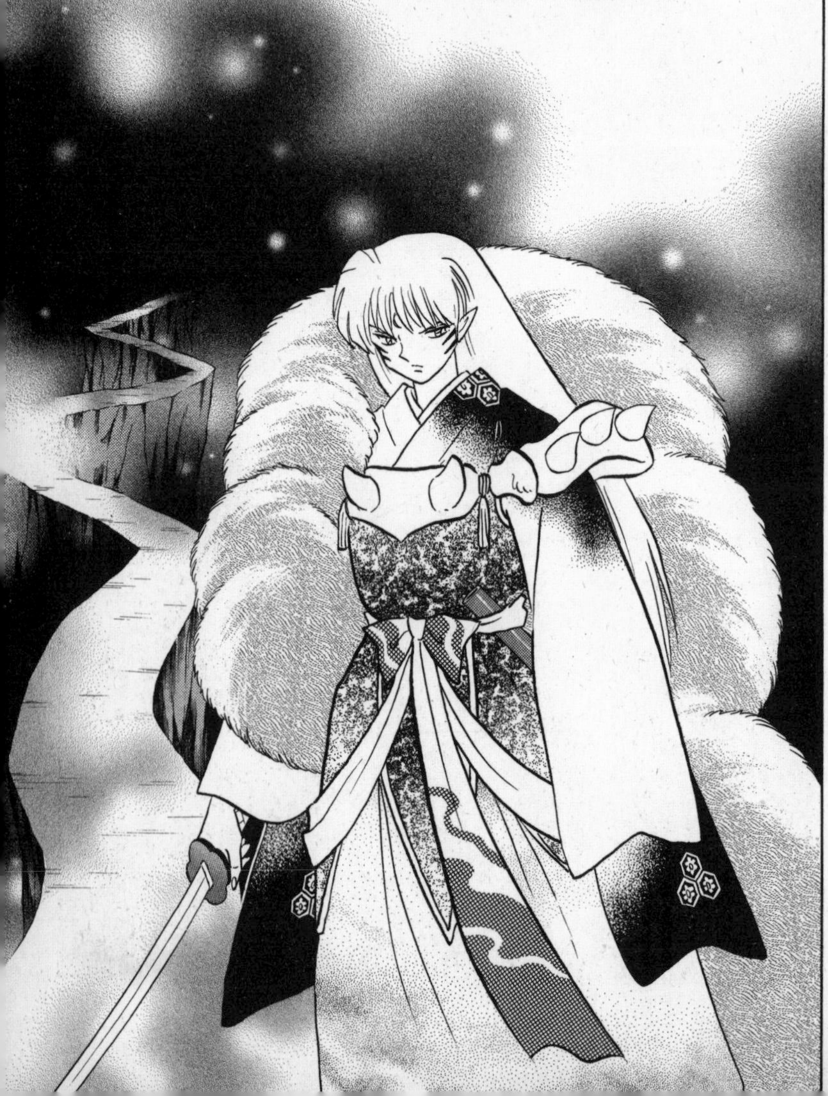

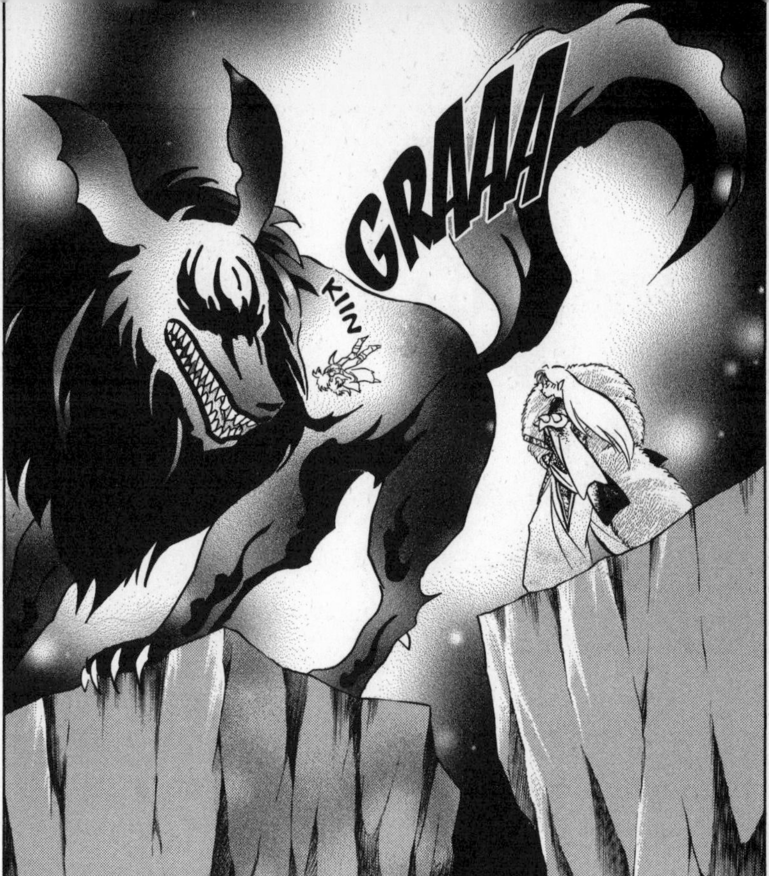
GRAAA
KIIN

2

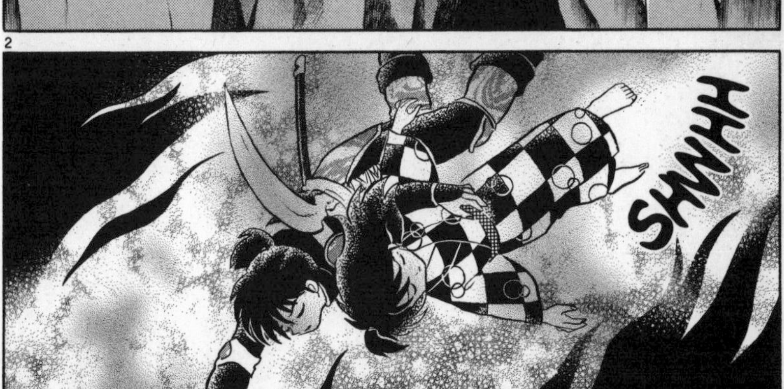
SHWHH

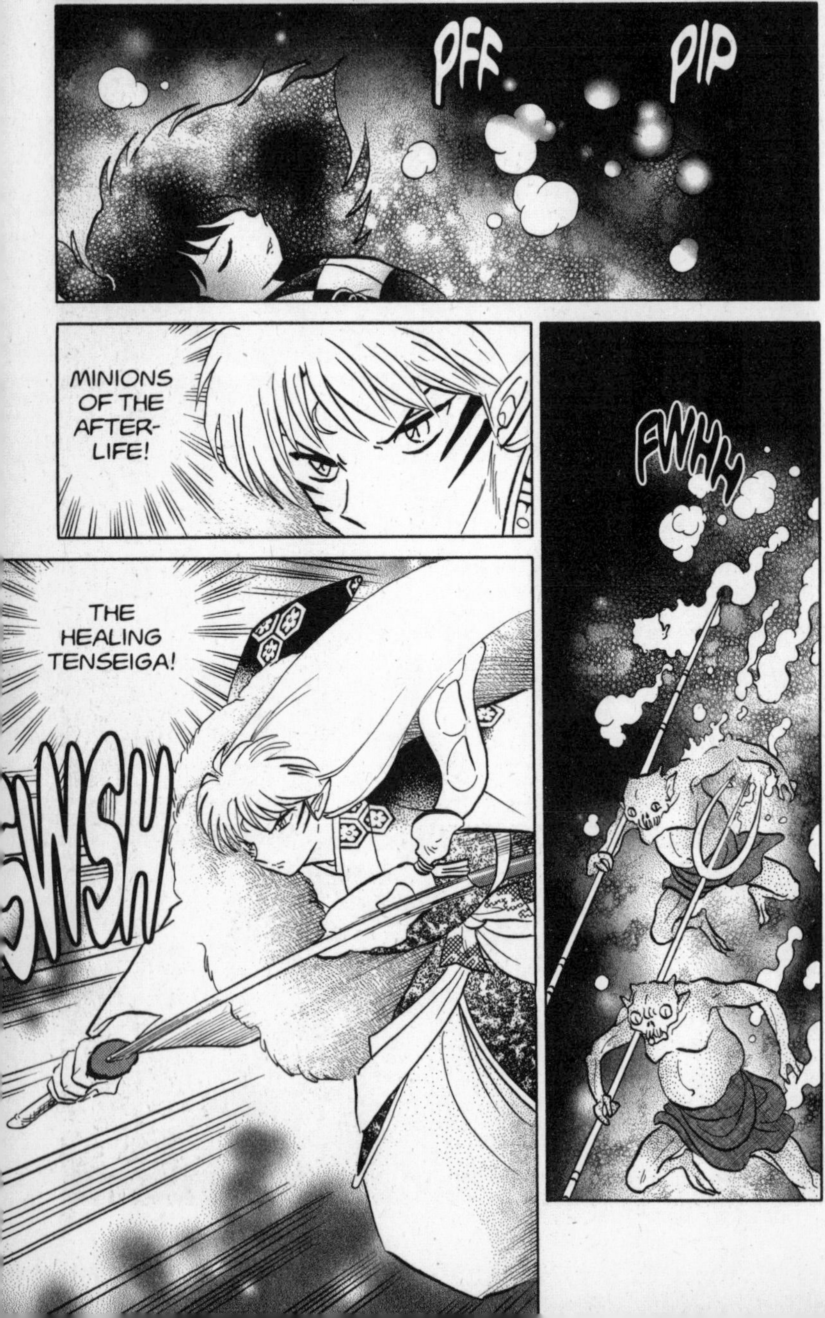
PIP
PFF
FWHH
MINIONS OF THE AFTER-LIFE!
THE HEALING TENSEIGA!
SWSH

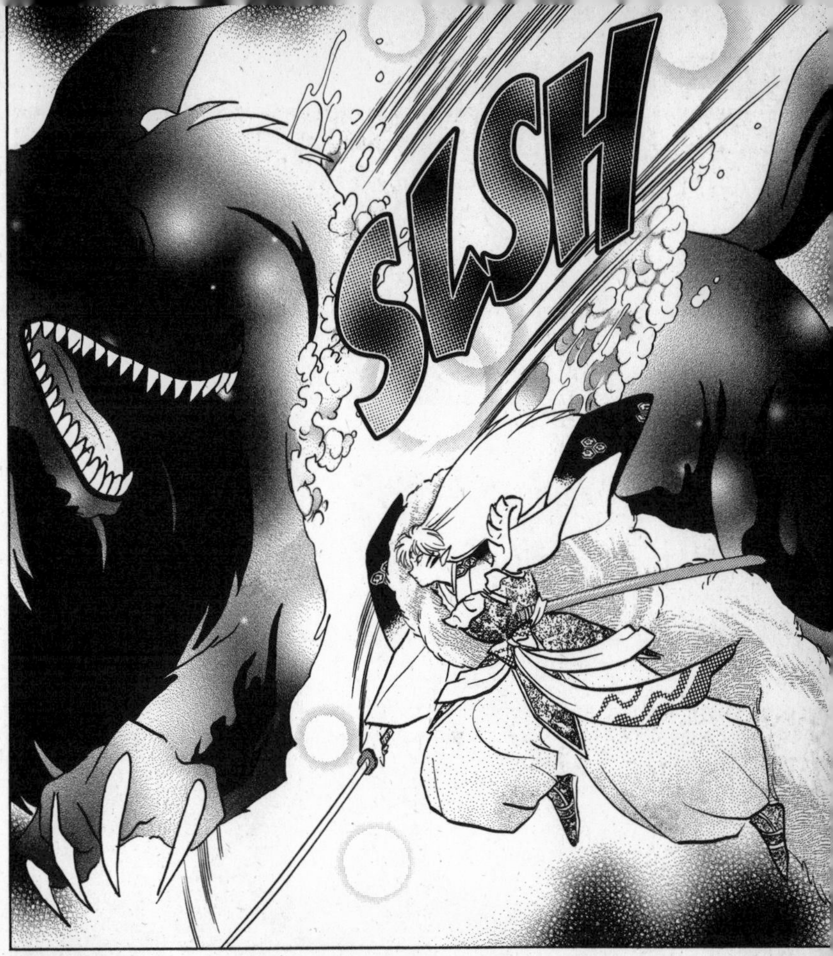
SLSH
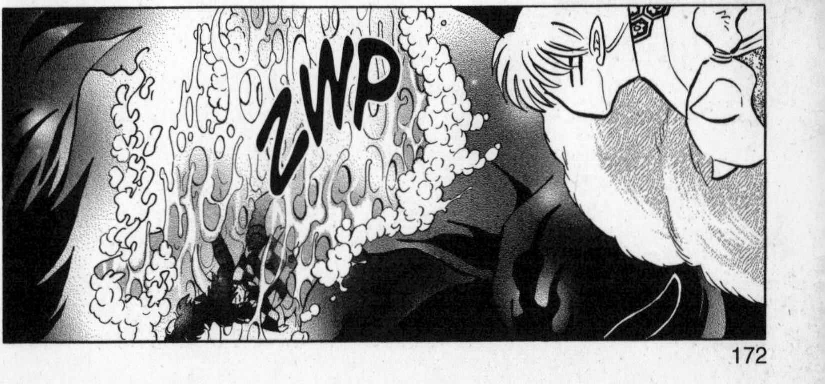
ZWP

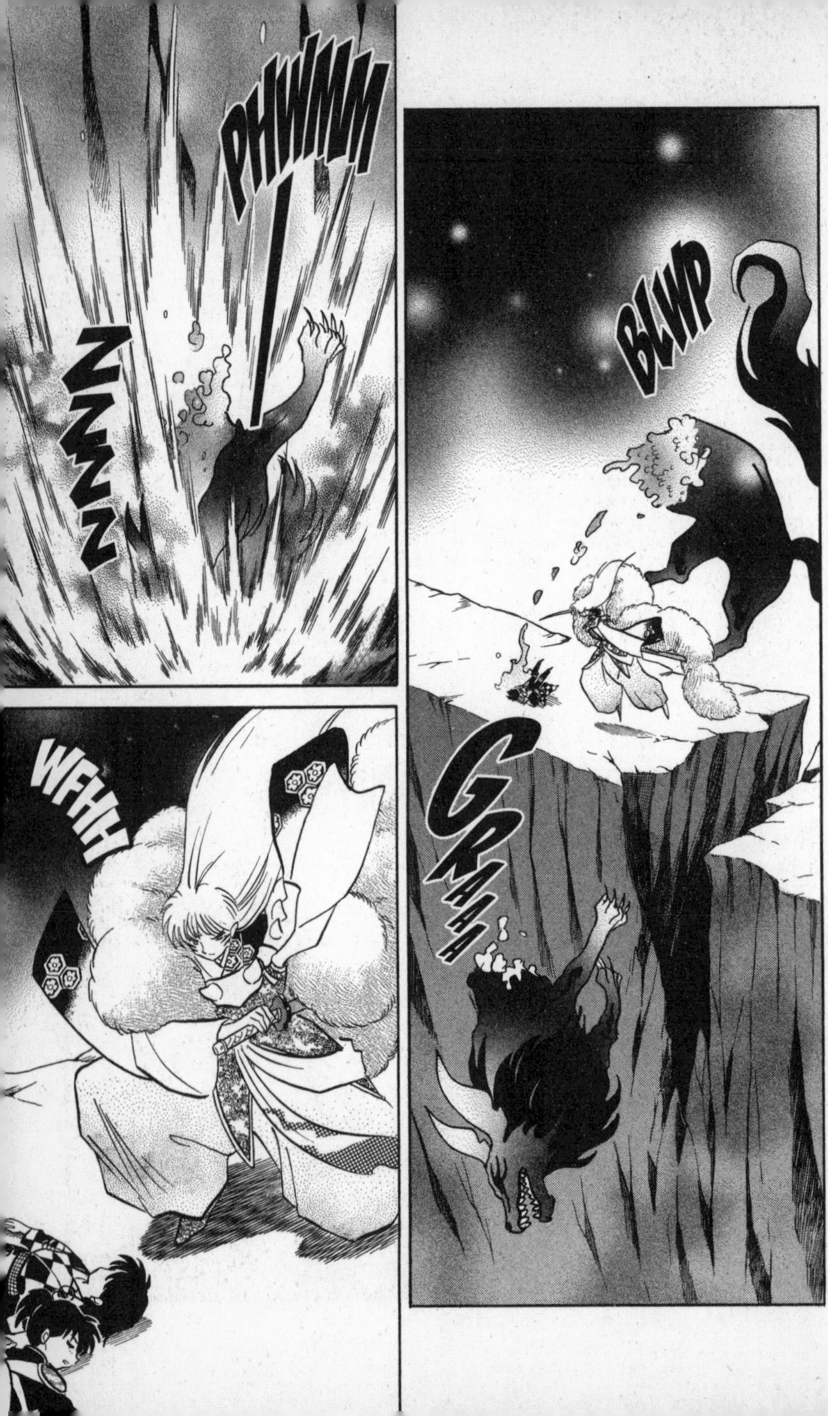
BLWP
GRAAAA
PHWNM
ZZZZ
WFHH

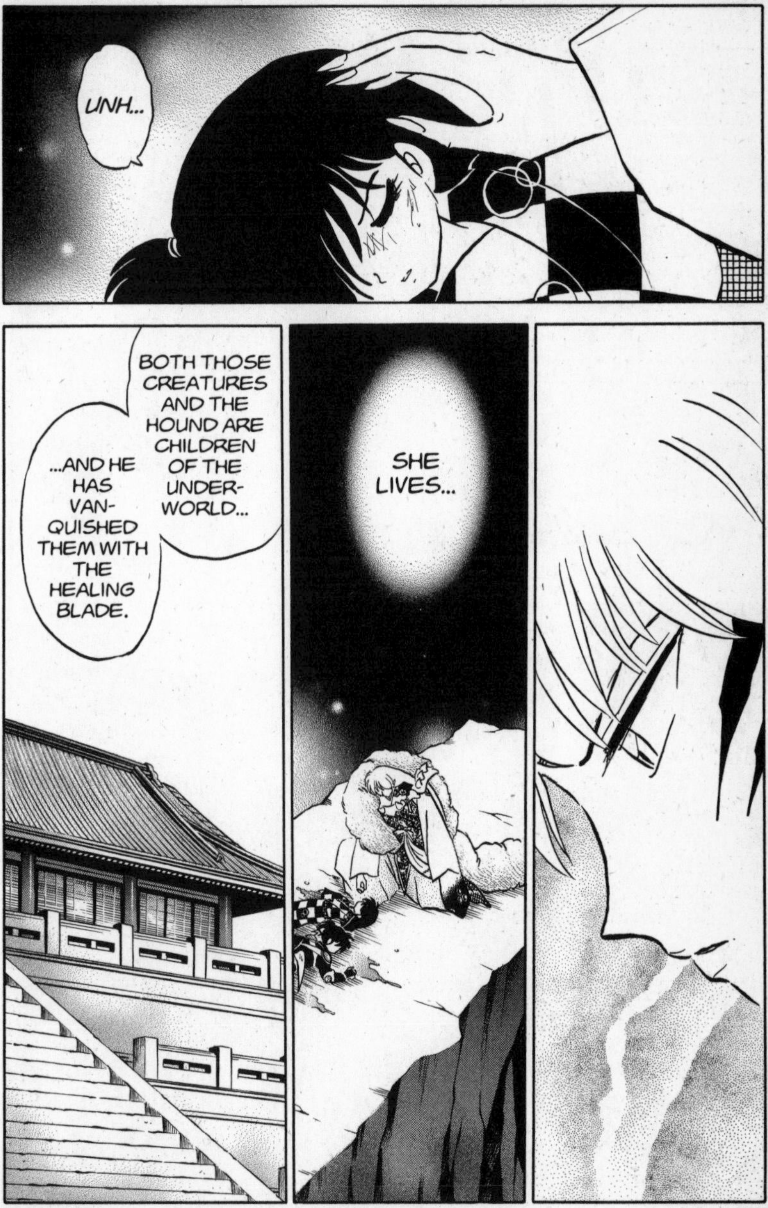
UNH...
SHE LIVES...
BOTH THOSE CREATURES AND THE HOUND ARE CHILDREN OF THE UNDER-WORLD...
...AND HE HAS VAN-QUISHED THEM WITH THE HEALING BLADE.

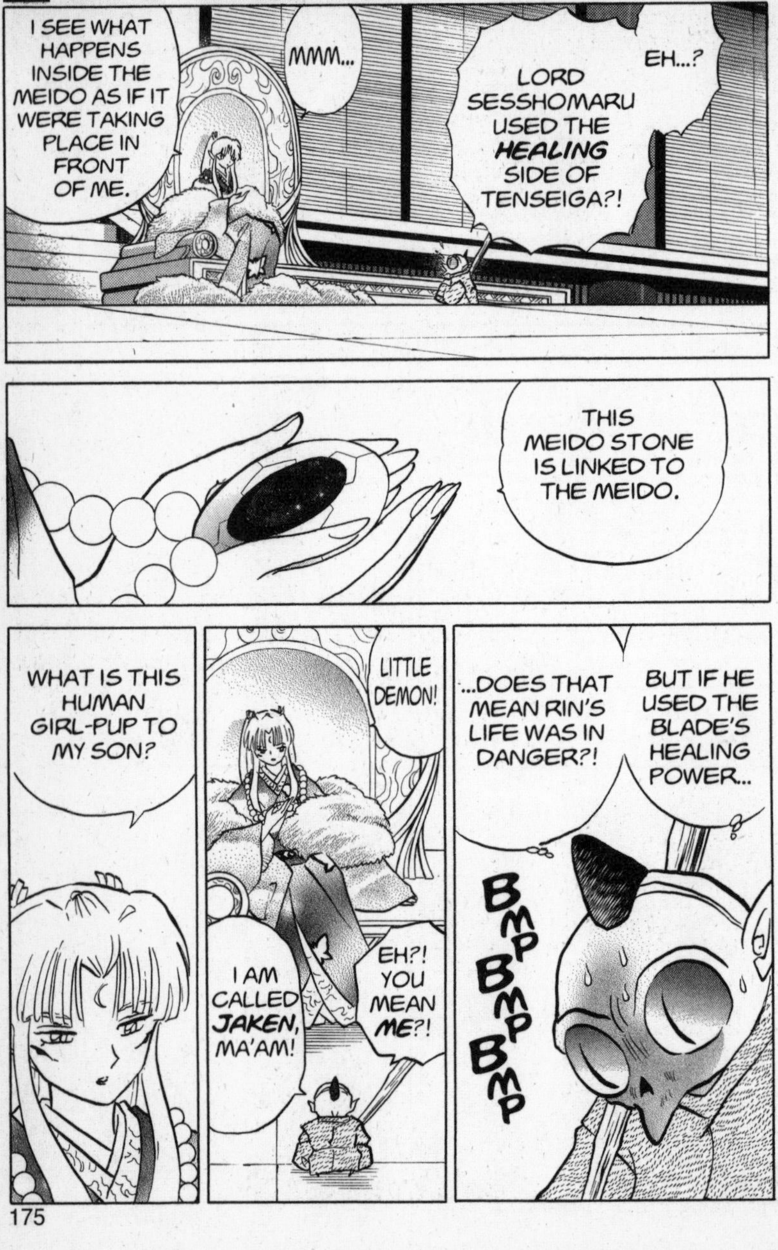
EH...?
LORD SESSHOMARU USED THE HEALING SIDE OF TENSEIGA?!
MMM...
I SEE WHAT HAPPENS INSIDE THE MEIDO AS IF IT WERE TAKING PLACE IN FRONT OF ME.
THIS MEIDO STONE IS LINKED TO THE MEIDO.
BUT IF HE USED THE BLADE'S HEALING POWER...
...DOES THAT MEAN RIN'S LIFE WAS IN DANGER?!
BMP BMP BMP
LITTLE DEMON!
EH?! YOU MEAN ME?!
I AM CALLED JAKEN, MA'AM!
WHAT IS THIS HUMAN GIRL-PUP TO MY SON?

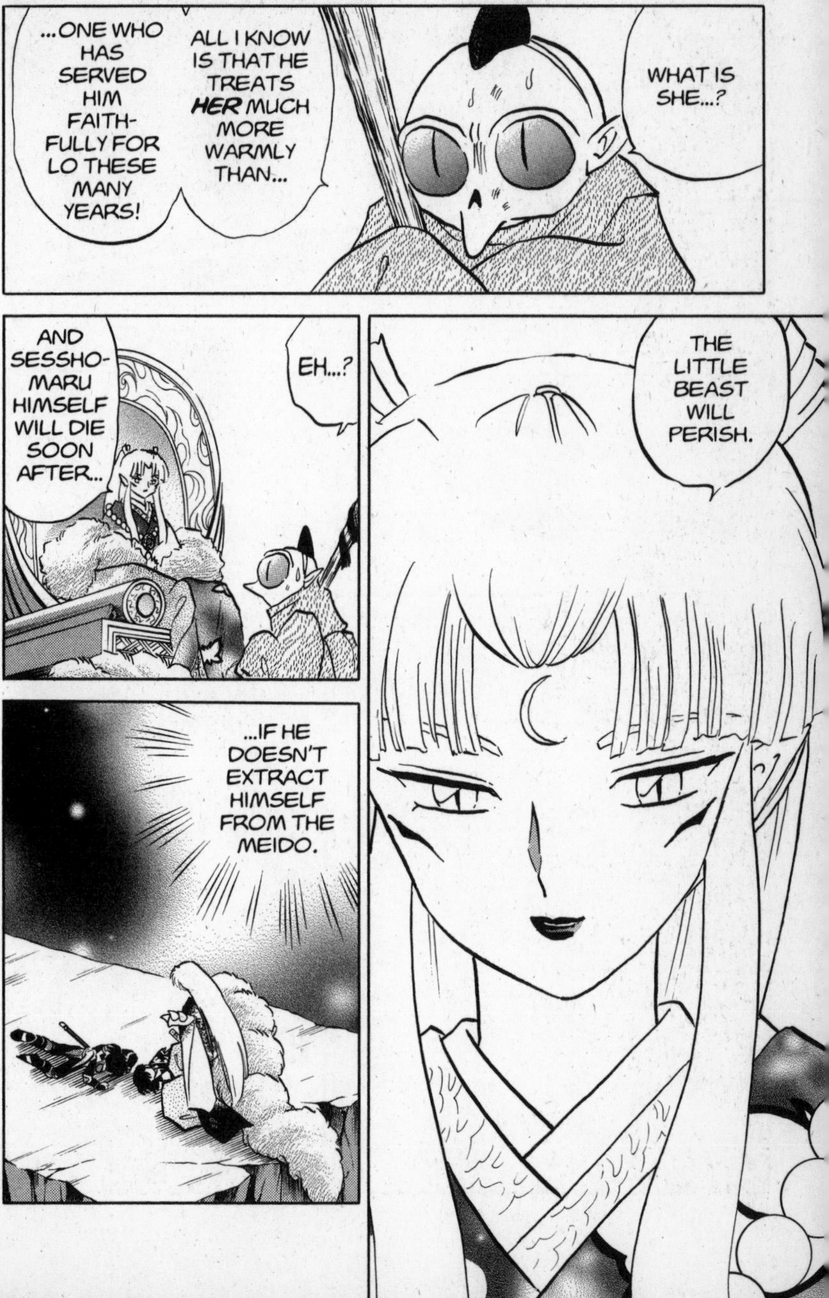
WHAT IS SHE...?
ALL I KNOW IS THAT HE TREATS **HER** MUCH MORE WARMLY THAN...
...ONE WHO HAS SERVED HIM FAITHFULLY FOR LO THESE MANY YEARS!
THE LITTLE BEAST WILL PERISH.
EH...?
AND SESSHOMARU HIMSELF WILL DIE SOON AFTER...
...IF HE DOESN'T EXTRACT HIMSELF FROM THE MEIDO.

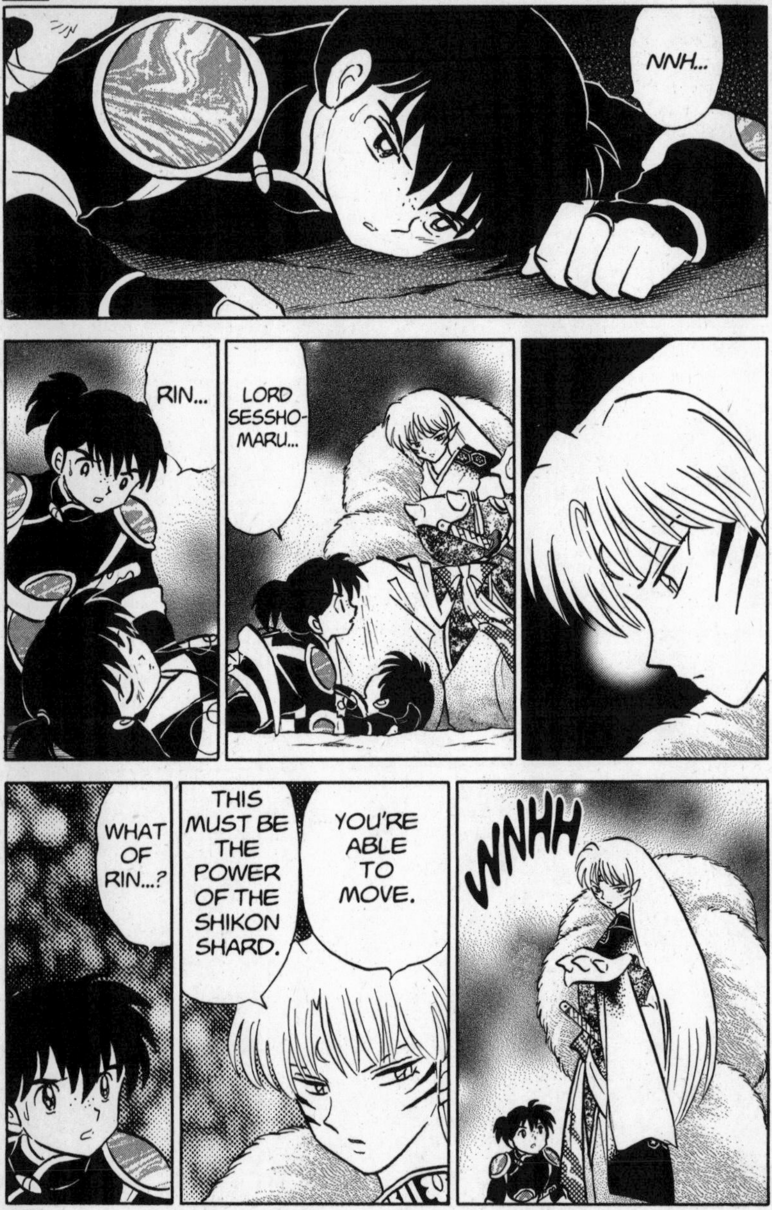
NNH...
LORD SESSHO-MARU...
RIN...
WNHH
YOU'RE ABLE TO MOVE.
THIS MUST BE THE POWER OF THE SHIKON SHARD.
WHAT OF RIN...?

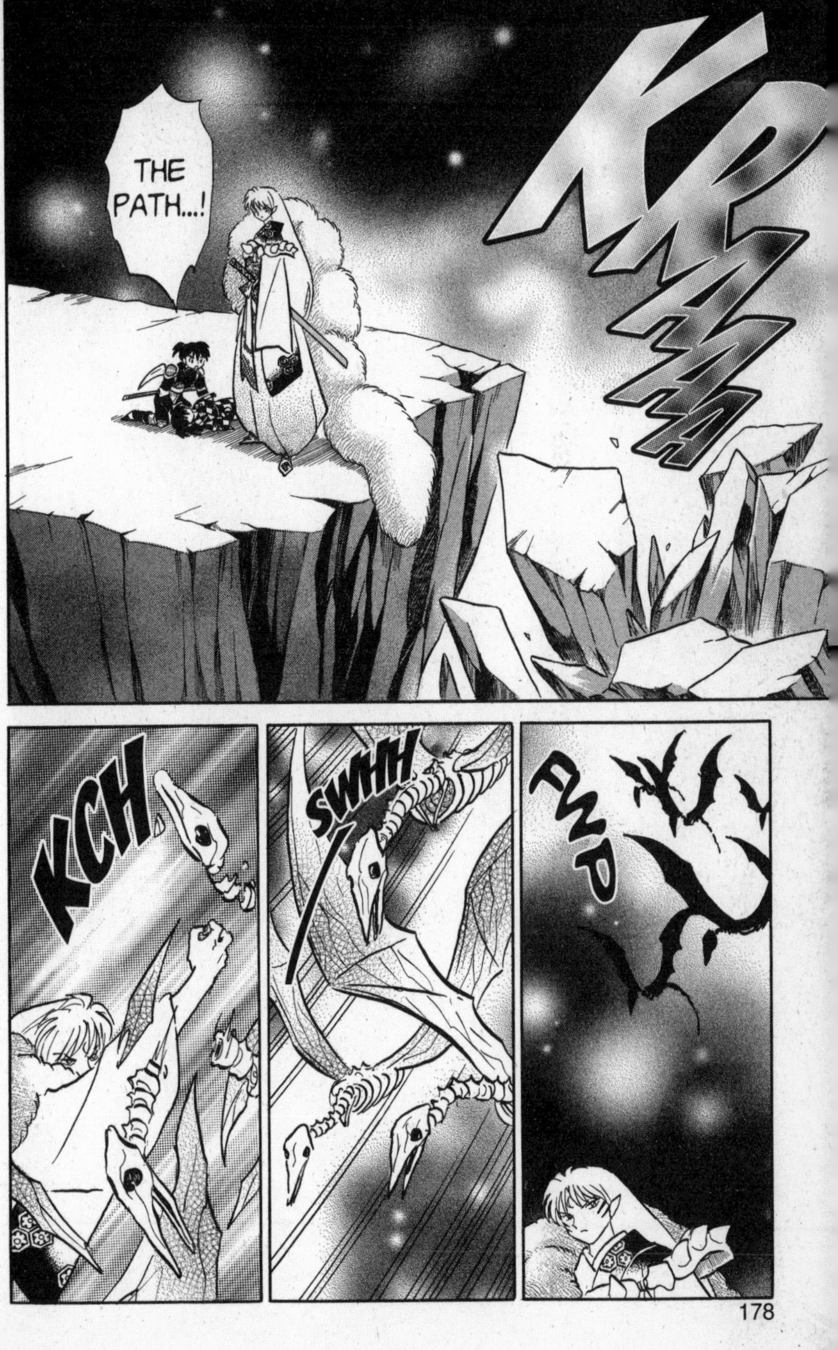
THE PATH...!
FWP
SWHH
KCH

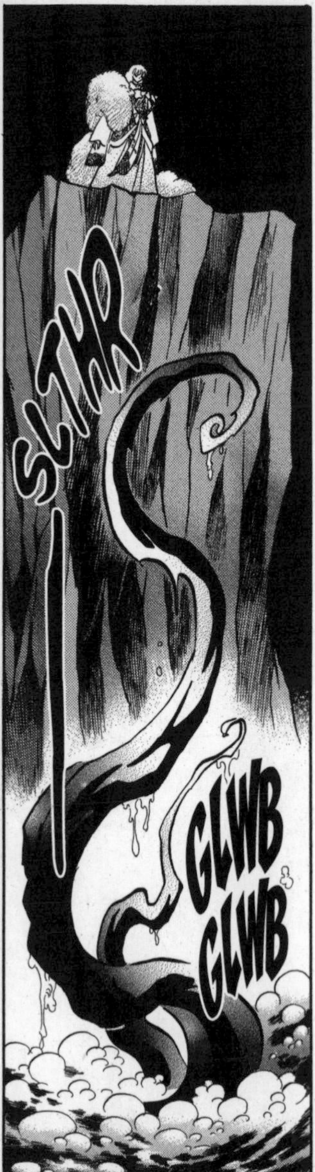
SLTHR
GLWB
GLWB
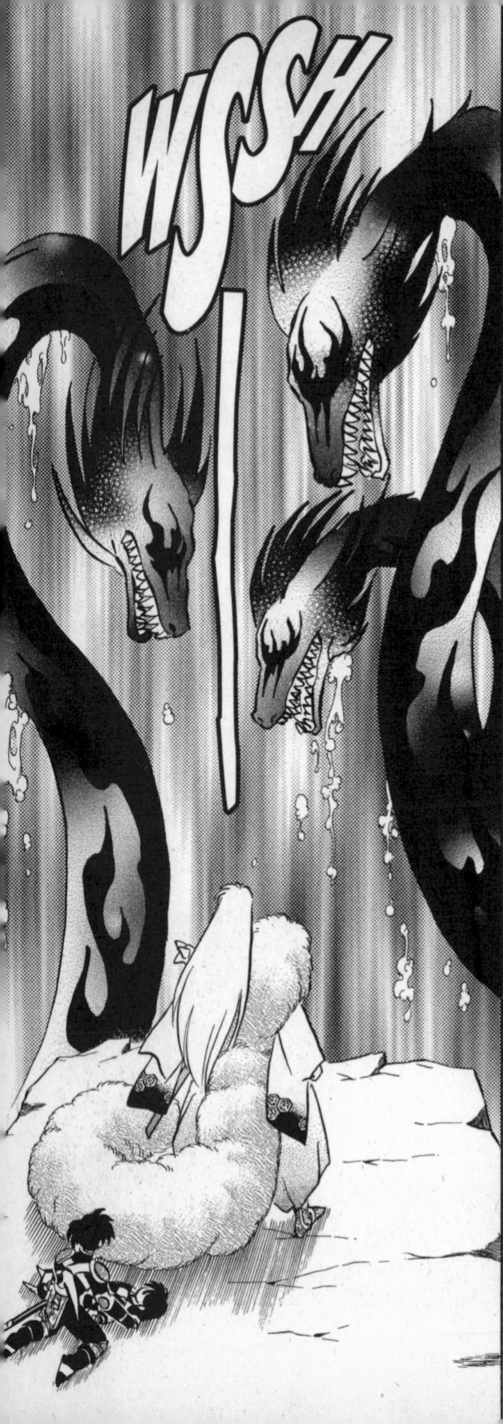
WSCH

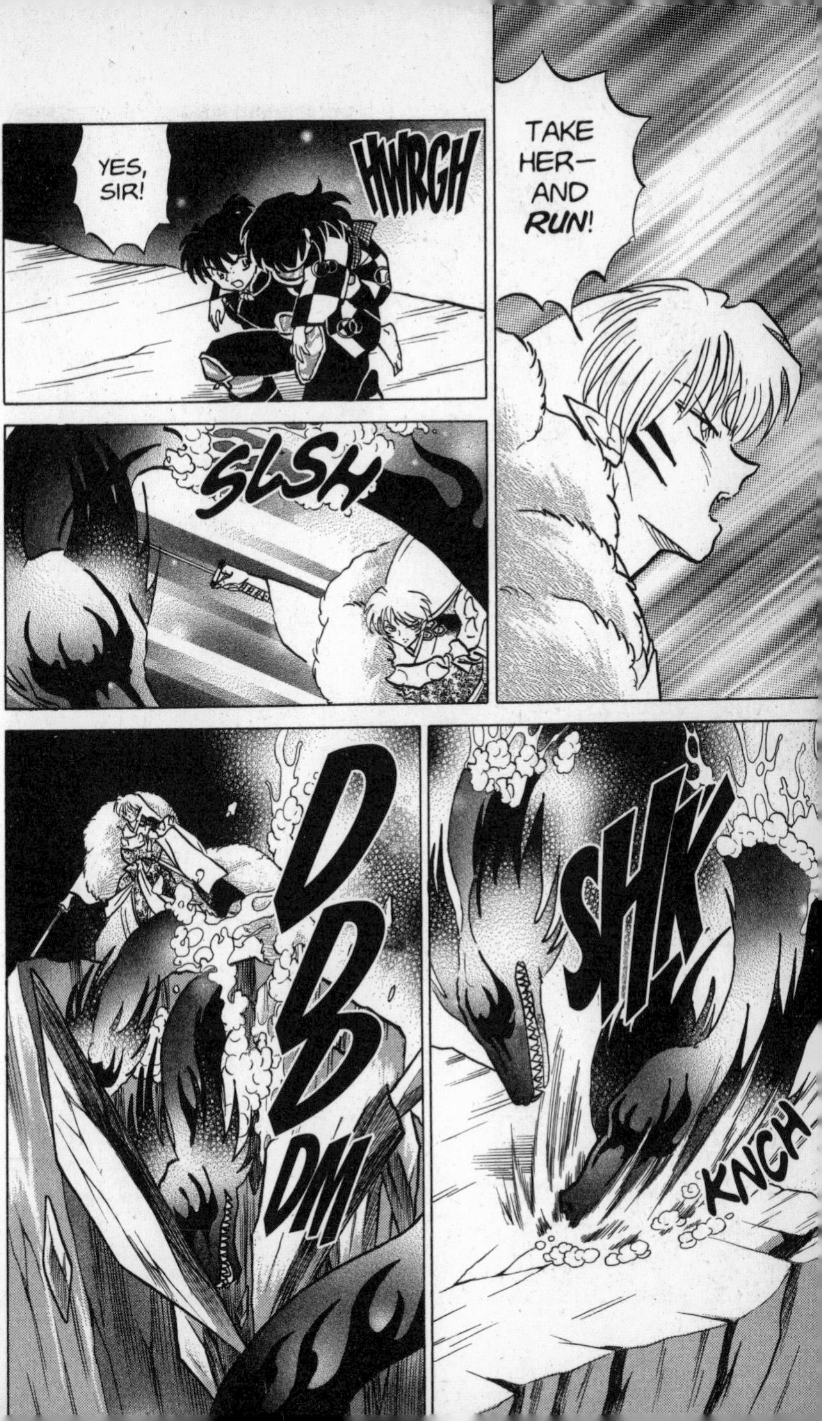
TAKE HER— AND RUN!
YES, SIR!
HWRGH
SLSH
SHK
KNCH

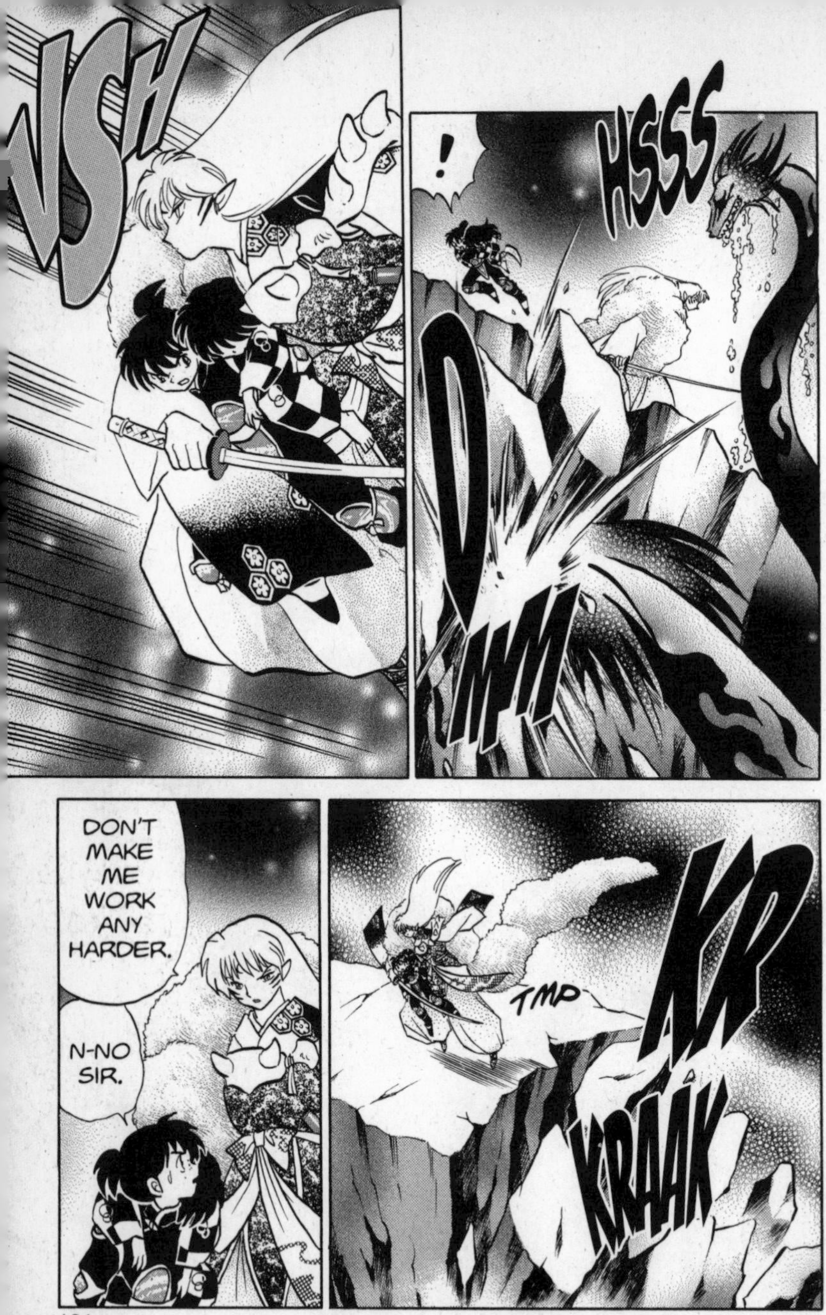
!
HSSS
DMM
VSH
KR
KRAAK
TMP
DON'T MAKE ME WORK ANY HARDER.
N-NO SIR.

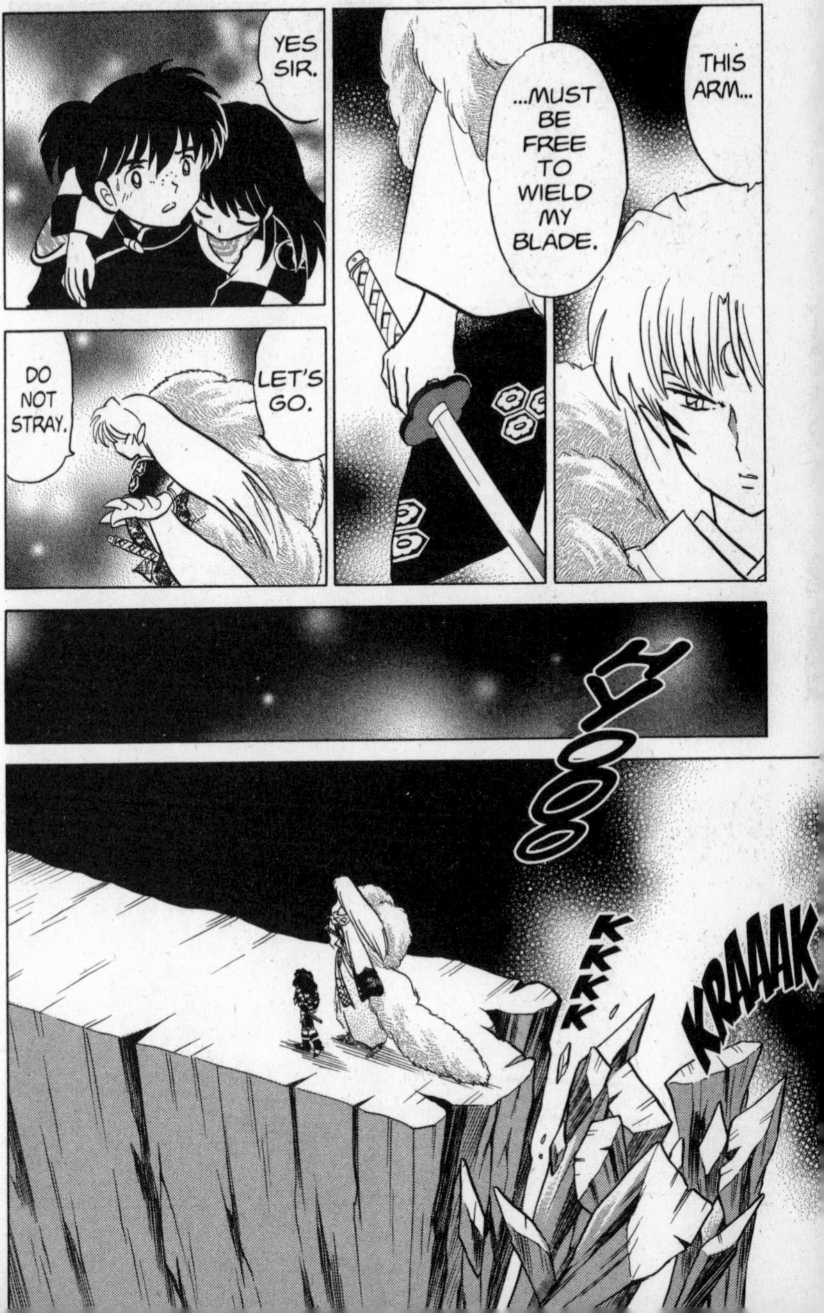
THIS ARM...
...MUST BE FREE TO WIELD MY BLADE.
YES SIR.
LET'S GO.
DO NOT STRAY.
ZOOOO
KRAAAK
KKKKK

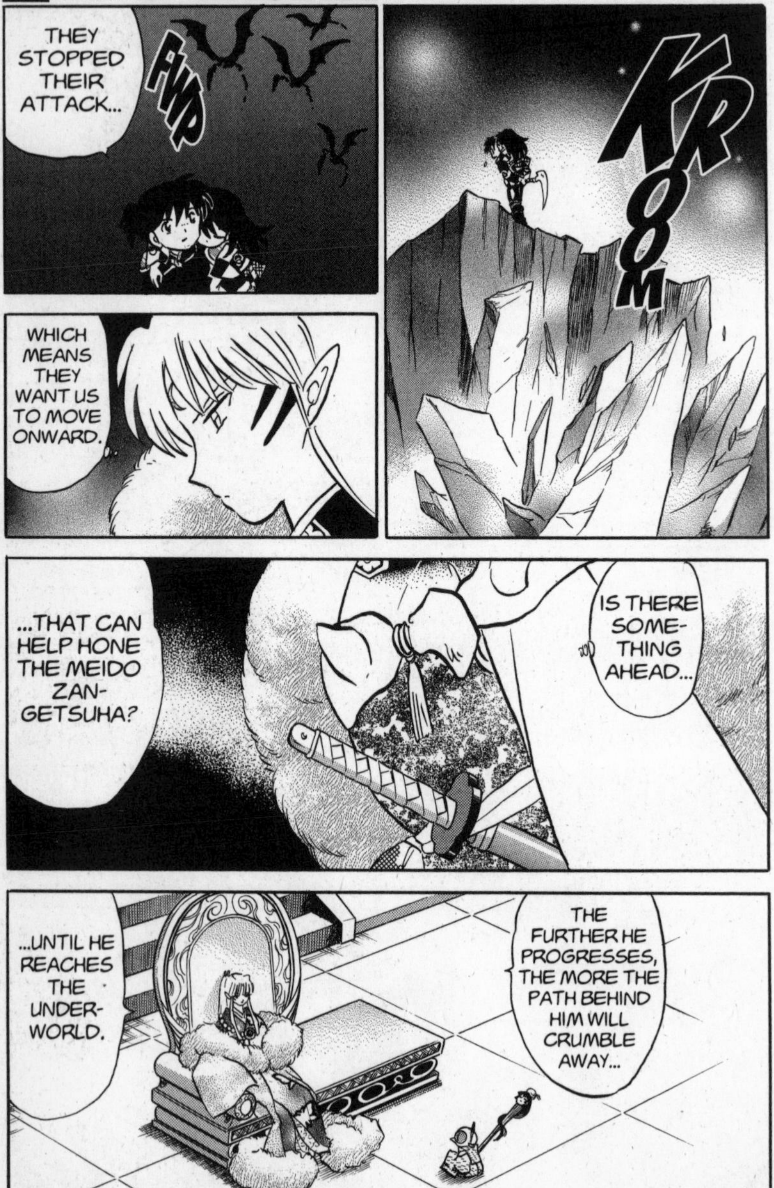
K'ROOM
FWP
THEY STOPPED THEIR ATTACK...
WHICH MEANS THEY WANT US TO MOVE ONWARD.
IS THERE SOME-THING AHEAD...
...THAT CAN HELP HONE THE MEIDO ZAN-GETSUHA?
THE FURTHER HE PROGRESSES, THE MORE THE PATH BEHIND HIM WILL CRUMBLE AWAY...
...UNTIL HE REACHES THE UNDER-WORLD.

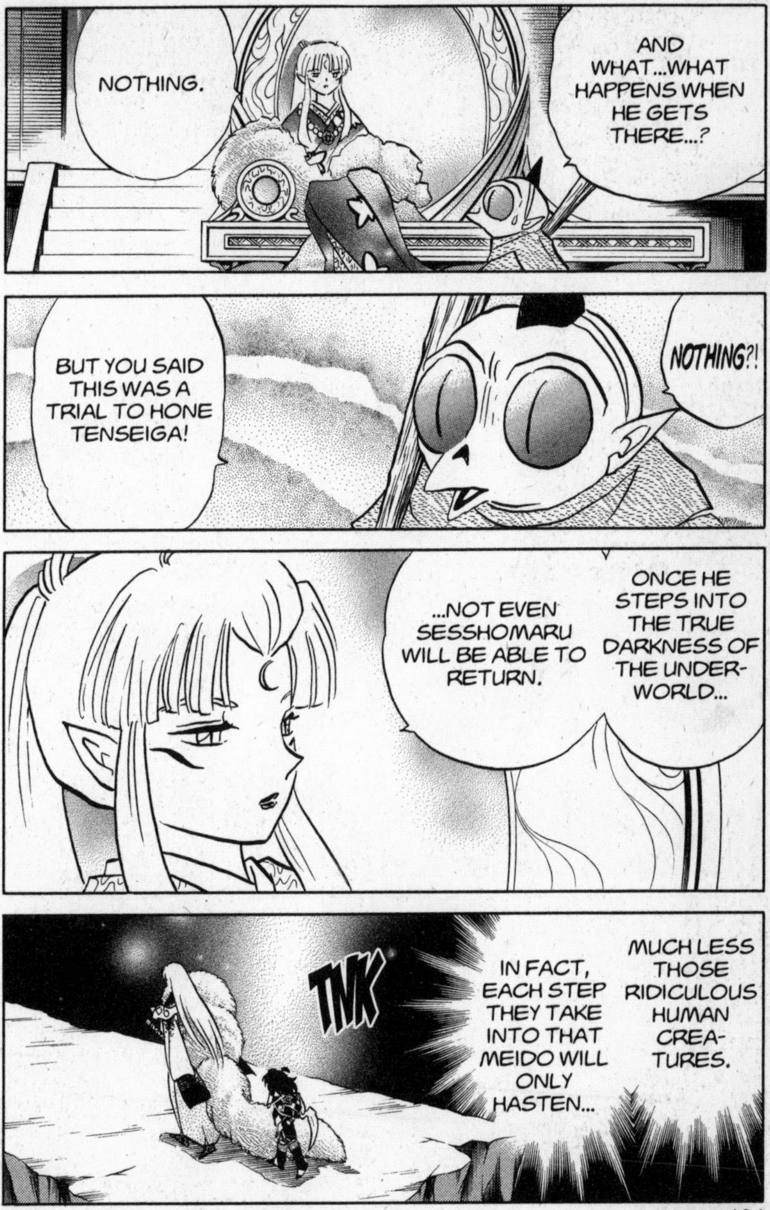
AND WHAT...WHAT HAPPENS WHEN HE GETS THERE...?
NOTHING.
NOTHING?!
BUT YOU SAID THIS WAS A TRIAL TO HONE TENSEIGA!
ONCE HE STEPS INTO THE TRUE DARKNESS OF THE UNDER-WORLD...
...NOT EVEN SESSHOMARU WILL BE ABLE TO RETURN.
MUCH LESS THOSE RIDICULOUS HUMAN CREA-TURES.
IN FACT, EACH STEP THEY TAKE INTO THAT MEIDO WILL ONLY HASTEN...
TMK

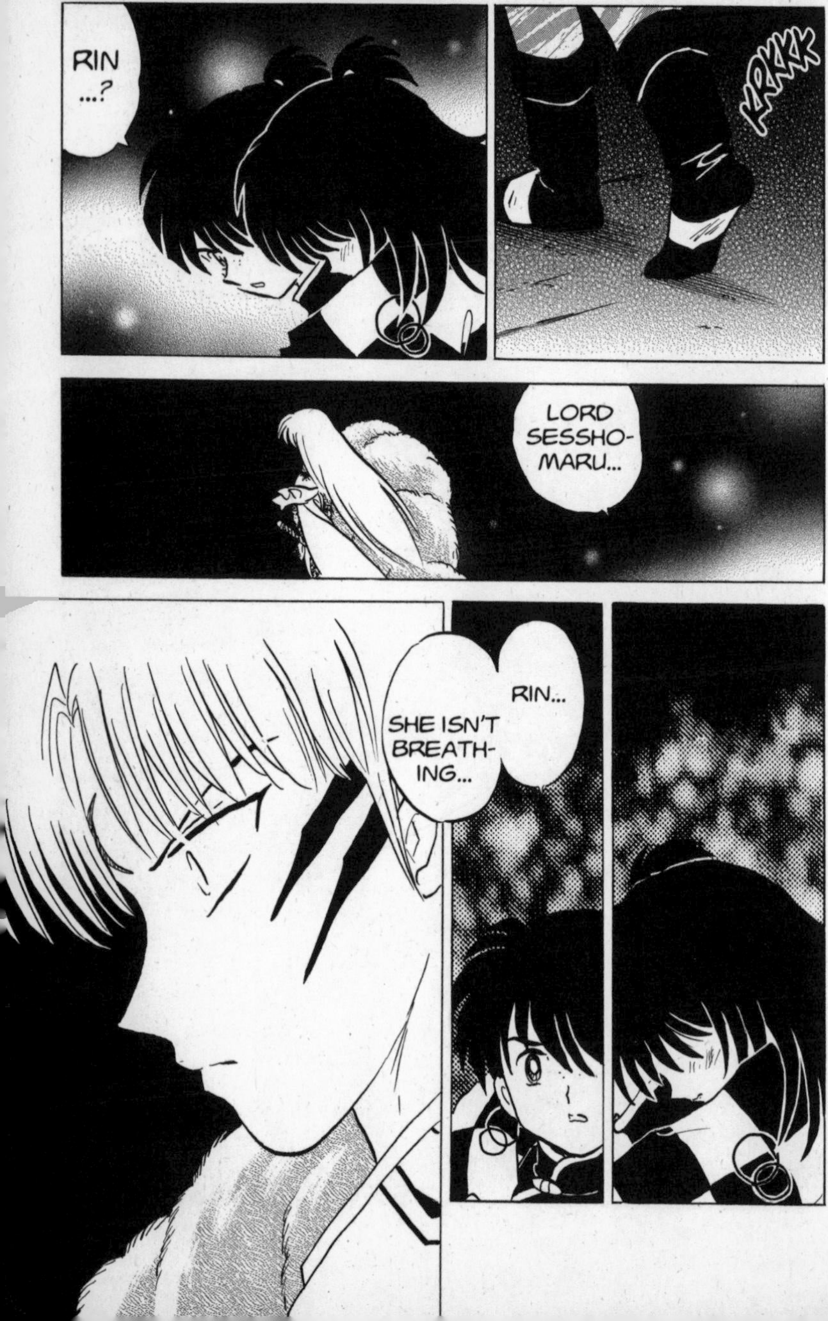
KRKKK
RIN ...?
LORD SESSHO-MARU...
RIN...
SHE ISN'T BREATH-ING...

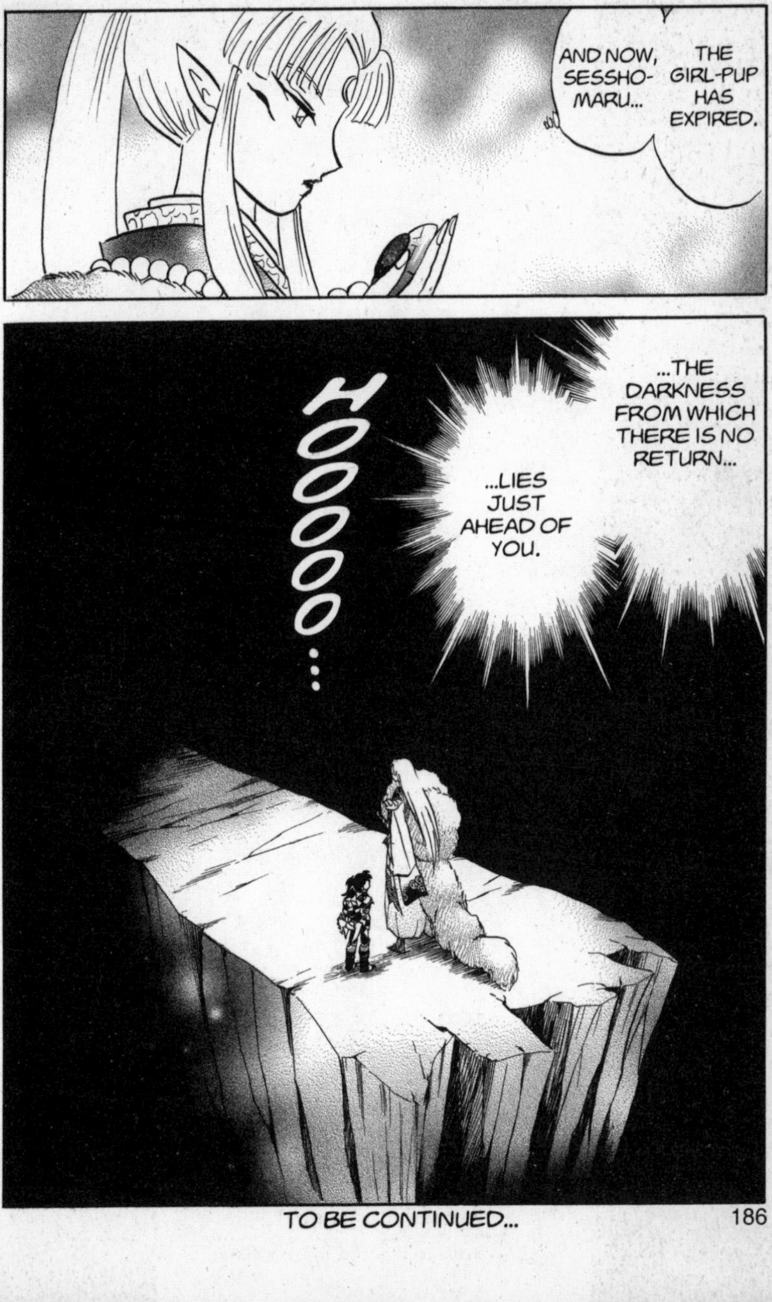
THE GIRL-PUP HAS EXPIRED.
AND NOW, SESSHO-MARU...
...THE DARKNESS FROM WHICH THERE IS NO RETURN...
...LIES JUST AHEAD OF YOU.
HOOOOOO...

TO BE CONTINUED...

INUYASHA

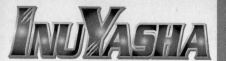

INUYASHA

VOL. 47

Shonen Sunday Edition

Story and Art by

RUMIKO TAKAHASHI

Original Japanese edition "INUYASHA"
published by SHOGAKUKAN Inc.

English Adaptation by Gerard Jones

Translation/Mari Morimoto
Touch-up Art & Lettering/Bill Schuch
Cover & Interior Graphic Design/Yuki Ameda
Editor/Annette Roman

VP, Production/Alvin Lu
VP, Sales & Product Marketing/Gonzalo Ferreyra
VP, Creative/Linda Espinosa
Publisher/Hyoe Narita

Printed in the U.S.A.

Published by VIZ Media, LLC
P.O. Box 77010
San Francisco, CA 94107

10 9 8 7 6 5 4 3 2 1
First printing, April 2010

RATED T+ FOR OLDER TEEN

PARENTAL ADVISORY
INUYASHA is rated T+ for Older Teen and is recommended for ages 16 and up. This volume contains violence.

ratings.viz.com

viz media

www.viz.com

SHONEN SUNDAY

WWW.SHONENSUNDAY.COM

TV SERIES & MOVIES ON DVD!

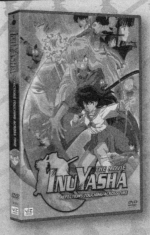
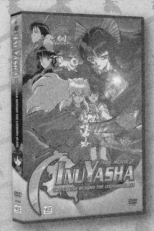
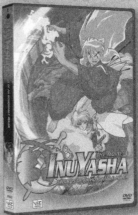
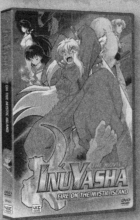

See more of the action in *Inuyasha* full-length movies

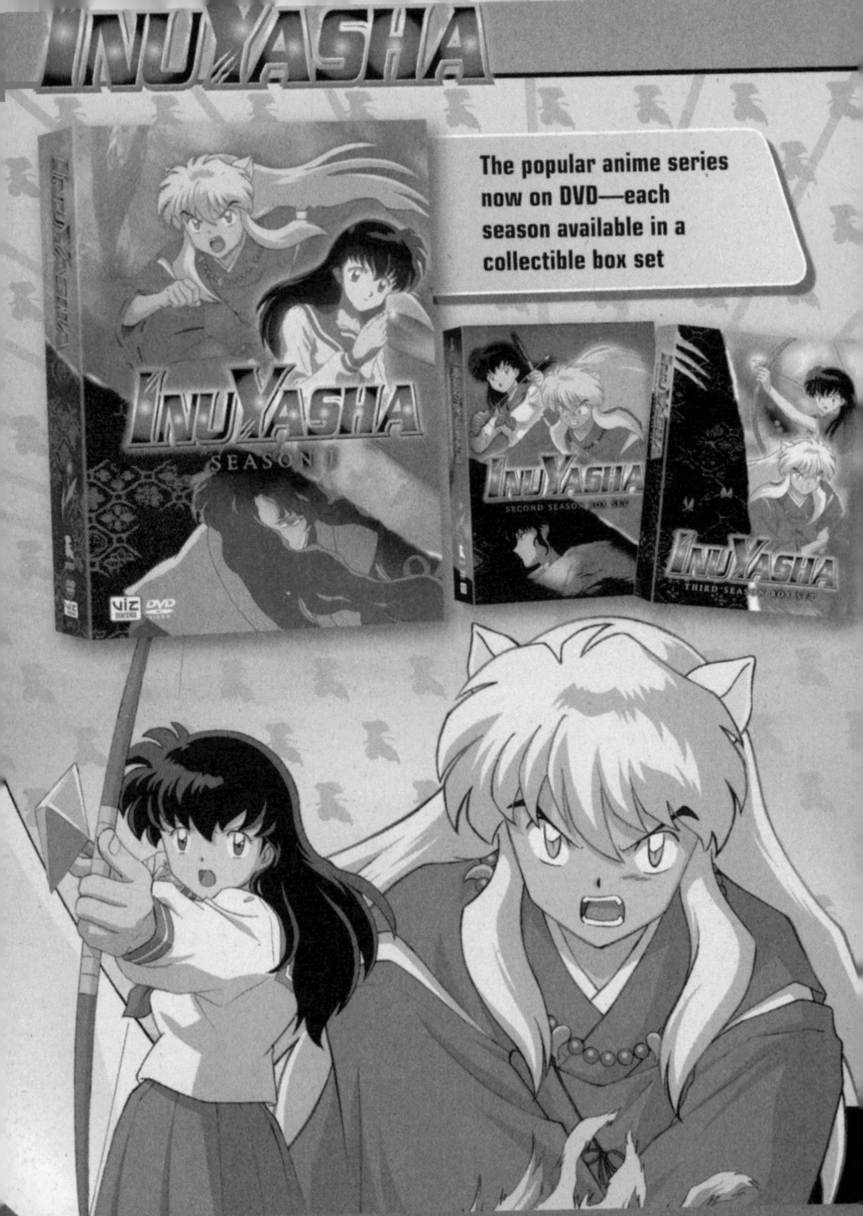
INUYASHA
The popular anime series now on DVD—each season available in a collectible box set
INUYASHA
SEASON 1
INUYASHA
INUYASHA

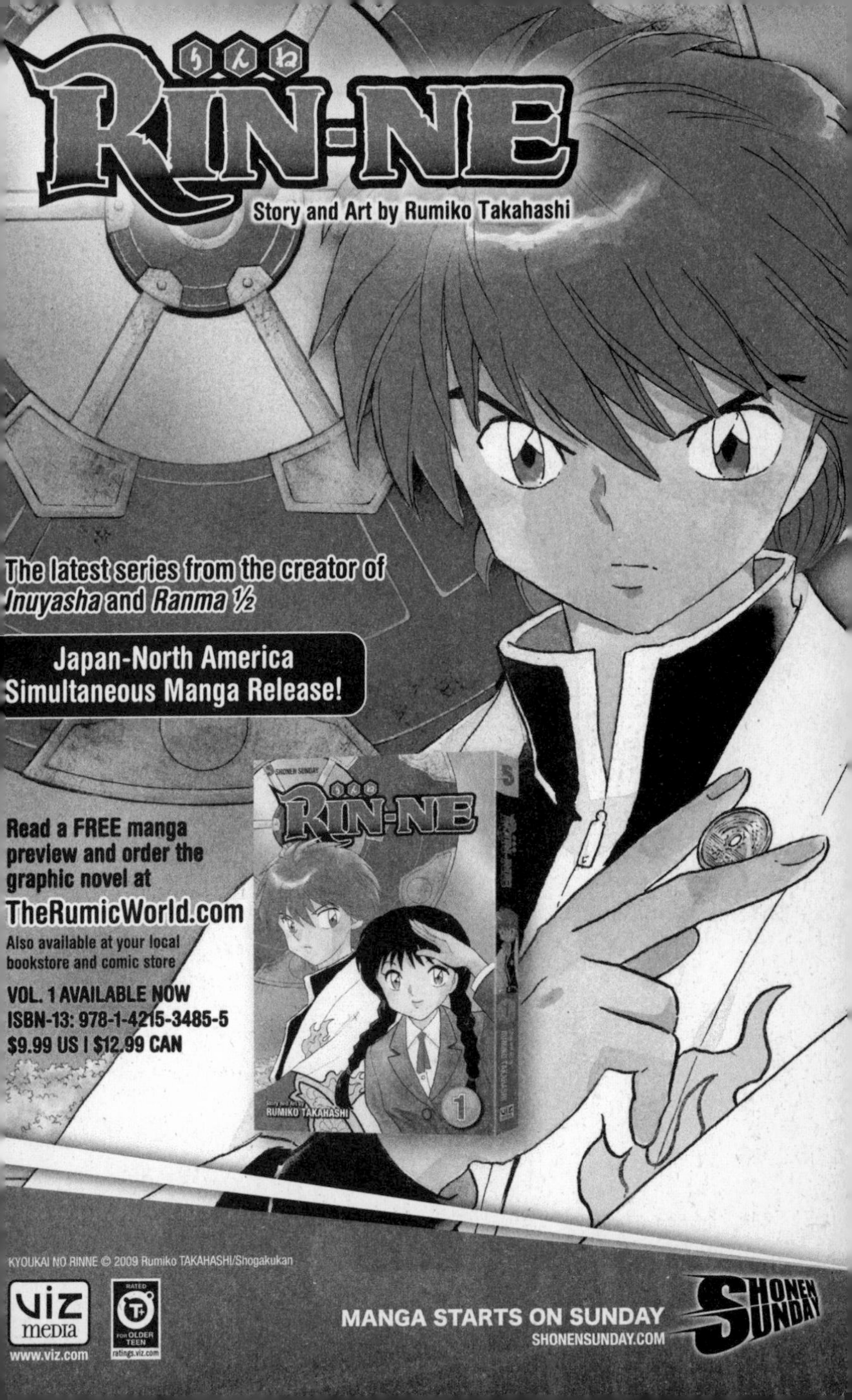

りんね
RIN-NE
Story and Art by Rumiko Takahashi
The latest series from the creator of
Inuyasha and Ranma ½
Japan-North America
Simultaneous Manga Release!
SHONEN SUNDAY
RIN-NE
Story and Art by
RUMIKO TAKAHASHI
1
Read a FREE manga
preview and order the
graphic novel at
TheRumicWorld.com
Also available at your local
bookstore and comic store
VOL. 1 AVAILABLE NOW
ISBN-13: 978-1-4215-3485-5
$9.99 US | $12.99 CAN
KYOUKAI NO RINNE © 2009 Rumiko TAKAHASHI/Shogakukan
viz media
www.viz.com
RATED T+ FOR OLDER TEEN
ratings.viz.com
MANGA STARTS ON SUNDAY
SHONENSUNDAY.COM
SHONEN SUNDAY

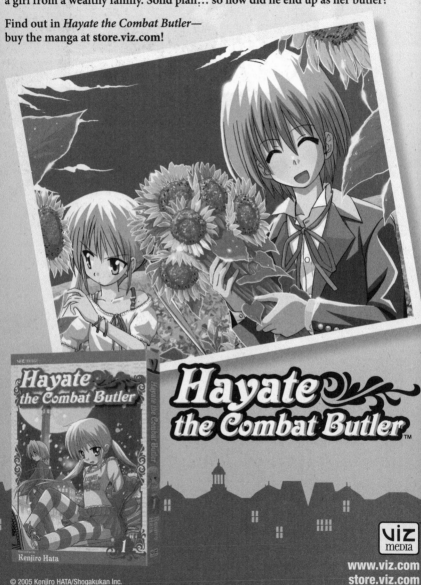

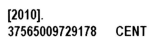

A DETEC...

...ervation
...mysteries
that leave the most seasoned law
enforcement officials baffled. But
when a strange chemical transforms
him from a high school teenager to a
grade schooler who no one takes
seriously, will this be one mystery
this sleuth can't solve?

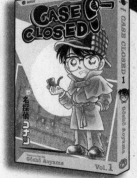

**Start your
graphic novel
collection today!**

www.viz.com
store.viz.com

©1994 Gosho AOYAMA/Shogakukan Inc.